MATT FRACTION AND TERRY DODSON

Present

ADVENTUREMAN™

VOLUME 1

"The END and EVERYTHING AFTER"

ADVENT

featuring

MATT FRACTION ★
AS THE WRITER.

TERRY DODSON ★
AS THE PENCILLER & COLORIST.

RACHEL DODSON ★
AS THE INKER.

CLAYTON COWLES ★
AS THE LETTERIST.

LEONARDO OLEA ★
AS THE DESIGNER.

**LAUREN SANKOVITCH
& TURNER LOBEY** ★
AS THE EDITORS.

DRAWN & COLORED WITH

 DODSONVISION® FRACTION INC. PRODUCTION ✱ Technirachel®

 COWLES STEREO ®
IN SELECTED COMICS

 DESIGN COMICS ASSOCIATION OF OLEA ®

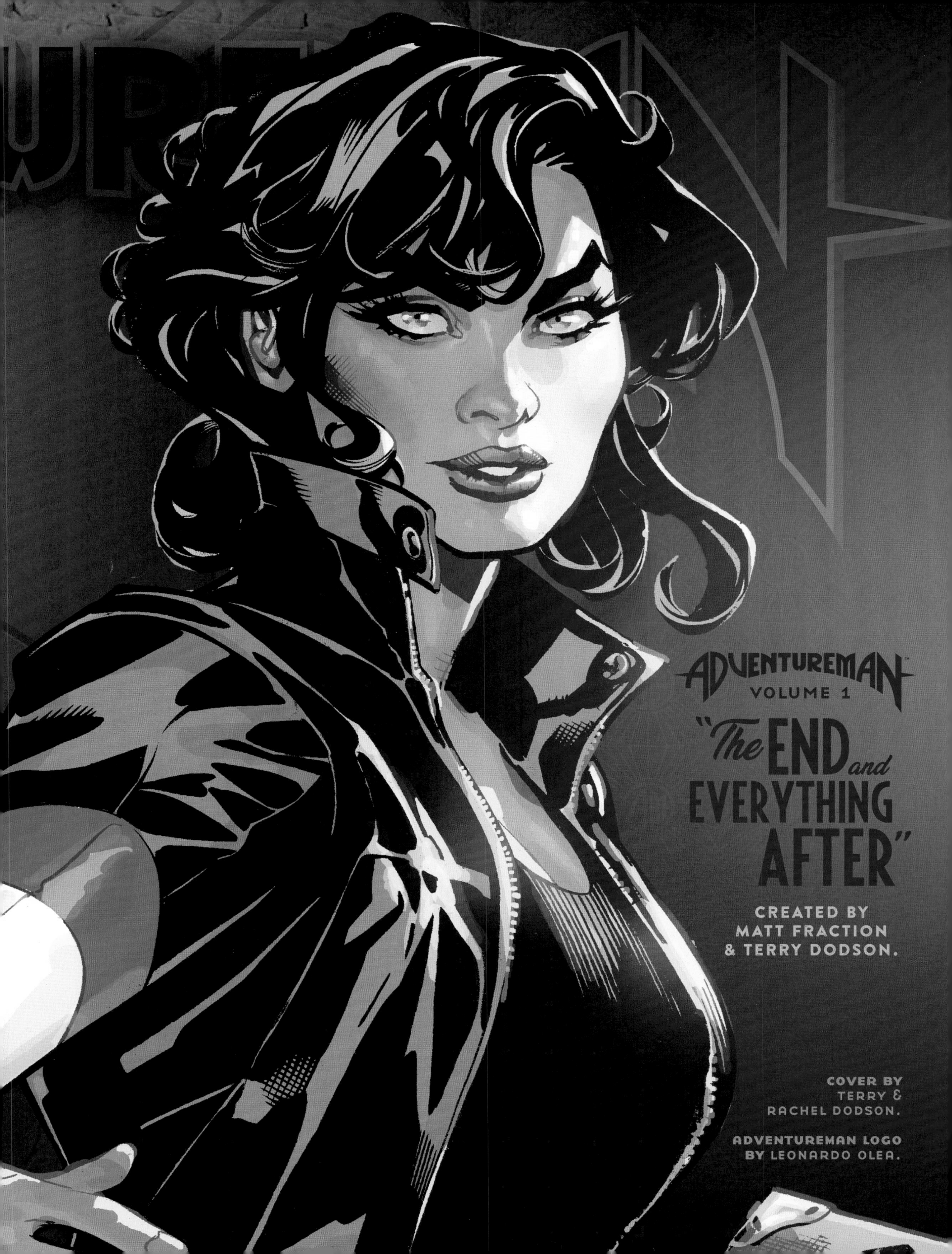

ADVENTUREMAN™
VOLUME 1

"The END and EVERYTHING AFTER"

CREATED BY
MATT FRACTION
& TERRY DODSON.

COVER BY
TERRY &
RACHEL DODSON.

ADVENTUREMAN LOGO
BY LEONARDO OLEA.

◁ SPECIAL THANKS ▷

Special thanks to **Eric Stephenson, Jeff Boison, Deanna Phelps** and everyone at *Image Comics*, **Philippe Hauri** and **Olivier Jalabert** at *Glènat*, **Lauren Sankovitch** for getting this project scheduled and getting the work out of us, **Turner Lobey** for getting us to the finish line, **Leonardo Olea** for creating the **ADVENTUREMAN** logo/monogram and designing this lovely book you are now holding, the color flatters - **Gilly Renk, Rich Ellis & Grey Allison**, and **Jeremiah Skipper**, and **Caitlin DiMotta** and **Amber Garza** for getting all our ducks in a row.

ADVENTUREMAN, VOL. 1. First printing. November 2020. Published by Image Comics, Inc. Office of publication: 2701 NW Vaughn St., Suite 780, Portland, OR 97210. Copyright © 2020 Milkfed Criminal Masterminds, Inc. and Terry Dodson. All rights reserved. Contains material originally published in single magazine form as ADVENTUREMAN #1-4. "Adventureman," its logos, and the likenesses of all characters herein are trademarks of Milkfed Criminal Masterminds, Inc. and Terry Dodson, unless otherwise noted. "Image" and the Image Comics logos are registered trademarks of Image Comics, Inc. No part of this publication may be reproduced or transmitted, in any form or by any means (except for short excerpts for journalistic or review purposes), without the express written permission of Milkfed Criminal Masterminds, Inc. and Terry Dodson, or Image Comics, Inc. All names, characters, events, and locales in this publication are entirely fictional. Any resemblance to actual persons (living or dead), events, or places, without satirical intent, is coincidental. Printed in Canada. For international rights, contact: foreignlicensing@imagecomics.com. ISBN: 978-1-5343-1712-3.

ADVENTUREMAN

"The END and EVERYTHING AFTER"

VOLUME 1

CHAPTER 1

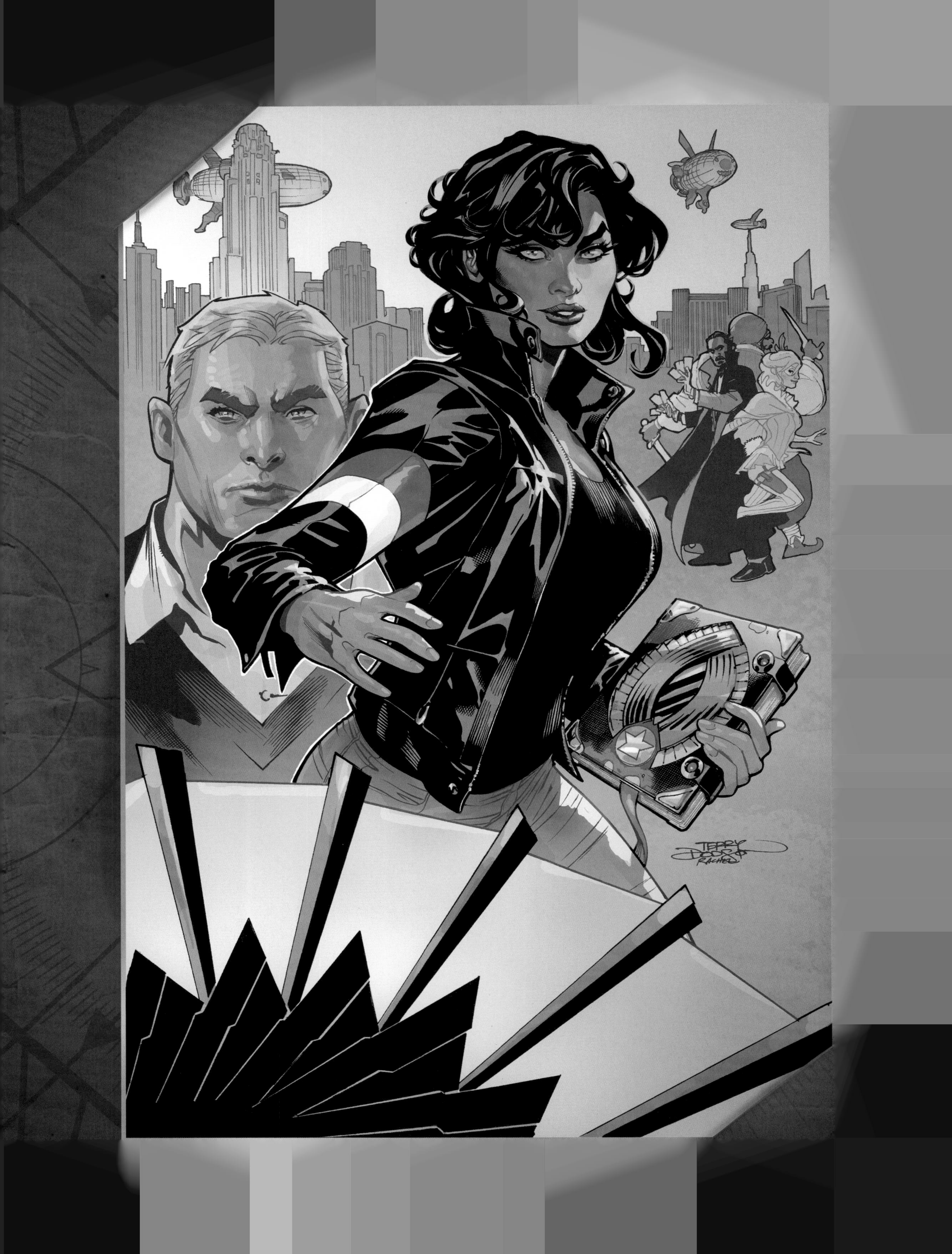
TERRY DODSON RACHEL

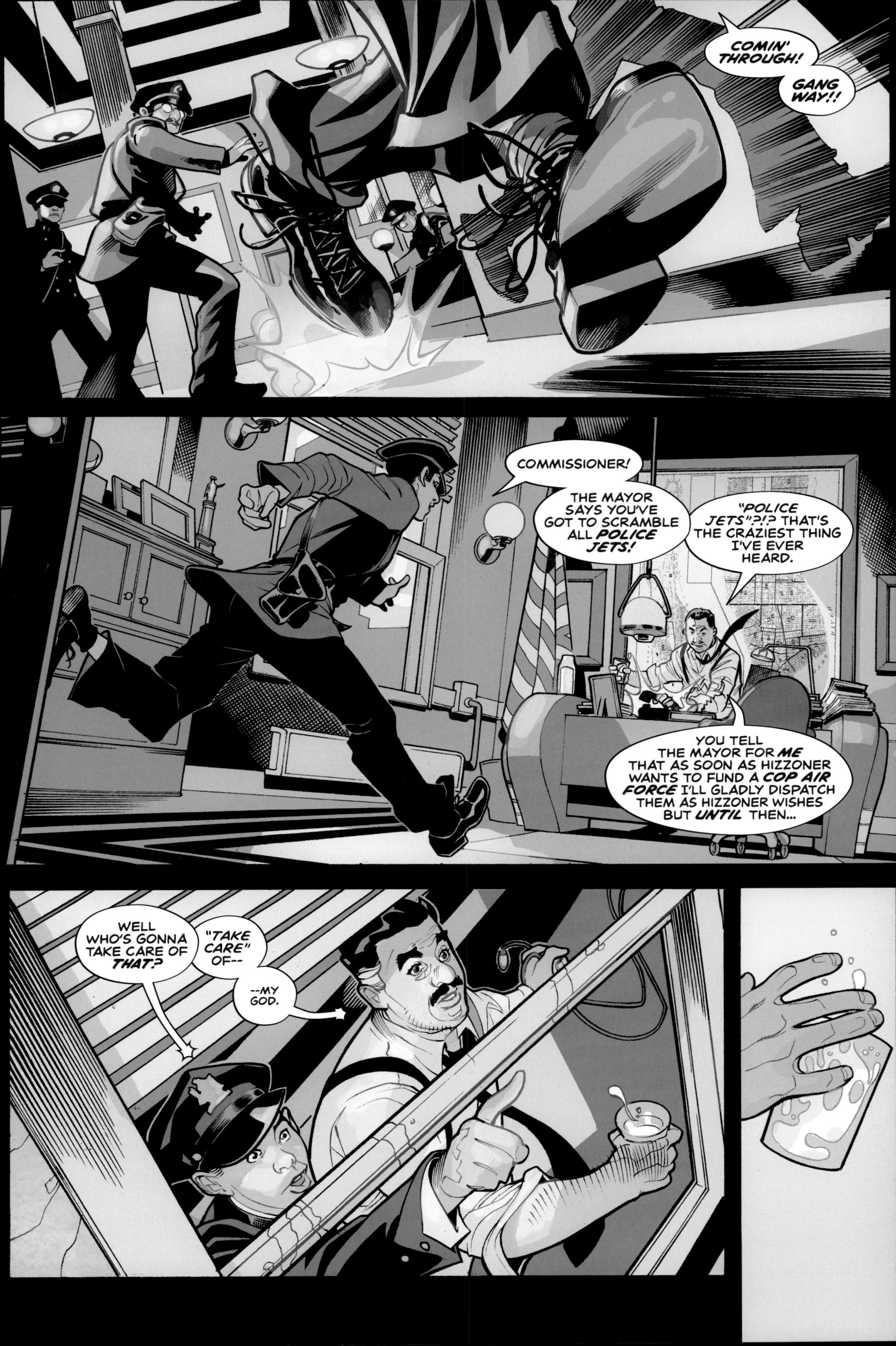
COMIN' THROUGH!
GANG WAY!!
COMMISSIONER!
THE MAYOR SAYS YOU'VE GOT TO SCRAMBLE ALL POLICE JETS!
"POLICE JETS"?!? THAT'S THE CRAZIEST THING I'VE EVER HEARD.
YOU TELL THE MAYOR FOR ME THAT AS SOON AS HIZZONER WANTS TO FUND A COP AIR FORCE I'LL GLADLY DISPATCH THEM AS HIZZONER WISHES BUT UNTIL THEN...
WELL WHO'S GONNA TAKE CARE OF THAT?
"TAKE CARE" OF--
--MY GOD.

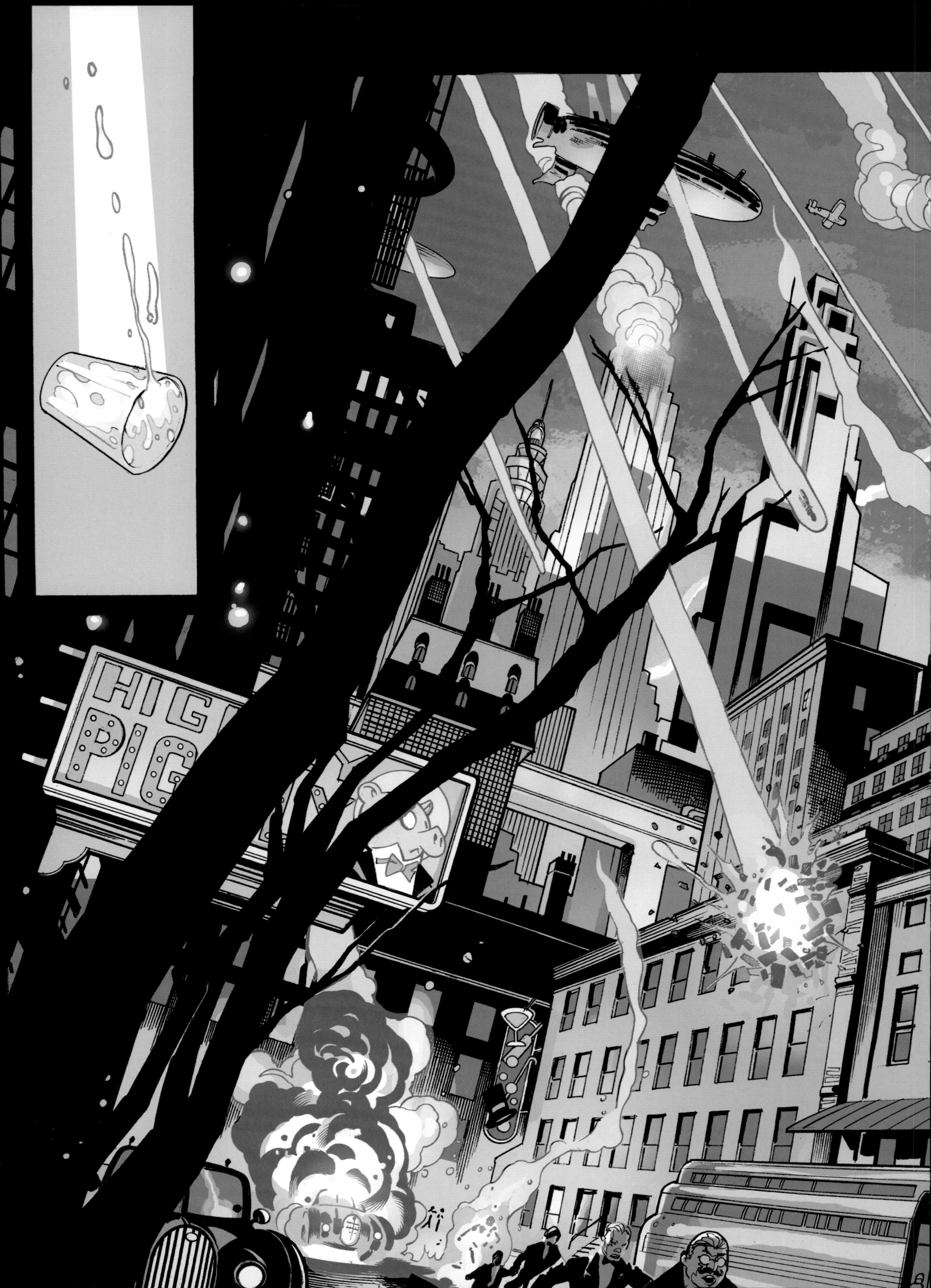
HIG
PIG

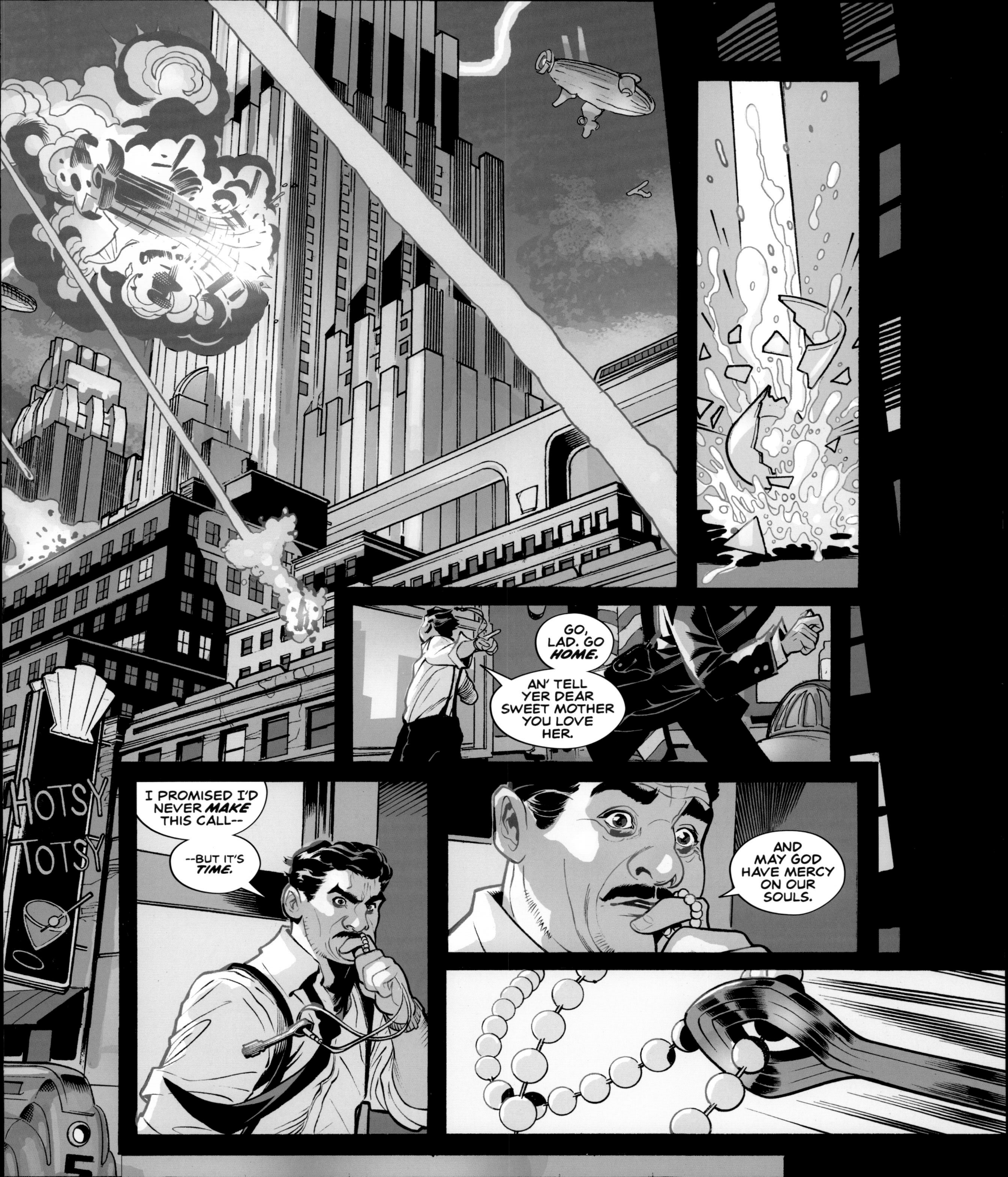
GO, LAD. GO *HOME.*
AN' TELL YER DEAR SWEET MOTHER YOU LOVE HER.
HOTSY TOTSY
I PROMISED I'D NEVER *MAKE* THIS CALL--
--BUT IT'S *TIME.*
AND MAY GOD HAVE MERCY ON OUR SOULS.

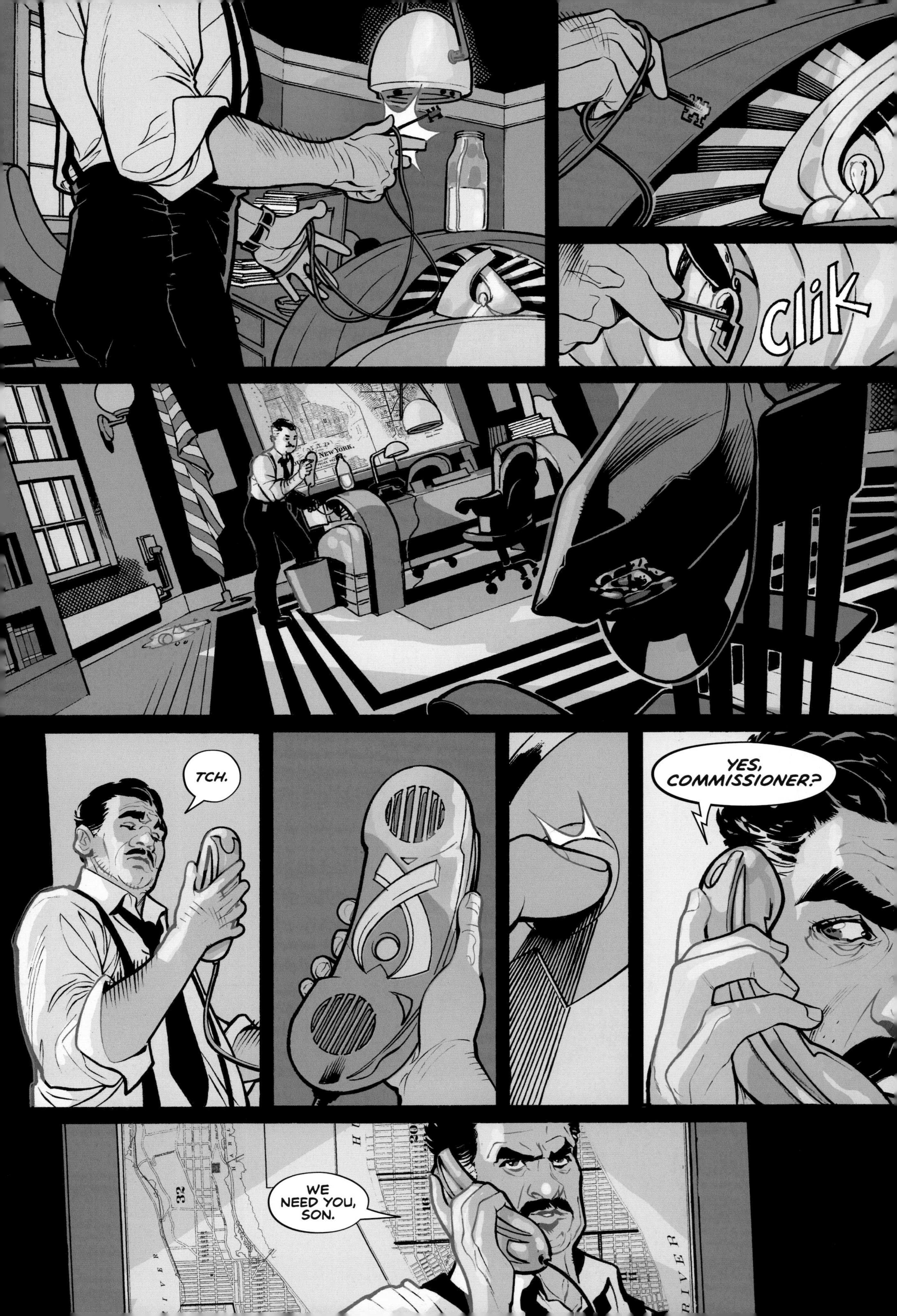
CLIK
TCH.
YES, COMMISSIONER?
WE NEED YOU, SON.

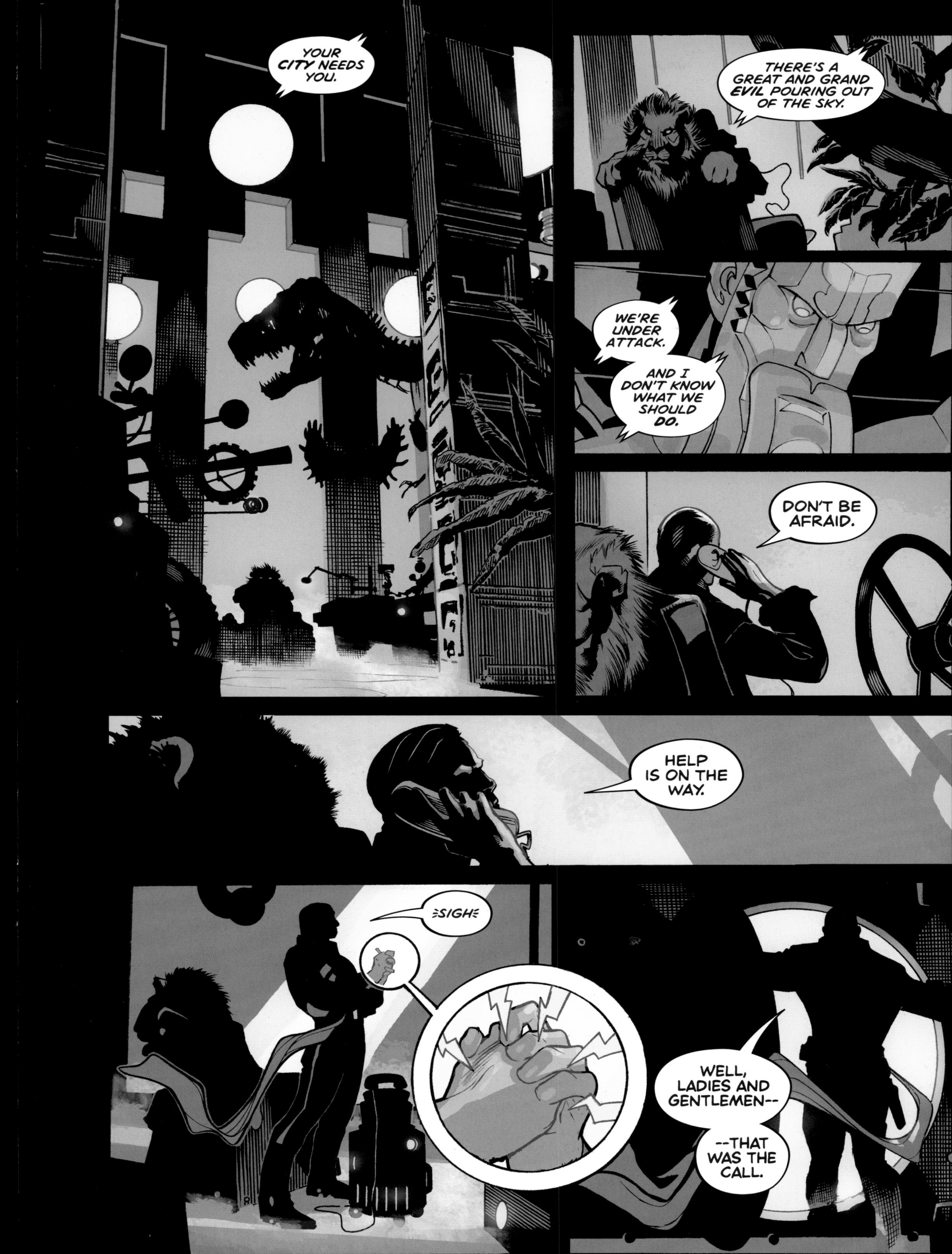
YOUR CITY NEEDS YOU.
THERE'S A GREAT AND GRAND EVIL POURING OUT OF THE SKY.
WE'RE UNDER ATTACK.
AND I DON'T KNOW WHAT WE SHOULD DO.
DON'T BE AFRAID.
HELP IS ON THE WAY.
SIGH
WELL, LADIES AND GENTLEMEN--
--THAT WAS THE CALL.

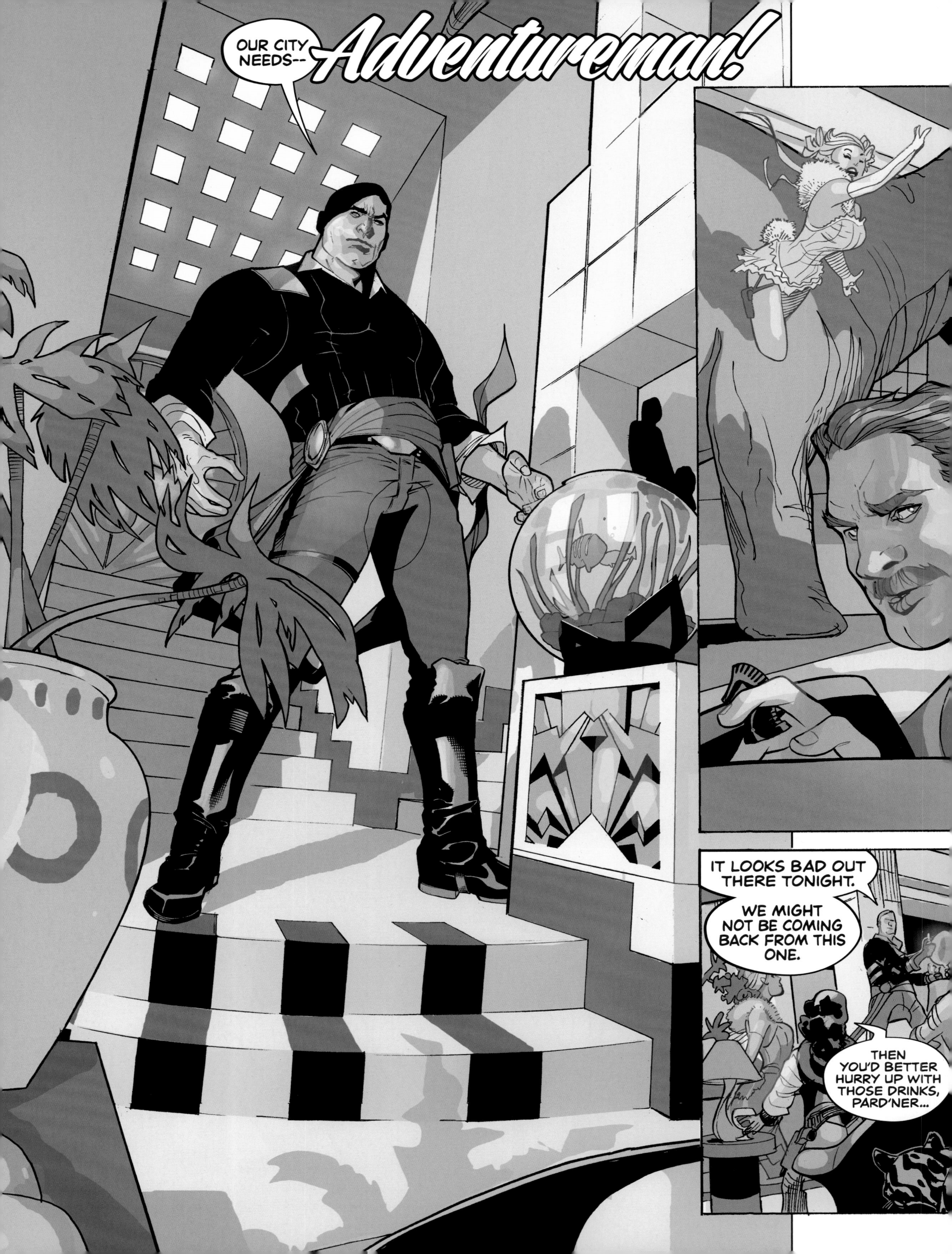
OUR CITY NEEDS--
Adventureman!
IT LOOKS BAD OUT THERE TONIGHT.
WE MIGHT NOT BE COMING BACK FROM THIS ONE.
THEN YOU'D BETTER HURRY UP WITH THOSE DRINKS, PARD'NER...

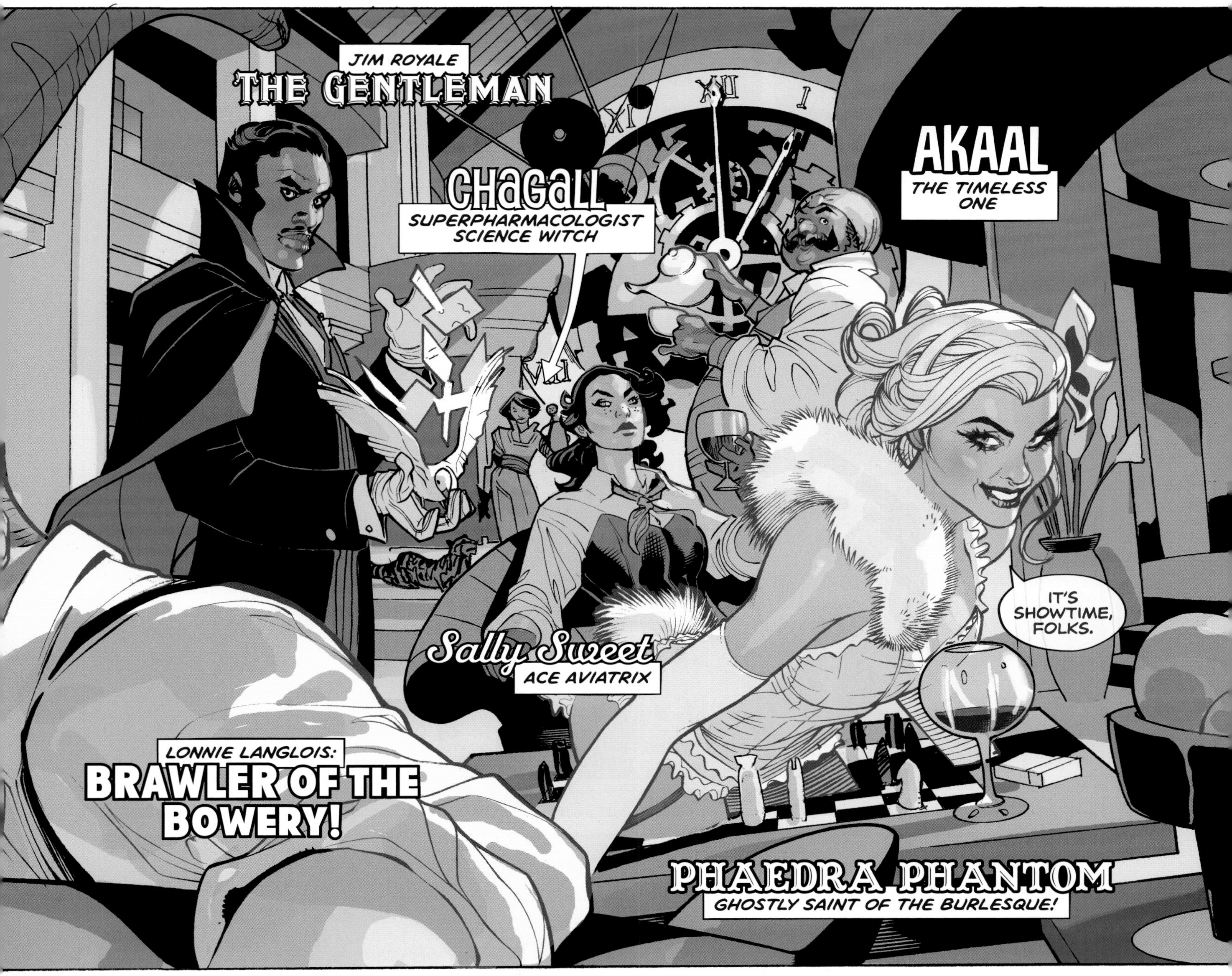
JIM ROYALE
THE GENTLEMAN
CHAGALL
SUPERPHARMACOLOGIST SCIENCE WITCH
AKAAL
THE TIMELESS ONE
IT'S SHOWTIME, FOLKS.
Sally Sweet
ACE AVIATRIX
LONNIE LANGLOIS:
BRAWLER OF THE BOWERY!
PHAEDRA PHANTOM
GHOSTLY SAINT OF THE BURLESQUE!

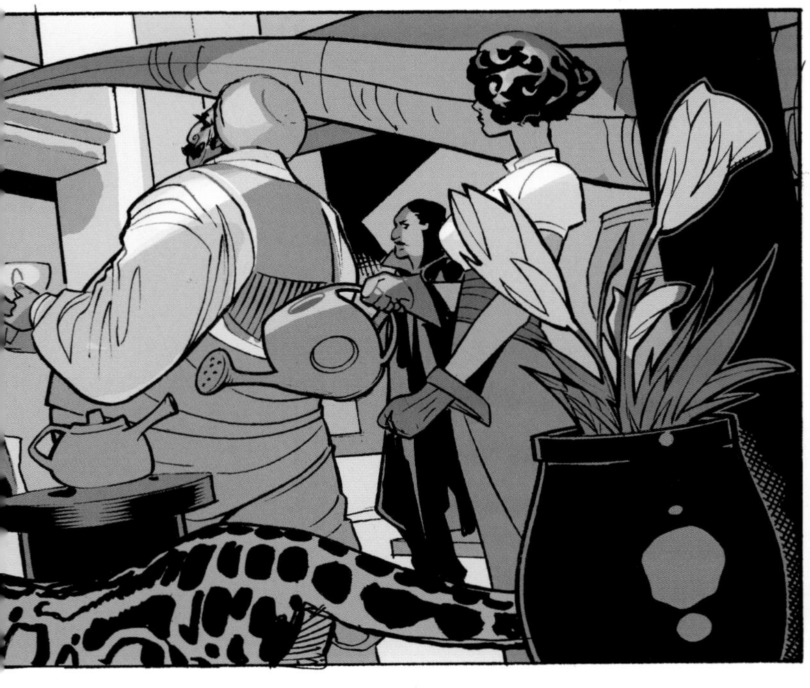

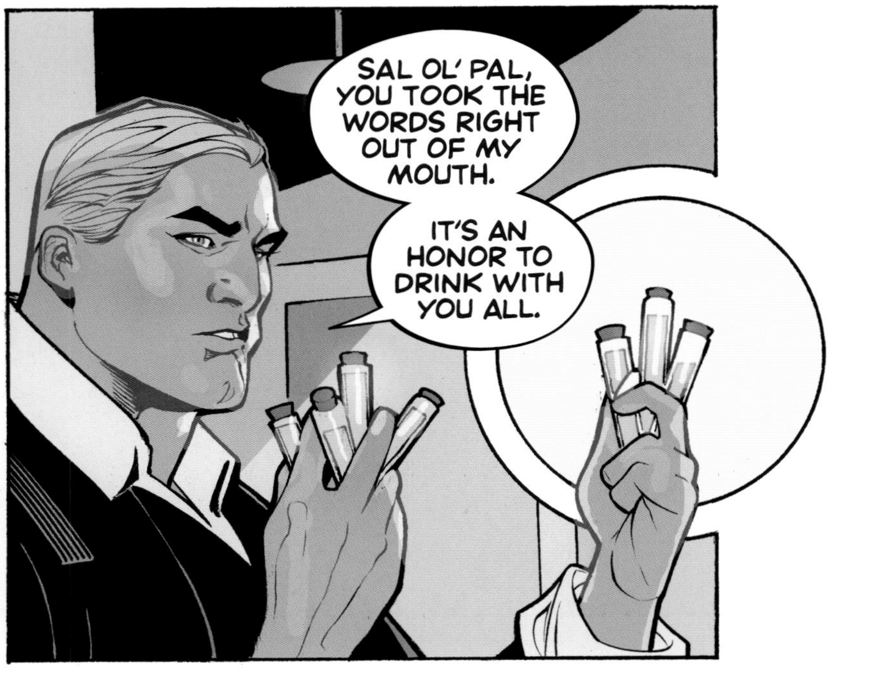
SAL OL' PAL, YOU TOOK THE WORDS RIGHT OUT OF MY MOUTH.
IT'S AN HONOR TO DRINK WITH YOU ALL.

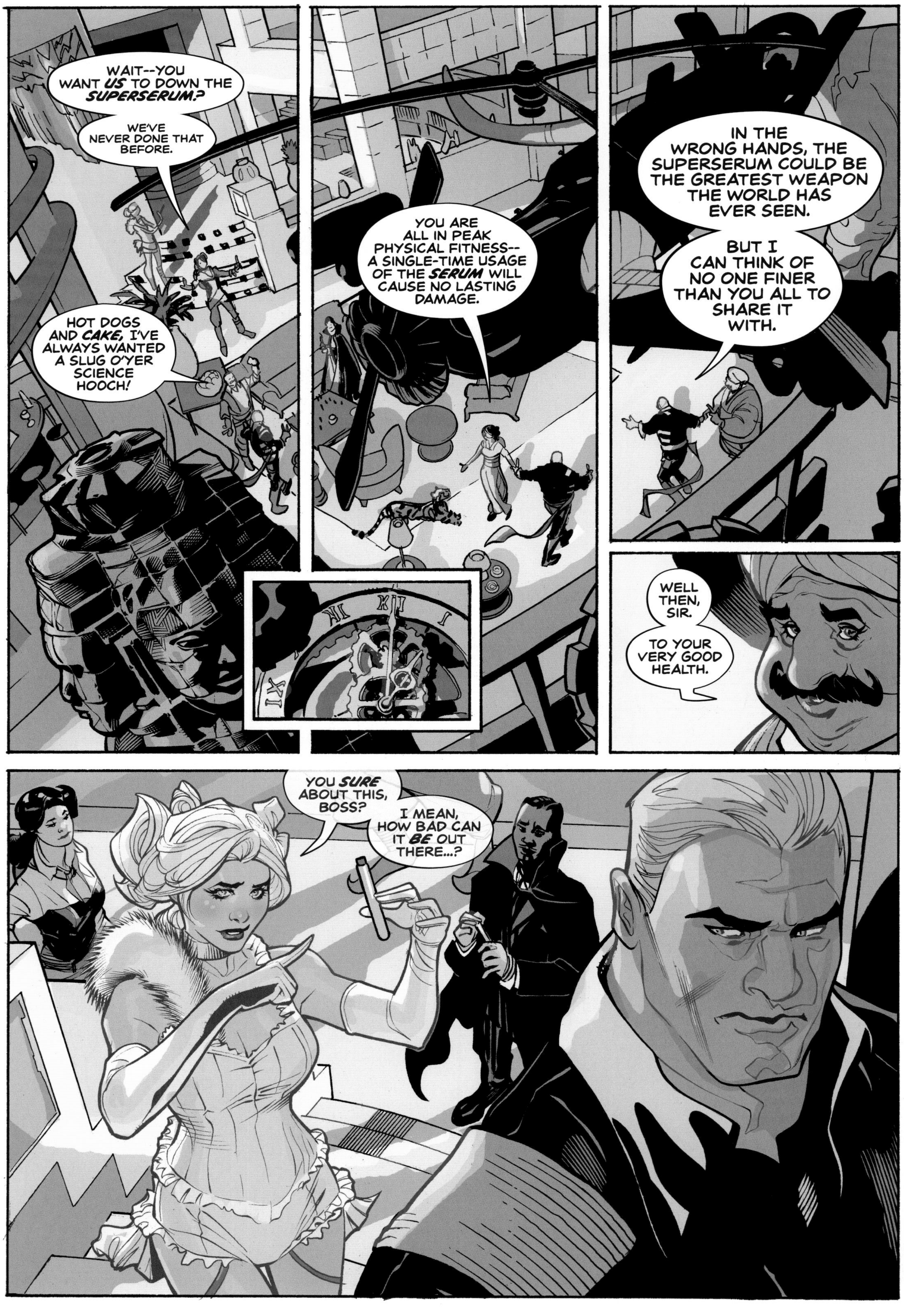
WAIT--YOU WANT US TO DOWN THE SUPERSERUM?
WE'VE NEVER DONE THAT BEFORE.
HOT DOGS AND CAKE, I'VE ALWAYS WANTED A SLUG O'YER SCIENCE HOOCH!
YOU ARE ALL IN PEAK PHYSICAL FITNESS-- A SINGLE-TIME USAGE OF THE SERUM WILL CAUSE NO LASTING DAMAGE.
IN THE WRONG HANDS, THE SUPERSERUM COULD BE THE GREATEST WEAPON THE WORLD HAS EVER SEEN.
BUT I CAN THINK OF NO ONE FINER THAN YOU ALL TO SHARE IT WITH.
WELL THEN, SIR.
TO YOUR VERY GOOD HEALTH.
YOU SURE ABOUT THIS, BOSS?
I MEAN, HOW BAD CAN IT BE OUT THERE...?

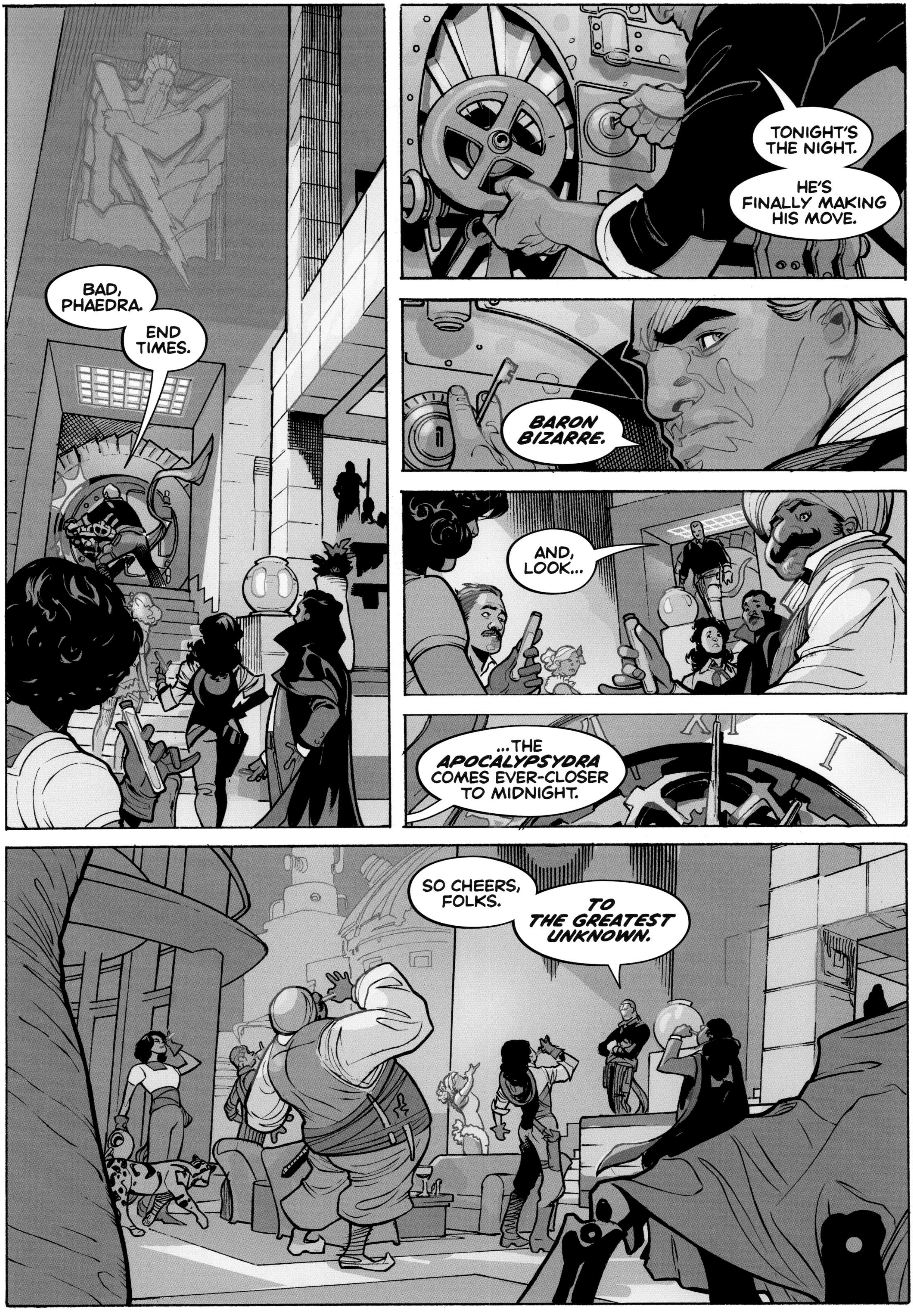
BAD, PHAEDRA.
END TIMES.
TONIGHT'S THE NIGHT.
HE'S FINALLY MAKING HIS MOVE.
BARON BIZARRE.
AND, LOOK...
...THE APOCALYPSYDRA COMES EVER-CLOSER TO MIDNIGHT.
SO CHEERS, FOLKS.
TO THE GREATEST UNKNOWN.

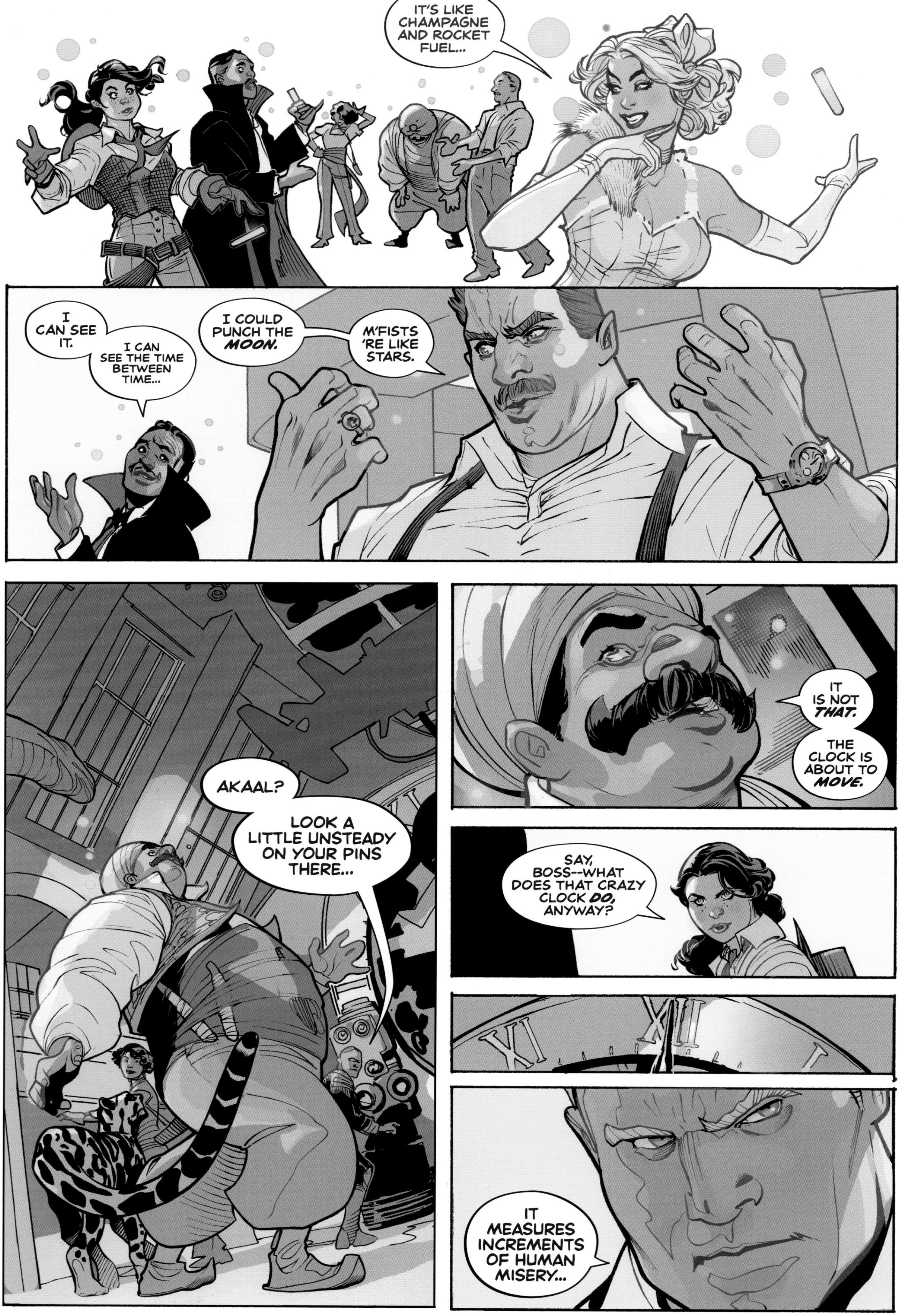
IT'S LIKE CHAMPAGNE AND ROCKET FUEL...
I CAN SEE IT.
I CAN SEE THE TIME BETWEEN TIME...
I COULD PUNCH THE ***MOON.***
M'FISTS 'RE LIKE STARS.
AKAAL?
LOOK A LITTLE UNSTEADY ON YOUR PINS THERE...
IT IS NOT ***THAT.***
THE CLOCK IS ABOUT TO ***MOVE.***
SAY, BOSS--WHAT DOES THAT CRAZY CLOCK ***DO,*** ANYWAY?
IT MEASURES INCREMENTS OF HUMAN MISERY...

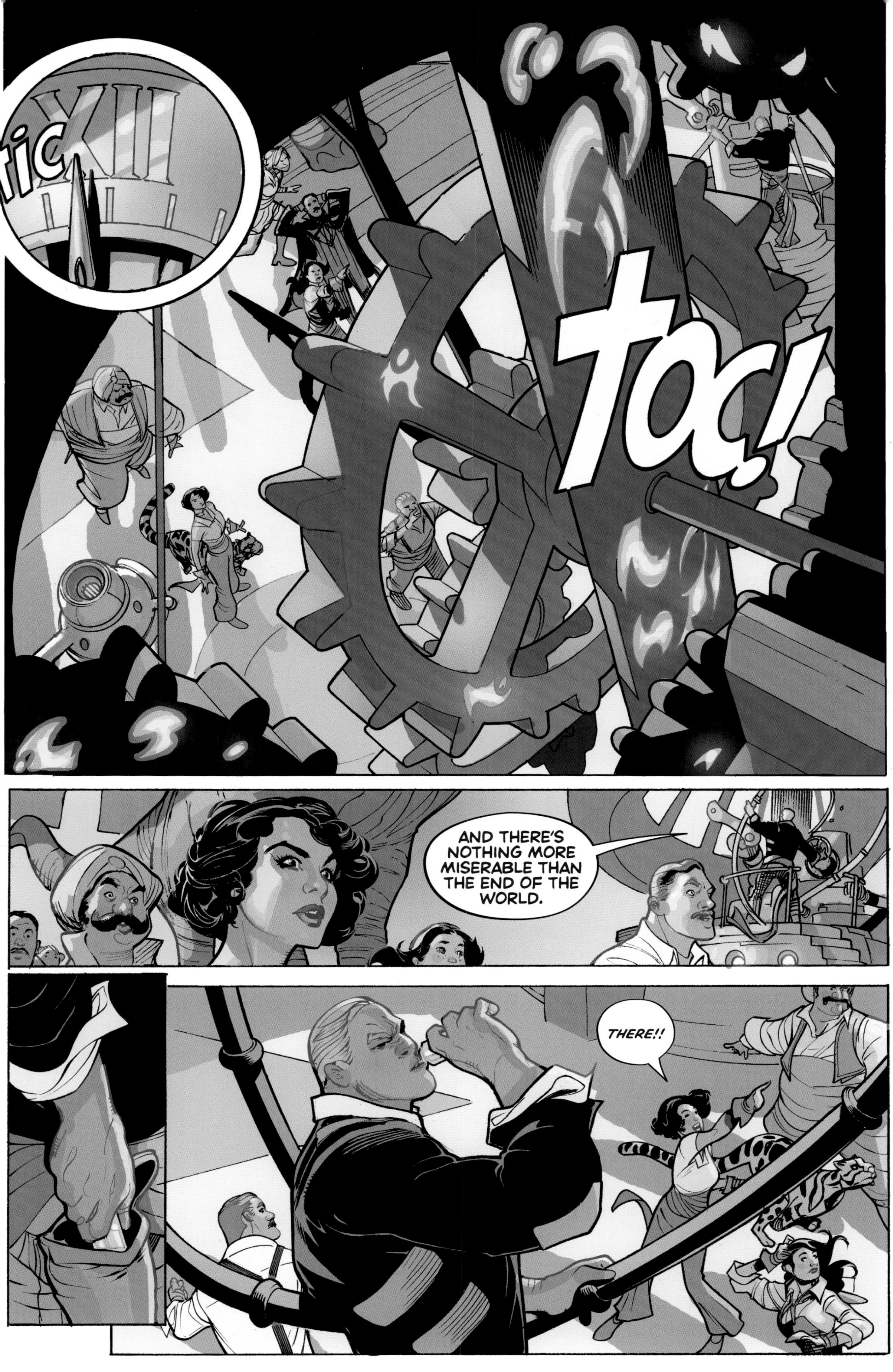
tic XIII
toc!
AND THERE'S NOTHING MORE MISERABLE THAN THE END OF THE WORLD.
THERE!!

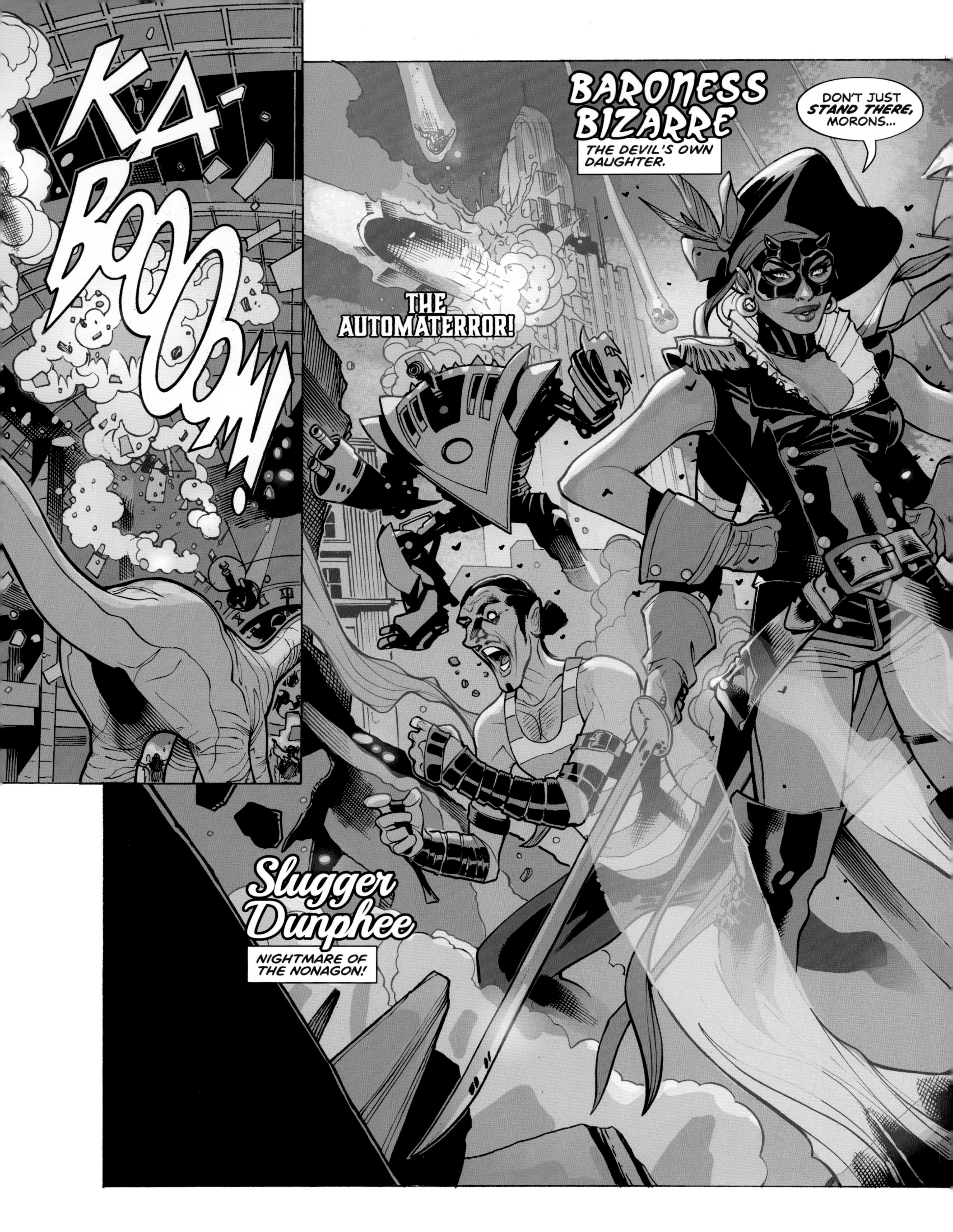
KA-BOOOOM!
BARONESS BIZARRE
THE DEVIL'S OWN DAUGHTER.
DON'T JUST STAND THERE, MORONS...
THE AUTOMATERROR!
Slugger Dunphee
NIGHTMARE OF THE NONAGON!

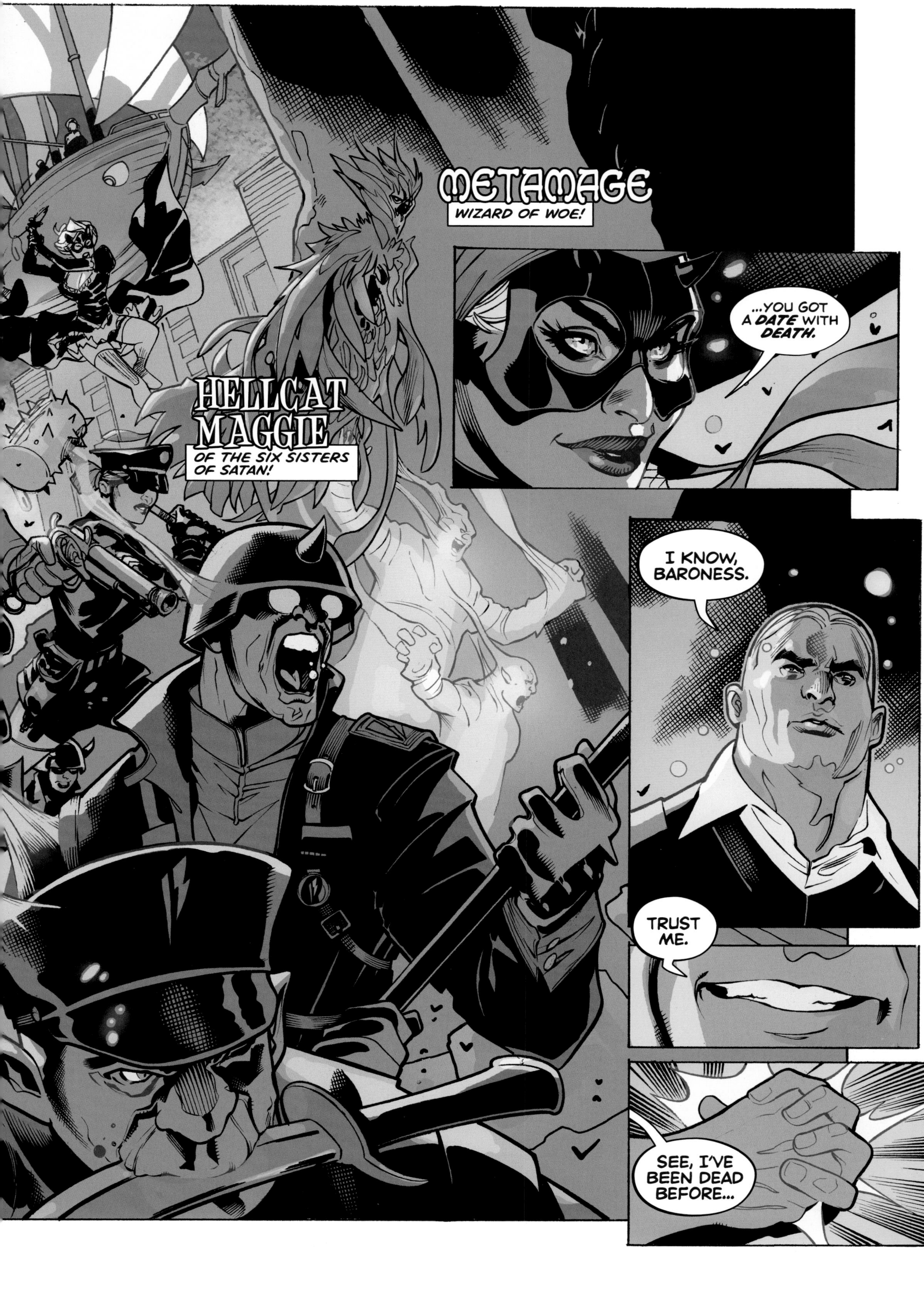
METAMAGE
WIZARD OF WOE!
HELLCAT MAGGIE
OF THE SIX SISTERS OF SATAN!
...YOU GOT A DATE WITH DEATH.
I KNOW, BARONESS.
TRUST ME.
SEE, I'VE BEEN DEAD BEFORE...

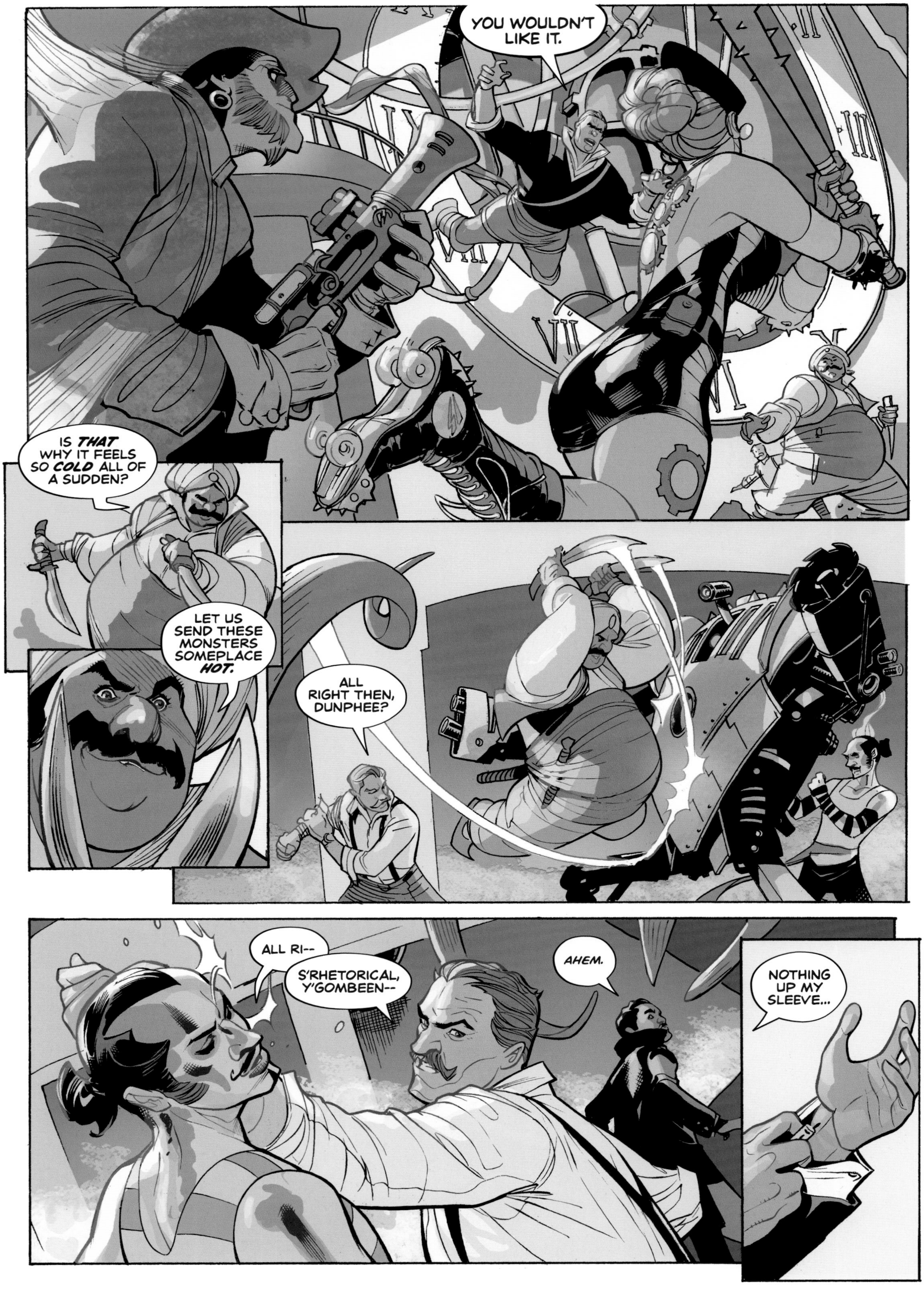
YOU WOULDN'T LIKE IT.
IS THAT WHY IT FEELS SO COLD ALL OF A SUDDEN?
LET US SEND THESE MONSTERS SOMEPLACE HOT.
ALL RIGHT THEN, DUNPHEE?
ALL RI--
S'RHETORICAL, Y'GOMBEEN--
AHEM.
NOTHING UP MY SLEEVE...

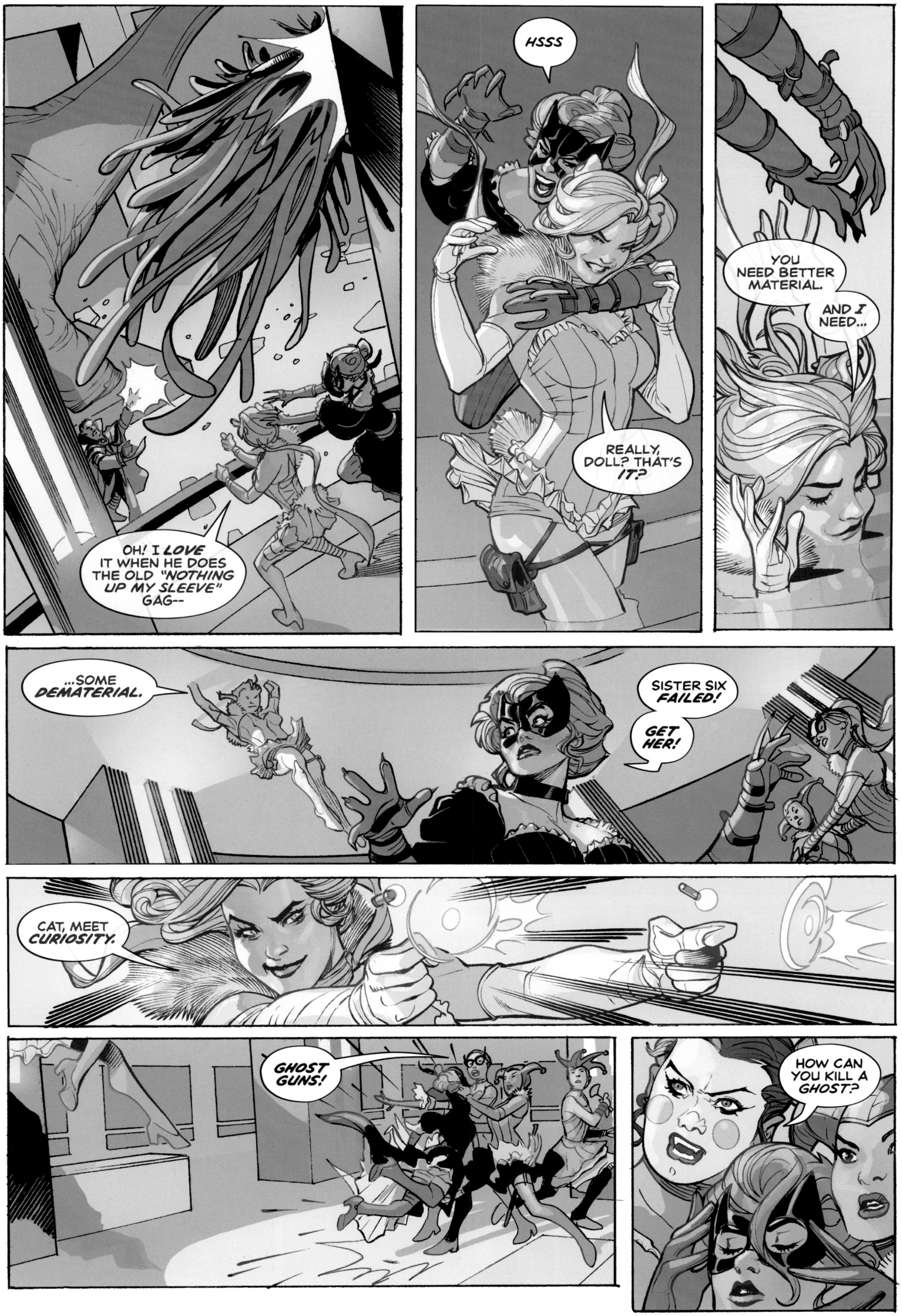
OH! I LOVE IT WHEN HE DOES THE OLD "NOTHING UP MY SLEEVE" GAG--
HSSS
REALLY, DOLL? THAT'S IT?
YOU NEED BETTER MATERIAL.
AND I NEED...
...SOME DEMATERIAL.
SISTER SIX FAILED!
GET HER!
CAT, MEET CURIOSITY.
GHOST GUNS!
HOW CAN YOU KILL A GHOST?

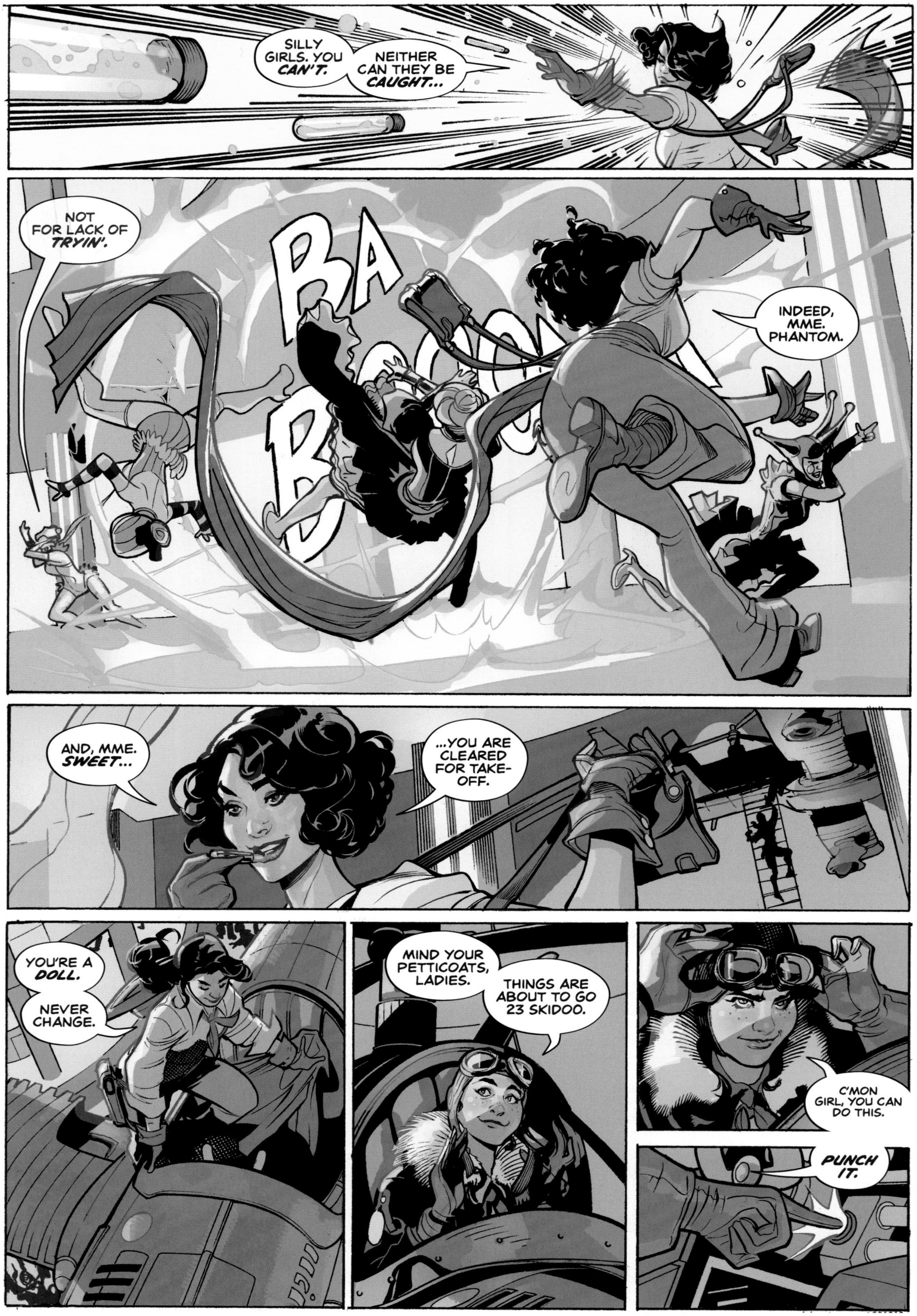
SILLY GIRLS. YOU *CAN'T.*
NEITHER CAN THEY BE *CAUGHT...*
NOT FOR LACK OF *TRYIN'.*
BA BOOM
INDEED, MME. PHANTOM.
AND, MME. *SWEET...*
...YOU ARE CLEARED FOR TAKE-OFF.
YOU'RE A *DOLL.*
NEVER CHANGE.
MIND YOUR PETTICOATS, LADIES.
THINGS ARE ABOUT TO GO 23 SKIDOO.
C'MON GIRL, YOU CAN DO THIS.
PUNCH IT.

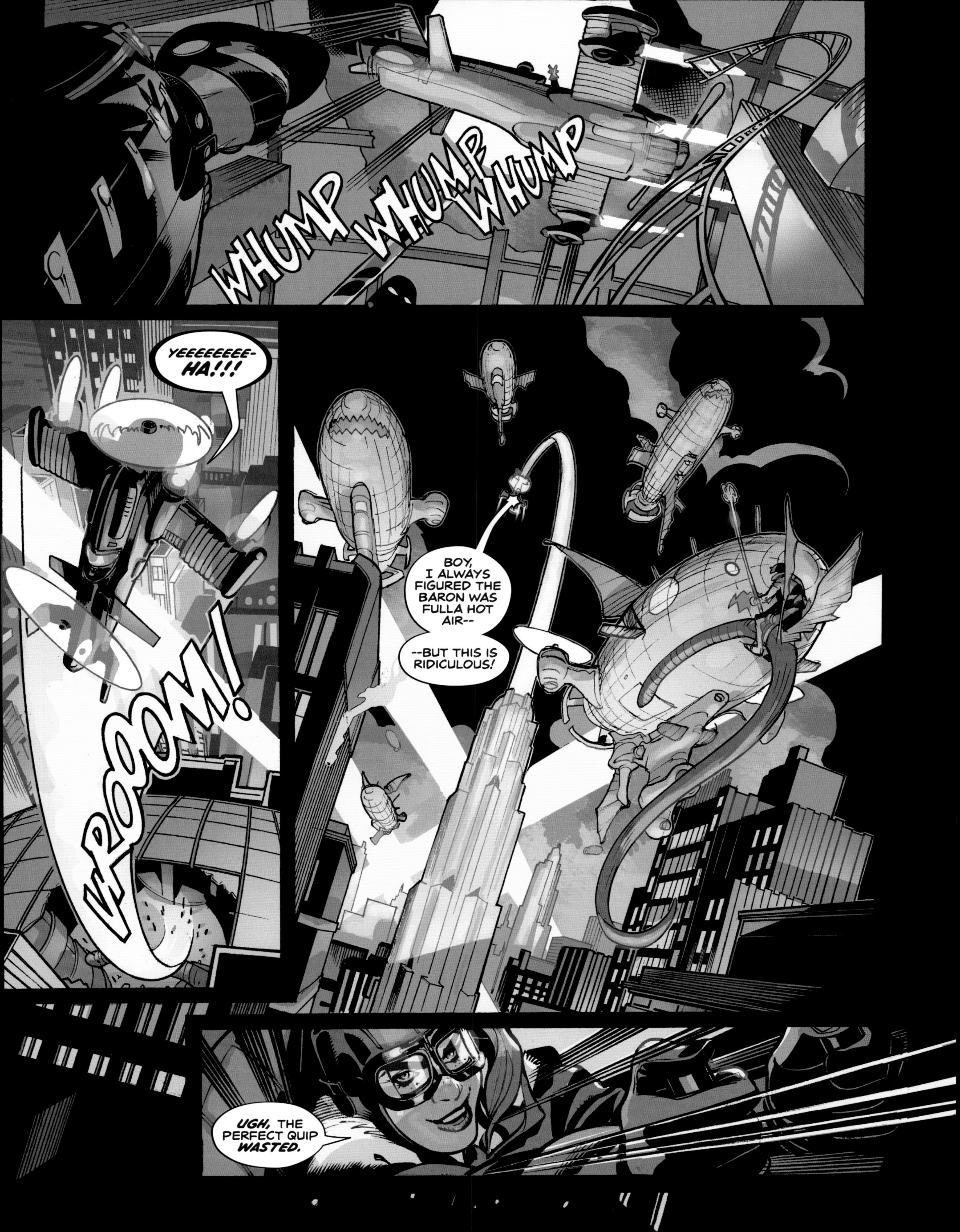
WHUMP WHUMP WHUMP
YEEEEEEEE-HA!!!
VROOOM!
BOY, I ALWAYS FIGURED THE BARON WAS FULLA HOT AIR--
--BUT THIS IS RIDICULOUS!
UGH, THE PERFECT QUIP WASTED.

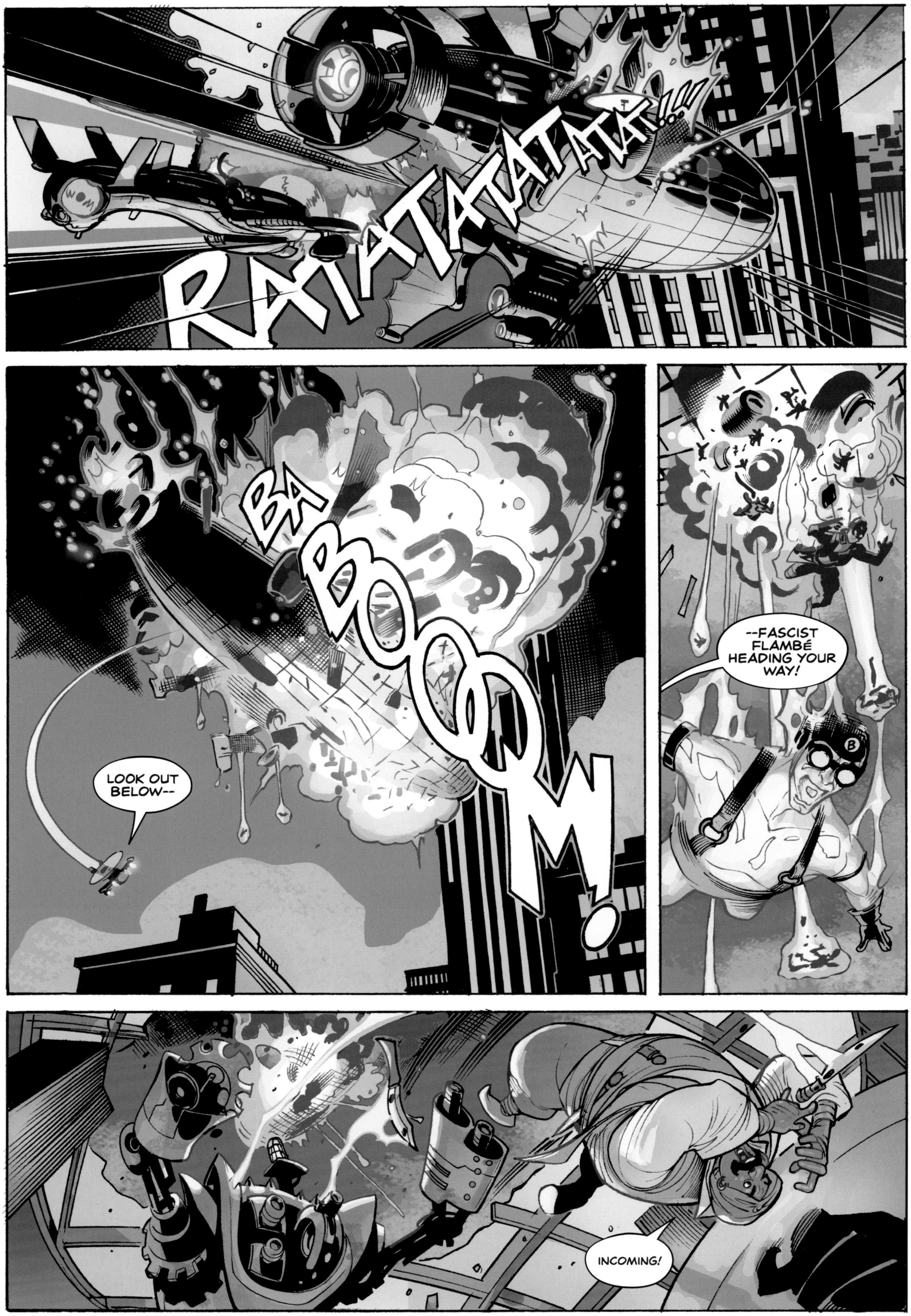
RATATATATATATATAT!!!!
BA BOOOOM!
LOOK OUT BELOW--
--FASCIST FLAMBÉ HEADING YOUR WAY!
INCOMING!

WHOOOMP!!!

HOW DANGLES THE DAGGER, DARLING DEAR?

FOOLISH GIRL--

--LOOK OUT!

HSSS

PSH. SO MUCH FOR CATLIKE REFLEXES.

RⁿᛏMS RⁿᛏMS RⁿᛏMS

�triangleᛁFFMRMᛏᛏ RⁿᛏMS ᛁFFMRMᛏᛏ RⁿᛏMS ᛁFFMRMᛏᛏ

JIM--

--S'TOO COLD TO REMEMBER--

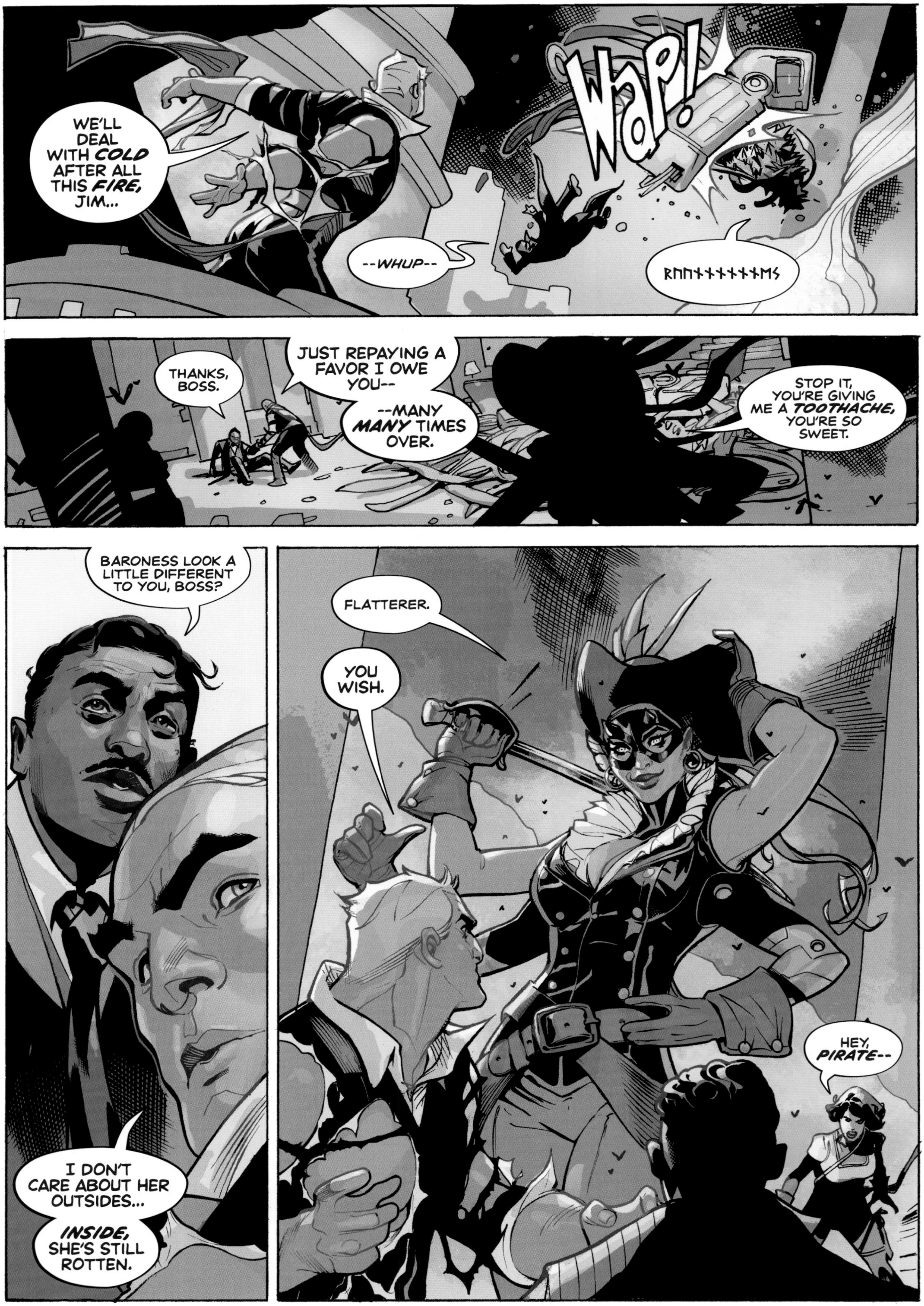
WE'LL DEAL WITH COLD AFTER ALL THIS FIRE, JIM...
WAP!
--WHUP--
THANKS, BOSS.
JUST REPAYING A FAVOR I OWE YOU--
--MANY MANY TIMES OVER.
STOP IT, YOU'RE GIVING ME A TOOTHACHE, YOU'RE SO SWEET.
BARONESS LOOK A LITTLE DIFFERENT TO YOU, BOSS?
I DON'T CARE ABOUT HER OUTSIDES...
INSIDE, SHE'S STILL ROTTEN.
FLATTERER.
YOU WISH.
HEY, PIRATE--

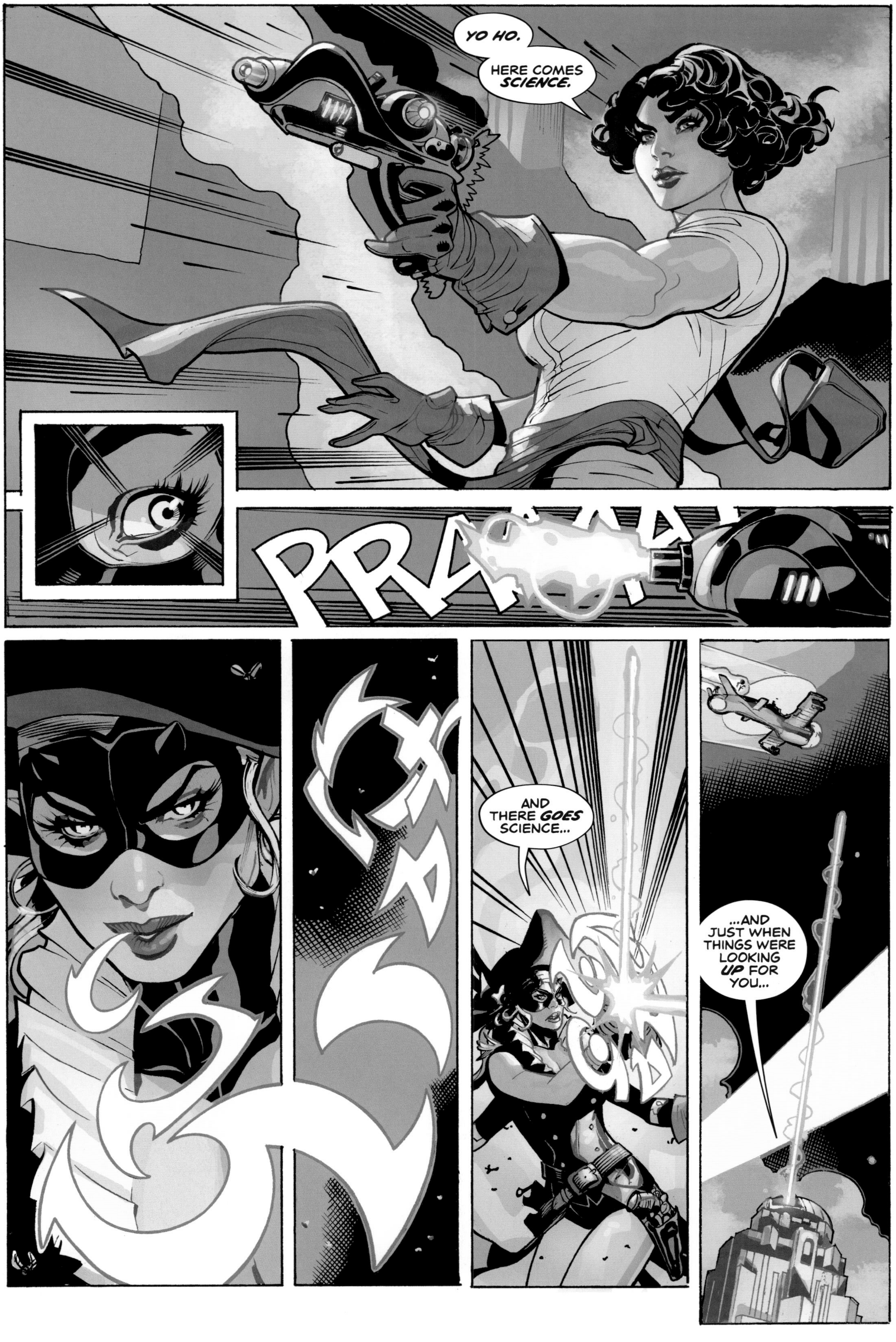
YO HO.
HERE COMES SCIENCE.
AND THERE GOES SCIENCE...
...AND JUST WHEN THINGS WERE LOOKING UP FOR YOU...

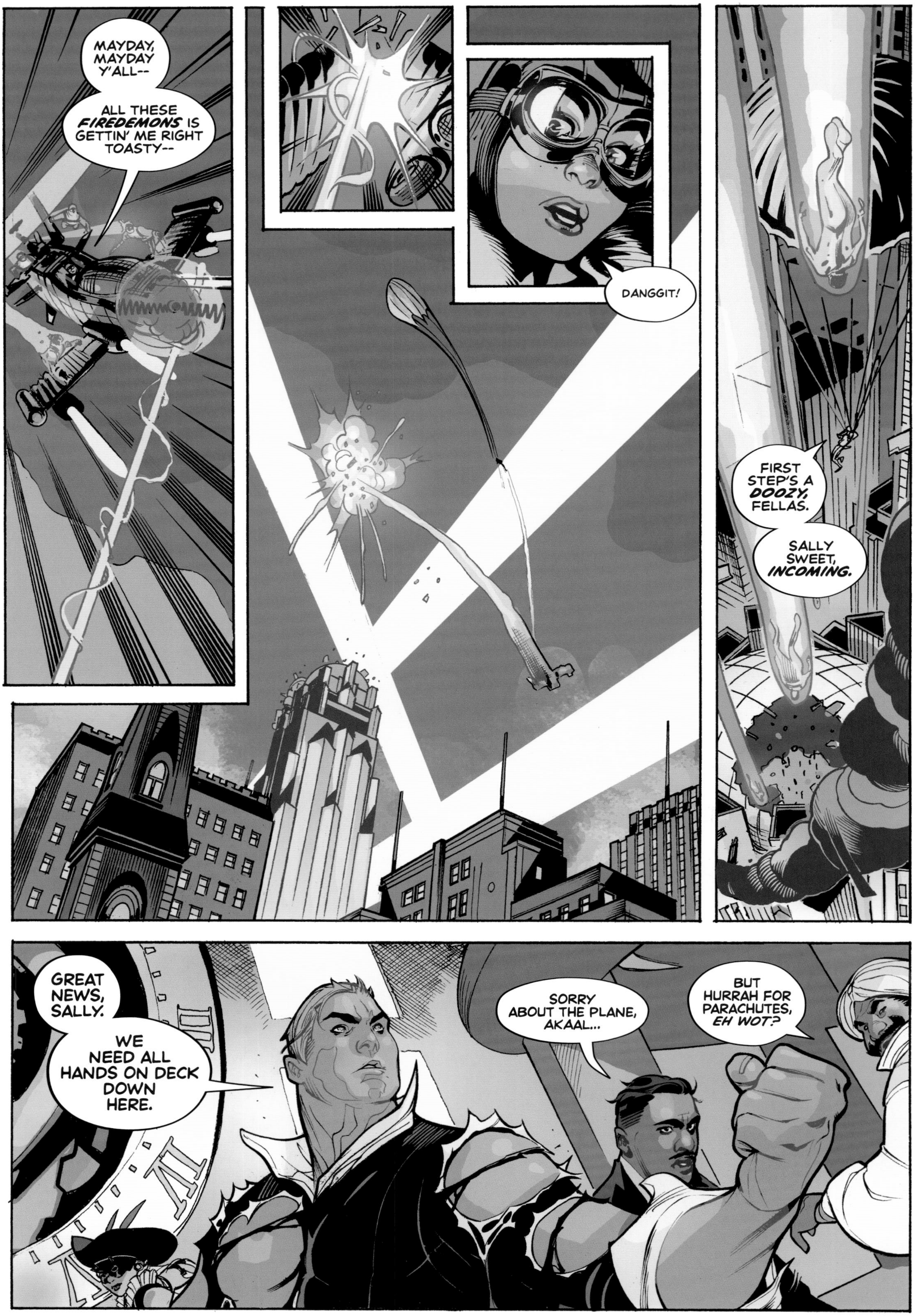
MAYDAY, MAYDAY Y'ALL--
ALL THESE FIREDEMONS IS GETTIN' ME RIGHT TOASTY--
DANGGIT!
FIRST STEP'S A DOOZY, FELLAS.
SALLY SWEET, INCOMING.
GREAT NEWS, SALLY.
WE NEED ALL HANDS ON DECK DOWN HERE.
SORRY ABOUT THE PLANE, AKAAL...
BUT HURRAH FOR PARACHUTES, EH WOT?

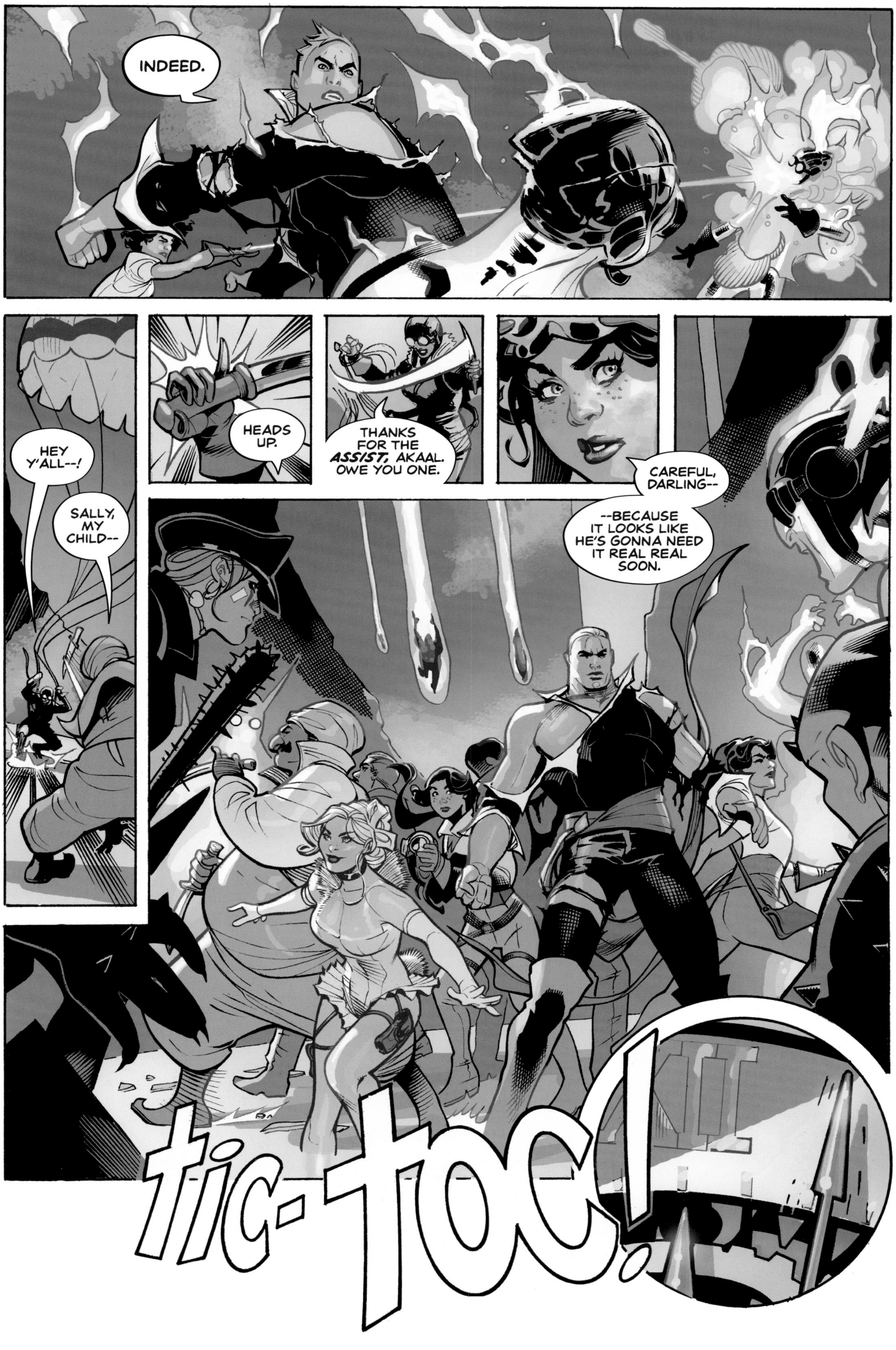
INDEED.
HEY Y'ALL--!
SALLY, MY CHILD--
HEADS UP.
THANKS FOR THE ASSIST, AKAAL. OWE YOU ONE.
CAREFUL, DARLING--
--BECAUSE IT LOOKS LIKE HE'S GONNA NEED IT REAL REAL SOON.
tic-toc!

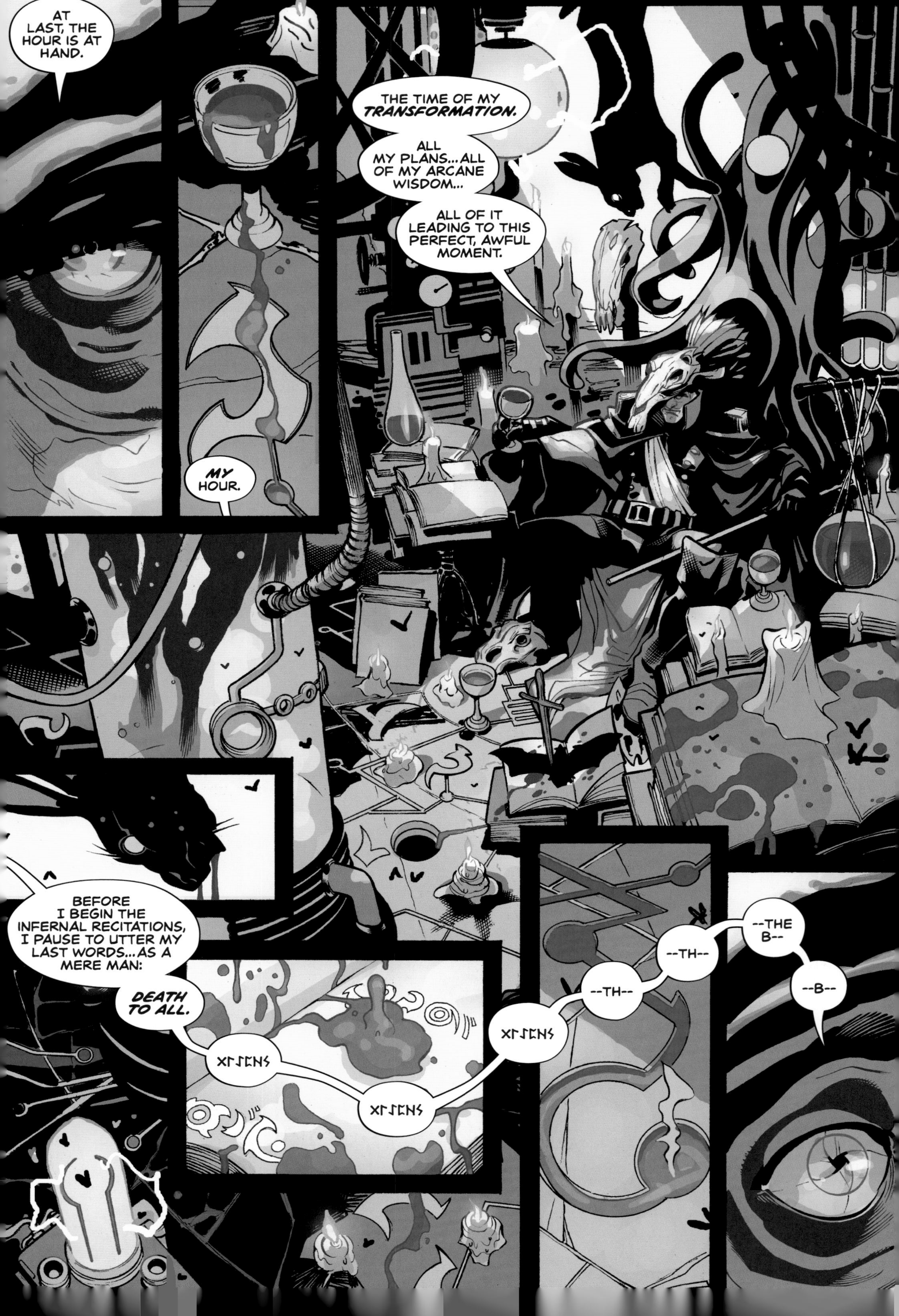

AT LAST, THE HOUR IS AT HAND.
THE TIME OF MY TRANSFORMATION.
ALL MY PLANS...ALL OF MY ARCANE WISDOM...
ALL OF IT LEADING TO THIS PERFECT, AWFUL MOMENT.
MY HOUR.
BEFORE I BEGIN THE INFERNAL RECITATIONS, I PAUSE TO UTTER MY LAST WORDS...AS A MERE MAN:
DEATH TO ALL.
--TH--
--TH--
--THE B--
--B--

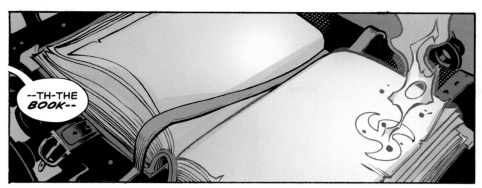

--TH-THE *BOOK*--

WHAT WAS *THAT?*

WHAT WAS WHAT, *MON AMI*...?

THAT SOUND.

LIKE BABIES MADE OF GLASS, SHATTERING...

TALK, FIEND!

WHAT MADNESS IS THIS?!?

BEHOLD--

--THE *JUDAS PRESS* STIRS FROM ITS SLUMBER!

THE *OBLITERATION BIBLE* IS WRITTEN!

tic-

AND YOUR *TIME*... ...IS UP.

toc!

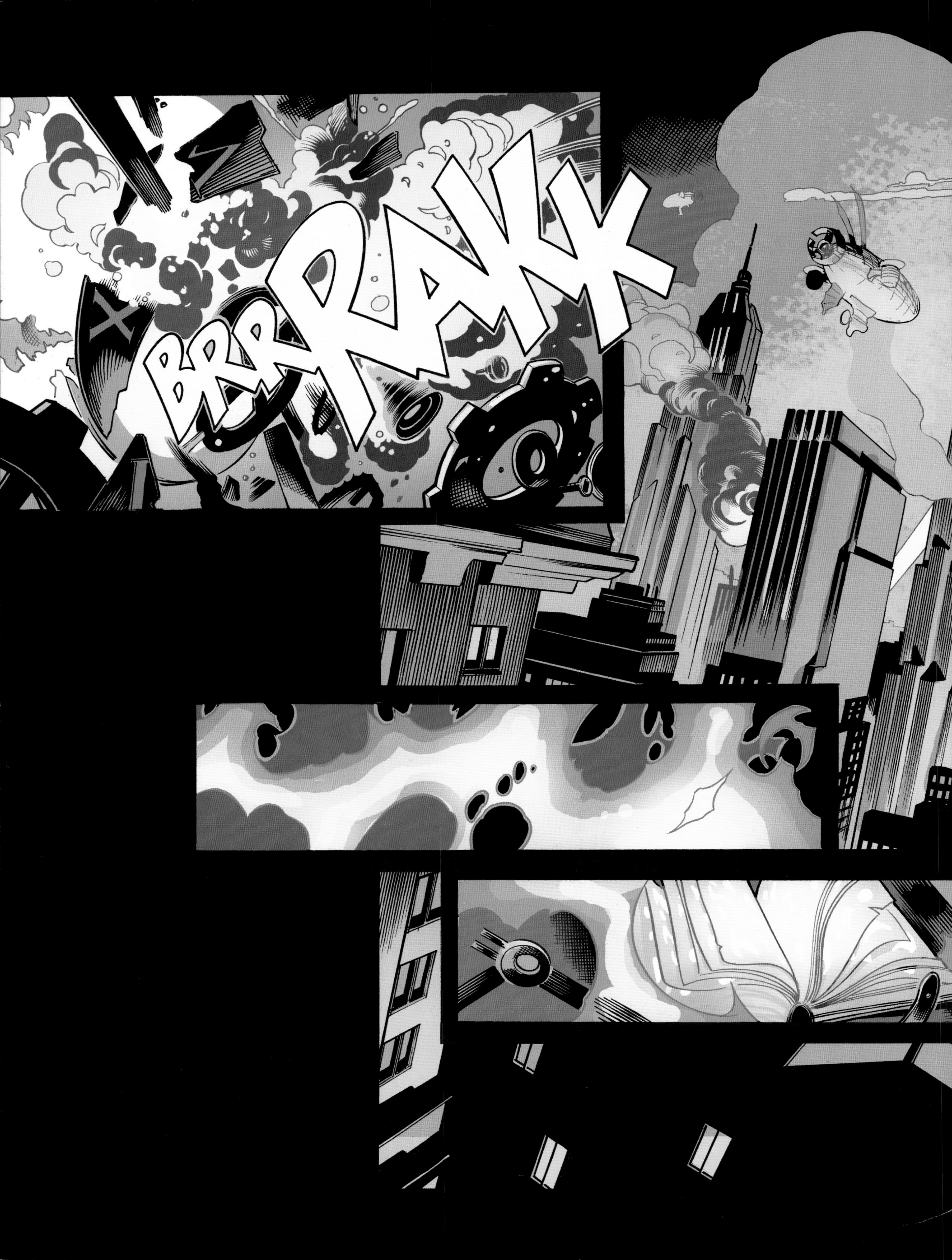
BRRRAKK

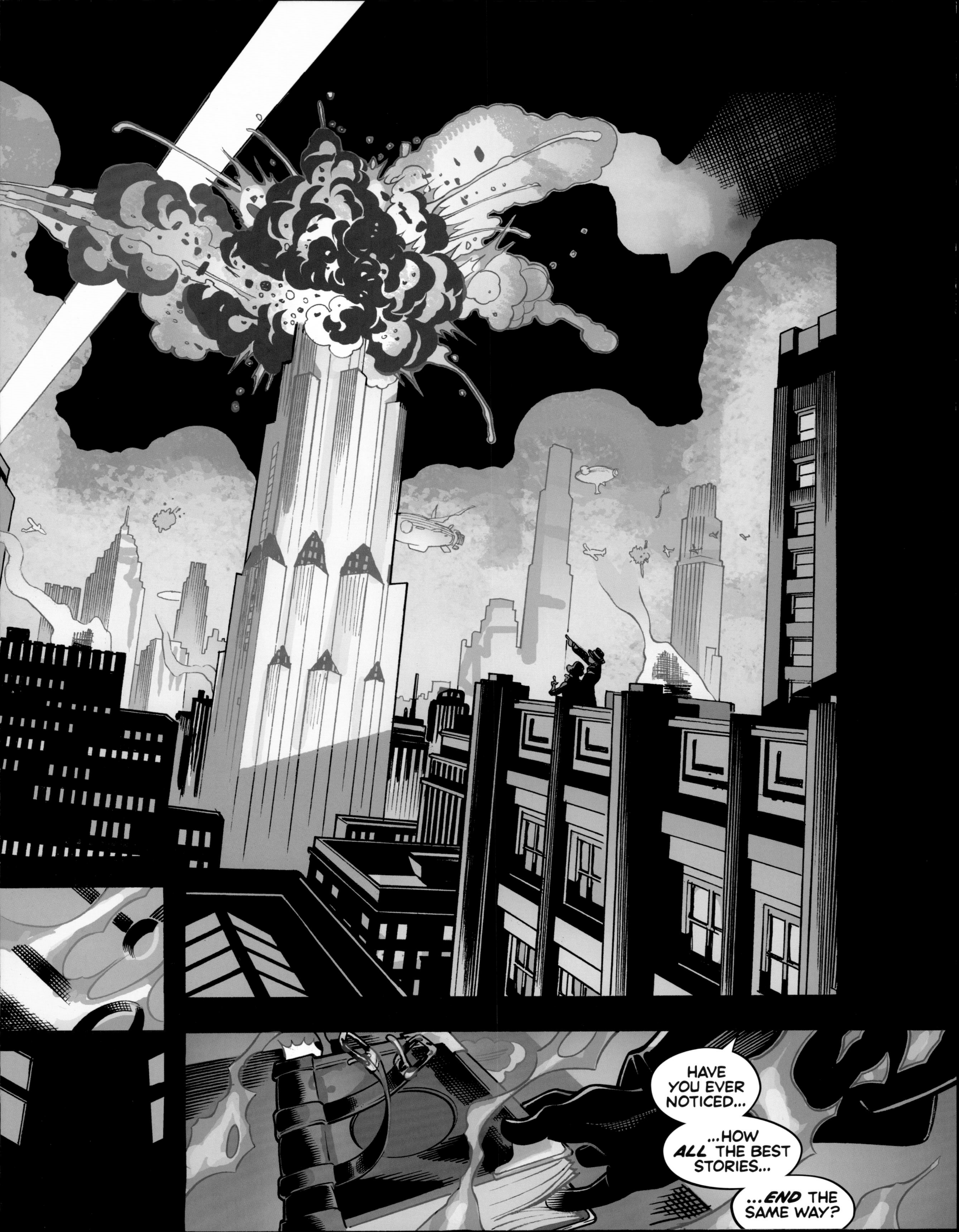
HAVE YOU EVER NOTICED...
...HOW ALL THE BEST STORIES...
...END THE SAME WAY?

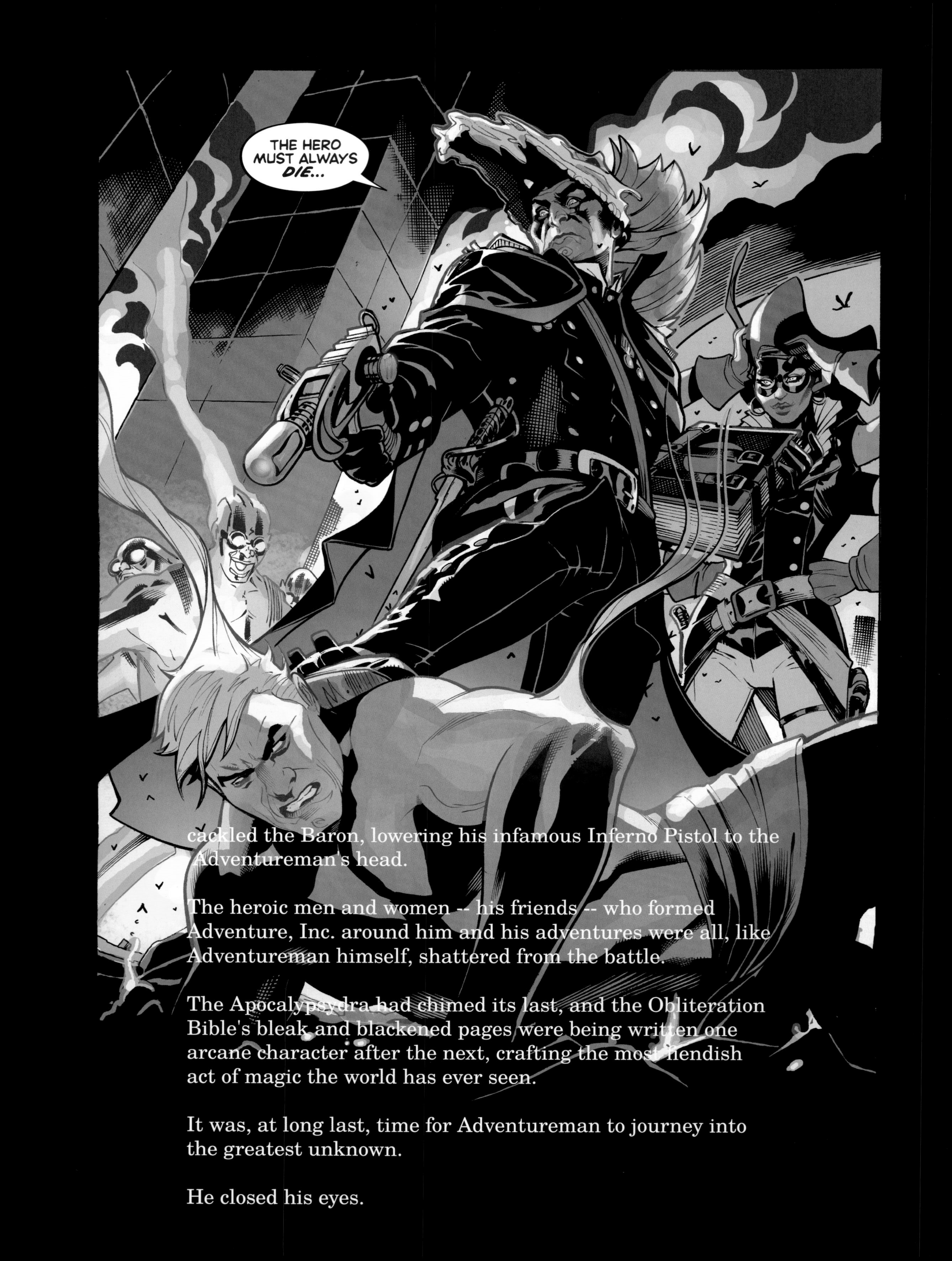
THE HERO MUST ALWAYS *DIE...*

cackled the Baron, lowering his infamous Inferno Pistol to the Adventureman's head.

The heroic men and women -- his friends -- who formed Adventure, Inc. around him and his adventures were all, like Adventureman himself, shattered from the battle.

The Apocalypsydra had chimed its last, and the Obliteration Bible's bleak and blackened pages were being written one arcane character after the next, crafting the most fiendish act of magic the world has ever seen.

It was, at long last, time for Adventureman to journey into the greatest unknown.

He closed his eyes.

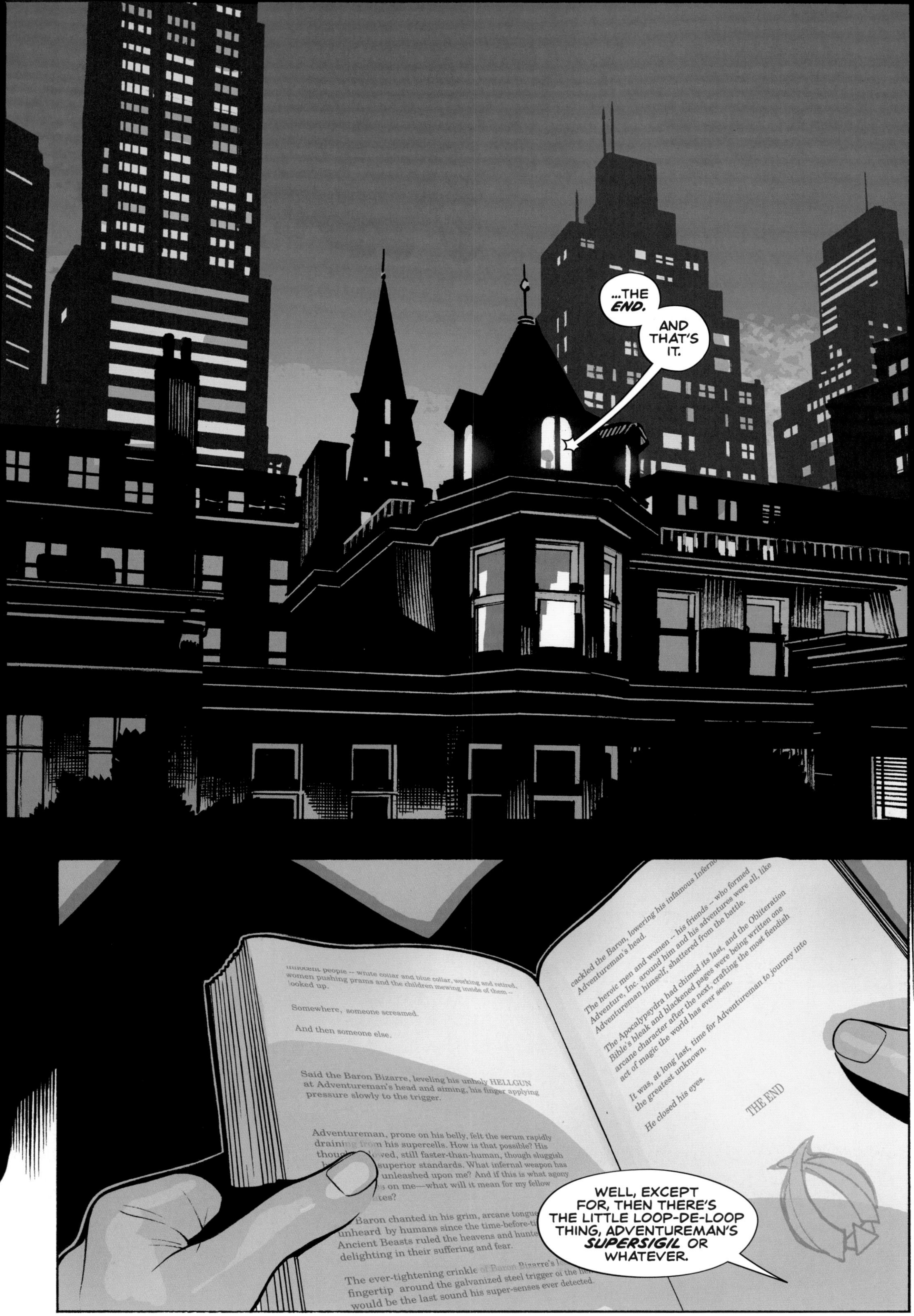
...THE END.
AND THAT'S IT.
Somewhere, someone screamed.
And then someone else.
Said the Baron Bizarre, leveling his unholy HELLGUN at Adventureman's head and aiming, his finger applying pressure slowly to the trigger.
He closed his eyes.
THE END
WELL, EXCEPT FOR, THEN THERE'S THE LITTLE LOOP-DE-LOOP THING, ADVENTUREMAN'S SUPERSIGIL OR WHATEVER.

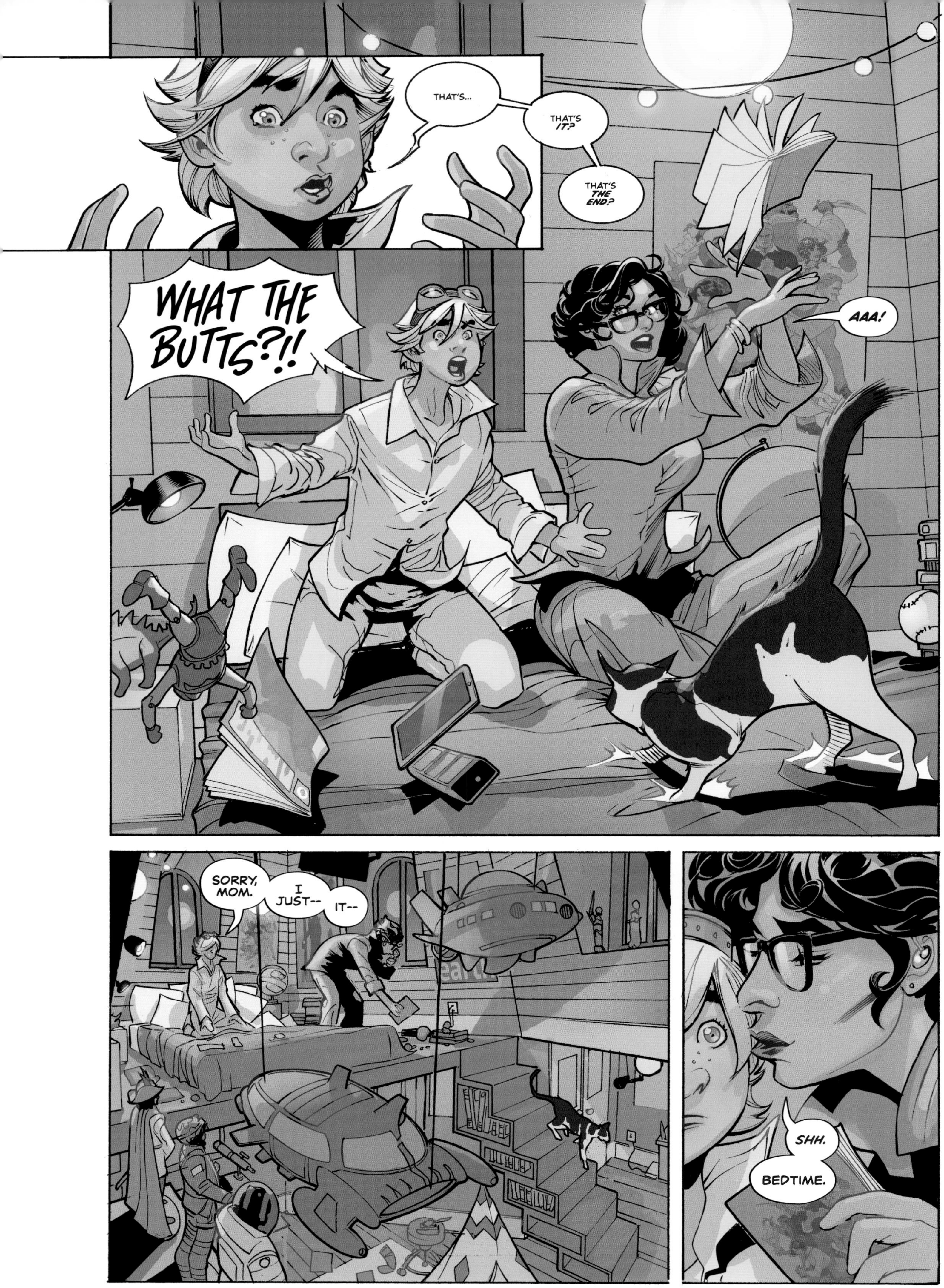
THAT'S...
THAT'S *IT?*
THAT'S *THE END?*
WHAT THE BUTTS?!!
AAA!
SORRY, MOM.
I JUST--
IT--
SHH.
BEDTIME.

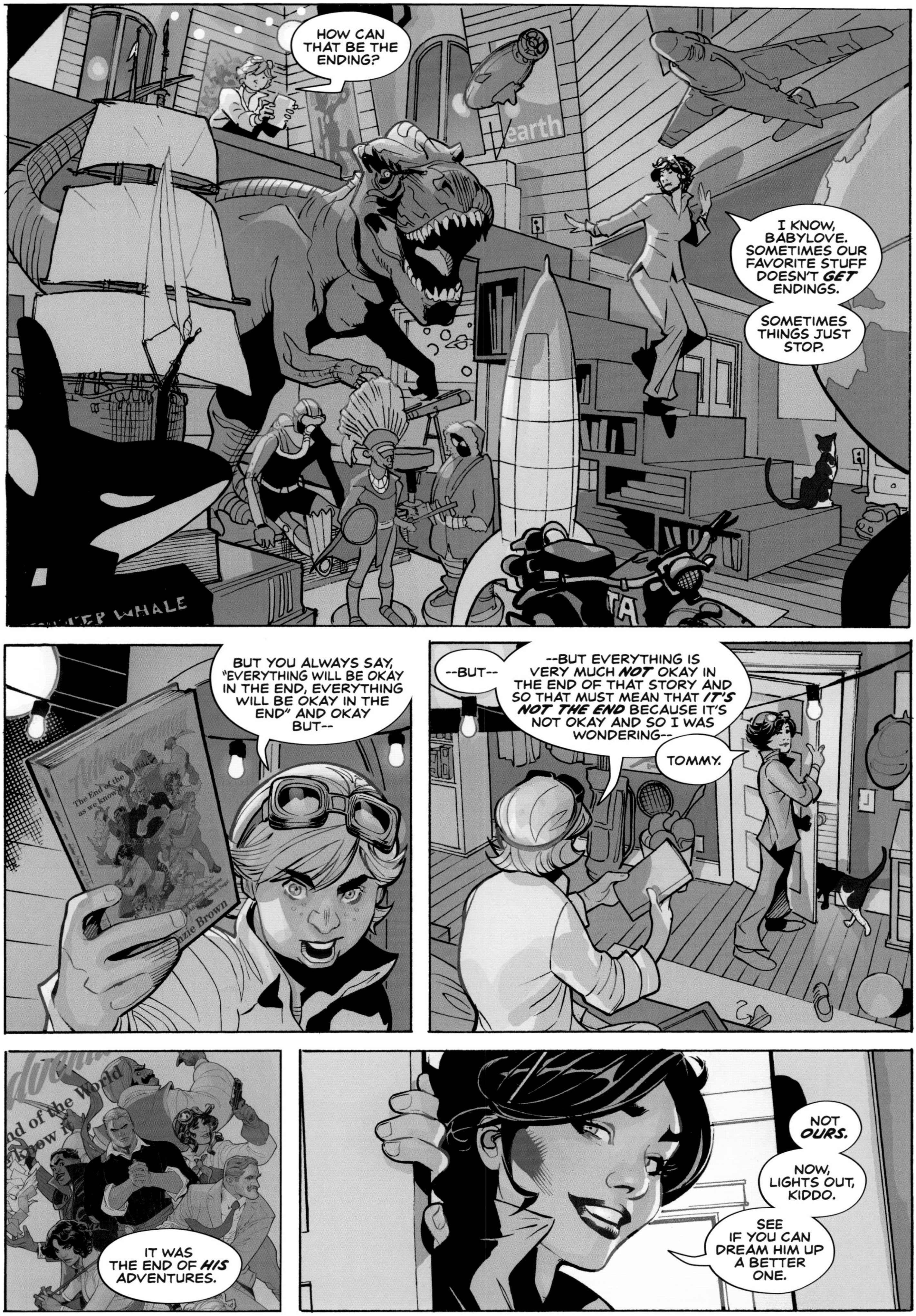
HOW CAN THAT BE THE ENDING?
earth
I KNOW, BABYLOVE. SOMETIMES OUR FAVORITE STUFF DOESN'T **GET** ENDINGS.
SOMETIMES THINGS JUST STOP.
BUT YOU ALWAYS SAY, "EVERYTHING WILL BE OKAY IN THE END, EVERYTHING WILL BE OKAY IN THE END" AND OKAY BUT--
--BUT--
--BUT EVERYTHING IS VERY MUCH **NOT** OKAY IN THE END OF THAT STORY AND SO THAT MUST MEAN THAT **IT'S NOT THE END** BECAUSE IT'S NOT OKAY AND SO I WAS WONDERING--
TOMMY.
IT WAS THE END OF **HIS** ADVENTURES.
NOT **OURS.**
NOW, LIGHTS OUT, KIDDO.
SEE IF YOU CAN DREAM HIM UP A BETTER ONE.

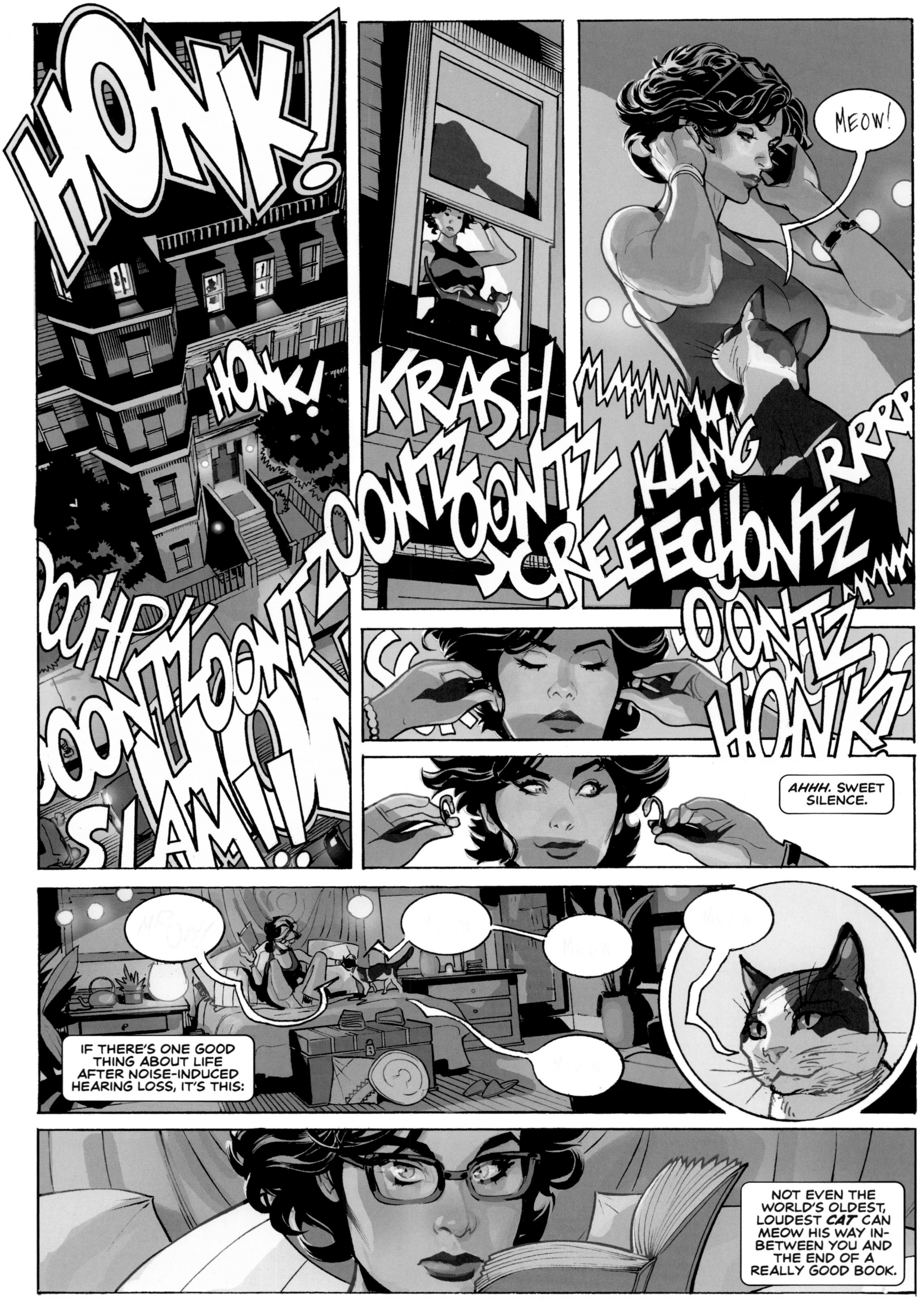
HONK!
MEOW!
HONK!
KRASH
OONTZ
KLANG
SCREEECH
OONTZ
OONTZ
HONK!
SLAM!
AHHH. SWEET SILENCE.
IF THERE'S ONE GOOD THING ABOUT LIFE AFTER NOISE-INDUCED HEARING LOSS, IT'S THIS:
NOT EVEN THE WORLD'S OLDEST, LOUDEST CAT CAN MEOW HIS WAY IN-BETWEEN YOU AND THE END OF A REALLY GOOD BOOK.

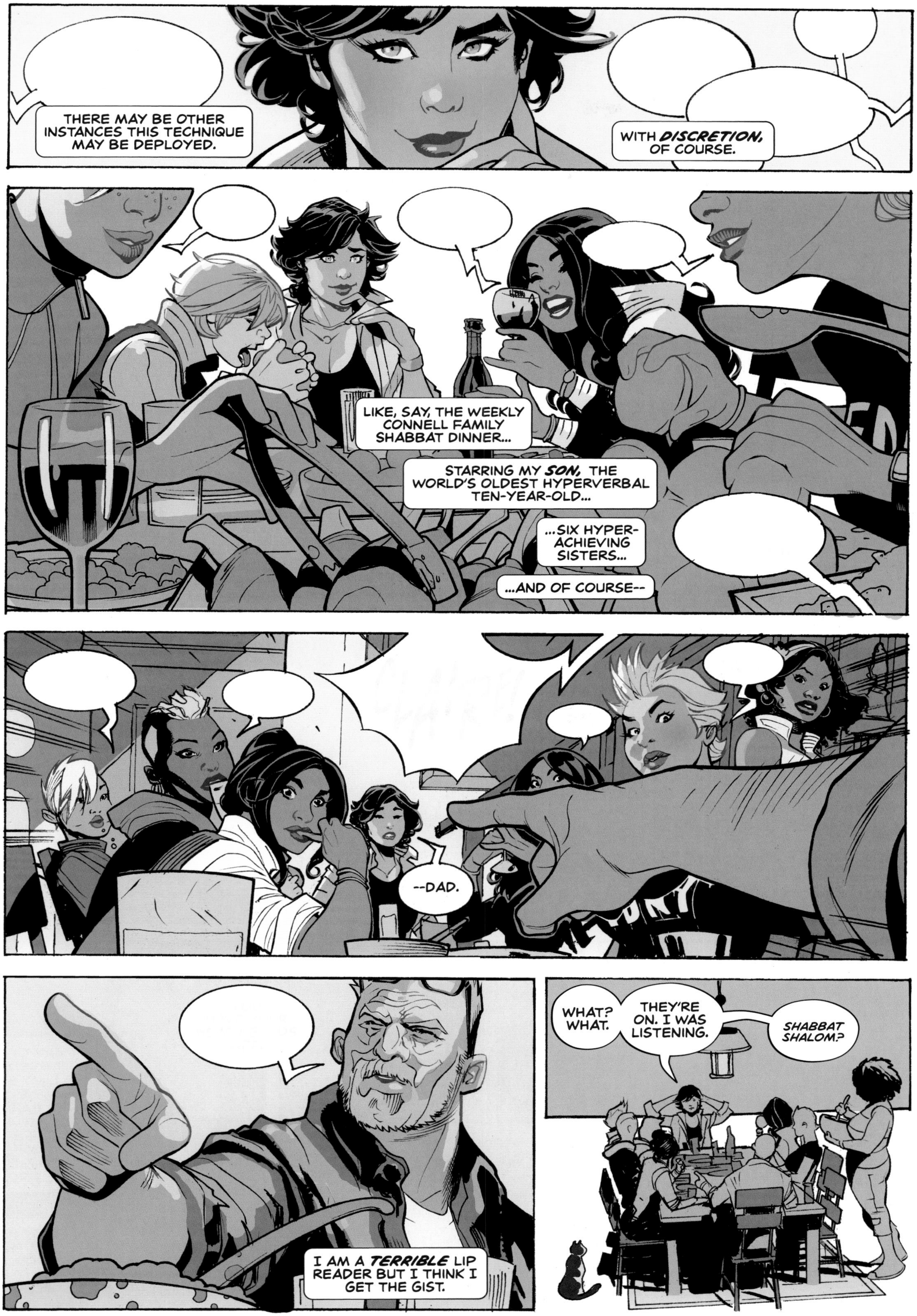
THERE MAY BE OTHER INSTANCES THIS TECHNIQUE MAY BE DEPLOYED.
WITH DISCRETION, OF COURSE.
LIKE, SAY, THE WEEKLY CONNELL FAMILY SHABBAT DINNER...
STARRING MY SON, THE WORLD'S OLDEST HYPERVERBAL TEN-YEAR-OLD...
...SIX HYPER-ACHIEVING SISTERS...
...AND OF COURSE--
--DAD.
I AM A TERRIBLE LIP READER BUT I THINK I GET THE GIST.
WHAT? WHAT.
THEY'RE ON. I WAS LISTENING.
SHABBAT SHALOM?

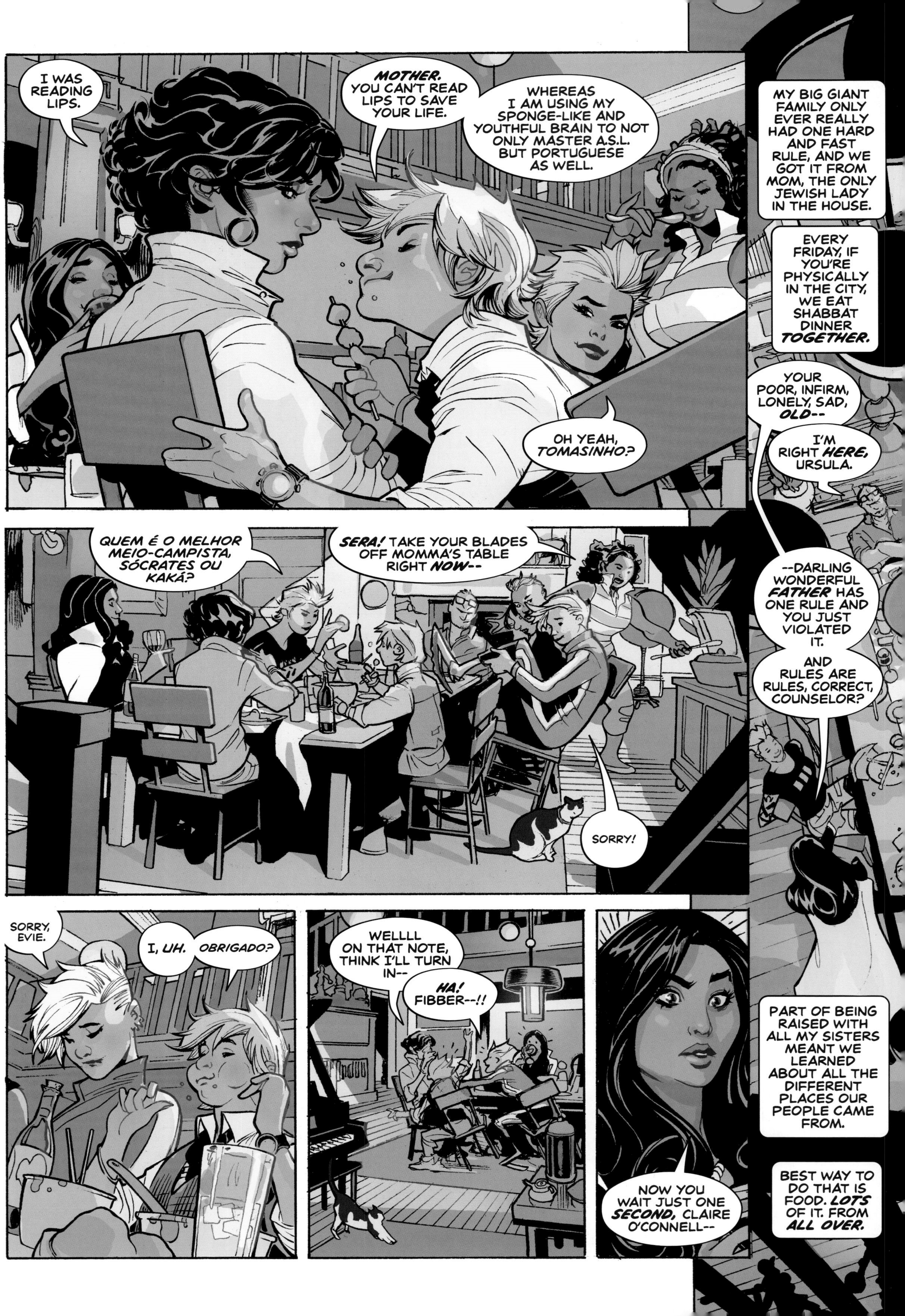
I WAS READING LIPS.
MOTHER. YOU CAN'T READ LIPS TO SAVE YOUR LIFE.
WHEREAS I AM USING MY SPONGE-LIKE AND YOUTHFUL BRAIN TO NOT ONLY MASTER A.S.L. BUT PORTUGUESE AS WELL.
OH YEAH, TOMASINHO?
MY BIG GIANT FAMILY ONLY EVER REALLY HAD ONE HARD AND FAST RULE, AND WE GOT IT FROM MOM, THE ONLY JEWISH LADY IN THE HOUSE.
EVERY FRIDAY, IF YOU'RE PHYSICALLY IN THE CITY, WE EAT SHABBAT DINNER TOGETHER.
YOUR POOR, INFIRM, LONELY, SAD, OLD--
I'M RIGHT HERE, URSULA.
QUEM É O MELHOR MEIO-CAMPISTA, SÓCRATES OU KAKÁ?
SERA! TAKE YOUR BLADES OFF MOMMA'S TABLE RIGHT NOW--
SORRY!
--DARLING WONDERFUL FATHER HAS ONE RULE AND YOU JUST VIOLATED IT.
AND RULES ARE RULES, CORRECT, COUNSELOR?
SORRY, EVIE.
I, UH.
OBRIGADO?
WELLLL ON THAT NOTE, THINK I'LL TURN IN--
HA! FIBBER--!!
NOW YOU WAIT JUST ONE SECOND, CLAIRE O'CONNELL--
PART OF BEING RAISED WITH ALL MY SISTERS MEANT WE LEARNED ABOUT ALL THE DIFFERENT PLACES OUR PEOPLE CAME FROM.
BEST WAY TO DO THAT IS FOOD. LOTS OF IT. FROM ALL OVER.

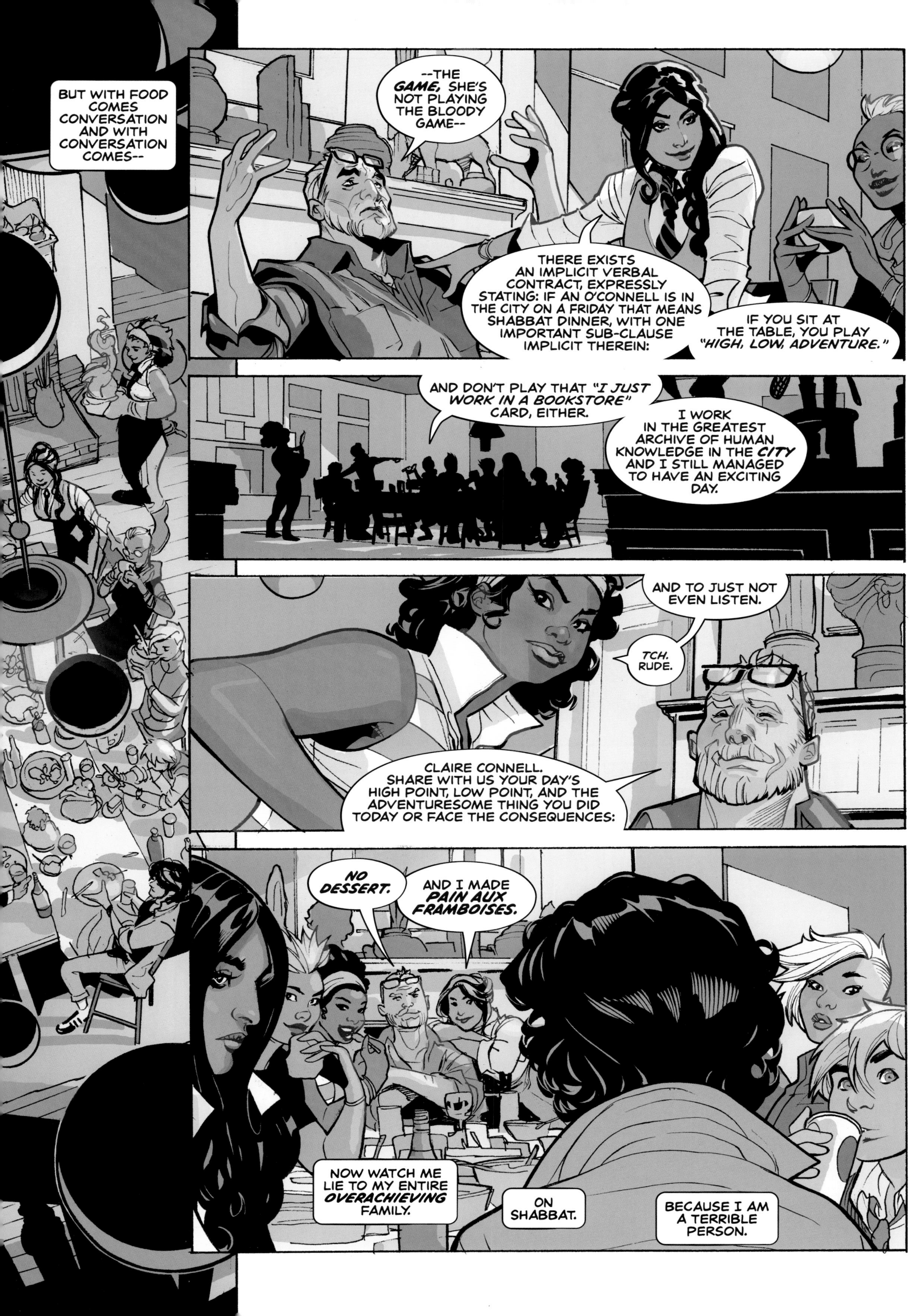
BUT WITH FOOD COMES CONVERSATION AND WITH CONVERSATION COMES--
--THE GAME, SHE'S NOT PLAYING THE BLOODY GAME--
THERE EXISTS AN IMPLICIT VERBAL CONTRACT, EXPRESSLY STATING: IF AN O'CONNELL IS IN THE CITY ON A FRIDAY THAT MEANS SHABBAT DINNER, WITH ONE IMPORTANT SUB-CLAUSE IMPLICIT THEREIN:
IF YOU SIT AT THE TABLE, YOU PLAY "HIGH, LOW, ADVENTURE."
AND DON'T PLAY THAT "I JUST WORK IN A BOOKSTORE" CARD, EITHER.
I WORK IN THE GREATEST ARCHIVE OF HUMAN KNOWLEDGE IN THE CITY AND I STILL MANAGED TO HAVE AN EXCITING DAY.
AND TO JUST NOT EVEN LISTEN.
TCH. RUDE.
CLAIRE CONNELL. SHARE WITH US YOUR DAY'S HIGH POINT, LOW POINT, AND THE ADVENTURESOME THING YOU DID TODAY OR FACE THE CONSEQUENCES:
NO DESSERT.
AND I MADE PAIN AUX FRAMBOISES.
NOW WATCH ME LIE TO MY ENTIRE OVERACHIEVING FAMILY.
ON SHABBAT.
BECAUSE I AM A TERRIBLE PERSON.

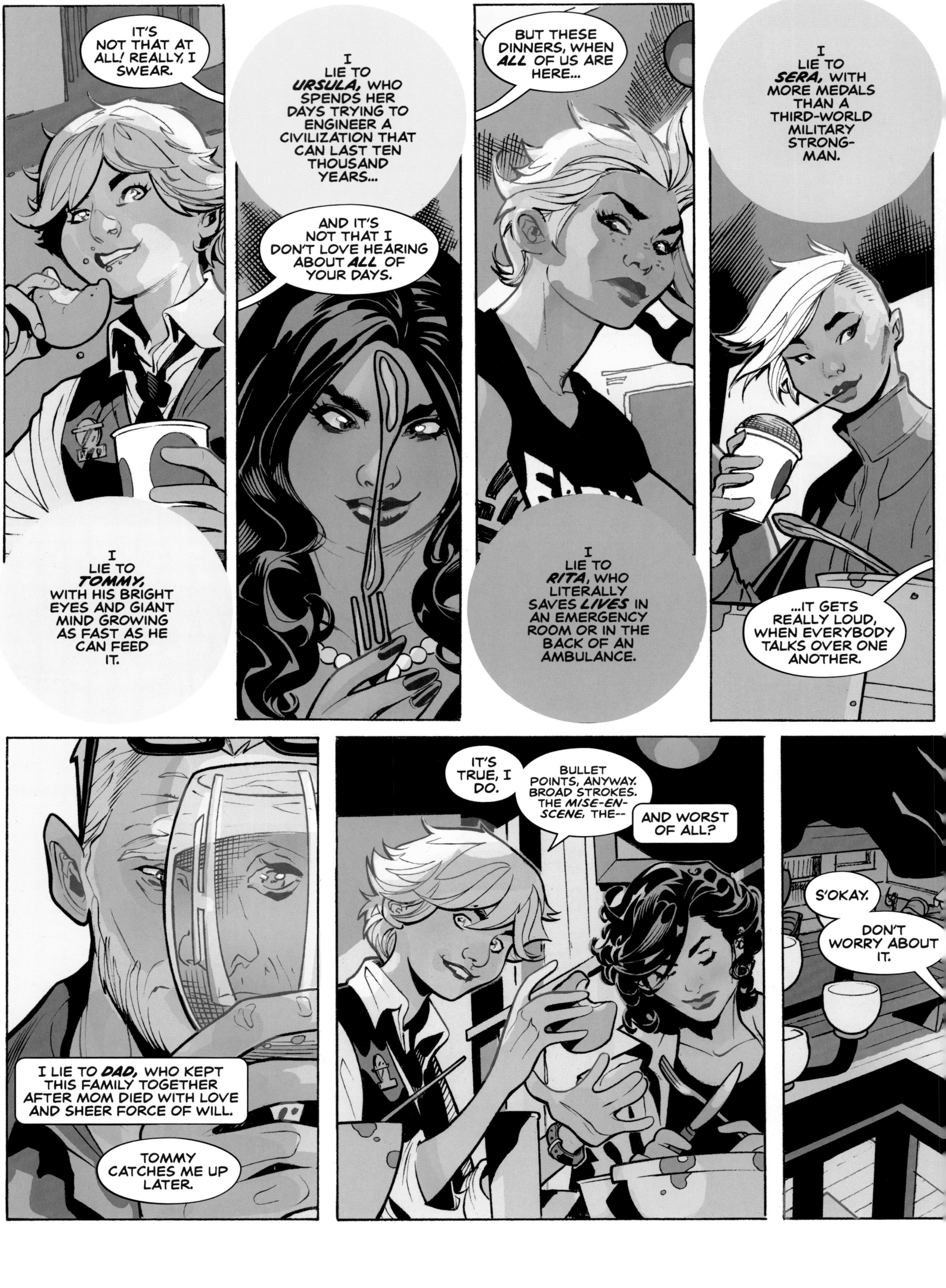
IT'S NOT THAT AT ALL! REALLY, I SWEAR.
I LIE TO TOMMY, WITH HIS BRIGHT EYES AND GIANT MIND GROWING AS FAST AS HE CAN FEED IT.
I LIE TO URSULA, WHO SPENDS HER DAYS TRYING TO ENGINEER A CIVILIZATION THAT CAN LAST TEN THOUSAND YEARS...
AND IT'S NOT THAT I DON'T LOVE HEARING ABOUT ALL OF YOUR DAYS.
BUT THESE DINNERS, WHEN ALL OF US ARE HERE...
I LIE TO RITA, WHO LITERALLY SAVES LIVES IN AN EMERGENCY ROOM OR IN THE BACK OF AN AMBULANCE.
I LIE TO SERA, WITH MORE MEDALS THAN A THIRD-WORLD MILITARY STRONG-MAN.
...IT GETS REALLY LOUD, WHEN EVERYBODY TALKS OVER ONE ANOTHER.
I LIE TO DAD, WHO KEPT THIS FAMILY TOGETHER AFTER MOM DIED WITH LOVE AND SHEER FORCE OF WILL.
TOMMY CATCHES ME UP LATER.
IT'S TRUE, I DO.
BULLET POINTS, ANYWAY. BROAD STROKES. THE MISE-EN-SCENE, THE--
AND WORST OF ALL?
S'OKAY.
DON'T WORRY ABOUT IT.

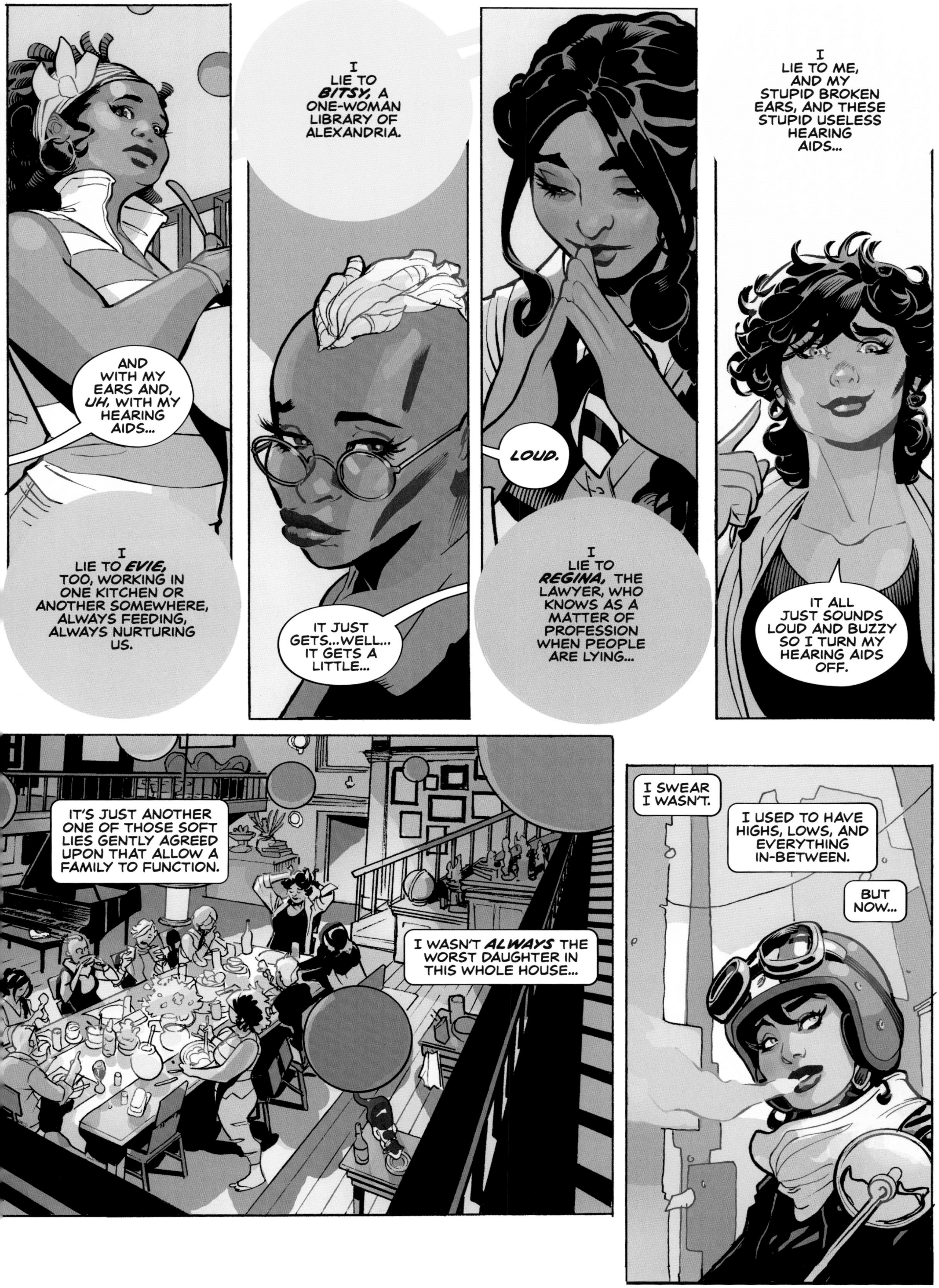
AND WITH MY EARS AND, *UH,* WITH MY HEARING AIDS...
I LIE TO *EVIE,* TOO, WORKING IN ONE KITCHEN OR ANOTHER SOMEWHERE, ALWAYS FEEDING, ALWAYS NURTURING US.
I LIE TO *BITSY,* A ONE-WOMAN LIBRARY OF ALEXANDRIA.
IT JUST GETS...WELL... IT GETS A LITTLE...
LOUD.
I LIE TO *REGINA,* THE LAWYER, WHO KNOWS AS A MATTER OF PROFESSION WHEN PEOPLE ARE LYING...
I LIE TO ME, AND MY STUPID BROKEN EARS, AND THESE STUPID USELESS HEARING AIDS...
IT ALL JUST SOUNDS LOUD AND BUZZY SO I TURN MY HEARING AIDS OFF.
IT'S JUST ANOTHER ONE OF THOSE SOFT LIES GENTLY AGREED UPON THAT ALLOW A FAMILY TO FUNCTION.
I WASN'T *ALWAYS* THE WORST DAUGHTER IN THIS WHOLE HOUSE...
I SWEAR I WASN'T.
I USED TO HAVE HIGHS, LOWS, AND EVERYTHING IN-BETWEEN.
BUT NOW...

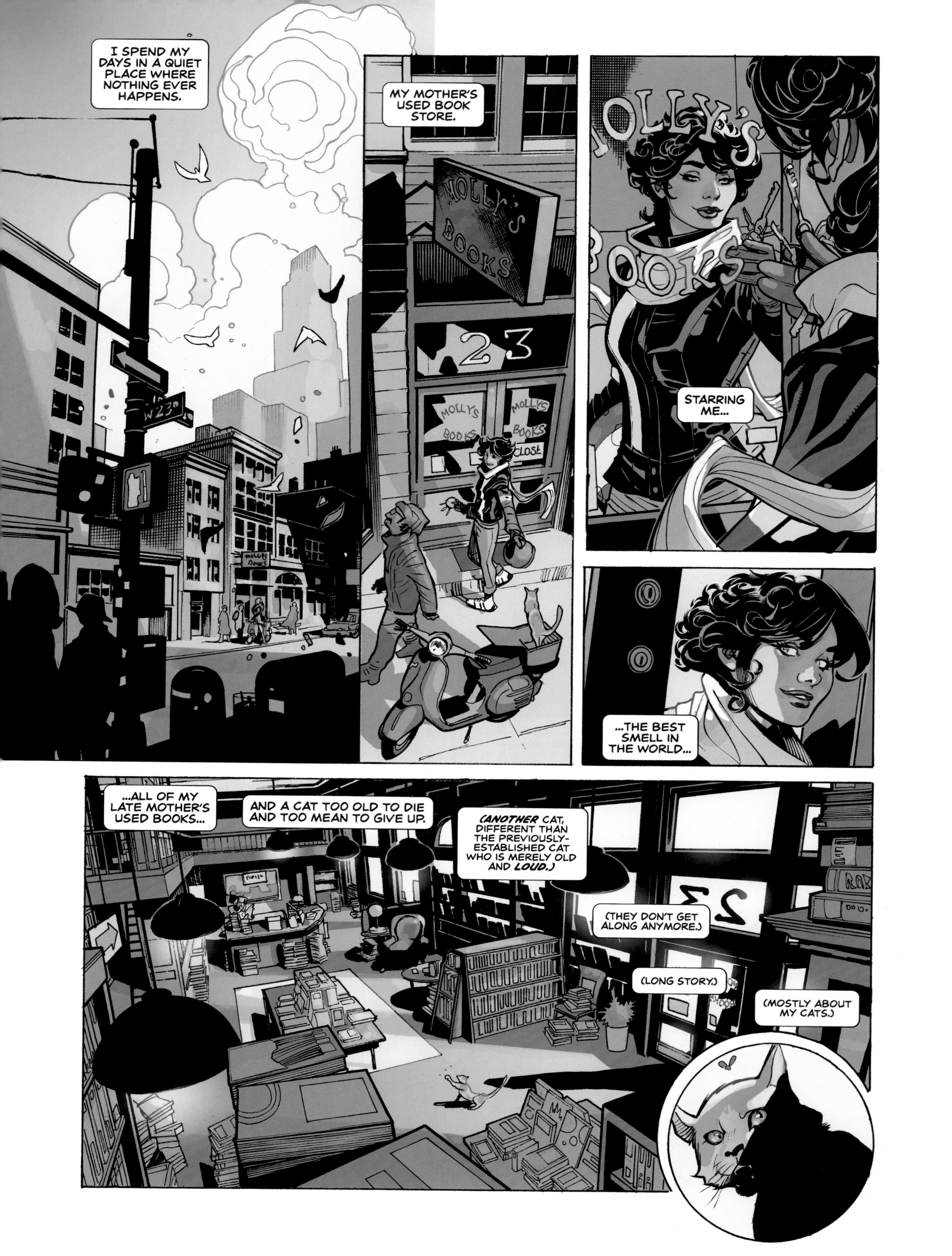
I SPEND MY DAYS IN A QUIET PLACE WHERE NOTHING EVER HAPPENS.
W 23
MY MOTHER'S USED BOOK STORE.
MOLLY'S BOOKS
23
MOLLY'S BOOKS
MOLLY'S BOOKS
CLOSE
MOLLY'S BOOKS
STARRING ME...
...THE BEST SMELL IN THE WORLD...
...ALL OF MY LATE MOTHER'S USED BOOKS...
AND A CAT TOO OLD TO DIE AND TOO MEAN TO GIVE UP.
(ANOTHER CAT, DIFFERENT THAN THE PREVIOUSLY-ESTABLISHED CAT WHO IS MERELY OLD AND LOUD.)
(THEY DON'T GET ALONG ANYMORE.)
(LONG STORY.)
(MOSTLY ABOUT MY CATS.)

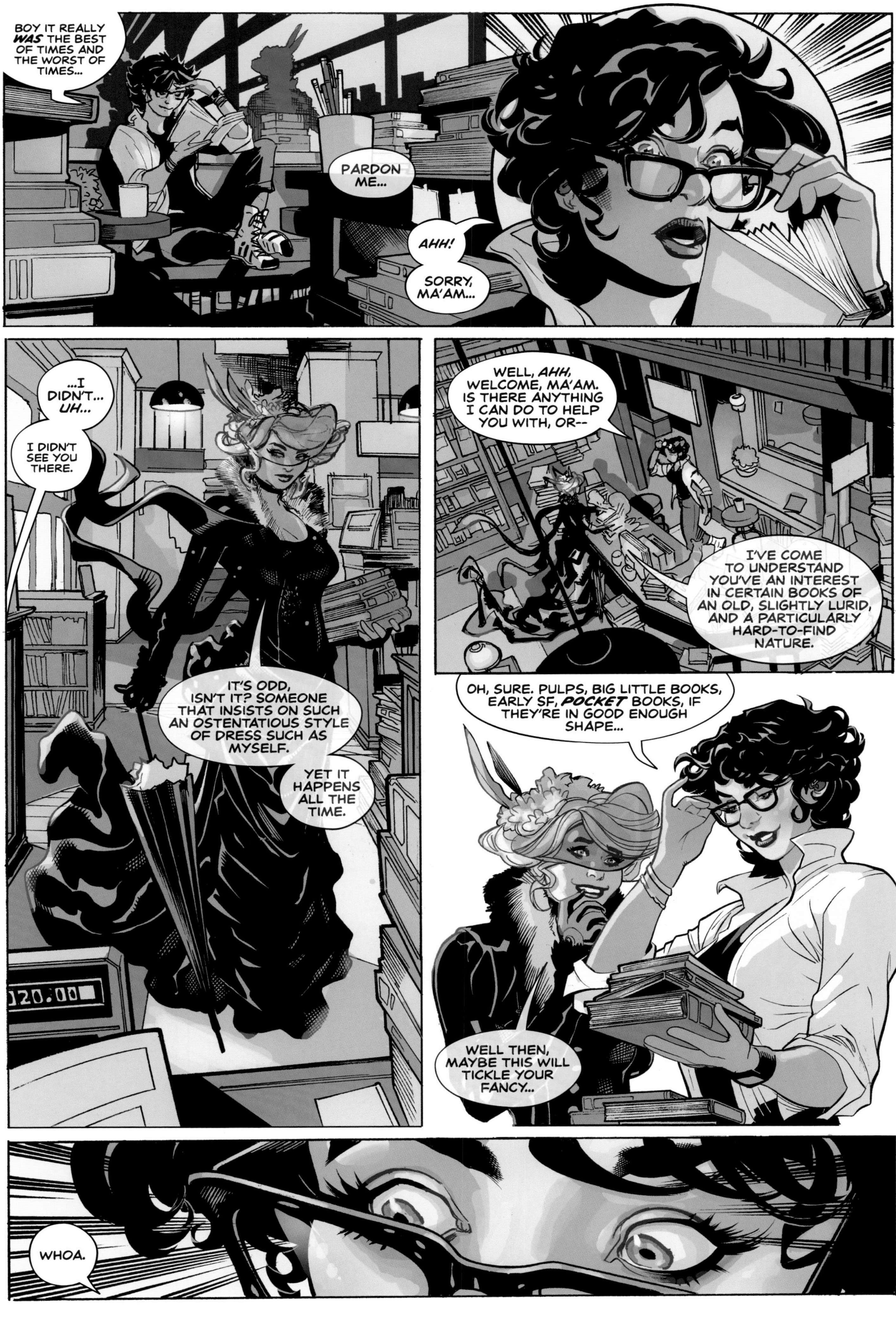
BOY IT REALLY *WAS* THE BEST OF TIMES AND THE WORST OF TIMES...
PARDON ME...
AHH!
SORRY, MA'AM...
...I DIDN'T... *UH*...
I DIDN'T SEE YOU THERE.
IT'S ODD, ISN'T IT? SOMEONE THAT INSISTS ON SUCH AN OSTENTATIOUS STYLE OF DRESS SUCH AS MYSELF.
YET IT HAPPENS ALL THE TIME.
WELL, *AHH,* WELCOME, MA'AM. IS THERE ANYTHING I CAN DO TO HELP YOU WITH, OR--
I'VE COME TO UNDERSTAND YOU'VE AN INTEREST IN CERTAIN BOOKS OF AN OLD, SLIGHTLY LURID, AND A PARTICULARLY HARD-TO-FIND NATURE.
OH, SURE. PULPS, BIG LITTLE BOOKS, EARLY SF, *POCKET* BOOKS, IF THEY'RE IN GOOD ENOUGH SHAPE...
WELL THEN, MAYBE THIS WILL TICKLE YOUR FANCY...
WHOA.

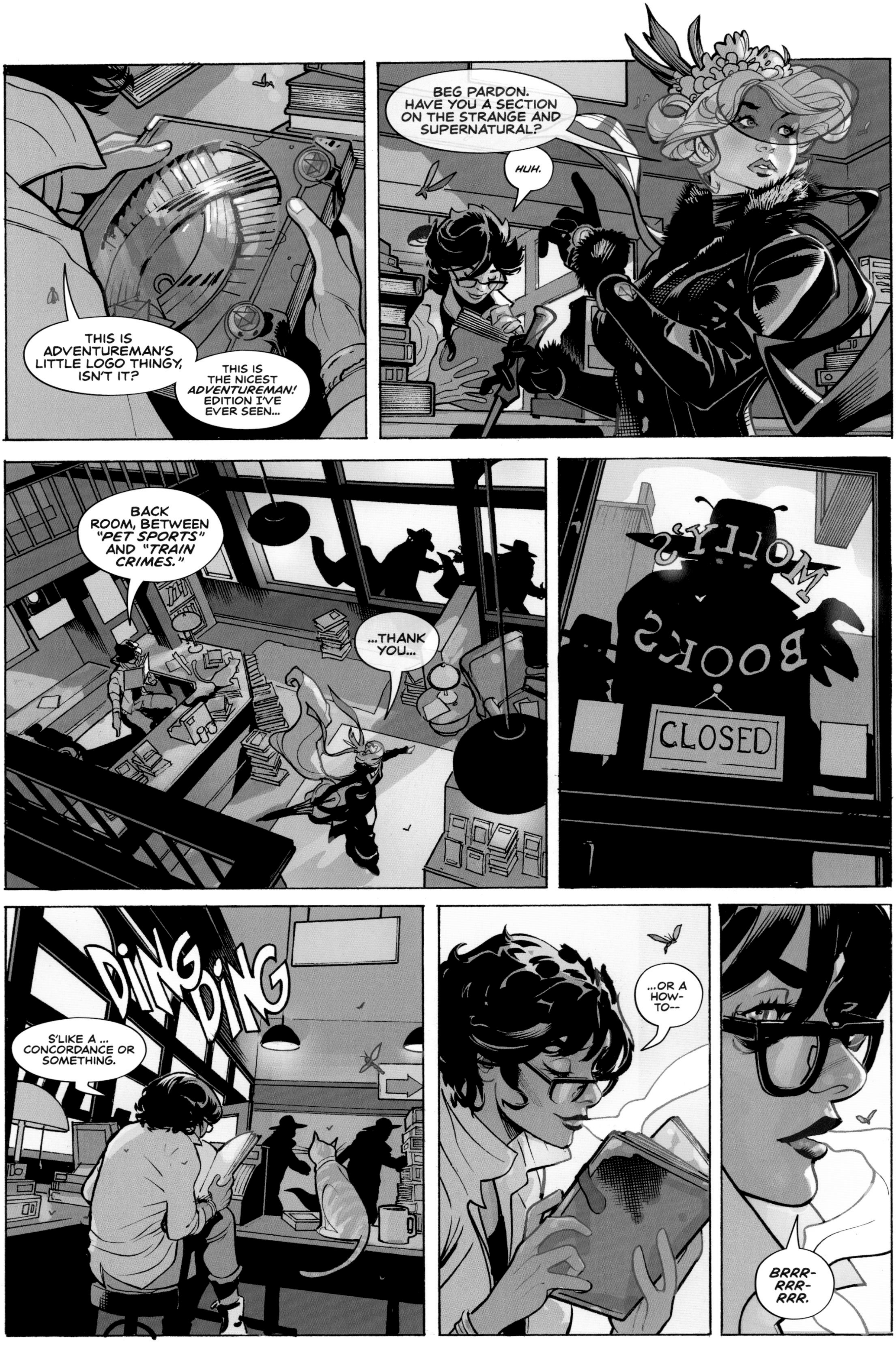
THIS IS ADVENTUREMAN'S LITTLE LOGO THINGY, ISN'T IT?
THIS IS THE NICEST ADVENTUREMAN! EDITION I'VE EVER SEEN...
BEG PARDON. HAVE YOU A SECTION ON THE STRANGE AND SUPERNATURAL?
HUH.
BACK ROOM, BETWEEN "PET SPORTS" AND "TRAIN CRIMES."
...THANK YOU...
MOLLY'S
BOOKS
CLOSED
DING DING
S'LIKE A ... CONCORDANCE OR SOMETHING.
...OR A HOW-TO--
BRRR-RRR-RRR.

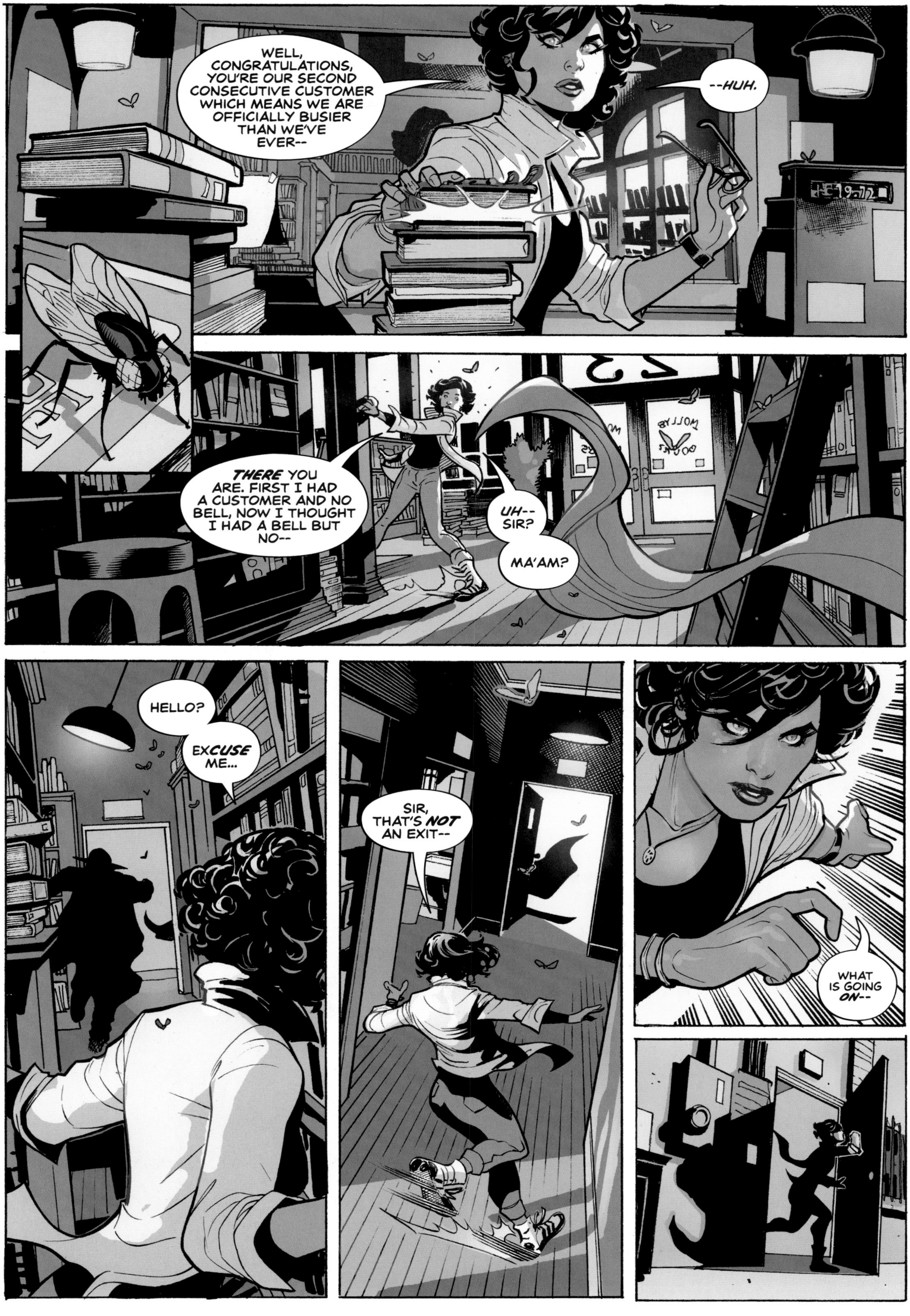
WELL, CONGRATULATIONS, YOU'RE OUR SECOND CONSECUTIVE CUSTOMER WHICH MEANS WE ARE OFFICIALLY BUSIER THAN WE'VE EVER--
--HUH.
THERE YOU ARE. FIRST I HAD A CUSTOMER AND NO BELL, NOW I THOUGHT I HAD A BELL BUT NO--
UH-- SIR?
MA'AM?
HELLO?
EXCUSE ME...
SIR, THAT'S NOT AN EXIT--
WHAT IS GOING ON--

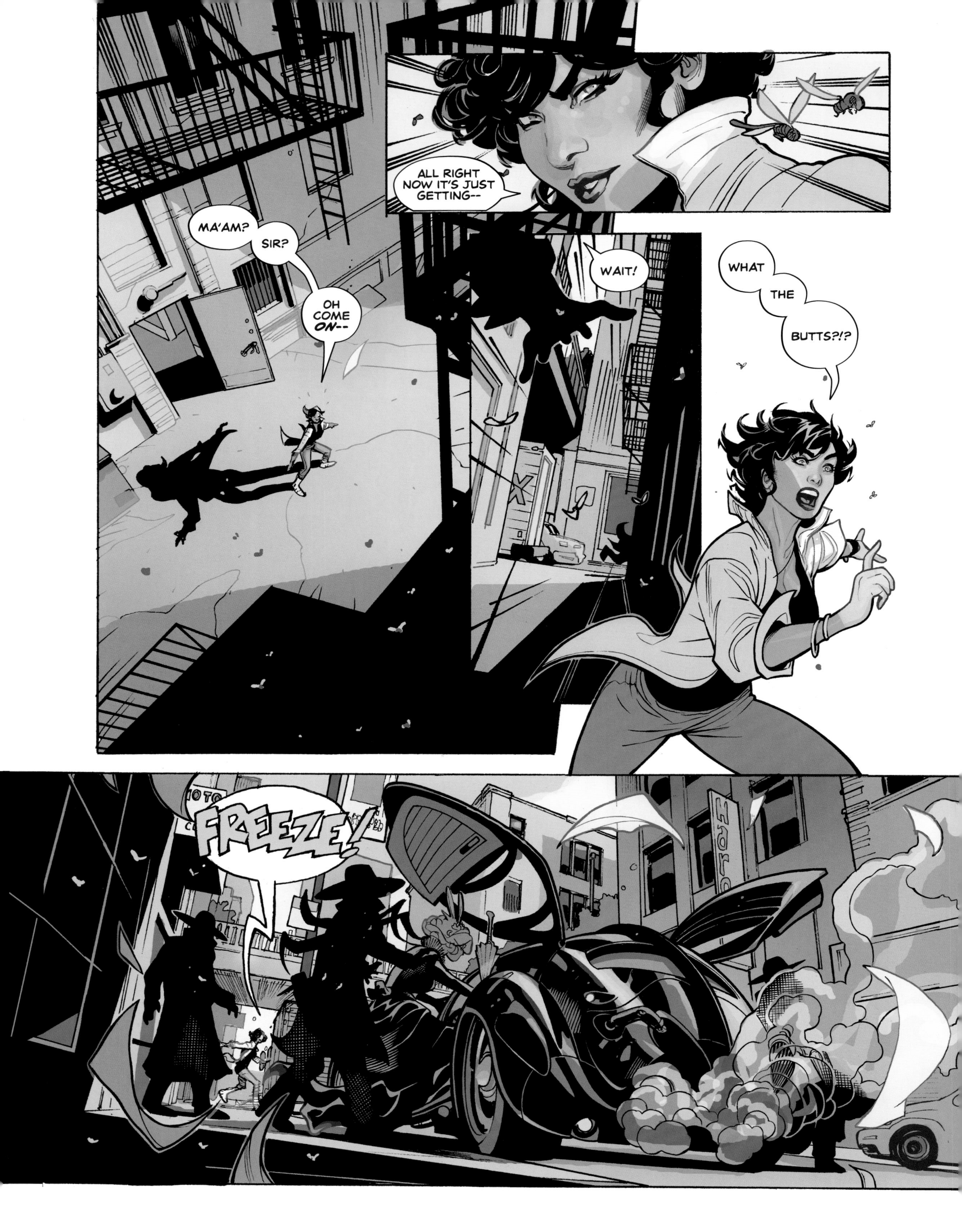
ALL RIGHT NOW IT'S JUST GETTING--
MA'AM?
SIR?
OH COME ON--
WAIT!
WHAT
THE
BUTTS?!?
FREEZE!

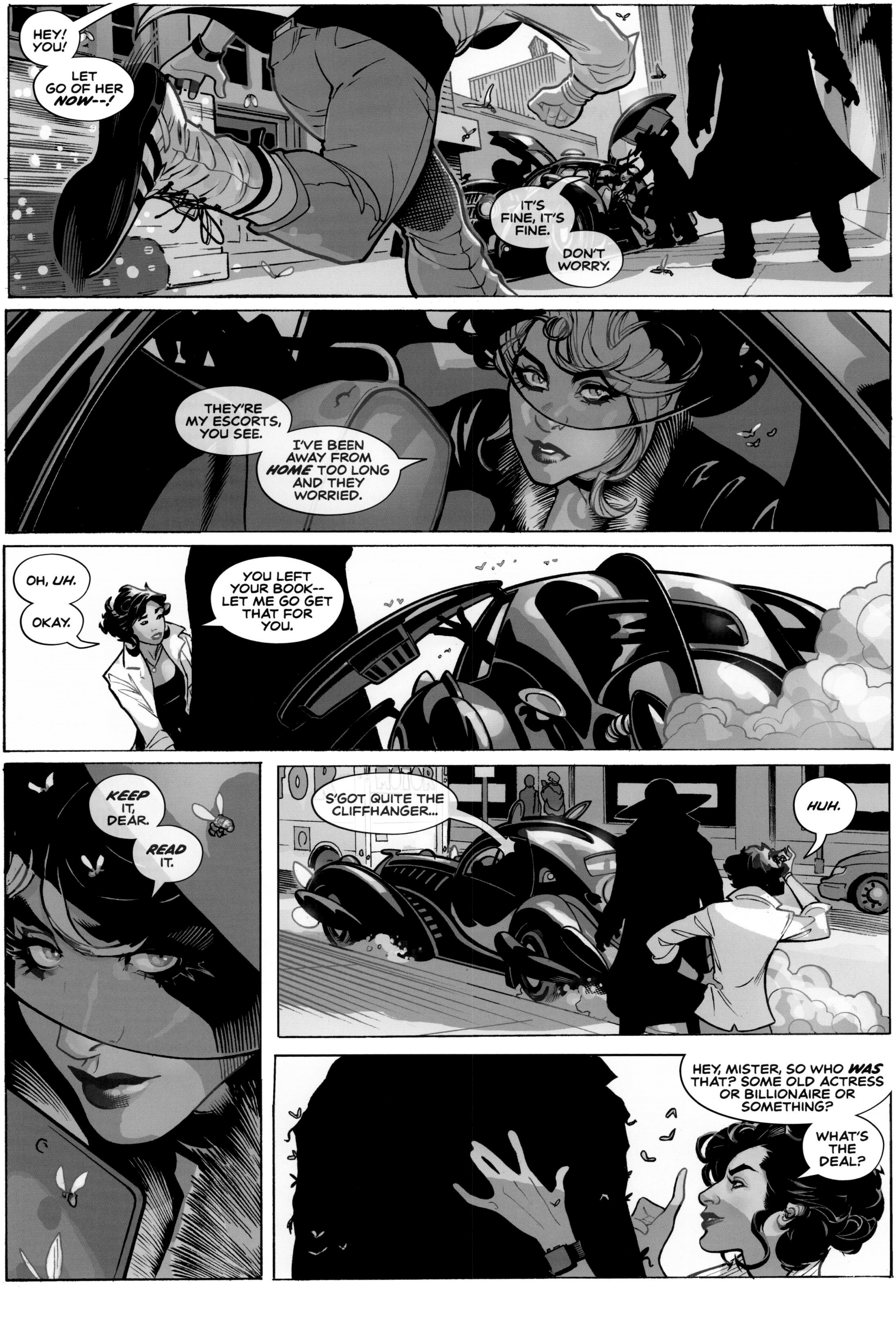
HEY! YOU!
LET GO OF HER NOW--!
IT'S FINE, IT'S FINE.
DON'T WORRY.
THEY'RE MY ESCORTS, YOU SEE.
I'VE BEEN AWAY FROM HOME TOO LONG AND THEY WORRIED.
OH, UH.
OKAY.
YOU LEFT YOUR BOOK-- LET ME GO GET THAT FOR YOU.
KEEP IT, DEAR.
READ IT.
S'GOT QUITE THE CLIFFHANGER...
HUH.
HEY, MISTER, SO WHO WAS THAT? SOME OLD ACTRESS OR BILLIONAIRE OR SOMETHING?
WHAT'S THE DEAL?

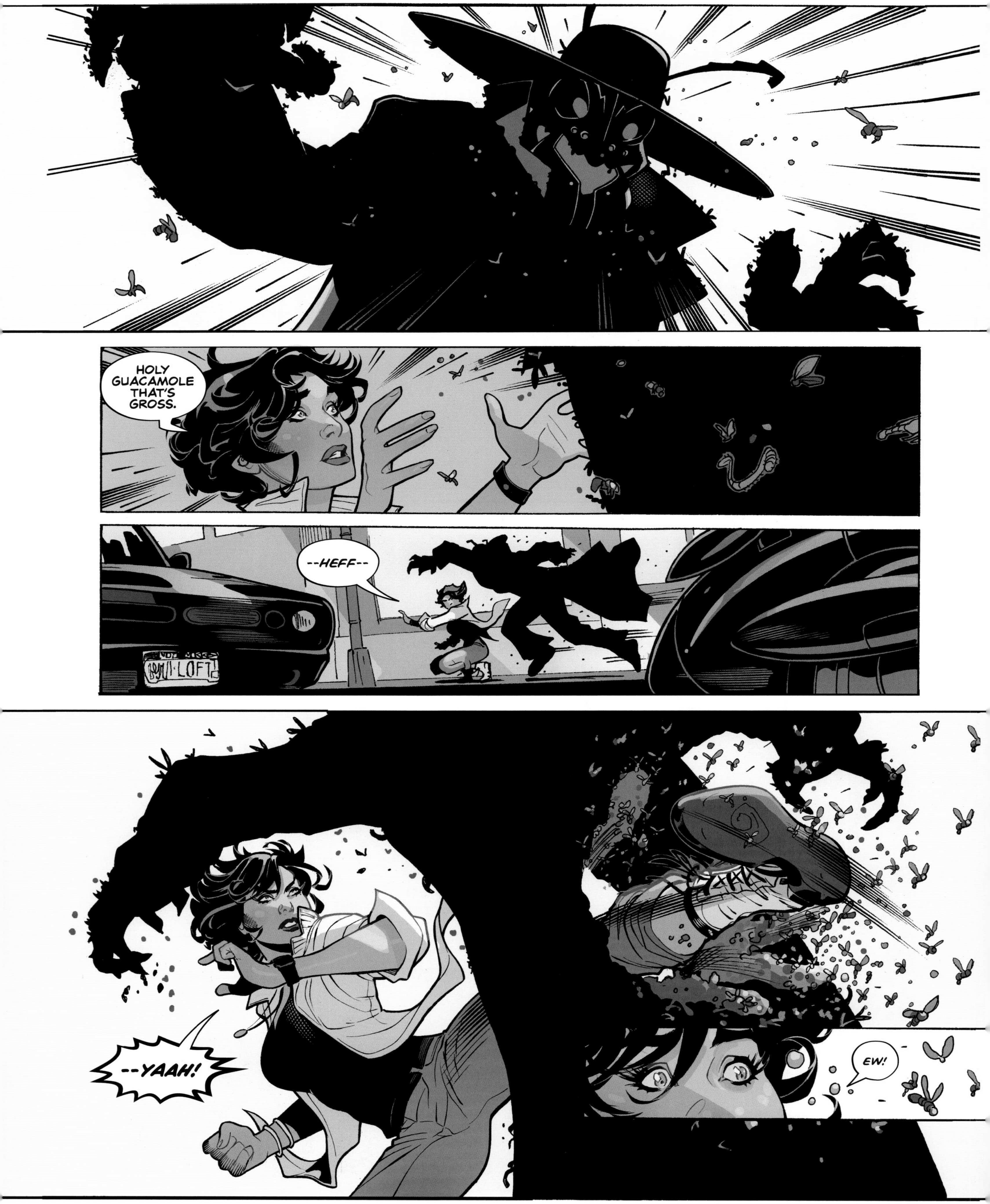
HOLY GUACAMOLE THAT'S GROSS.
--HEFF--
--YAAH!
EW!

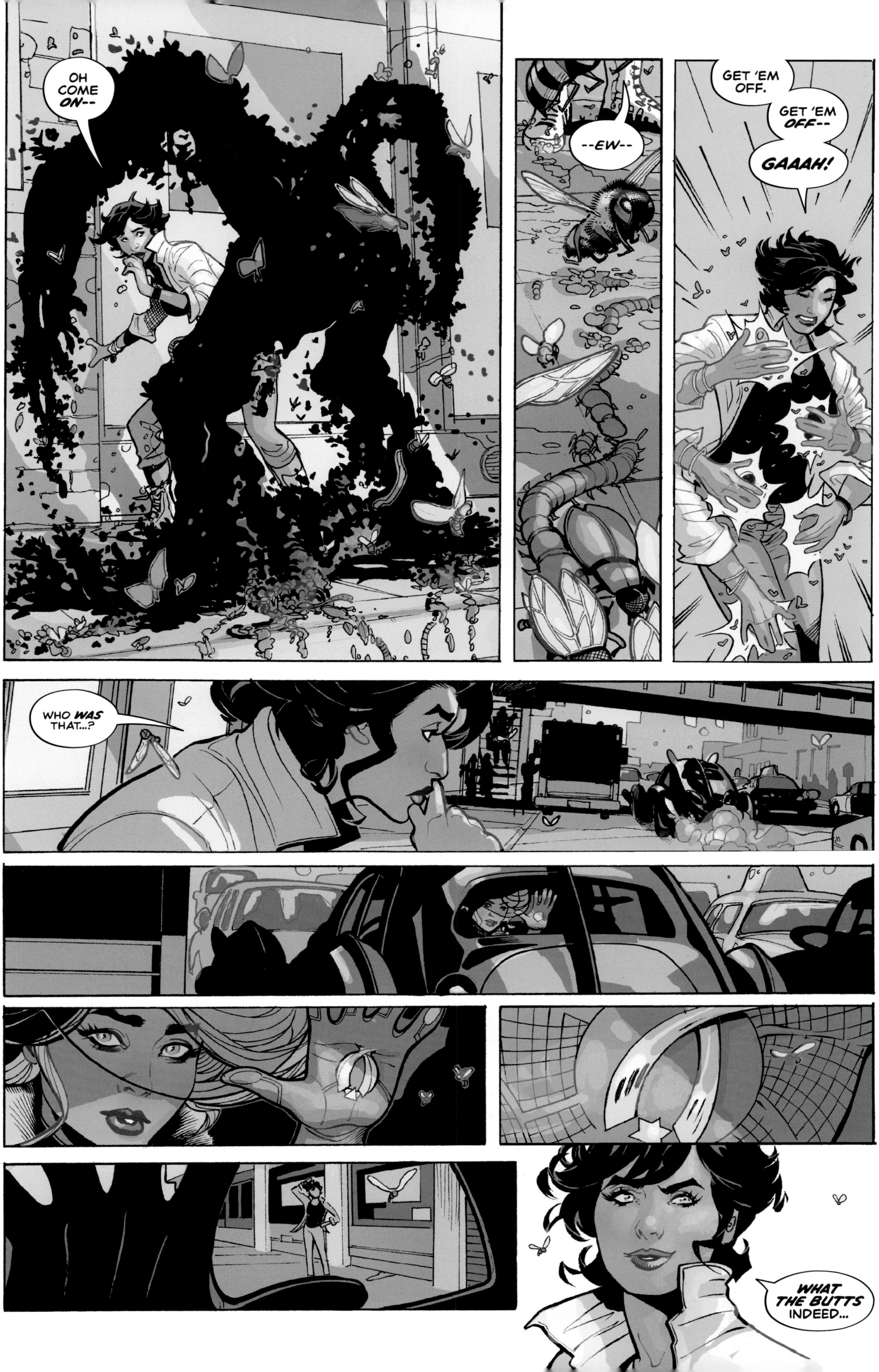
OH COME ON--
--EW--
GET 'EM OFF.
GET 'EM OFF--
GAAAH!
WHO WAS THAT...?
WHAT THE BUTTS INDEED...

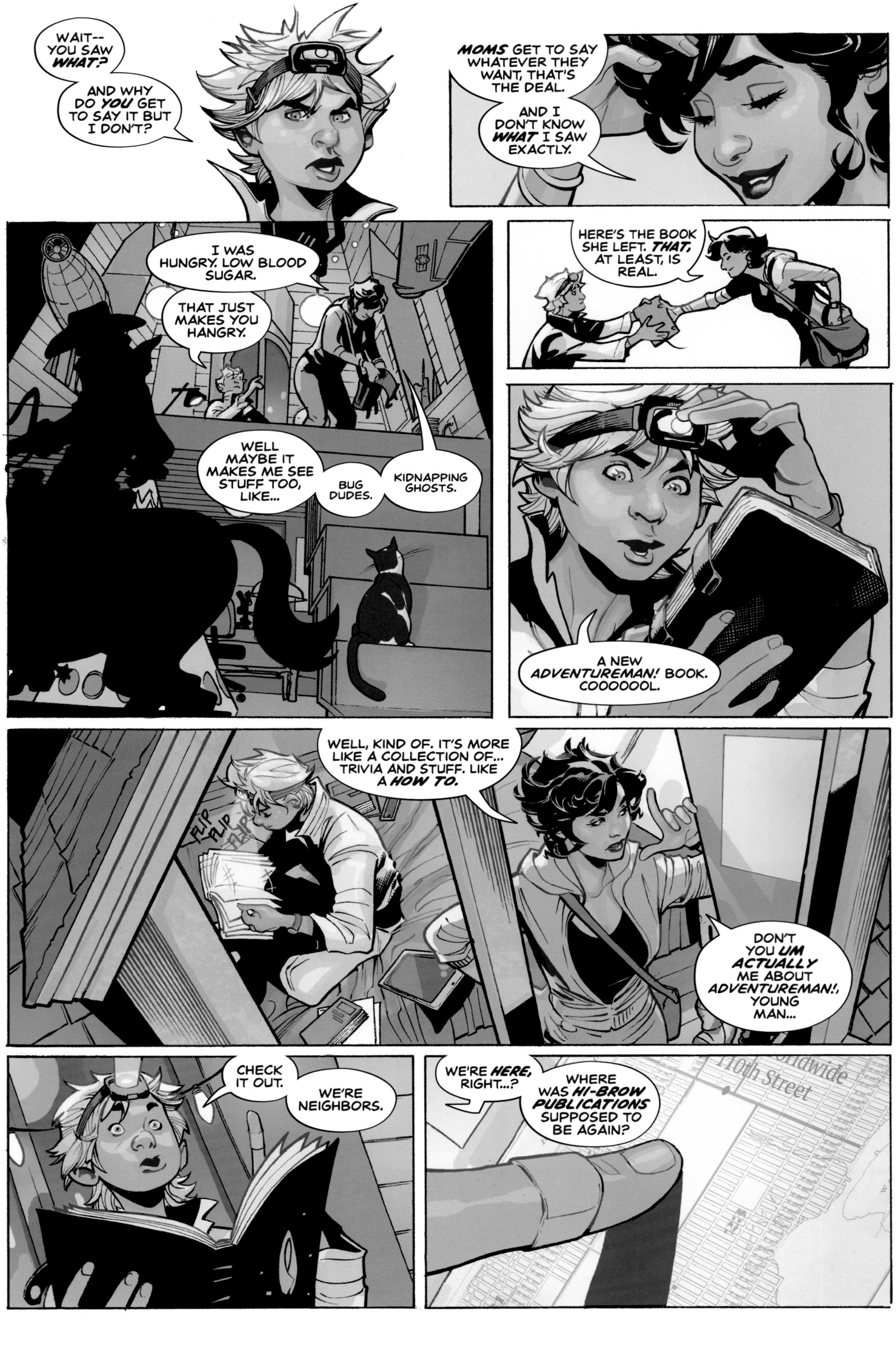
WAIT-- YOU SAW WHAT?
AND WHY DO YOU GET TO SAY IT BUT I DON'T?
MOMS GET TO SAY WHATEVER THEY WANT, THAT'S THE DEAL.
AND I DON'T KNOW WHAT I SAW EXACTLY.
I WAS HUNGRY. LOW BLOOD SUGAR.
THAT JUST MAKES YOU HANGRY.
WELL MAYBE IT MAKES ME SEE STUFF TOO, LIKE...
BUG DUDES.
KIDNAPPING GHOSTS.
HERE'S THE BOOK SHE LEFT. THAT, AT LEAST, IS REAL.
A NEW ADVENTUREMAN! BOOK. COOOOOOL.
WELL, KIND OF. IT'S MORE LIKE A COLLECTION OF... TRIVIA AND STUFF. LIKE A HOW TO.
FLIP FLIP FLIP
DON'T YOU UM ACTUALLY ME ABOUT ADVENTUREMAN!, YOUNG MAN...
CHECK IT OUT.
WE'RE NEIGHBORS.
WE'RE HERE, RIGHT...?
WHERE WAS HI-BROW PUBLICATIONS SUPPOSED TO BE AGAIN?
110th Street

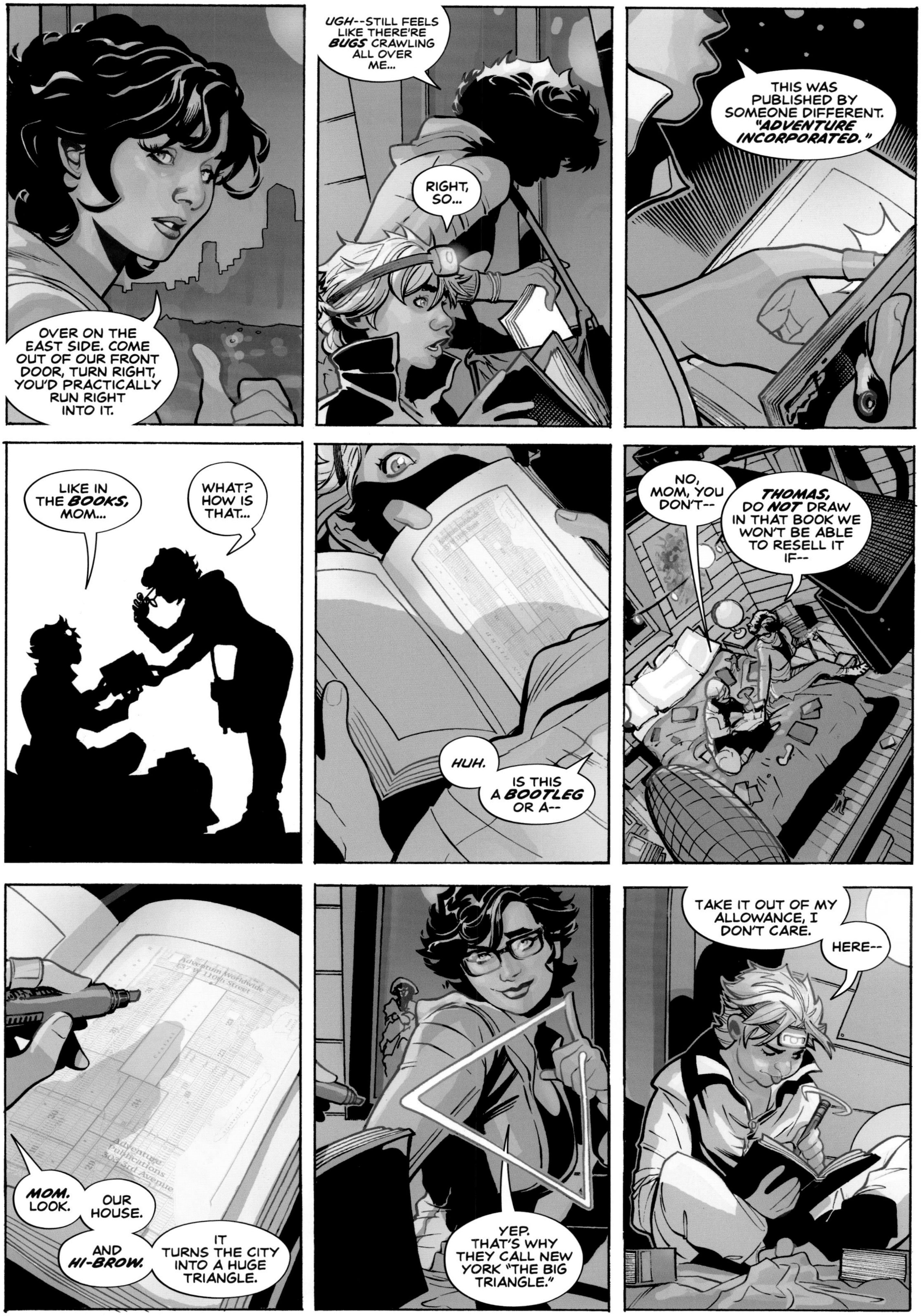

OVER ON THE EAST SIDE. COME OUT OF OUR FRONT DOOR, TURN RIGHT, YOU'D PRACTICALLY RUN RIGHT INTO IT.
UGH--STILL FEELS LIKE THERE'RE BUGS CRAWLING ALL OVER ME...
RIGHT, SO...
THIS WAS PUBLISHED BY SOMEONE DIFFERENT. "ADVENTURE INCORPORATED."
LIKE IN THE BOOKS, MOM...
WHAT? HOW IS THAT...
HUH.
IS THIS A BOOTLEG OR A--
NO, MOM, YOU DON'T--
THOMAS, DO NOT DRAW IN THAT BOOK WE WON'T BE ABLE TO RESELL IT IF--
MOM. LOOK.
OUR HOUSE.
AND HI-BROW.
IT TURNS THE CITY INTO A HUGE TRIANGLE.
YEP. THAT'S WHY THEY CALL NEW YORK "THE BIG TRIANGLE."
TAKE IT OUT OF MY ALLOWANCE, I DON'T CARE.
HERE--

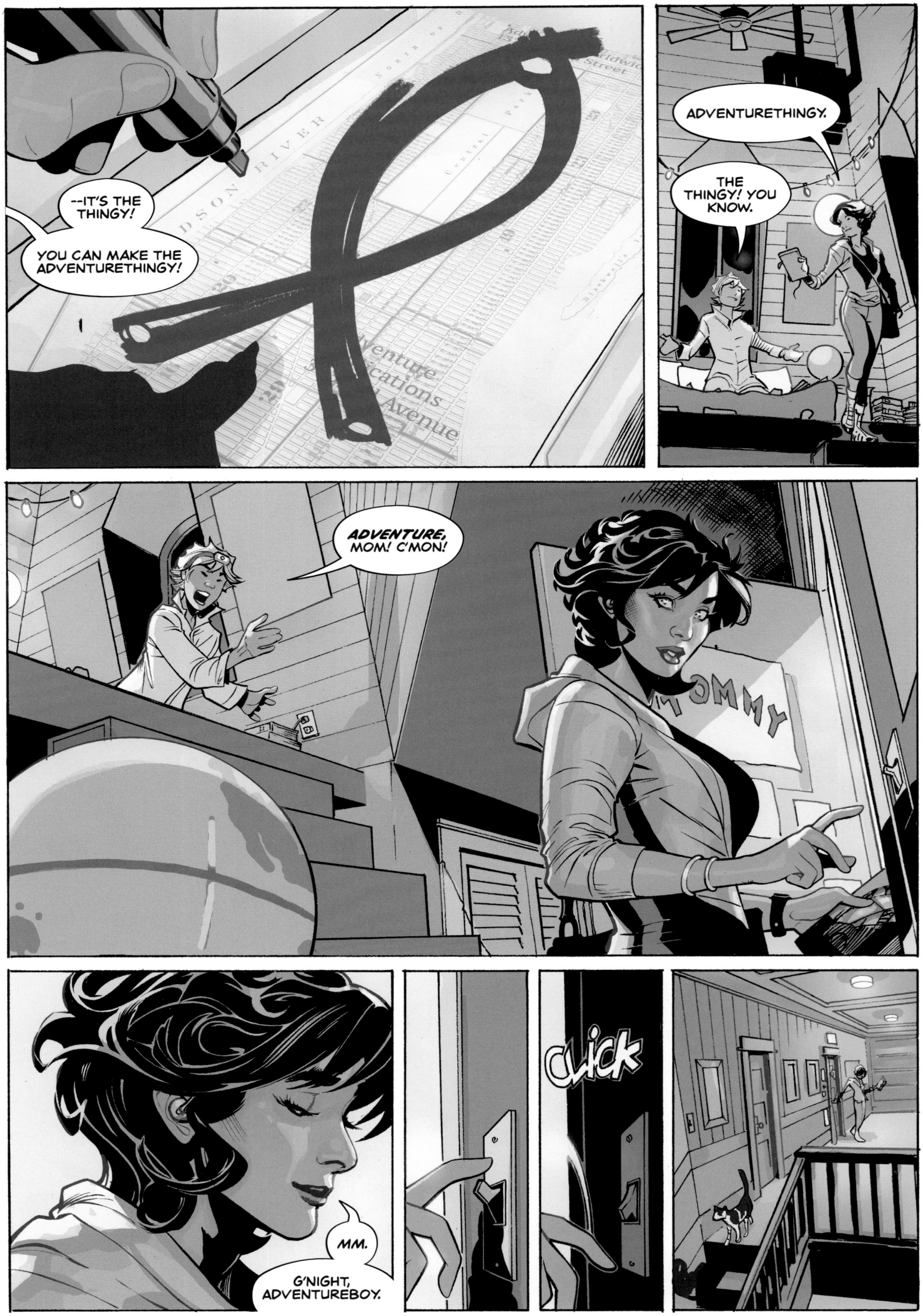

--IT'S THE THINGY!
YOU CAN MAKE THE ADVENTURETHINGY!
ADVENTURETHINGY.
THE THINGY! YOU KNOW.
ADVENTURE, MOM! C'MON!
MM.
G'NIGHT, ADVENTUREBOY.
CLICK

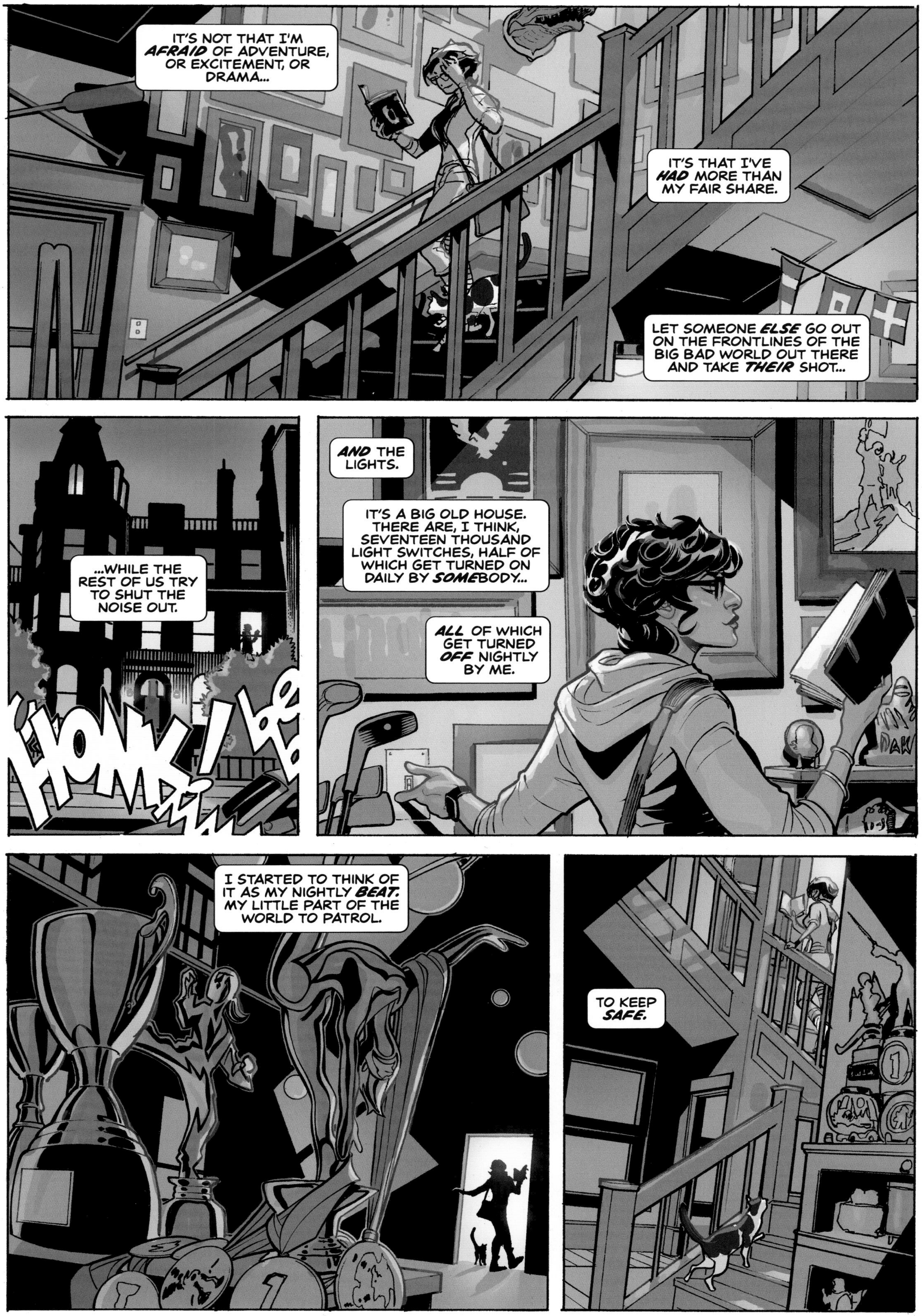
IT'S NOT THAT I'M AFRAID OF ADVENTURE, OR EXCITEMENT, OR DRAMA...
IT'S THAT I'VE HAD MORE THAN MY FAIR SHARE.
LET SOMEONE ELSE GO OUT ON THE FRONTLINES OF THE BIG BAD WORLD OUT THERE AND TAKE THEIR SHOT...
...WHILE THE REST OF US TRY TO SHUT THE NOISE OUT.
HONK!
AND THE LIGHTS.
IT'S A BIG OLD HOUSE. THERE ARE, I THINK, SEVENTEEN THOUSAND LIGHT SWITCHES, HALF OF WHICH GET TURNED ON DAILY BY SOMEBODY...
ALL OF WHICH GET TURNED OFF NIGHTLY BY ME.
I STARTED TO THINK OF IT AS MY NIGHTLY BEAT. MY LITTLE PART OF THE WORLD TO PATROL.
TO KEEP SAFE.

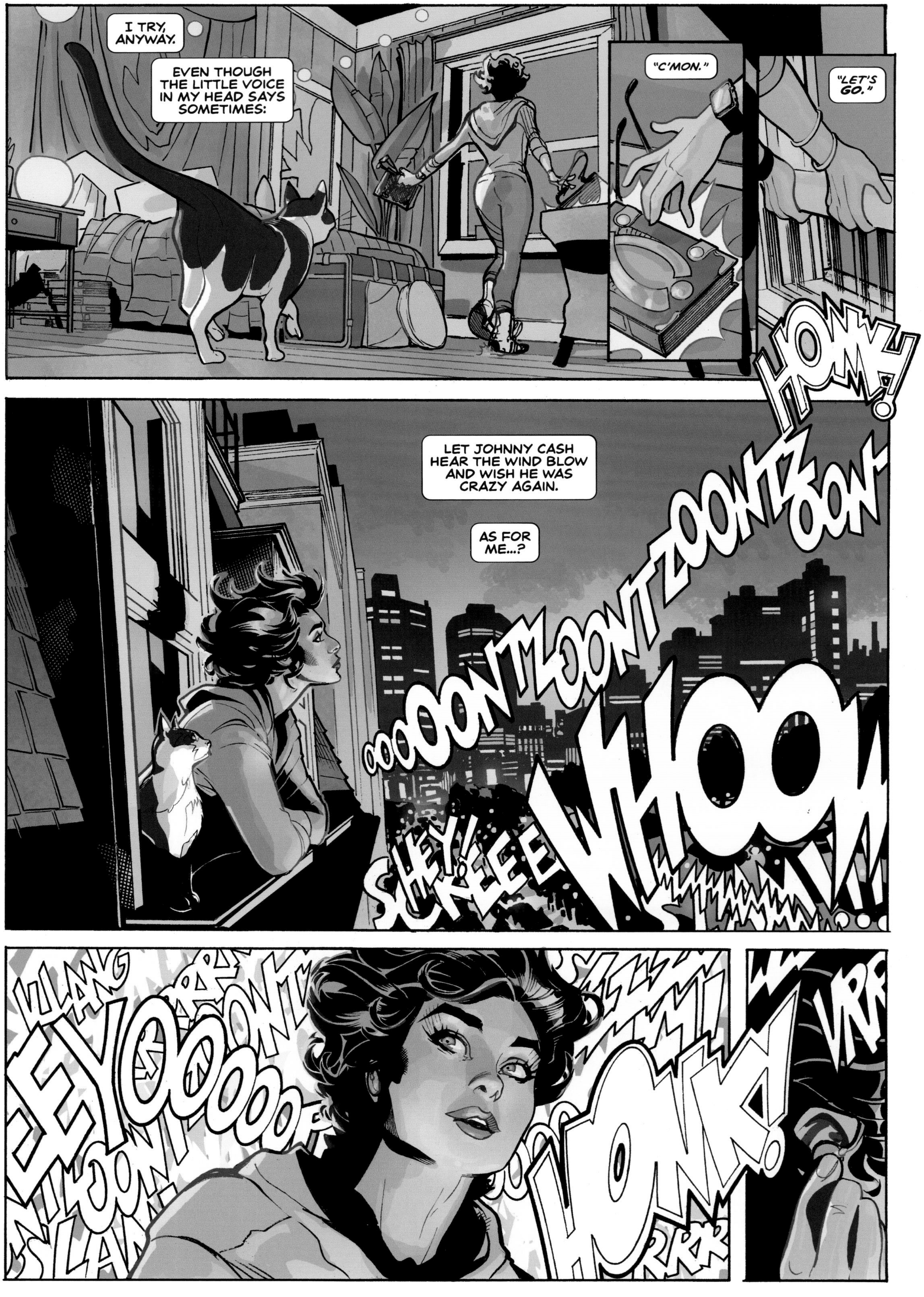
I TRY, ANYWAY.
EVEN THOUGH THE LITTLE VOICE IN MY HEAD SAYS SOMETIMES:
"C'MON."
"LET'S GO."
HONK!
LET JOHNNY CASH HEAR THE WIND BLOW AND WISH HE WAS CRAZY AGAIN.
AS FOR ME...?
OOOOONTZOONTZOONTZOONTZOON
HEY!
SKREEEE
WHOOM
HONK!

I'LL TAKE A QUIET LIFE...

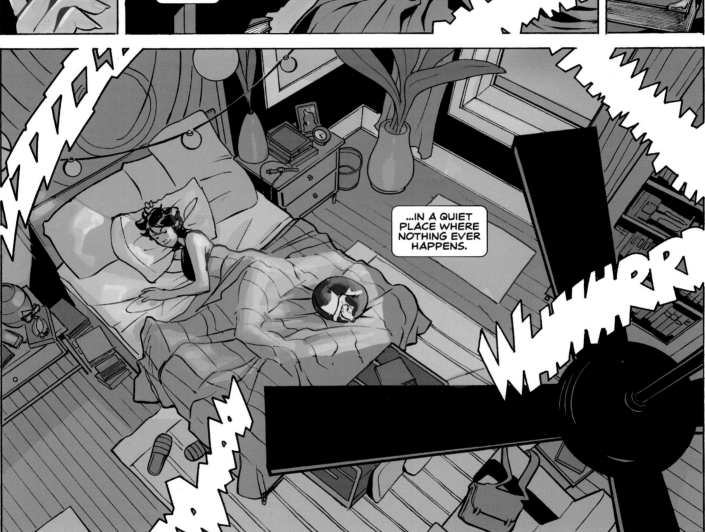

...IN A QUIET PLACE WHERE NOTHING EVER HAPPENS.

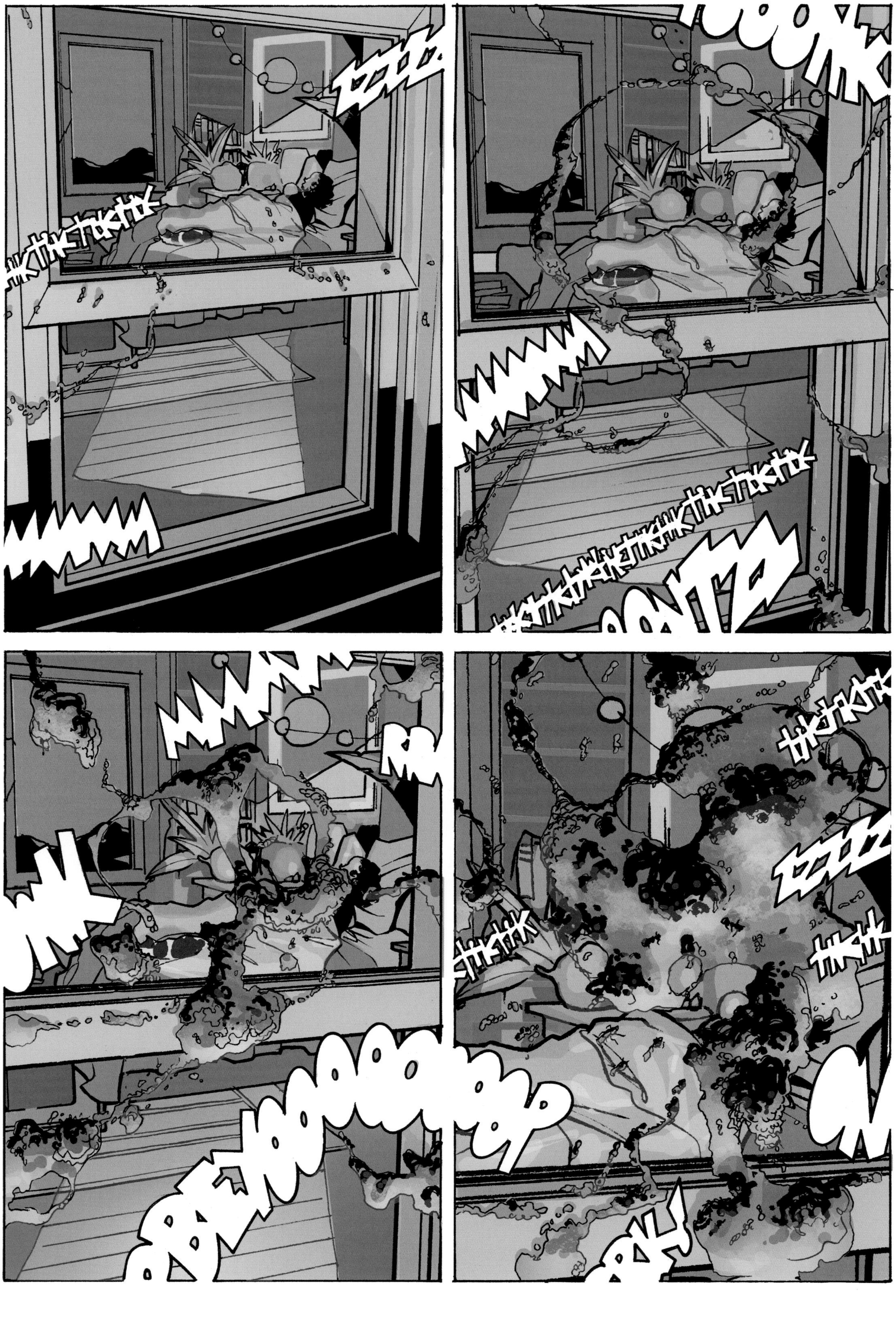

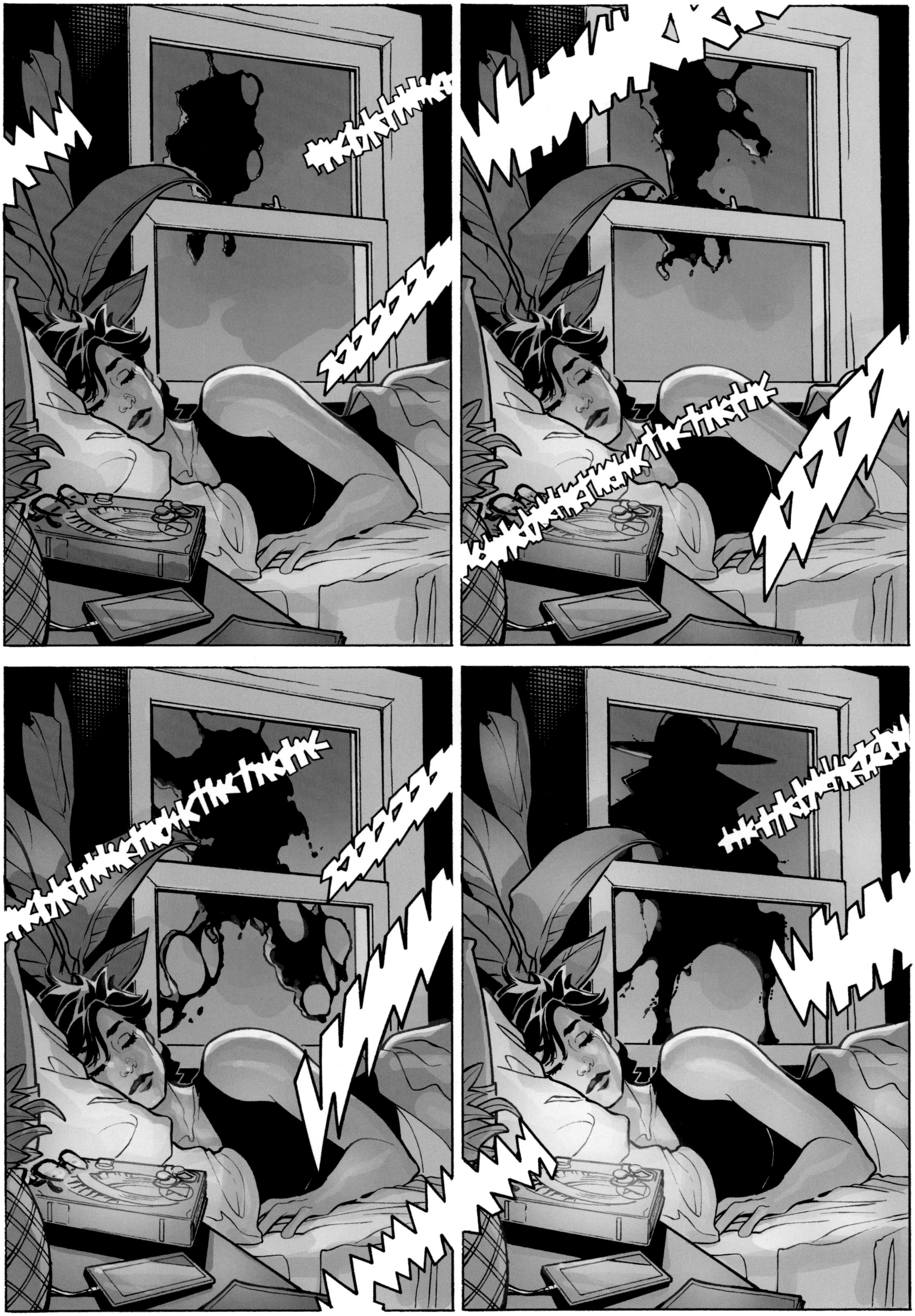

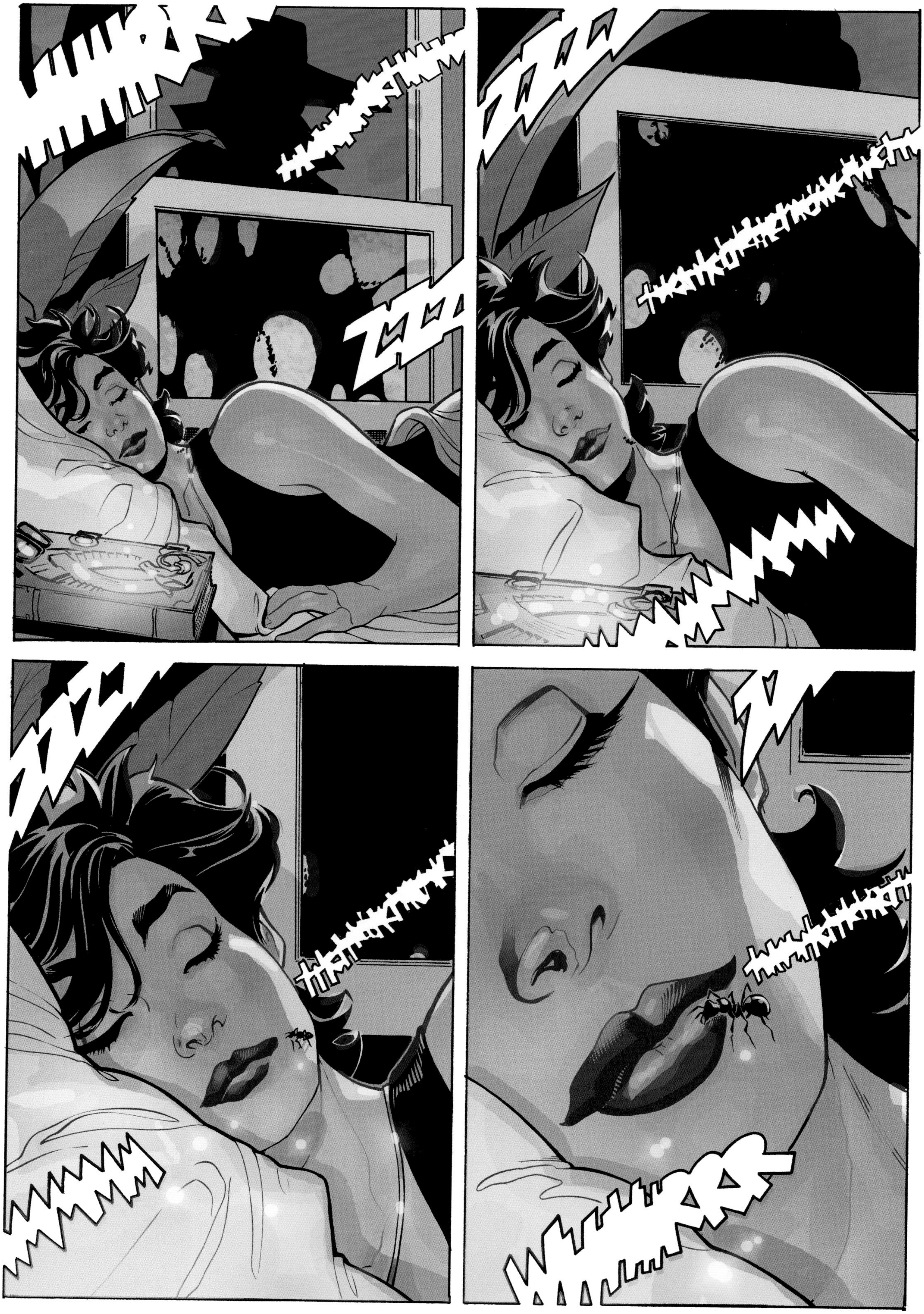

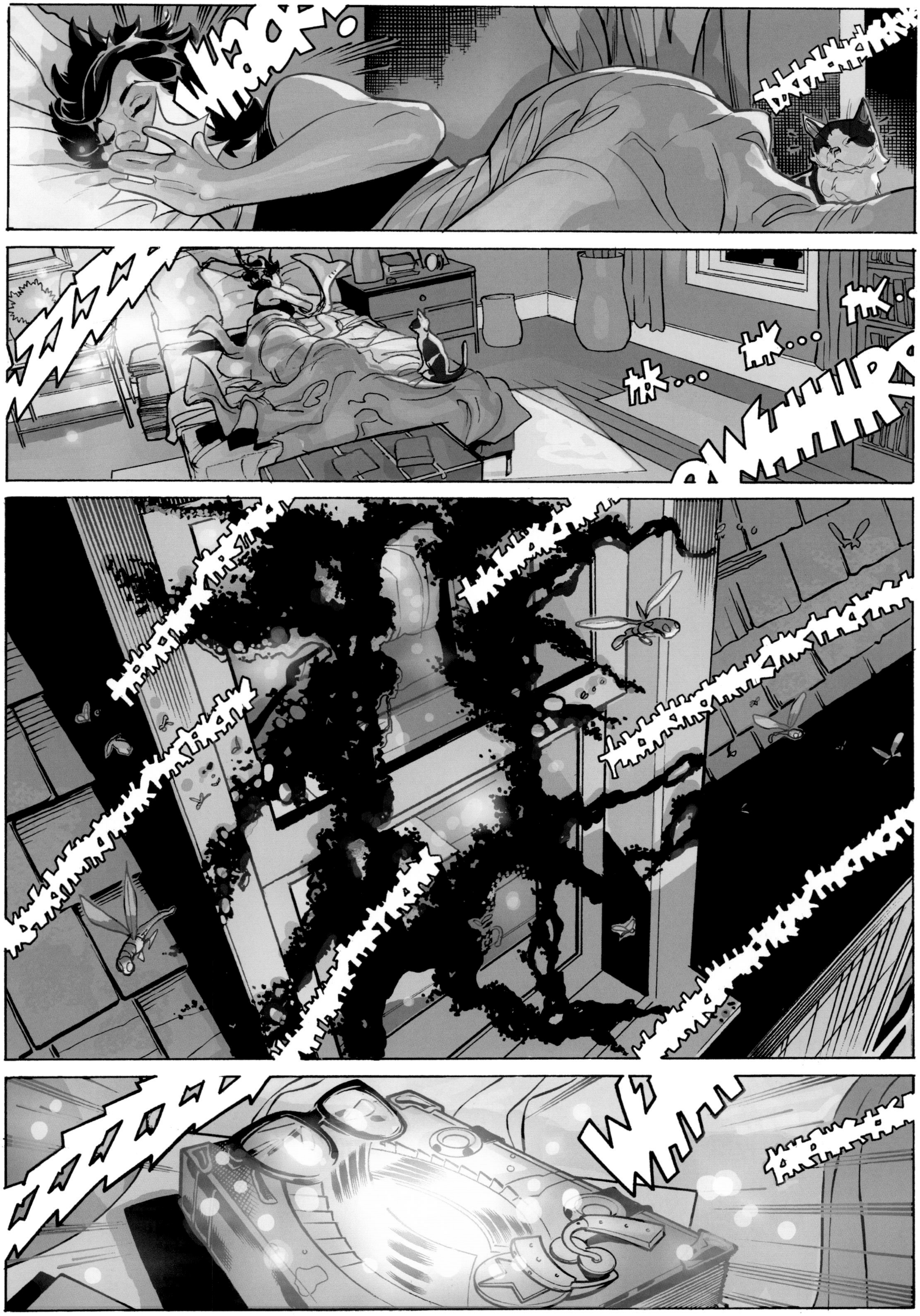
WHOOF!
TIK...
TIK...
TIK...

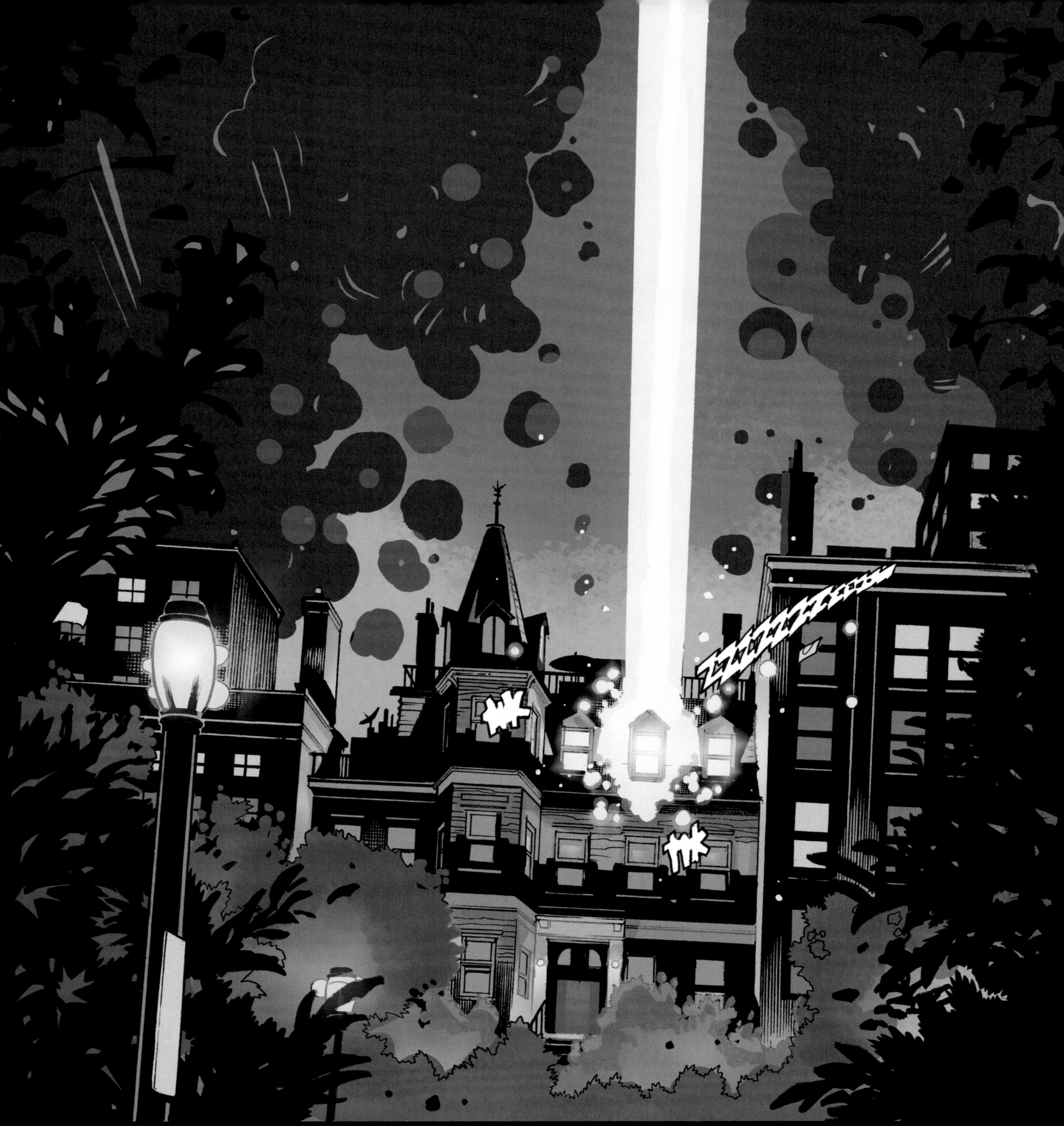

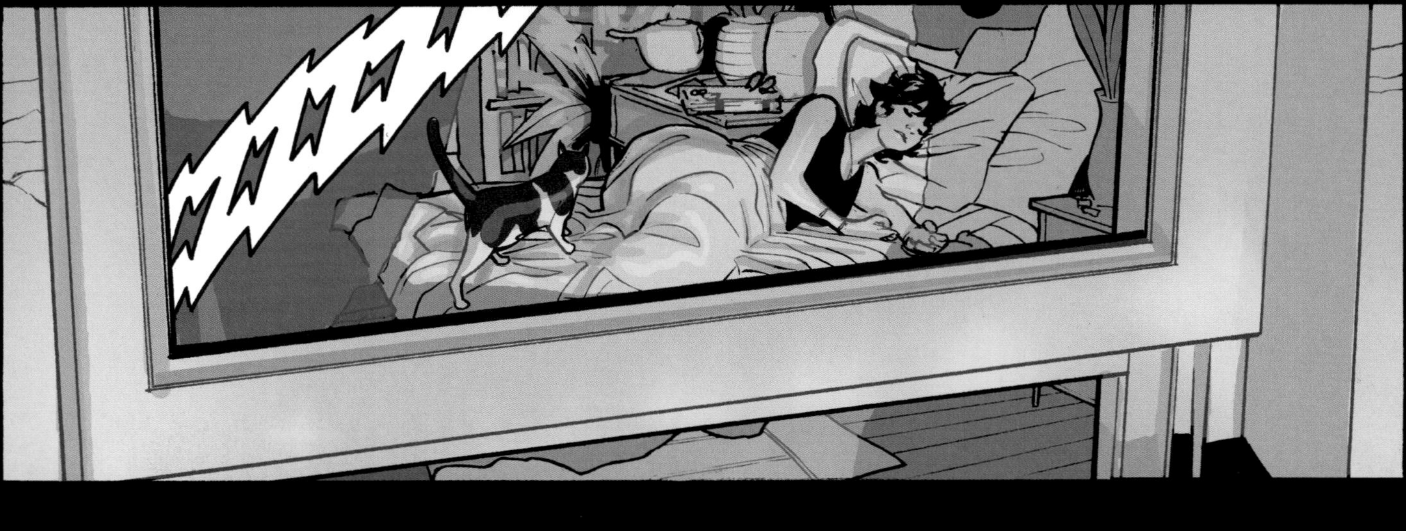

ADVENTUREMAN

"The END and EVERYTHING AFTER"

VOLUME 1

CHAPTER

2

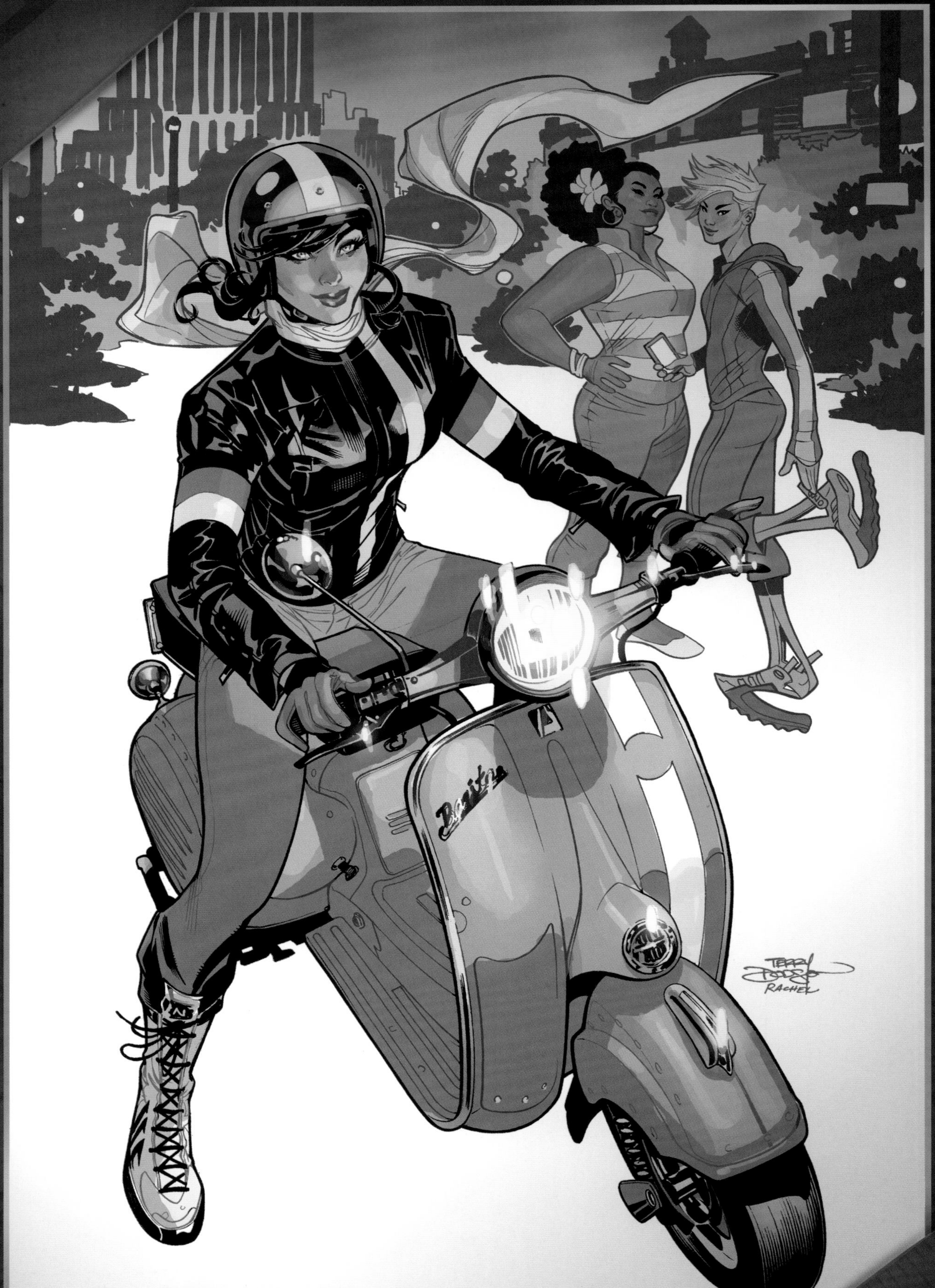

ORIGINAL COVER
FOR ISSUE 2

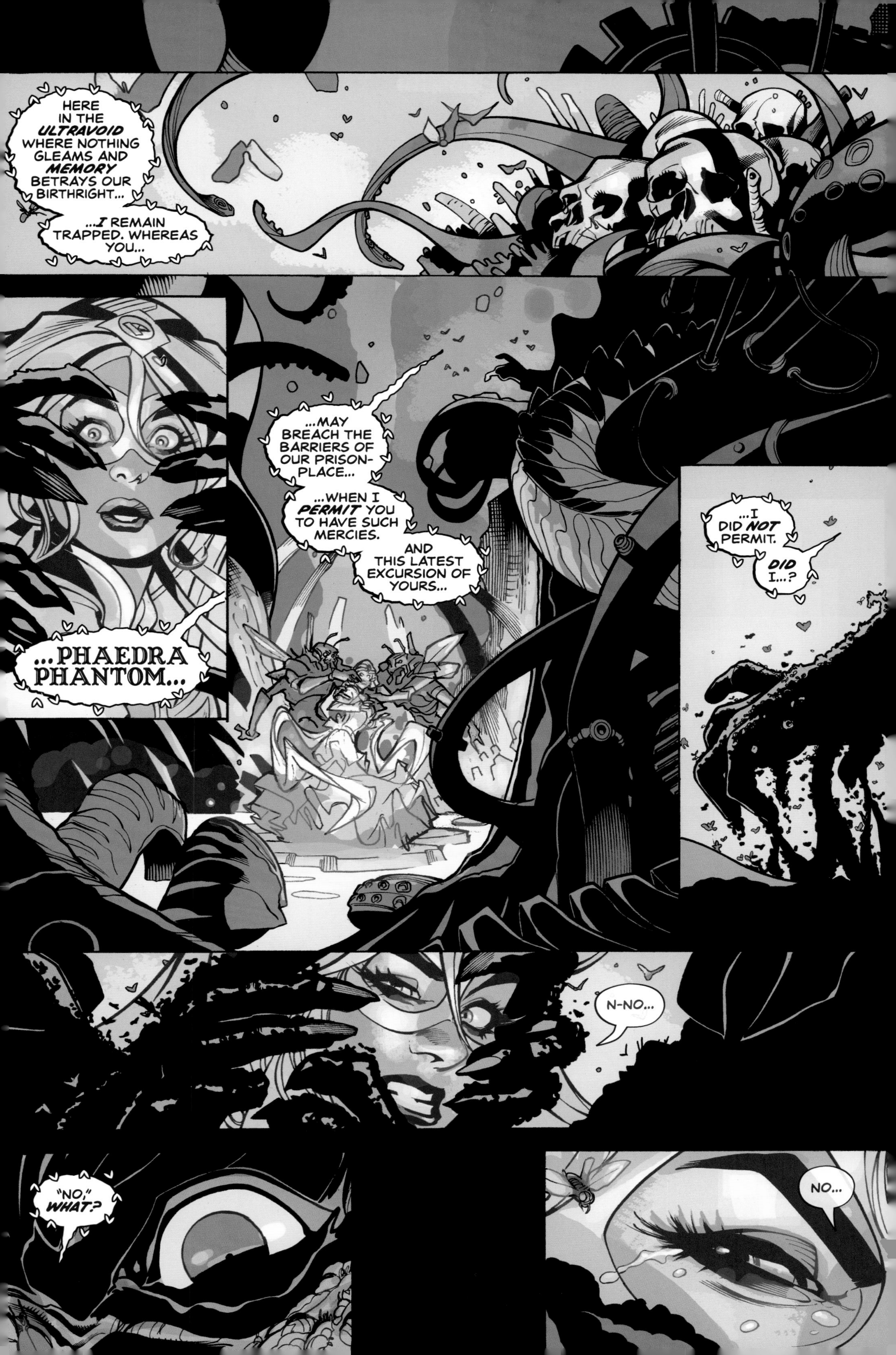

HERE IN THE ULTRAVOID WHERE NOTHING GLEAMS AND MEMORY BETRAYS OUR BIRTHRIGHT...
...I REMAIN TRAPPED. WHEREAS YOU...
...PHAEDRA PHANTOM...
...MAY BREACH THE BARRIERS OF OUR PRISON-PLACE...
...WHEN I PERMIT YOU TO HAVE SUCH MERCIES.
AND THIS LATEST EXCURSION OF YOURS...
...I DID NOT PERMIT.
DID I...?
N-NO...
"NO," WHAT?
NO...

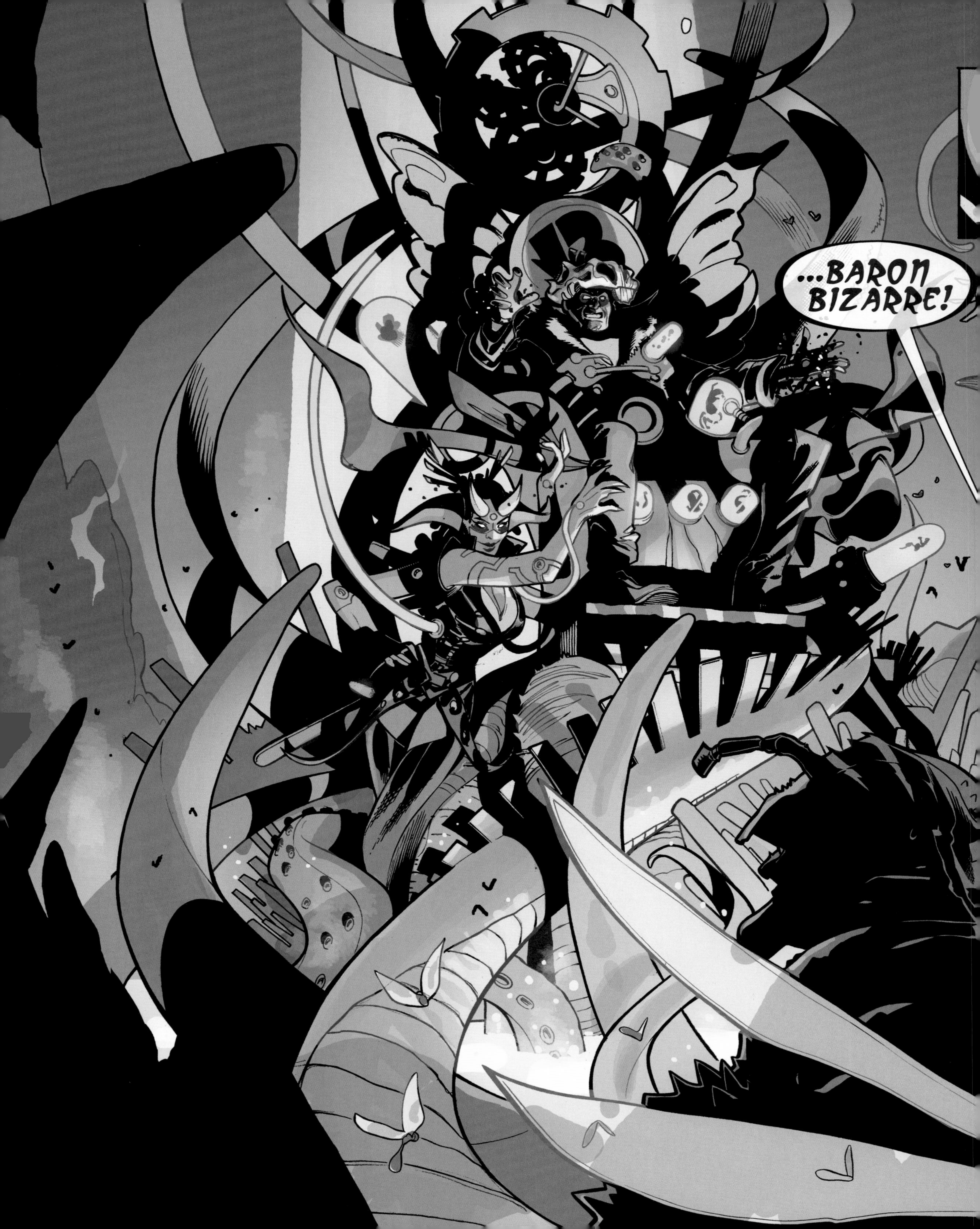
...BARON BIZARRE!

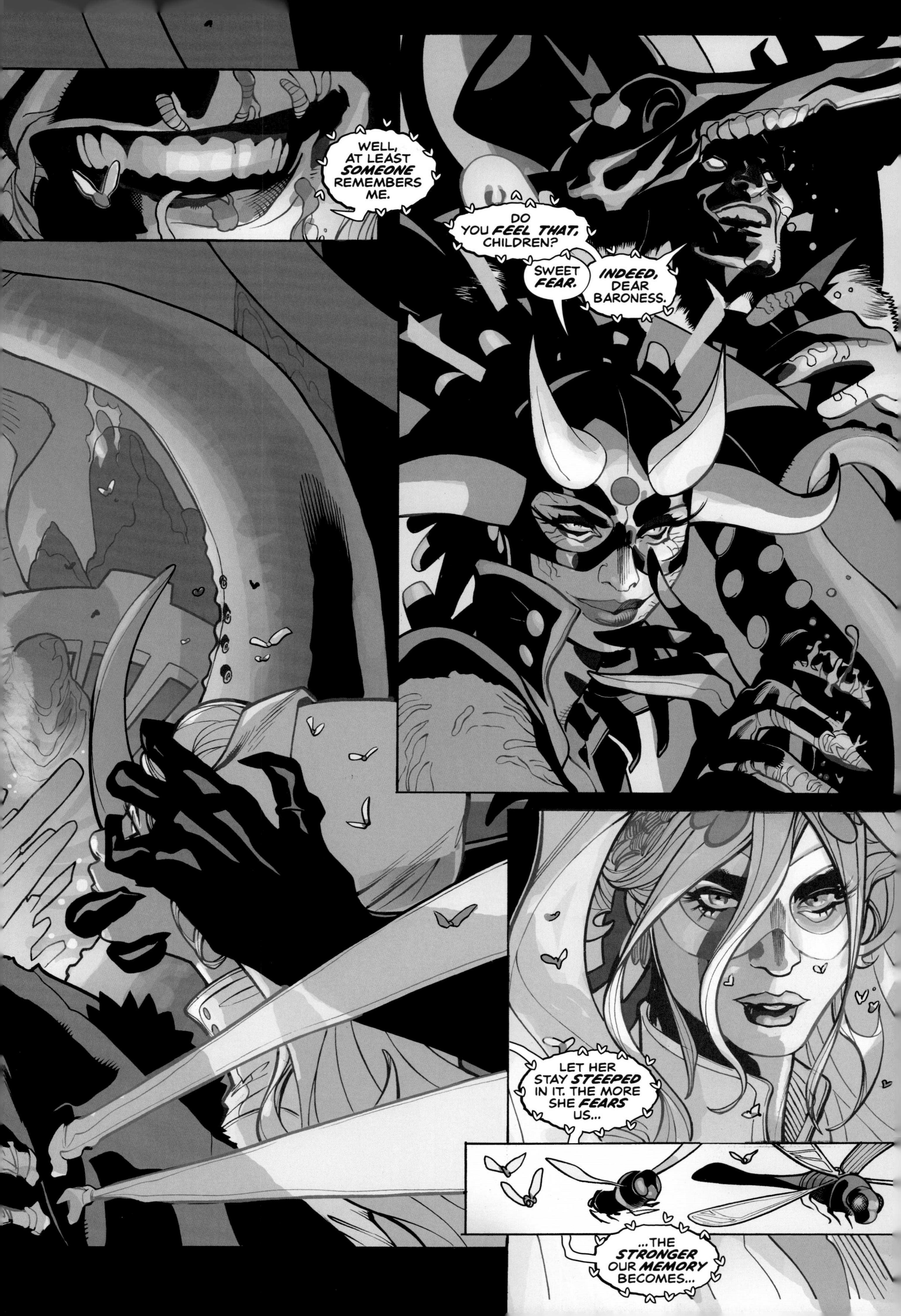
WELL, AT LEAST SOMEONE REMEMBERS ME.
DO YOU FEEL THAT, CHILDREN?
SWEET FEAR.
INDEED, DEAR BARONESS.
LET HER STAY STEEPED IN IT. THE MORE SHE FEARS US...
...THE STRONGER OUR MEMORY BECOMES...

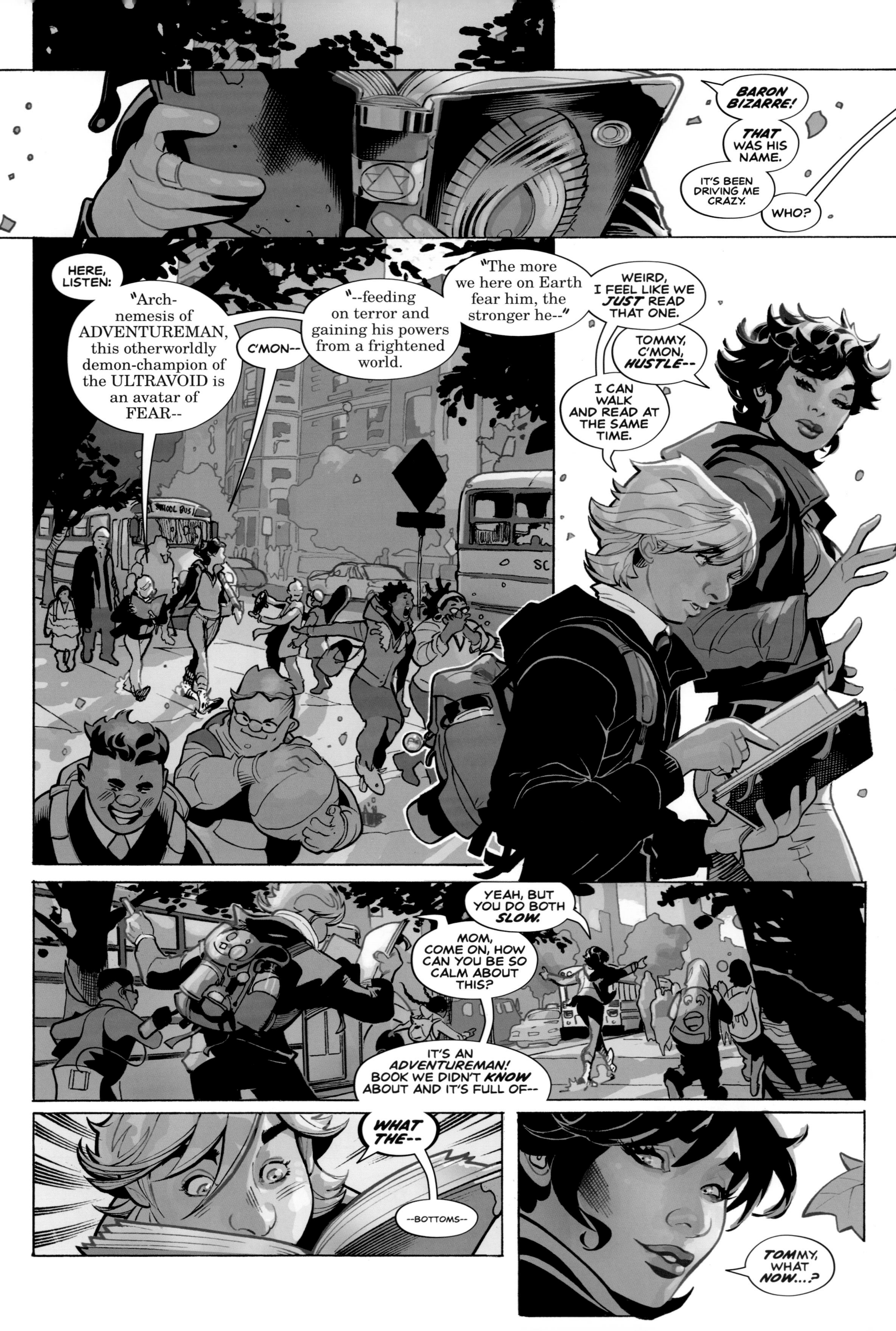
BARON BIZARRE!
THAT WAS HIS NAME.
IT'S BEEN DRIVING ME CRAZY.
WHO?
HERE, LISTEN:
"Arch-nemesis of ADVENTUREMAN, this otherworldly demon-champion of the ULTRAVOID is an avatar of FEAR--
C'MON--
"--feeding on terror and gaining his powers from a frightened world.
"The more we here on Earth fear him, the stronger he--"
WEIRD, I FEEL LIKE WE JUST READ THAT ONE.
TOMMY, C'MON, HUSTLE--
I CAN WALK AND READ AT THE SAME TIME.
YEAH, BUT YOU DO BOTH SLOW.
MOM, COME ON, HOW CAN YOU BE SO CALM ABOUT THIS?
IT'S AN ADVENTUREMAN! BOOK WE DIDN'T KNOW ABOUT AND IT'S FULL OF--
WHAT THE--
--BOTTOMS--
TOMMY, WHAT NOW...?

THEY GIVE THE *ADDRESS* FOR *ADVENTUM WORLDWIDE!* ADVENTUREMAN'S *HEADQUARTERS!*

WHAT? THEY NEVER SAID THAT IN THE BOOKS.

IT WAS ALWAYS "A stately tower north of the park" OR "That regal spire atop the city like a crown"...

AND LOOK-- --IT'S THE SAME ADDRESS AS THE PUBLISHERS OF *THIS.*

DO YOU THINK *ADVENTUREMAN* HIMSELF *PUBLISHED* IT AND--

I *THINK* THE SCHOOL BELL'S ABOUT TO RING, YOUNG MAN.

HOW CAN YOU BE THINKING ABOUT *SCHOOL* AT A TIME LIKE THIS?!?

TOMMY, I--

AAAH!

RIIINN... R'III...GH!

WHY DIDN'T YOU TELL ME I WAS GONNA BE LATE?!?

BYYYYYYEEEEEE--!

THAT *KID.*

I SWEAR.

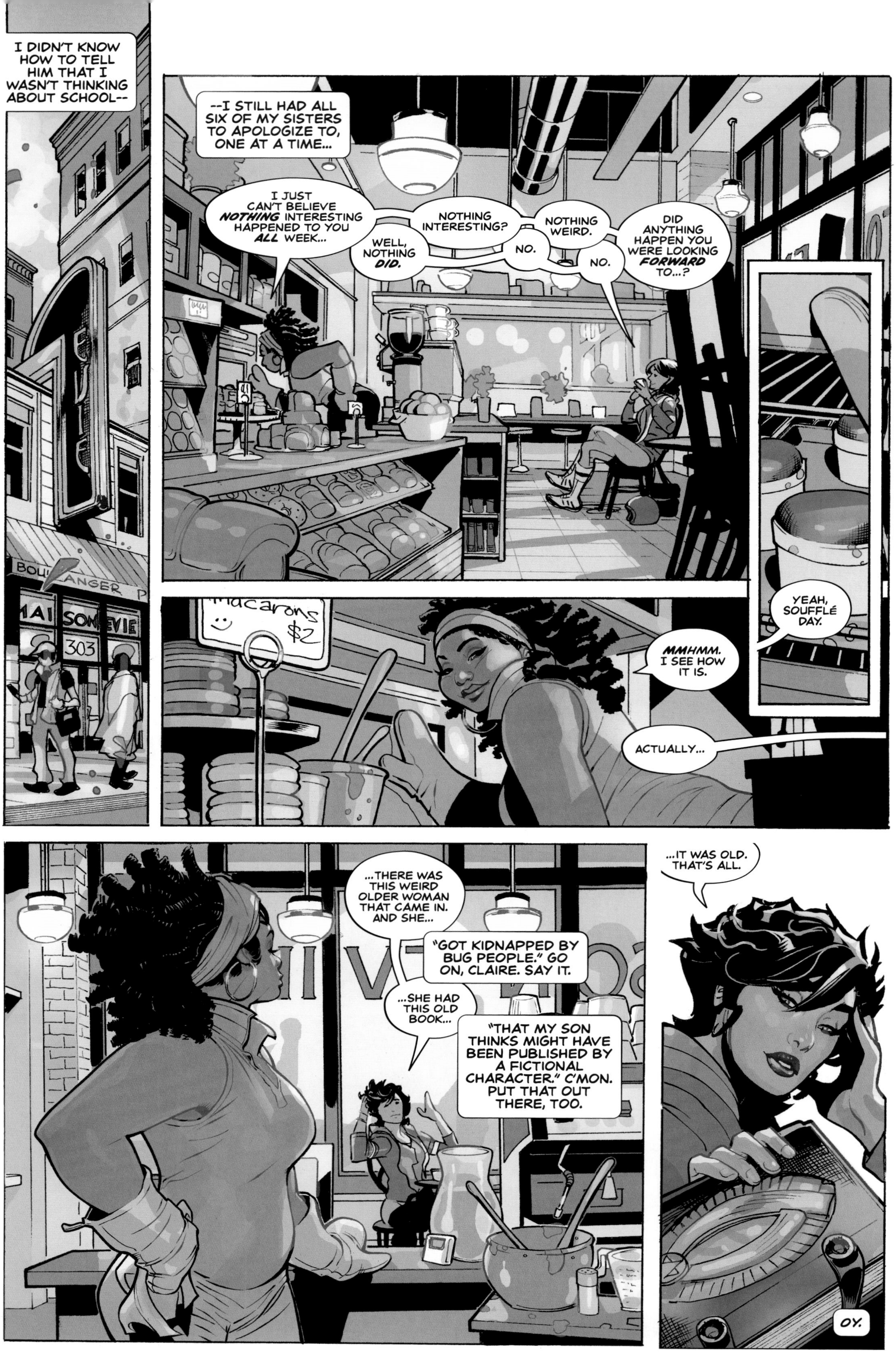

I DIDN'T KNOW HOW TO TELL HIM THAT I WASN'T THINKING ABOUT SCHOOL--
BOULANGER
MAISON DE VIE
303
--I STILL HAD ALL SIX OF MY SISTERS TO APOLOGIZE TO, ONE AT A TIME...
I JUST CAN'T BELIEVE NOTHING INTERESTING HAPPENED TO YOU ALL WEEK...
WELL, NOTHING DID.
NOTHING INTERESTING?
NO.
NOTHING WEIRD.
NO.
DID ANYTHING HAPPEN YOU WERE LOOKING FORWARD TO...?
YEAH, SOUFFLÉ DAY.
Macarons $2
MMHMM. I SEE HOW IT IS.
ACTUALLY...
...THERE WAS THIS WEIRD OLDER WOMAN THAT CAME IN. AND SHE...
"GOT KIDNAPPED BY BUG PEOPLE." GO ON, CLAIRE. SAY IT.
...SHE HAD THIS OLD BOOK...
"THAT MY SON THINKS MIGHT HAVE BEEN PUBLISHED BY A FICTIONAL CHARACTER." C'MON. PUT THAT OUT THERE, TOO.
...IT WAS OLD. THAT'S ALL.
OY.

FOR A WOMAN SURROUNDED BY BOOKS ALL DAY LONG...

...YOU SURE DON'T KNOW HOW TO TELL A GOOD STORY.

in peak physical form. This is accomplished by Adventureman's dedication to a rigorous and highly specific set of isometric exercises blending the worlds of medical science and the lost and arcane arts practiced by martial artists, monks, and adepts of

CLAIRE...?

MM.

with whom Adventureman shared in a kind of knowledge exchange between their cultures or societies and our own. When first

OKAY THEN.

I'M JUST GONNA SIT MYSELF DOWN FOR A BIT, SLOW AND QUIET...

HEY YOU GUYS DID I MISS SOUFFLÉ DAY I'M SORRY I RAN FROM UP--

OH.

EEP.

=SIGH=...

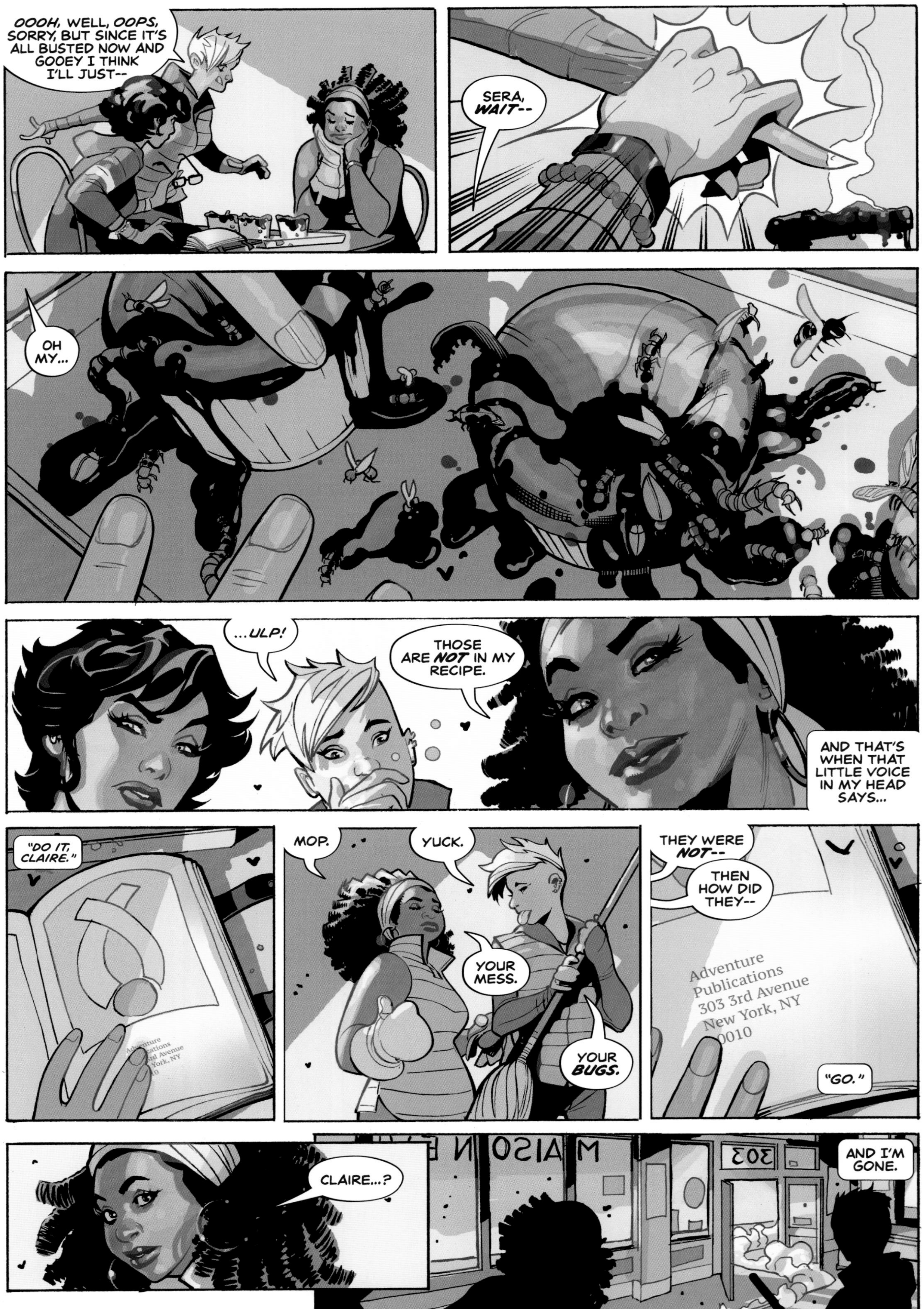
OOOH, WELL, OOPS, SORRY, BUT SINCE IT'S ALL BUSTED NOW AND GOOEY I THINK I'LL JUST--
SERA, WAIT--
OH MY...
...ULP!
THOSE ARE NOT IN MY RECIPE.
AND THAT'S WHEN THAT LITTLE VOICE IN MY HEAD SAYS...
"DO IT, CLAIRE."
Adventure Publications 303 3rd Avenue New York, NY 10010
MOP.
YUCK.
YOUR MESS.
YOUR BUGS.
THEY WERE NOT--
THEN HOW DID THEY--
Adventure Publications 303 3rd Avenue New York, NY 10010
"GO."
CLAIRE...?
MAISON
303
AND I'M GONE.

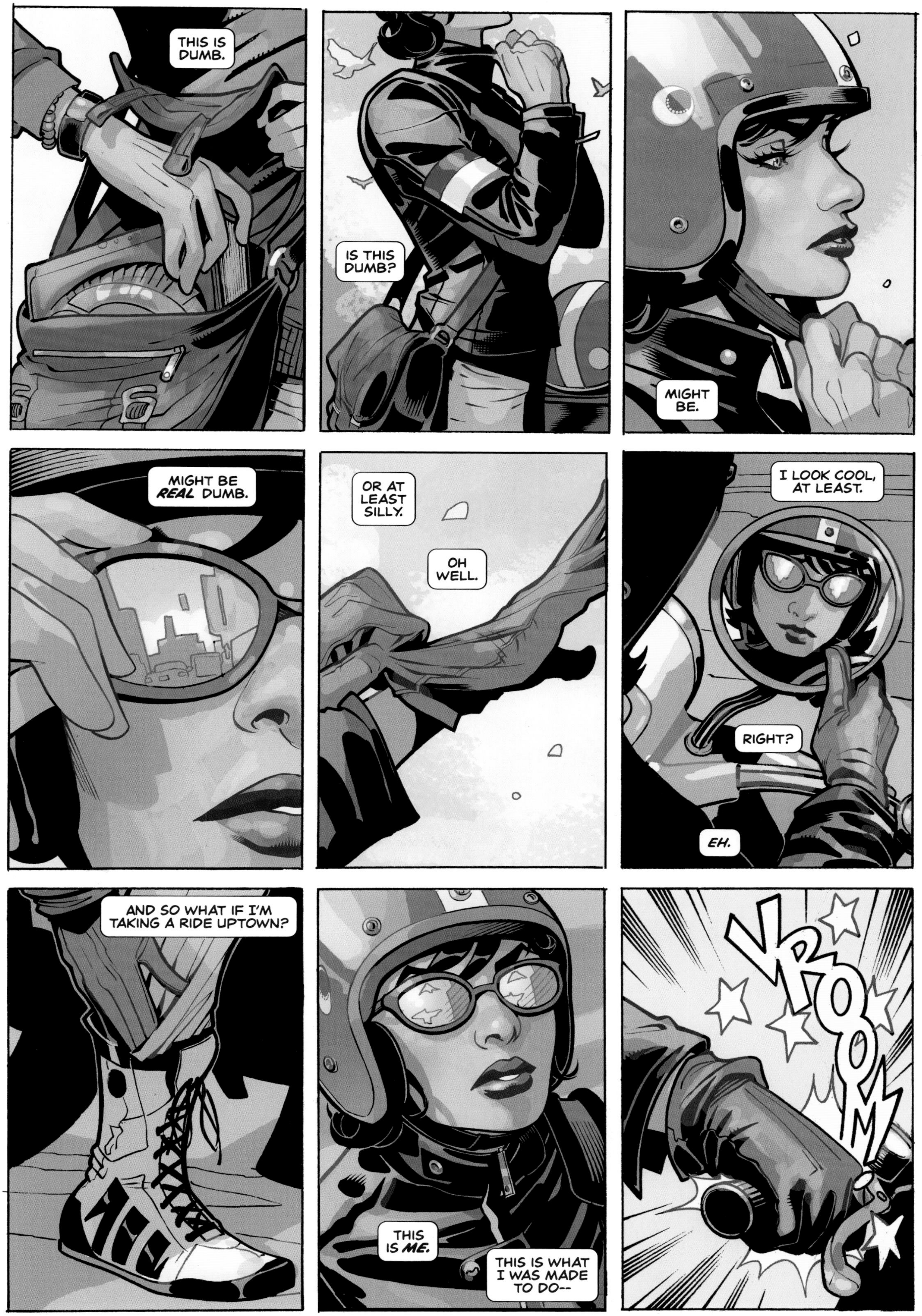
THIS IS DUMB.
IS THIS DUMB?
MIGHT BE.
MIGHT BE REAL DUMB.
OR AT LEAST SILLY.
OH WELL.
I LOOK COOL, AT LEAST.
RIGHT?
EH.
AND SO WHAT IF I'M TAKING A RIDE UPTOWN?
THIS IS ME.
THIS IS WHAT I WAS MADE TO DO--
VROOM

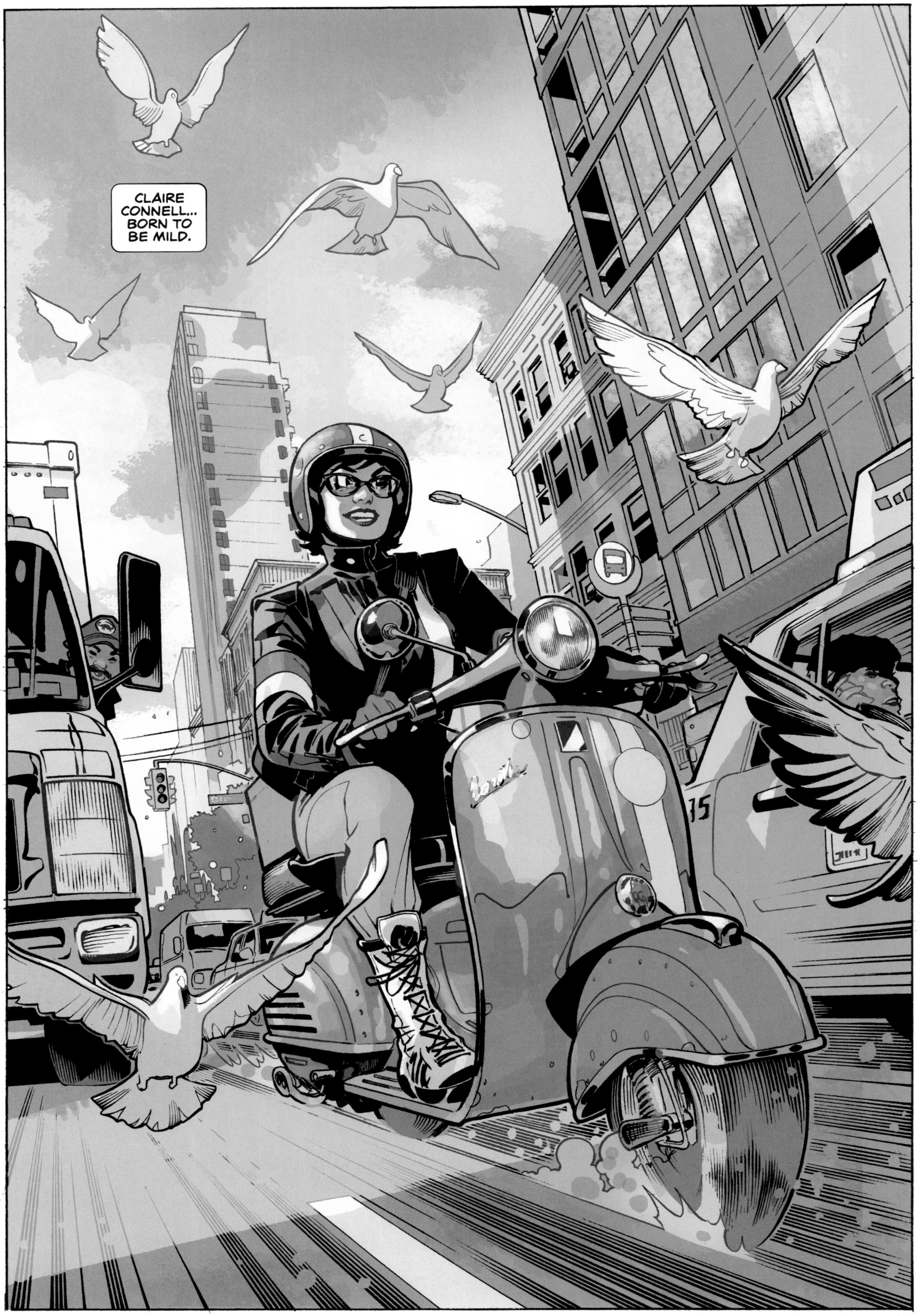
CLAIRE CONNELL... BORN TO BE MILD.

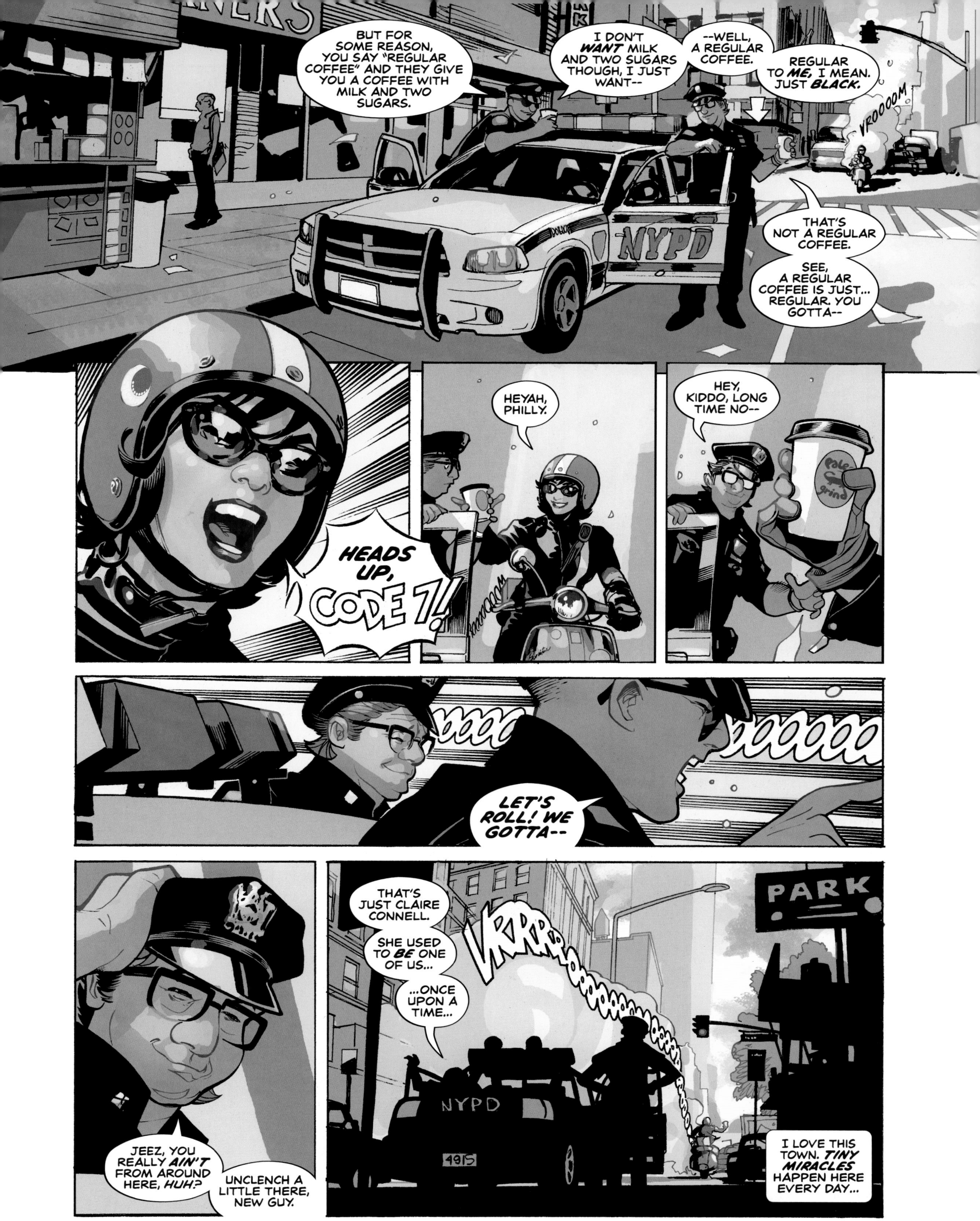
BUT FOR SOME REASON, YOU SAY "REGULAR COFFEE" AND THEY GIVE YOU A COFFEE WITH MILK AND TWO SUGARS.
I DON'T WANT MILK AND TWO SUGARS THOUGH, I JUST WANT--
--WELL, A REGULAR COFFEE.
REGULAR TO ME, I MEAN. JUST BLACK.
VROOOOM
THAT'S NOT A REGULAR COFFEE.
SEE, A REGULAR COFFEE IS JUST... REGULAR. YOU GOTTA--
NYPD
HEADS UP, CODE 7!
HEYAH, PHILLY.
HEY, KIDDO, LONG TIME NO--
LET'S ROLL! WE GOTTA--
JEEZ, YOU REALLY AIN'T FROM AROUND HERE, HUH?
UNCLENCH A LITTLE THERE, NEW GUY.
THAT'S JUST CLAIRE CONNELL.
SHE USED TO BE ONE OF US...
...ONCE UPON A TIME...
PARK
NYPD
4915
I LOVE THIS TOWN. TINY MIRACLES HAPPEN HERE EVERY DAY...

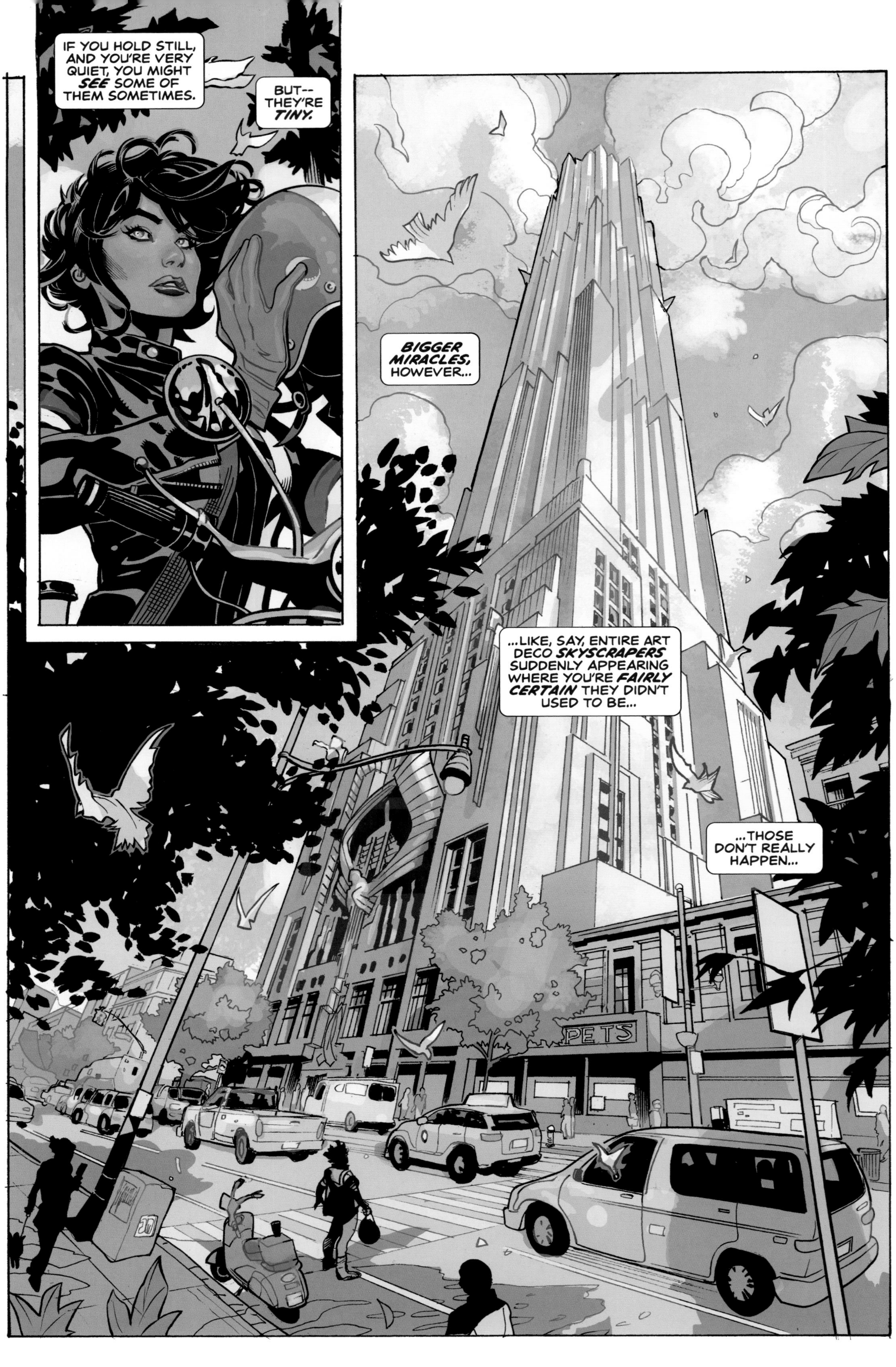
IF YOU HOLD STILL, AND YOU'RE VERY QUIET, YOU MIGHT SEE SOME OF THEM SOMETIMES.
BUT-- THEY'RE TINY.
BIGGER MIRACLES, HOWEVER...
...LIKE, SAY, ENTIRE ART DECO SKYSCRAPERS SUDDENLY APPEARING WHERE YOU'RE FAIRLY CERTAIN THEY DIDN'T USED TO BE...
...THOSE DON'T REALLY HAPPEN...
PETS

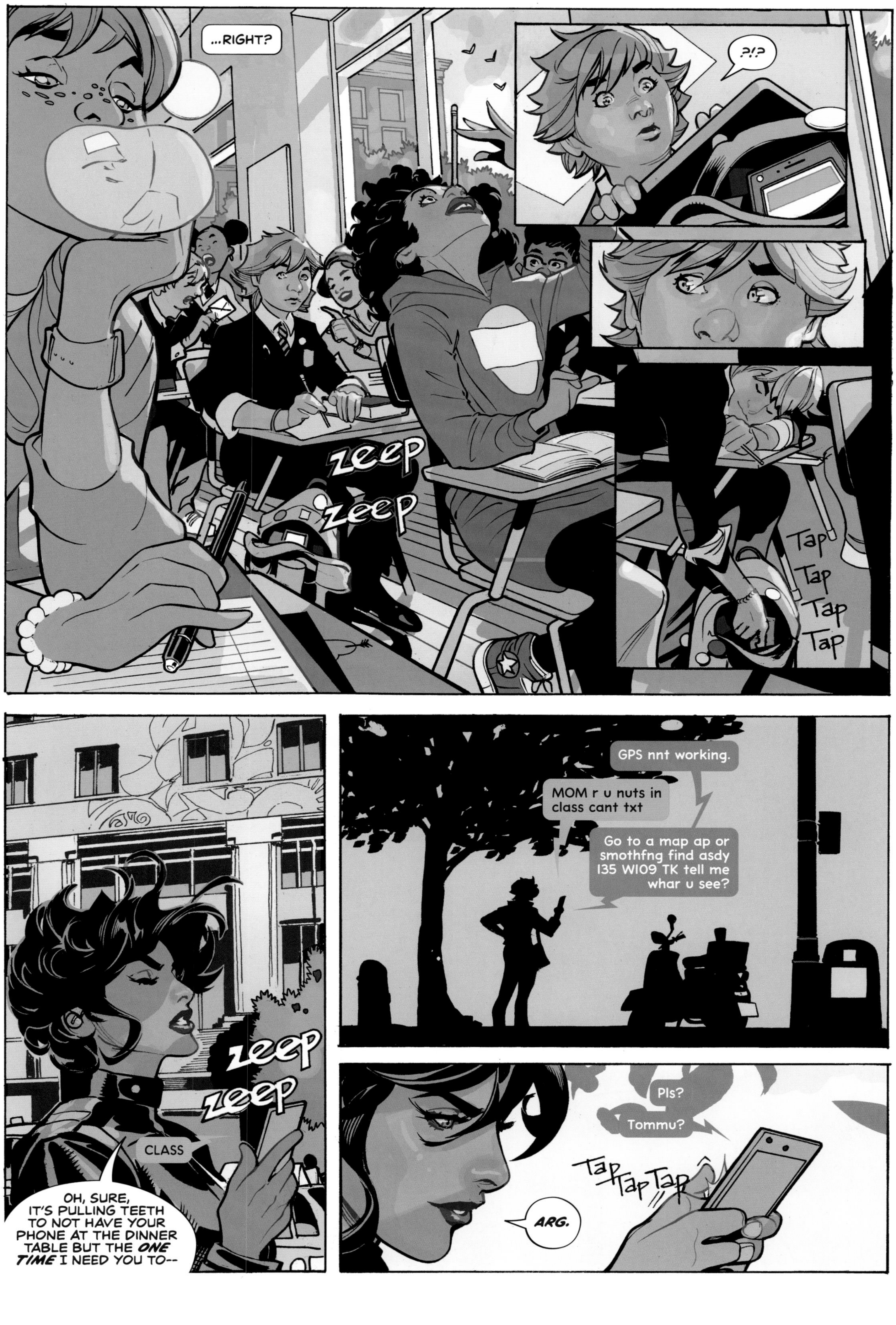
...RIGHT?
?!?
zeep
zeep
Tap
Tap
Tap
Tap
zeep
zeep
CLASS
OH, SURE, IT'S PULLING TEETH TO NOT HAVE YOUR PHONE AT THE DINNER TABLE BUT THE ONE TIME I NEED YOU TO--
GPS nnt working.
MOM r u nuts in class cant txt
Go to a map ap or smothfng find asdy 135 W109 TK tell me whar u see?
Pls?
Tommu?
TapTapTap
ARG.

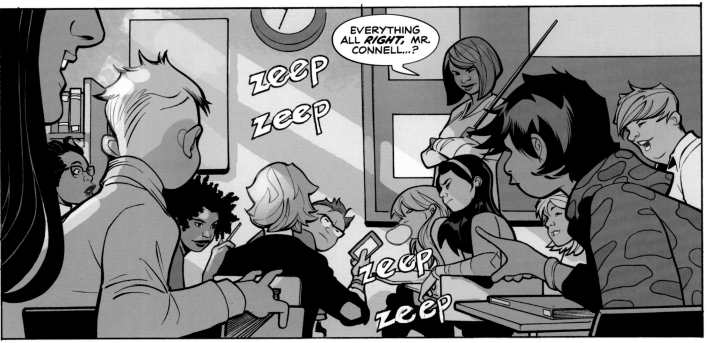

EVERYTHING ALL *RIGHT,* MR. CONNELL...?

ZEEP
ZEEP

ZEEP

ZEEP

WE CAN *WAIT,* I'M SURE.

NO, MA'AM. SORRY, MA'AM.

ZEEP ZEEP

ZEEP ZEEP

OH I CANNOT BE*LIEVE* THAT KID, FOLLOWING THE CLASS RULES LIKE THAT ON ME, HIS *OWN MOTHER*...

OKAY, CLAIRE, YOU'VE GONE FROM *DUMB* TO *SILLY*...

...WHY NOT GO TO OUTRIGHT *CRAZY?*

EXCUSE ME--SIR...?

HOW LONG HAS THAT *BUILDING* BEEN THERE?

...UHHH...

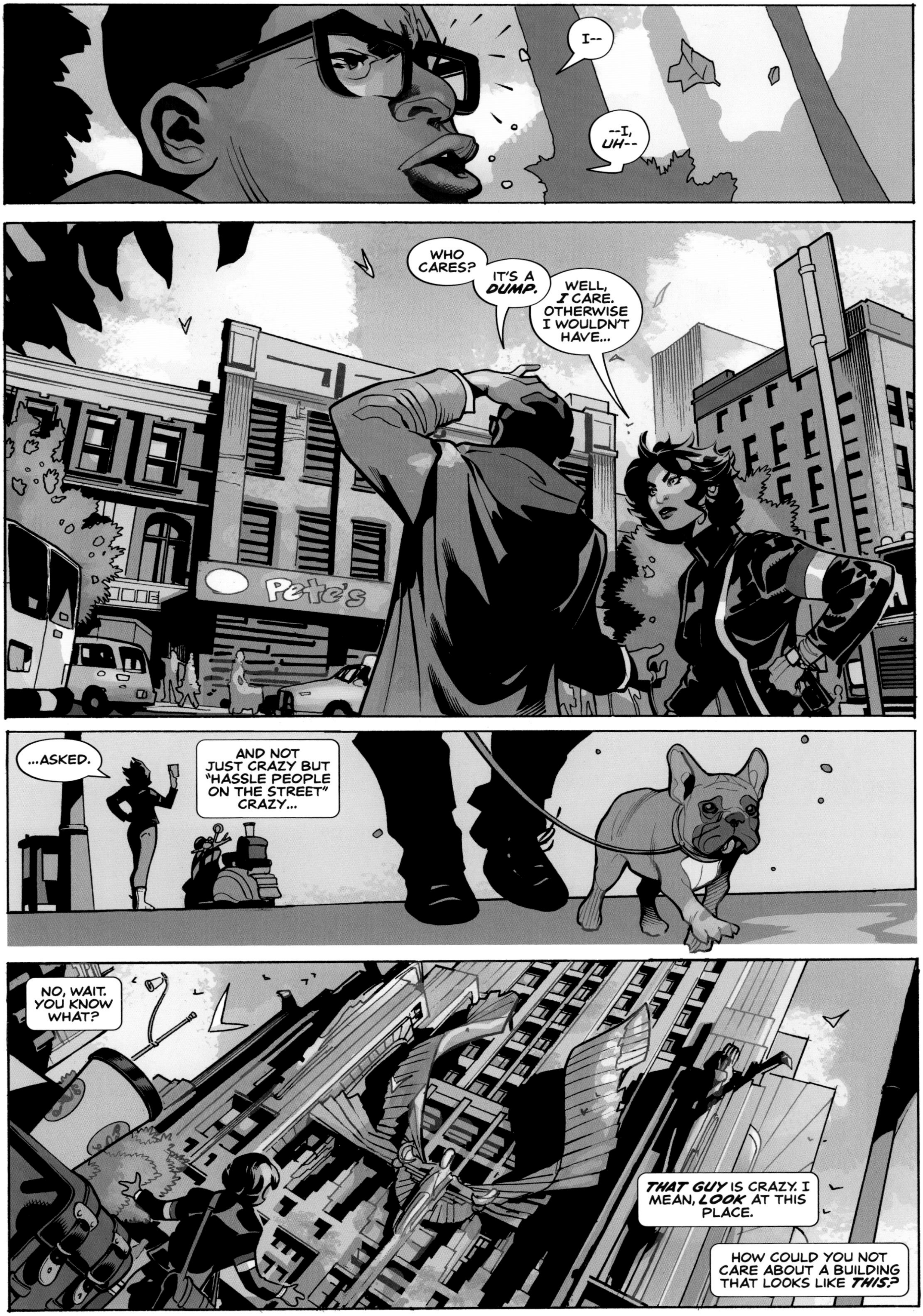
I--
--I, UH--
WHO CARES?
IT'S A DUMP.
WELL, I CARE. OTHERWISE I WOULDN'T HAVE...
Pete's
...ASKED.
AND NOT JUST CRAZY BUT "HASSLE PEOPLE ON THE STREET" CRAZY...
NO, WAIT. YOU KNOW WHAT?
THAT GUY IS CRAZY. I MEAN, LOOK AT THIS PLACE.
HOW COULD YOU NOT CARE ABOUT A BUILDING THAT LOOKS LIKE THIS?

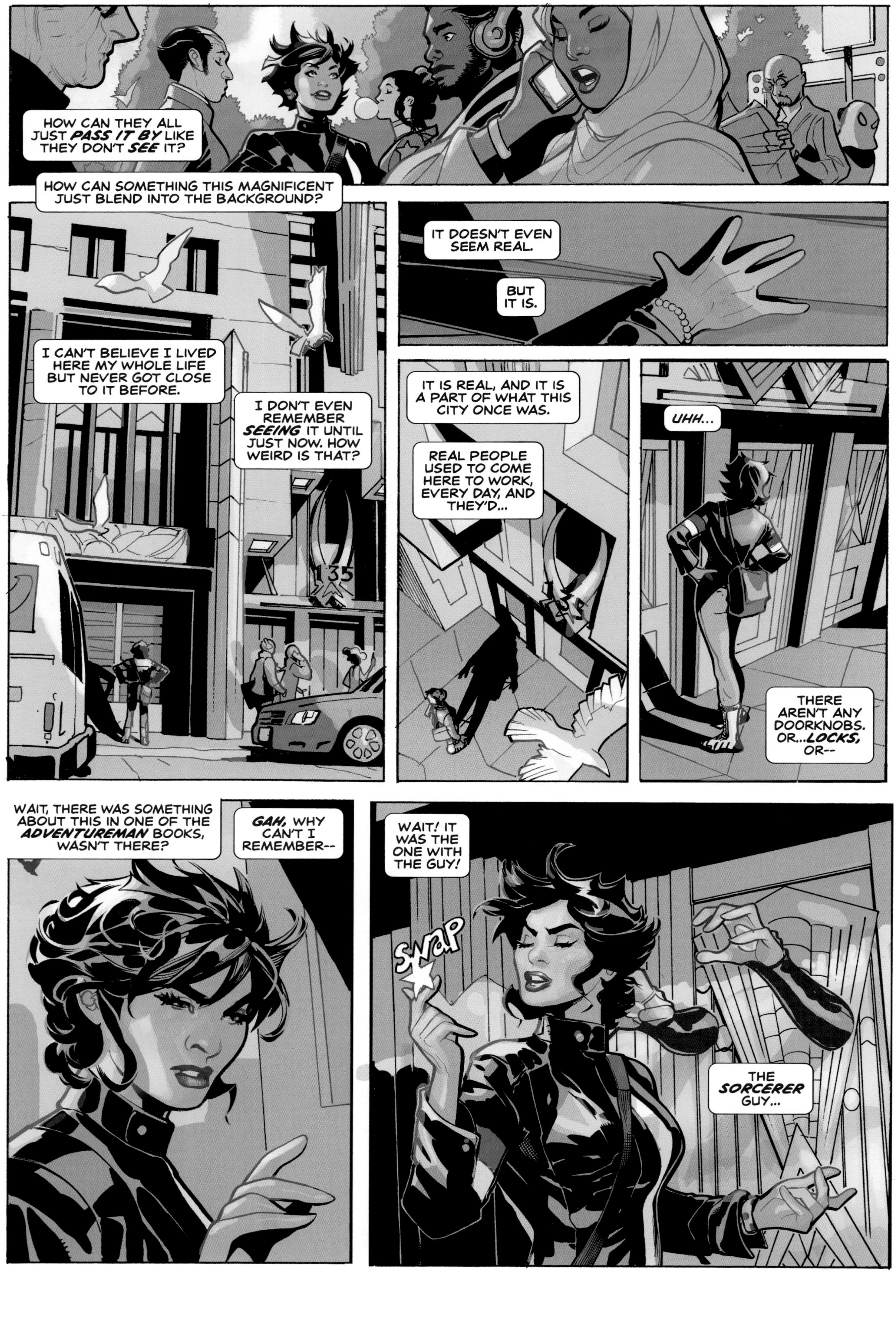
HOW CAN THEY ALL JUST PASS IT BY LIKE THEY DON'T SEE IT?
HOW CAN SOMETHING THIS MAGNIFICENT JUST BLEND INTO THE BACKGROUND?
I CAN'T BELIEVE I LIVED HERE MY WHOLE LIFE BUT NEVER GOT CLOSE TO IT BEFORE.
I DON'T EVEN REMEMBER SEEING IT UNTIL JUST NOW. HOW WEIRD IS THAT?
135
IT DOESN'T EVEN SEEM REAL.
BUT IT IS.
IT IS REAL, AND IT IS A PART OF WHAT THIS CITY ONCE WAS.
REAL PEOPLE USED TO COME HERE TO WORK, EVERY DAY, AND THEY'D...
UHH...
THERE AREN'T ANY DOORKNOBS. OR...LOCKS, OR--
WAIT, THERE WAS SOMETHING ABOUT THIS IN ONE OF THE ADVENTUREMAN BOOKS, WASN'T THERE?
GAH, WHY CAN'T I REMEMBER--
WAIT! IT WAS THE ONE WITH THE GUY!
SNAP
THE SORCERER GUY...

Panting and sweating, the Fancy Man runs, the sounds of the heels of his bespoke Italian boots tapping upon the concrete a staccato rat-tat-tat, matching the tempo of his ever-quickening heart.

How odd, thinks Gentleman Jim Royale. *There's no traffic.*

No, indeed: the only thing the fancy man hears as he runs are the sounds he makes trying to flee the ever-encroaching shadows.

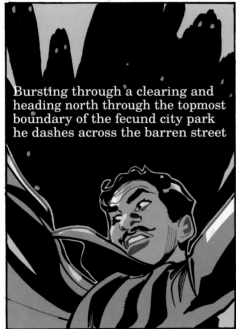

Bursting through a clearing and heading north through the topmost boundary of the fecund city park he dashes across the barren street

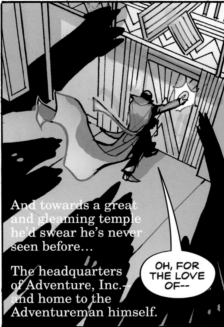

And towards a great and gleaming temple he'd swear he's never seen before...

The headquarters of Adventure, Inc.-- and home to the Adventureman himself.

OH, FOR THE LOVE OF--

WE USUALLY HAVE A STRICT *NO SOLICITORS* POLICY...

...BUT FOR YOU WE'LL MAKE AN EXCEPTION!

WHOA--

WHAT THE *BUTTS?*

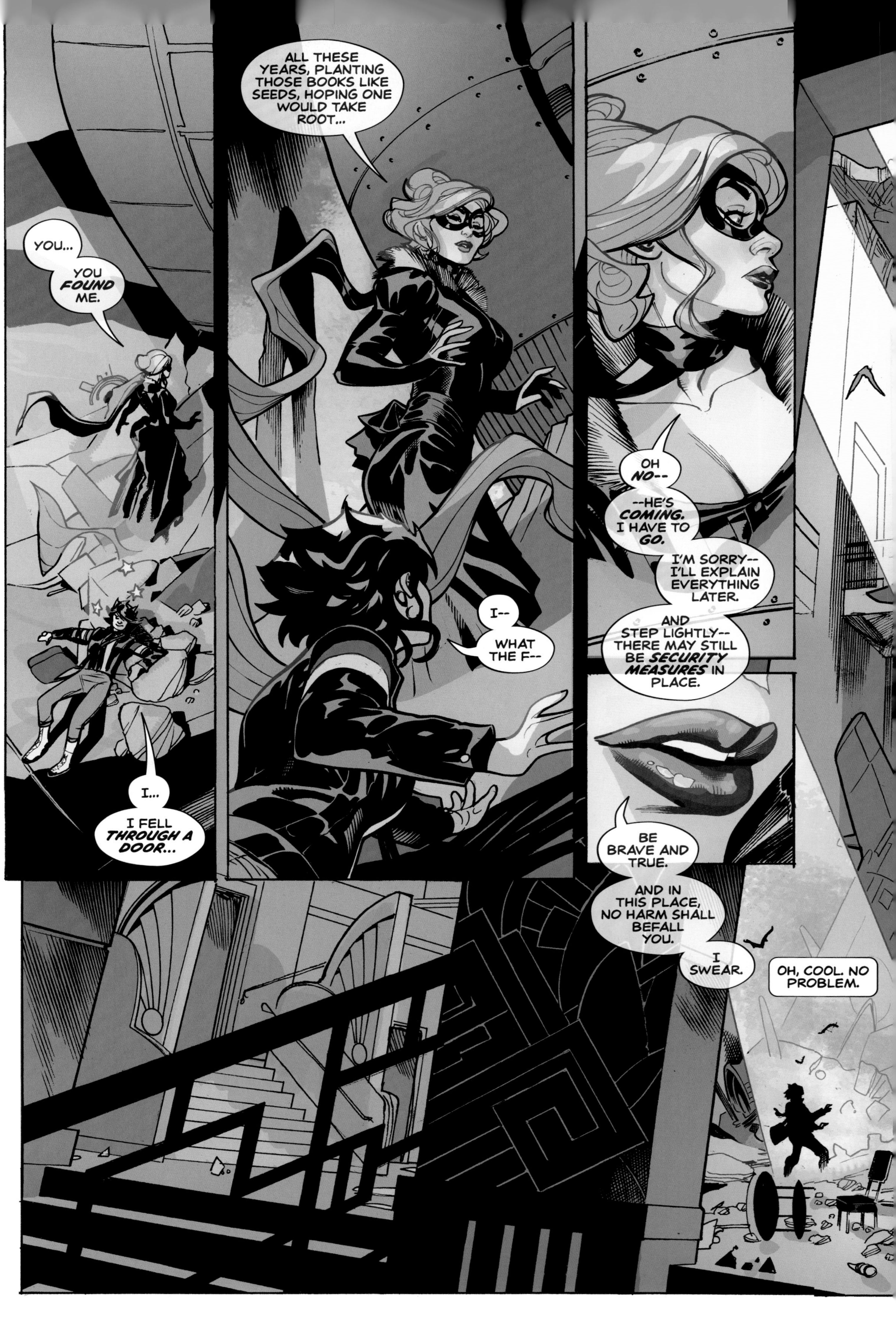
YOU...
YOU FOUND ME.
I...
I FELL THROUGH A DOOR...
ALL THESE YEARS, PLANTING THOSE BOOKS LIKE SEEDS, HOPING ONE WOULD TAKE ROOT...
I--
WHAT THE F--
OH NO--
--HE'S COMING. I HAVE TO GO.
I'M SORRY-- I'LL EXPLAIN EVERYTHING LATER.
AND STEP LIGHTLY-- THERE MAY STILL BE SECURITY MEASURES IN PLACE.
BE BRAVE AND TRUE.
AND IN THIS PLACE, NO HARM SHALL BEFALL YOU.
I SWEAR.
OH, COOL. NO PROBLEM.

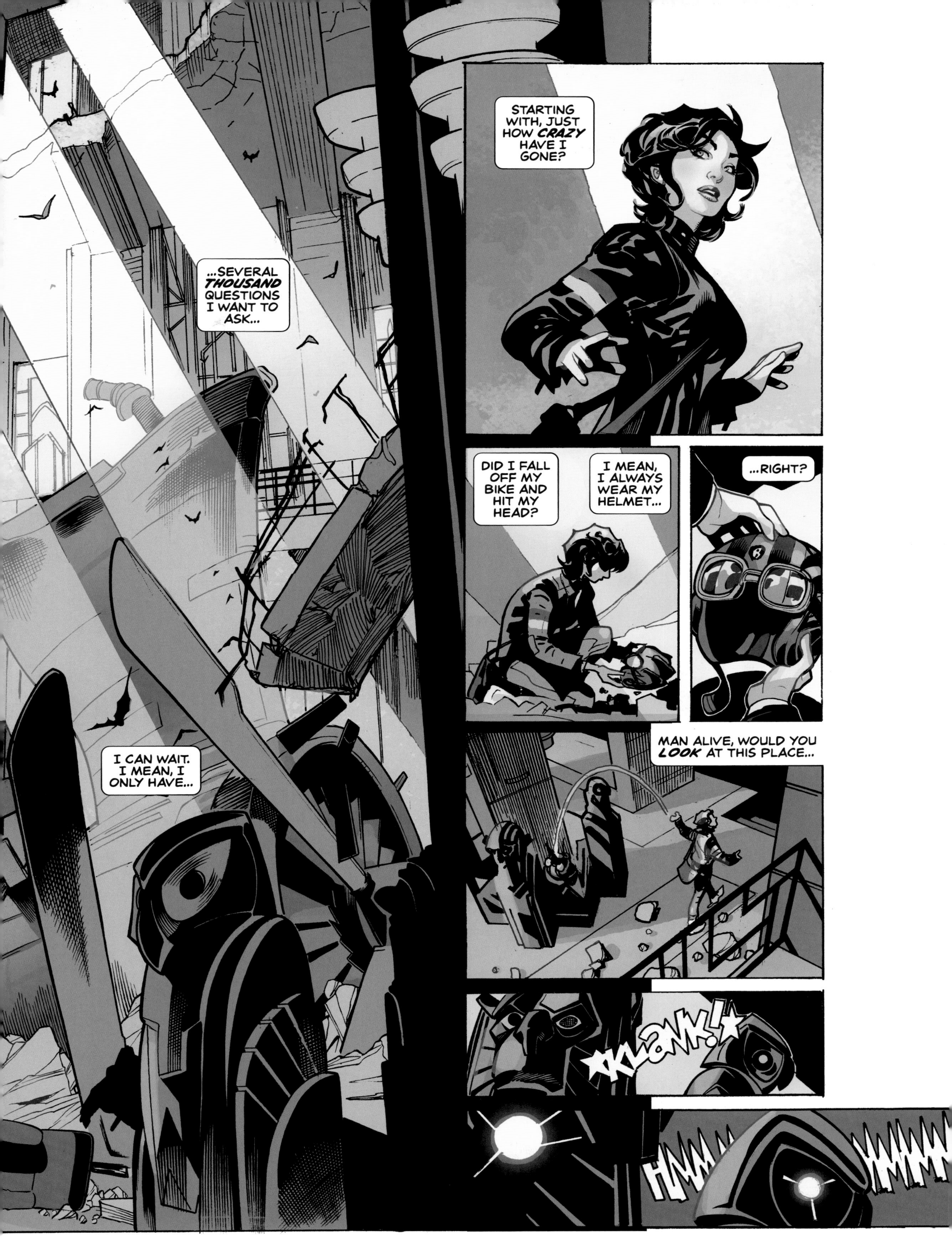
I CAN WAIT. I MEAN, I ONLY HAVE...
...SEVERAL THOUSAND QUESTIONS I WANT TO ASK...
STARTING WITH, JUST HOW CRAZY HAVE I GONE?
DID I FALL OFF MY BIKE AND HIT MY HEAD?
I MEAN, I ALWAYS WEAR MY HELMET...
...RIGHT?
MAN ALIVE, WOULD YOU LOOK AT THIS PLACE...
KLANK!

WWWWUUHHRRR

KVOK!

UM.

"THERE MAY STILL BE SECURITY MEASURES IN PLACE," THE NICE GHOST-LADY SAID.

AAAAAH--

YEAH.

NO DUH.

HIIIII--

--YAH!

KRUK!

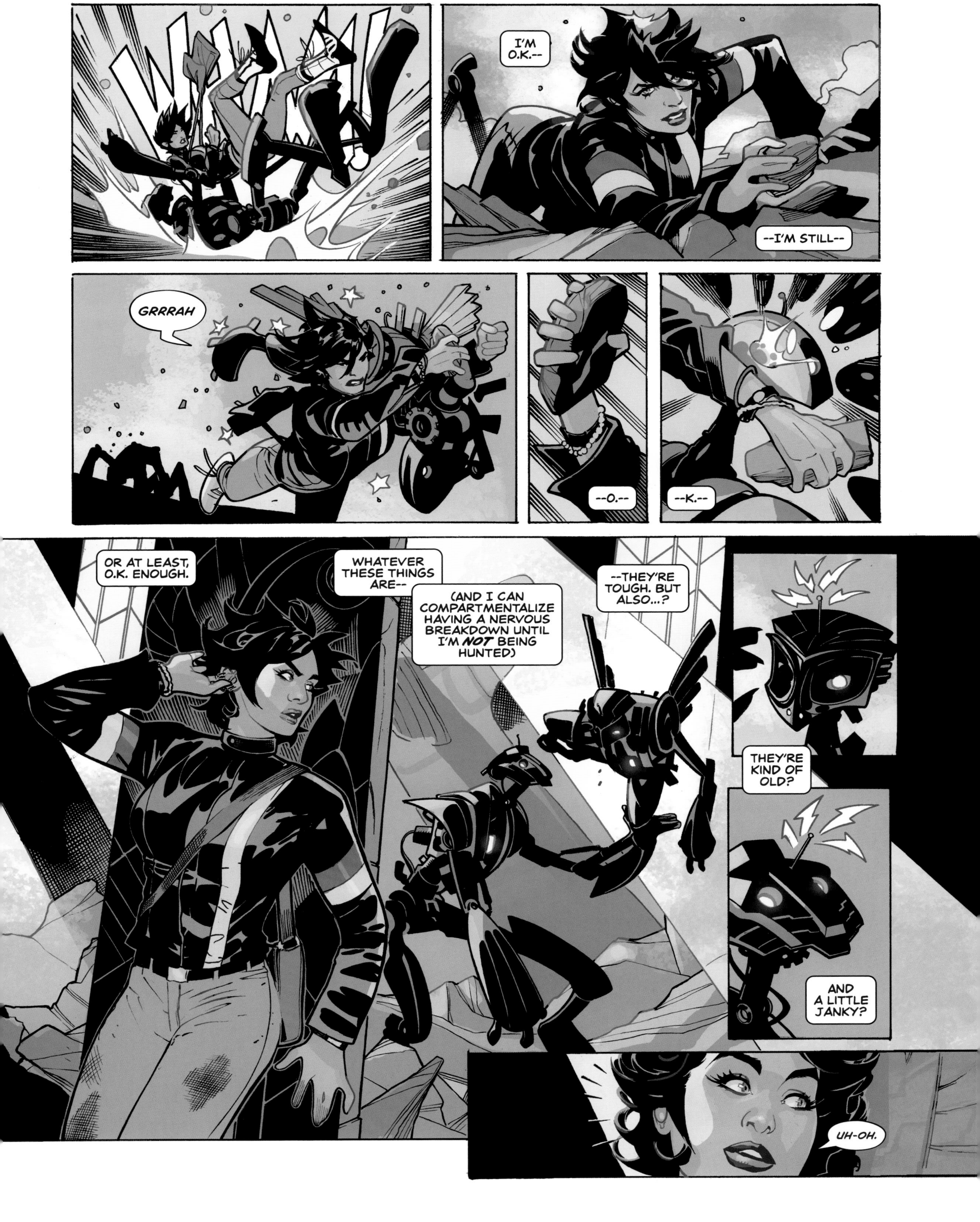
I'M O.K.--
--I'M STILL--
GRRRAH
--O.--
--K.--
OR AT LEAST, O.K. ENOUGH.
WHATEVER THESE THINGS ARE--
(AND I CAN COMPARTMENTALIZE HAVING A NERVOUS BREAKDOWN UNTIL I'M *NOT* BEING HUNTED)
--THEY'RE TOUGH. BUT ALSO...?
THEY'RE KIND OF OLD?
AND A LITTLE JANKY?
UH-OH.

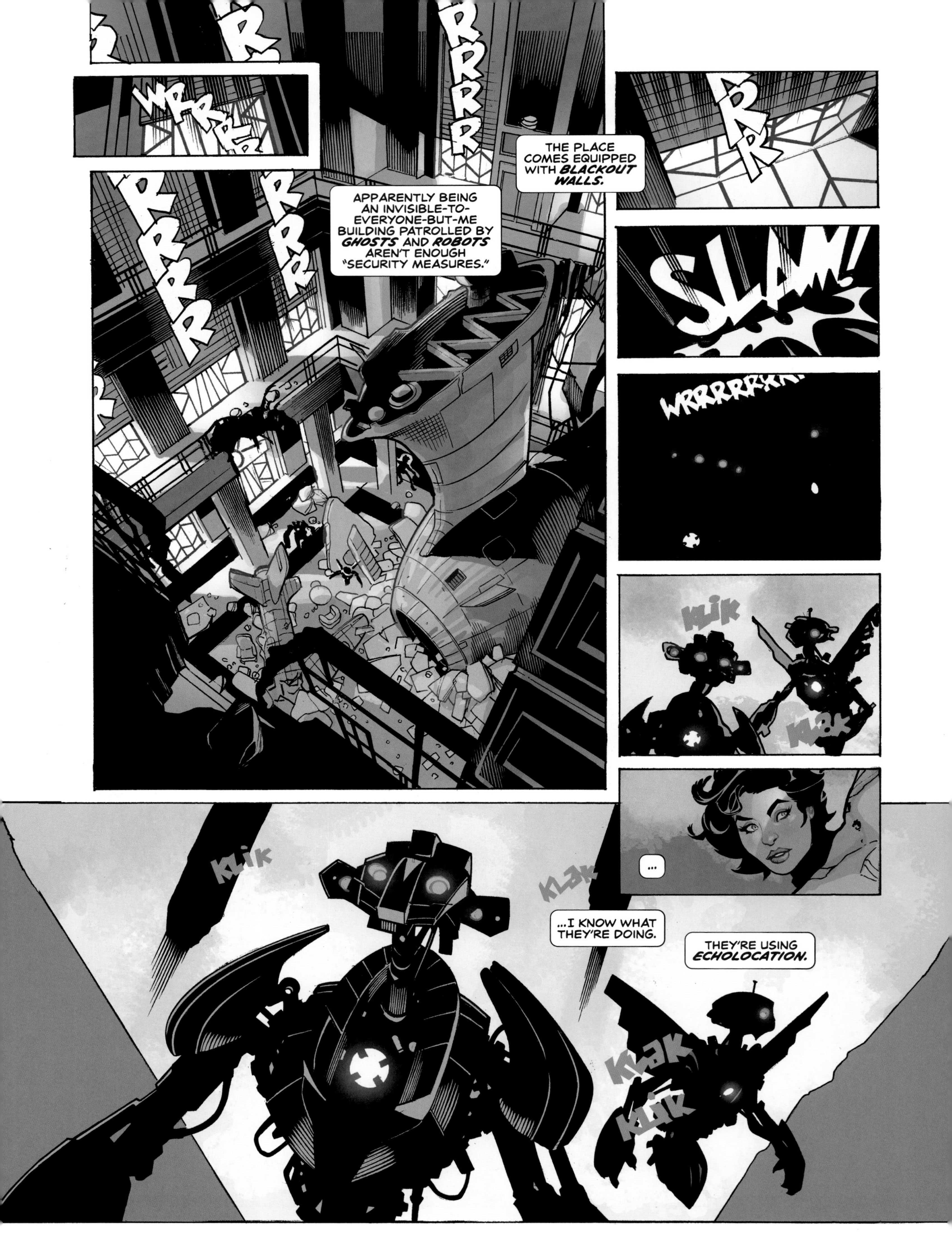
WRRR
RRRRR
THE PLACE COMES EQUIPPED WITH BLACKOUT WALLS.
APPARENTLY BEING AN INVISIBLE-TO-EVERYONE-BUT-ME BUILDING PATROLLED BY GHOSTS AND ROBOTS AREN'T ENOUGH "SECURITY MEASURES."
SLAM!
KLIK
KLAK
...
KLIK
KLAK
...I KNOW WHAT THEY'RE DOING.
THEY'RE USING ECHOLOCATION.
KLAK
KLIK

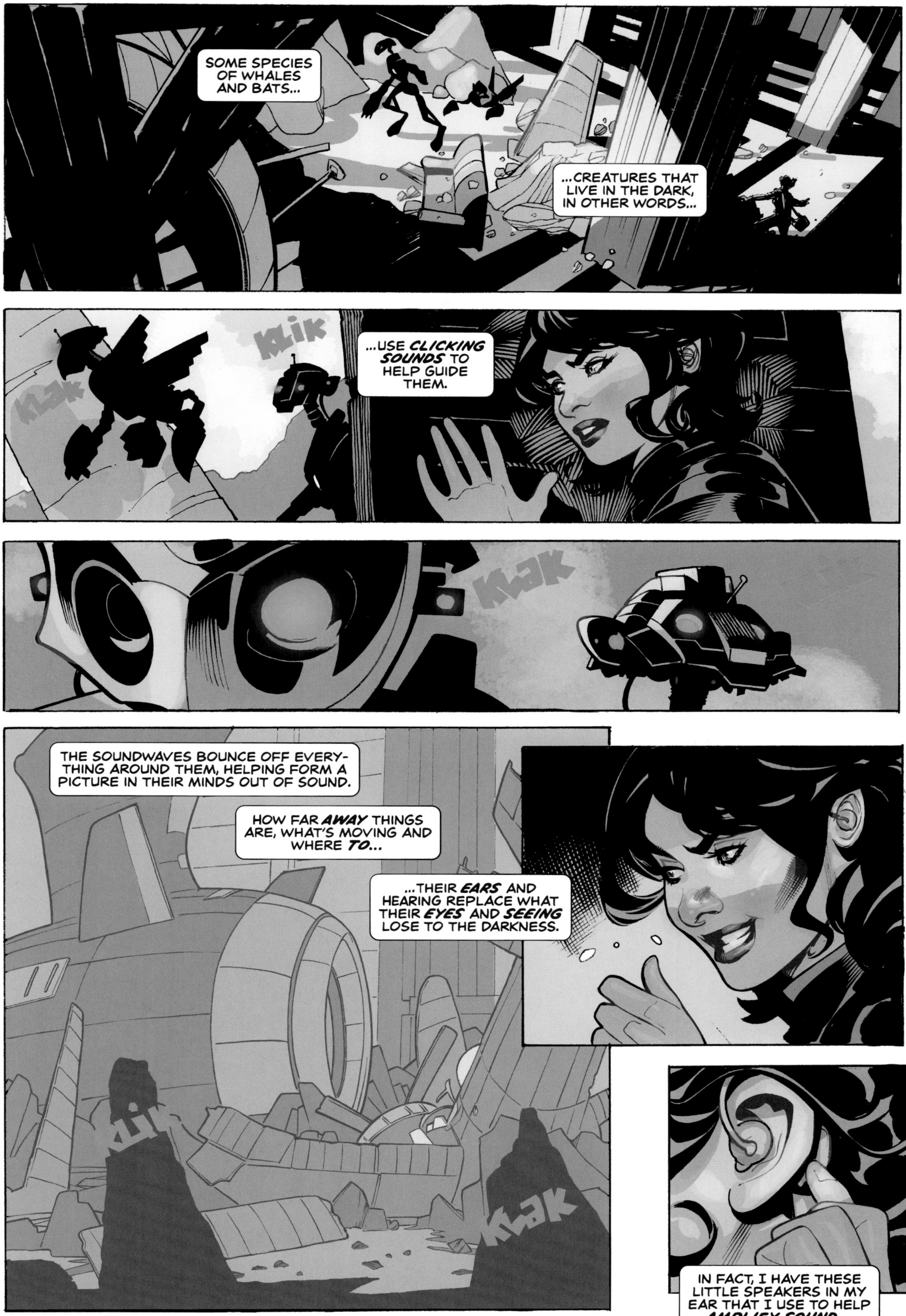
SOME SPECIES OF WHALES AND BATS...
...CREATURES THAT LIVE IN THE DARK, IN OTHER WORDS...
KLIK
KLAK
...USE CLICKING SOUNDS TO HELP GUIDE THEM.
KLAK
THE SOUNDWAVES BOUNCE OFF EVERY-THING AROUND THEM, HELPING FORM A PICTURE IN THEIR MINDS OUT OF SOUND.
HOW FAR AWAY THINGS ARE, WHAT'S MOVING AND WHERE TO...
...THEIR EARS AND HEARING REPLACE WHAT THEIR EYES AND SEEING LOSE TO THE DARKNESS.
KLIK
KLAK
IN FACT, I HAVE THESE LITTLE SPEAKERS IN MY EAR THAT I USE TO HELP AMPLIFY SOUND...

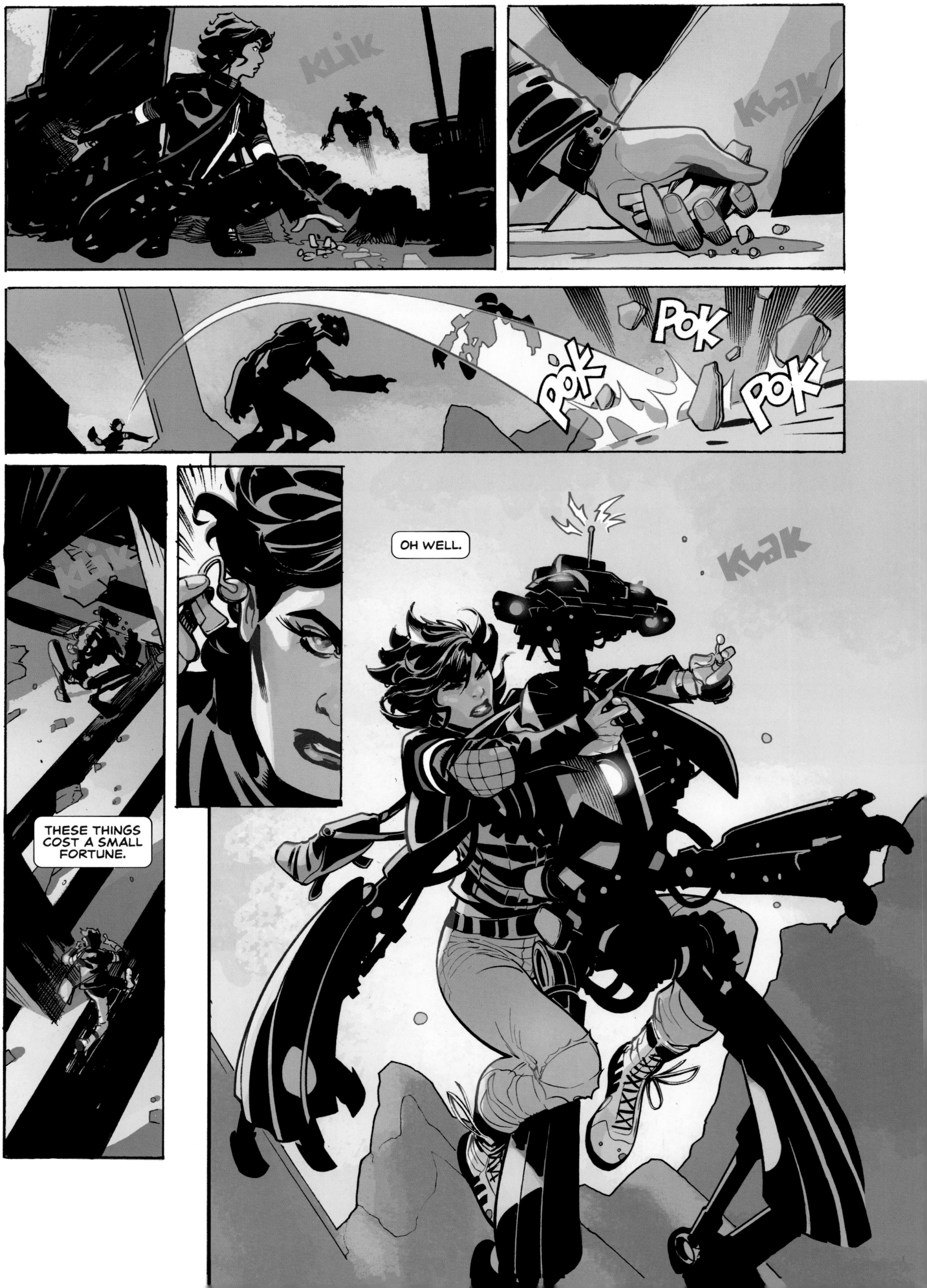
KLIK
KLAK
POK
POK
POK
KLIK
THESE THINGS COST A SMALL FORTUNE.
OH WELL.
KLAK

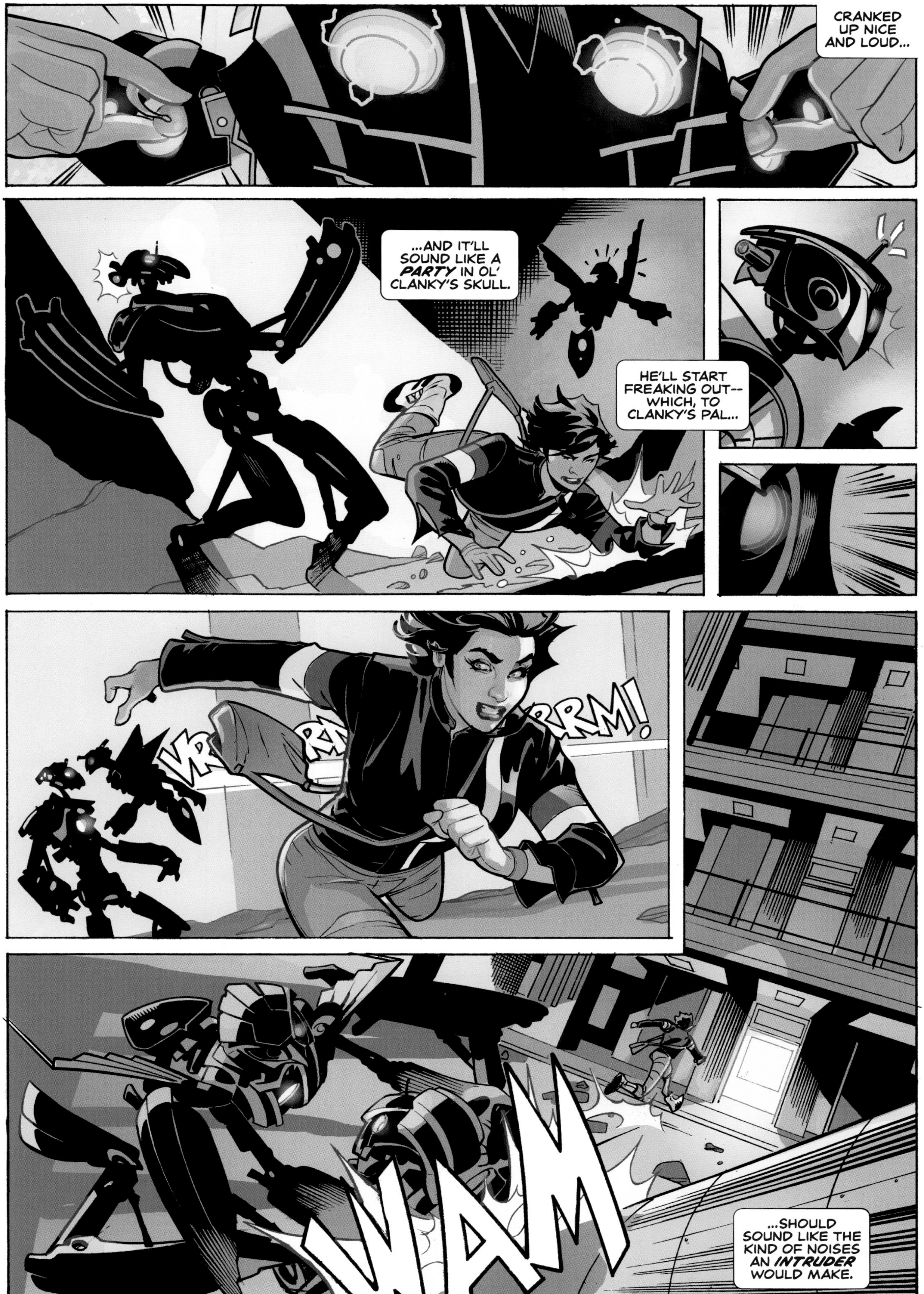
CRANKED UP NICE AND LOUD...
...AND IT'LL SOUND LIKE A *PARTY* IN OL' CLANKY'S SKULL.
HE'LL START FREAKING OUT-- WHICH, TO CLANKY'S PAL...
VRRRRRRRRM!
...SHOULD SOUND LIKE THE KIND OF NOISES AN *INTRUDER* WOULD MAKE.
WAM

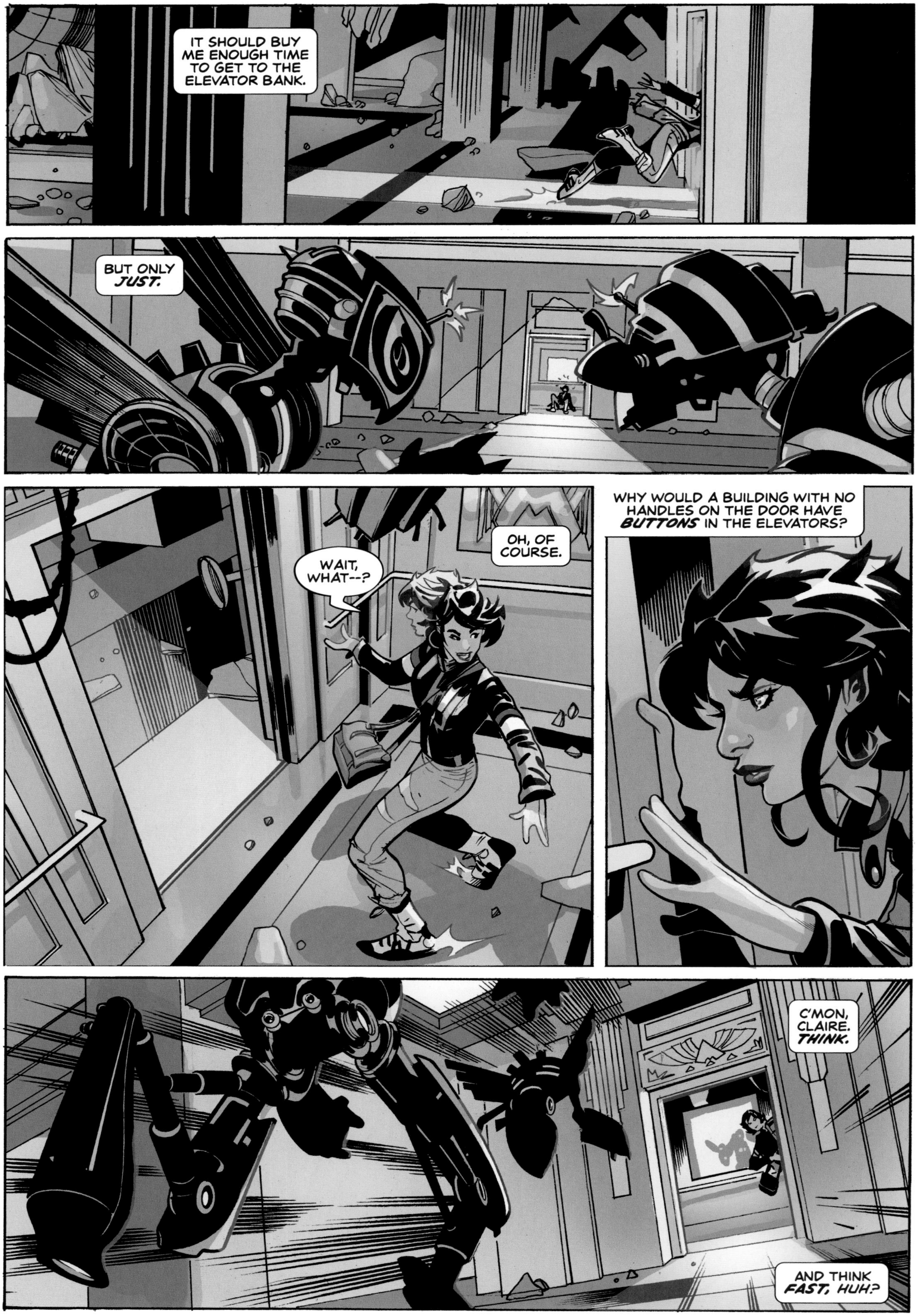
IT SHOULD BUY ME ENOUGH TIME TO GET TO THE ELEVATOR BANK.
BUT ONLY *JUST.*
WAIT, WHAT--?
OH, OF COURSE.
WHY WOULD A BUILDING WITH NO HANDLES ON THE DOOR HAVE *BUTTONS* IN THE ELEVATORS?
C'MON, CLAIRE. *THINK.*
AND THINK *FAST,* HUH?

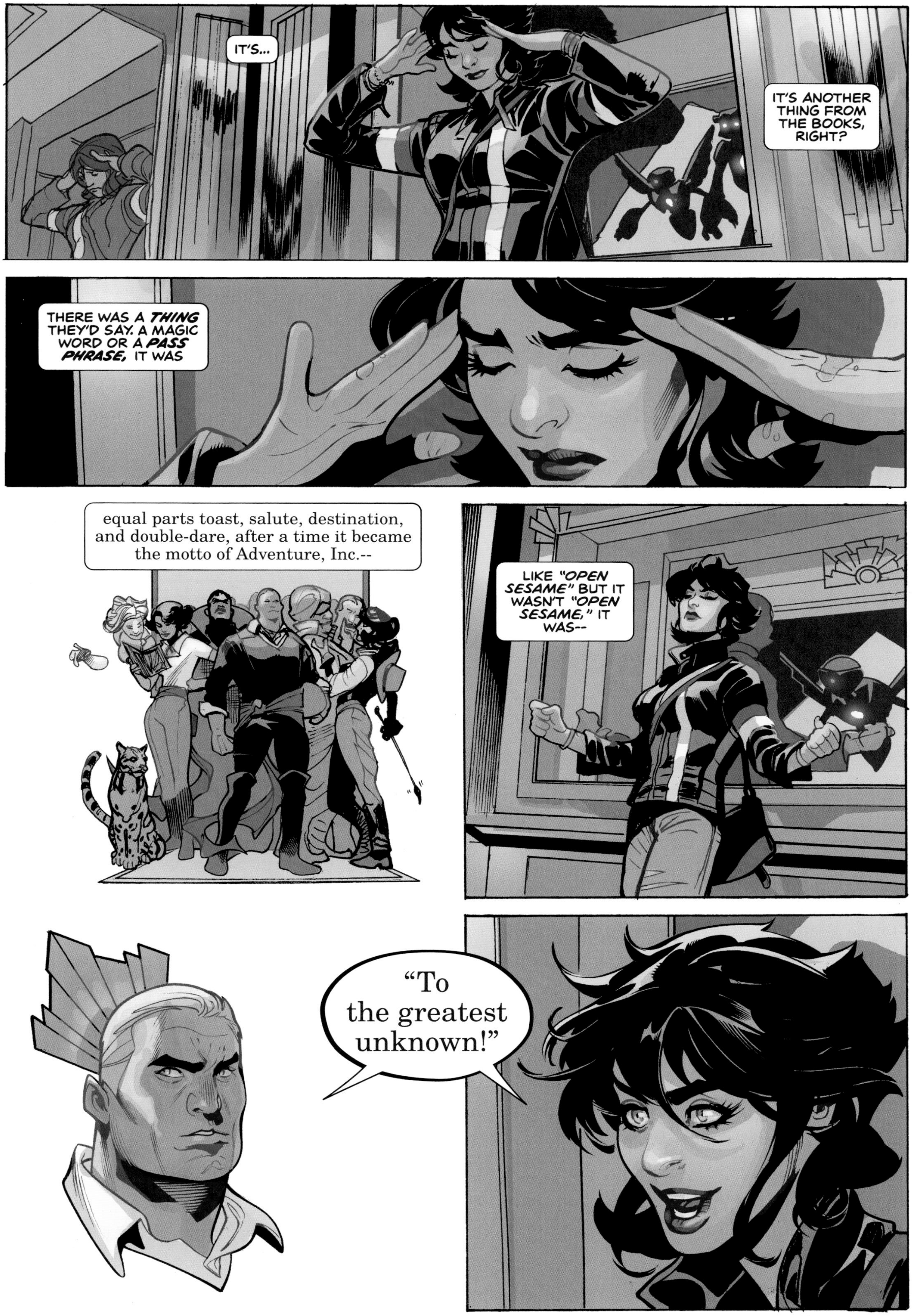

IT'S...
IT'S ANOTHER THING FROM THE BOOKS, RIGHT?
THERE WAS A THING THEY'D SAY. A MAGIC WORD OR A PASS PHRASE, IT WAS
equal parts toast, salute, destination, and double-dare, after a time it became the motto of Adventure, Inc.--
LIKE "OPEN SESAME" BUT IT WASN'T "OPEN SESAME," IT WAS--
"To the greatest unknown!"

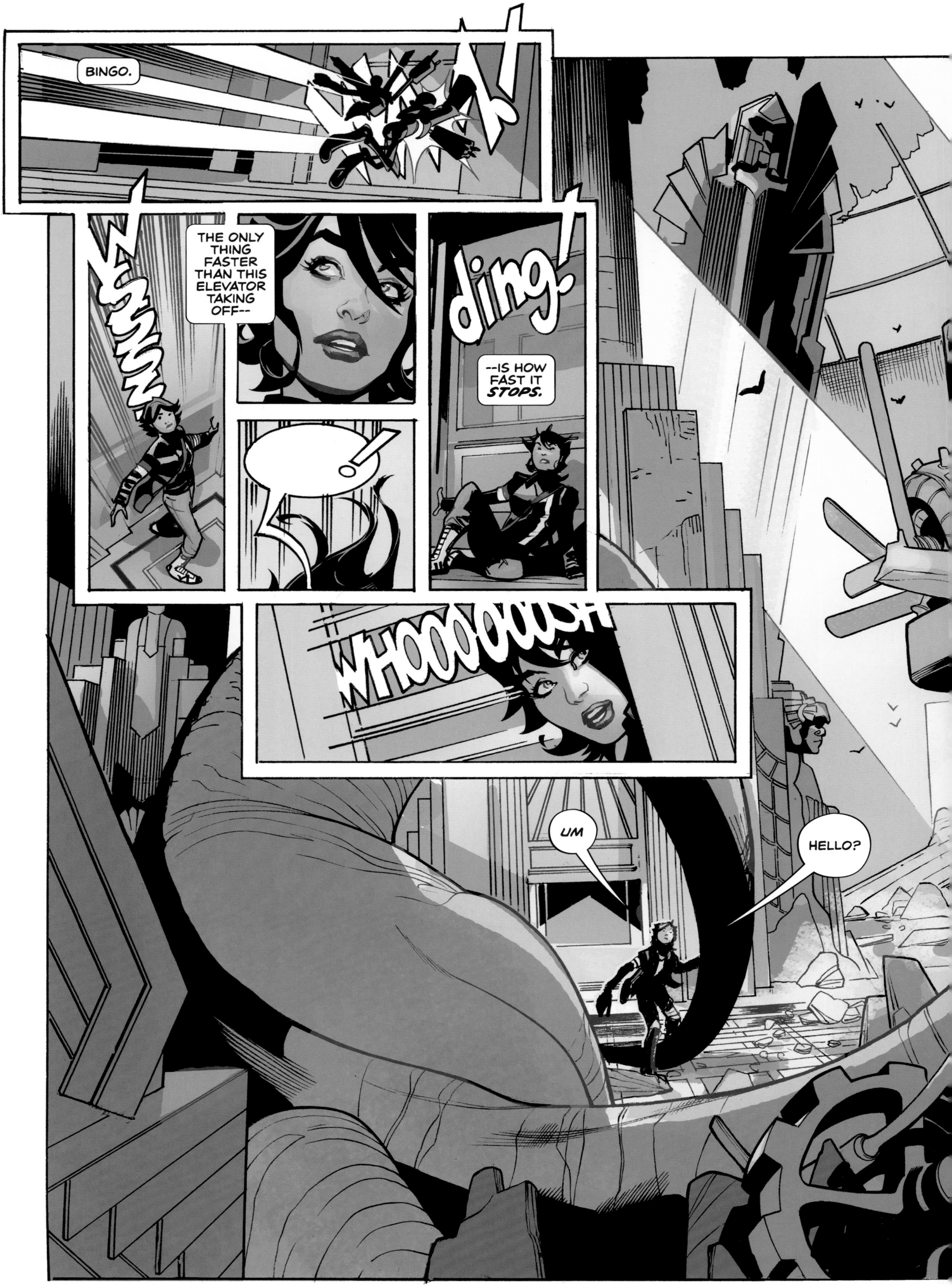
BINGO.
THE ONLY THING FASTER THAN THIS ELEVATOR TAKING OFF--
ding!
--IS HOW FAST IT *STOPS.*
!
WHOOOOOOSH
UM
HELLO?

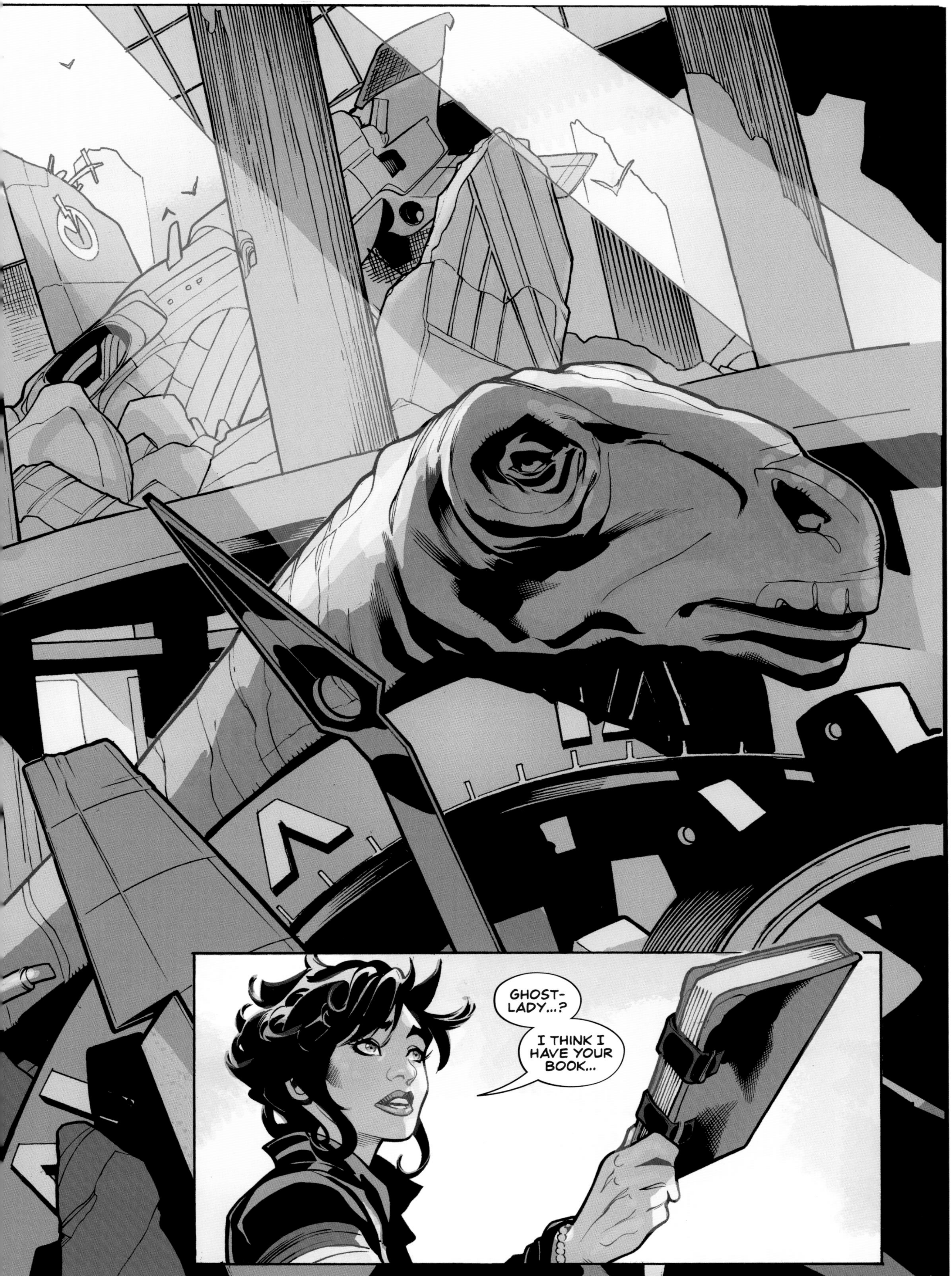
GHOST-LADY...?
I THINK I HAVE YOUR BOOK...

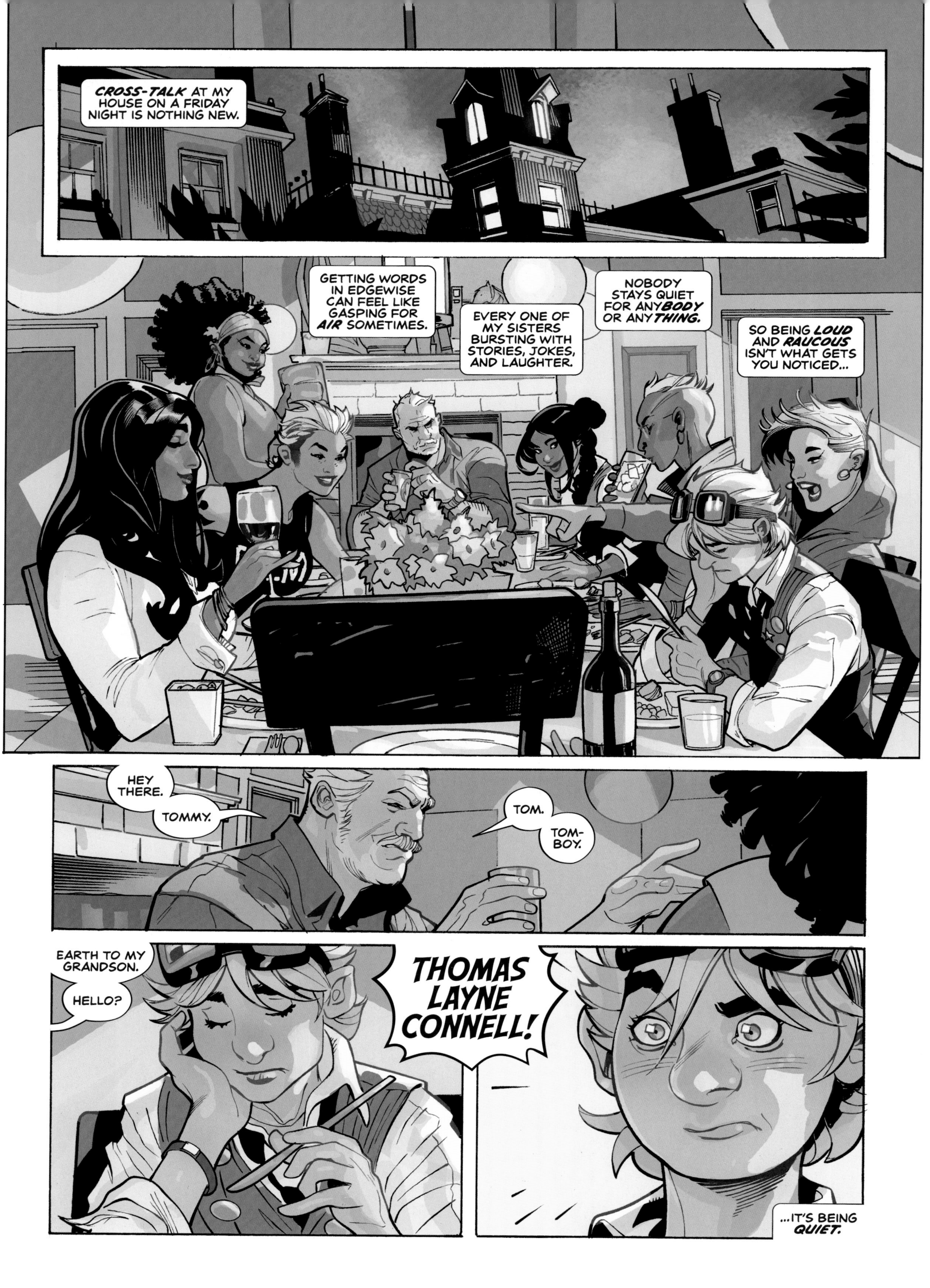

CROSS-TALK AT MY HOUSE ON A FRIDAY NIGHT IS NOTHING NEW.
GETTING WORDS IN EDGEWISE CAN FEEL LIKE GASPING FOR AIR SOMETIMES.
EVERY ONE OF MY SISTERS BURSTING WITH STORIES, JOKES, AND LAUGHTER.
NOBODY STAYS QUIET FOR ANYBODY OR ANYTHING.
SO BEING LOUD AND RAUCOUS ISN'T WHAT GETS YOU NOTICED...
HEY THERE.
TOMMY.
TOM.
TOM-BOY.
EARTH TO MY GRANDSON.
HELLO?
THOMAS LAYNE CONNELL!
...IT'S BEING QUIET.

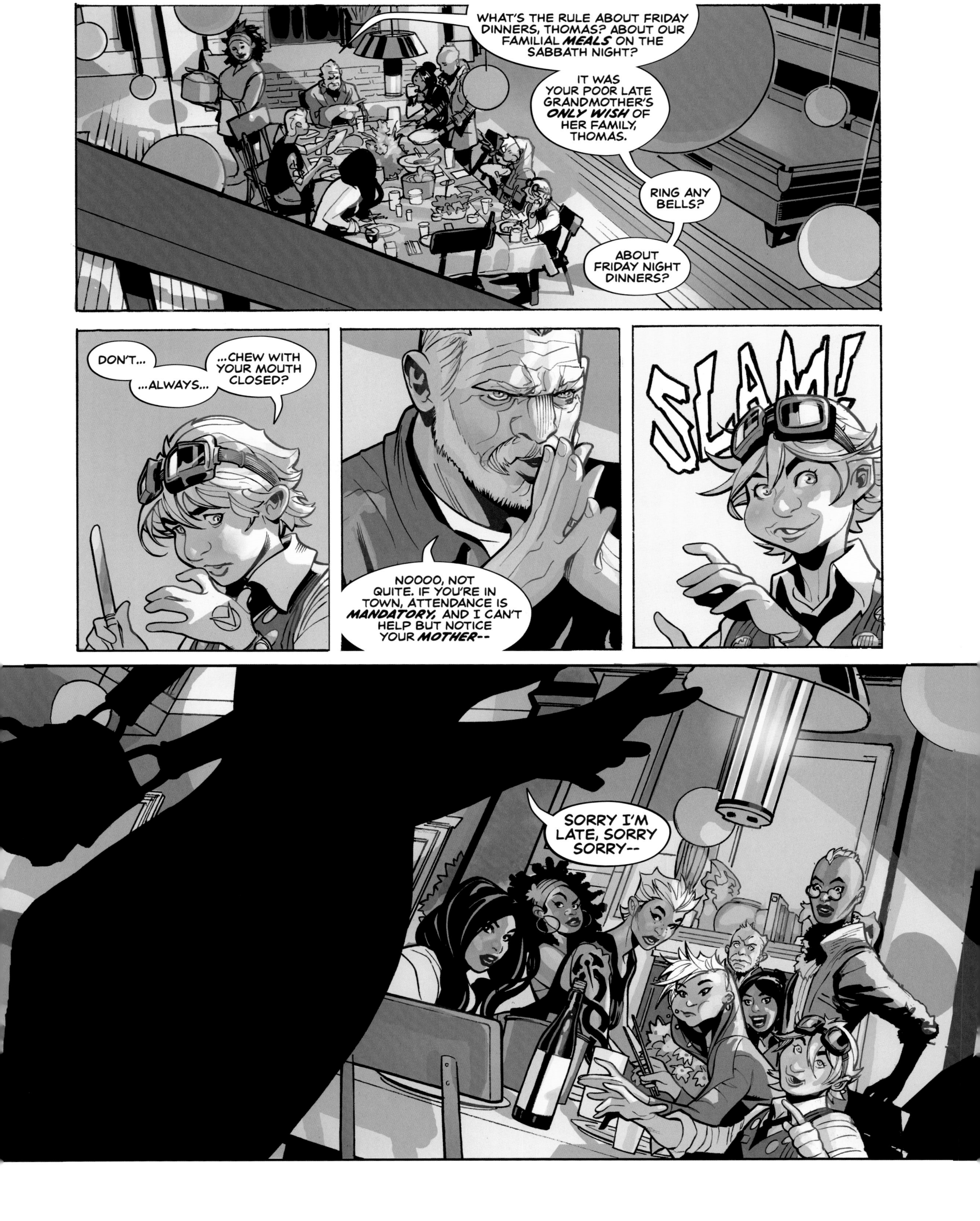
WHAT'S THE RULE ABOUT FRIDAY DINNERS, THOMAS? ABOUT OUR FAMILIAL **MEALS** ON THE SABBATH NIGHT?
IT WAS YOUR POOR LATE GRANDMOTHER'S **ONLY WISH** OF HER FAMILY, THOMAS.
RING ANY BELLS?
ABOUT FRIDAY NIGHT DINNERS?
DON'T...
...ALWAYS...
...CHEW WITH YOUR MOUTH CLOSED?
NOOOO, NOT QUITE. IF YOU'RE IN TOWN, ATTENDANCE IS **MANDATORY,** AND I CAN'T HELP BUT NOTICE YOUR **MOTHER--**
SLAM!
SORRY I'M LATE, SORRY SORRY--

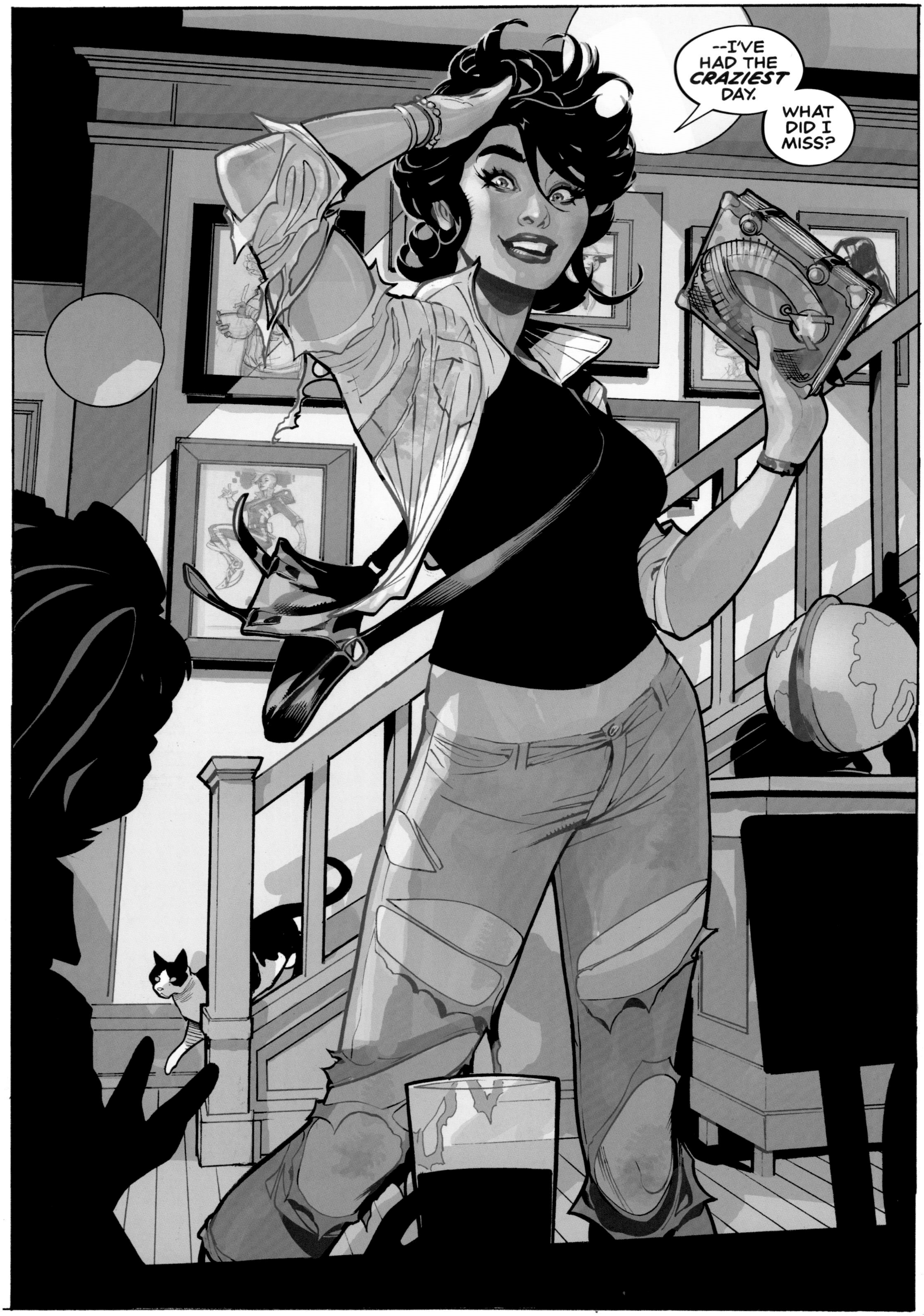
--I'VE HAD THE *CRAZIEST* DAY.
WHAT DID I MISS?

ADVENTUREMAN

"The END and EVERYTHING AFTER"

VOLUME 1

CHAPTER

 # 3

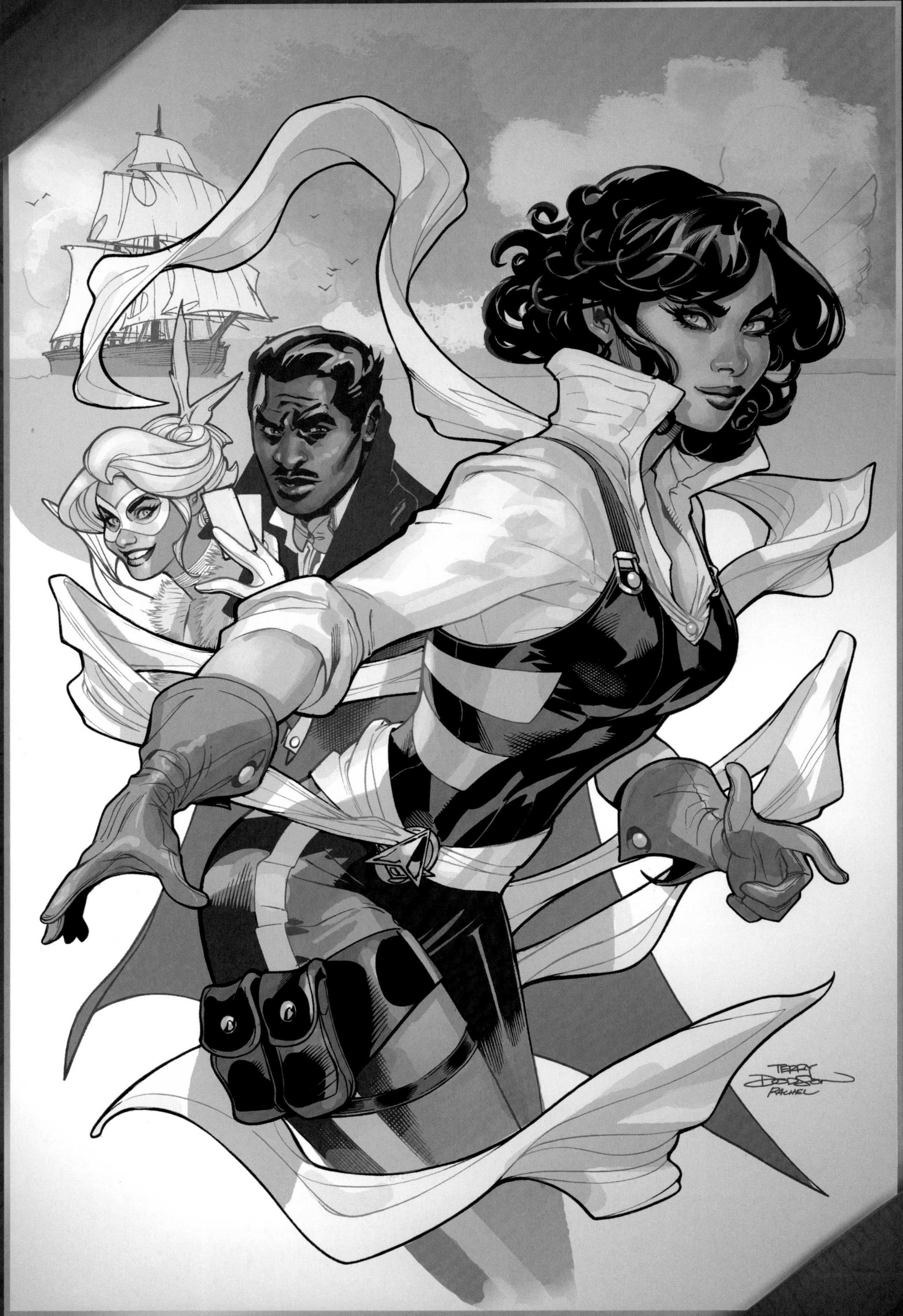
TERRY
DODSON
RACHEL

ORIGINAL COVER
FOR ISSUE 3

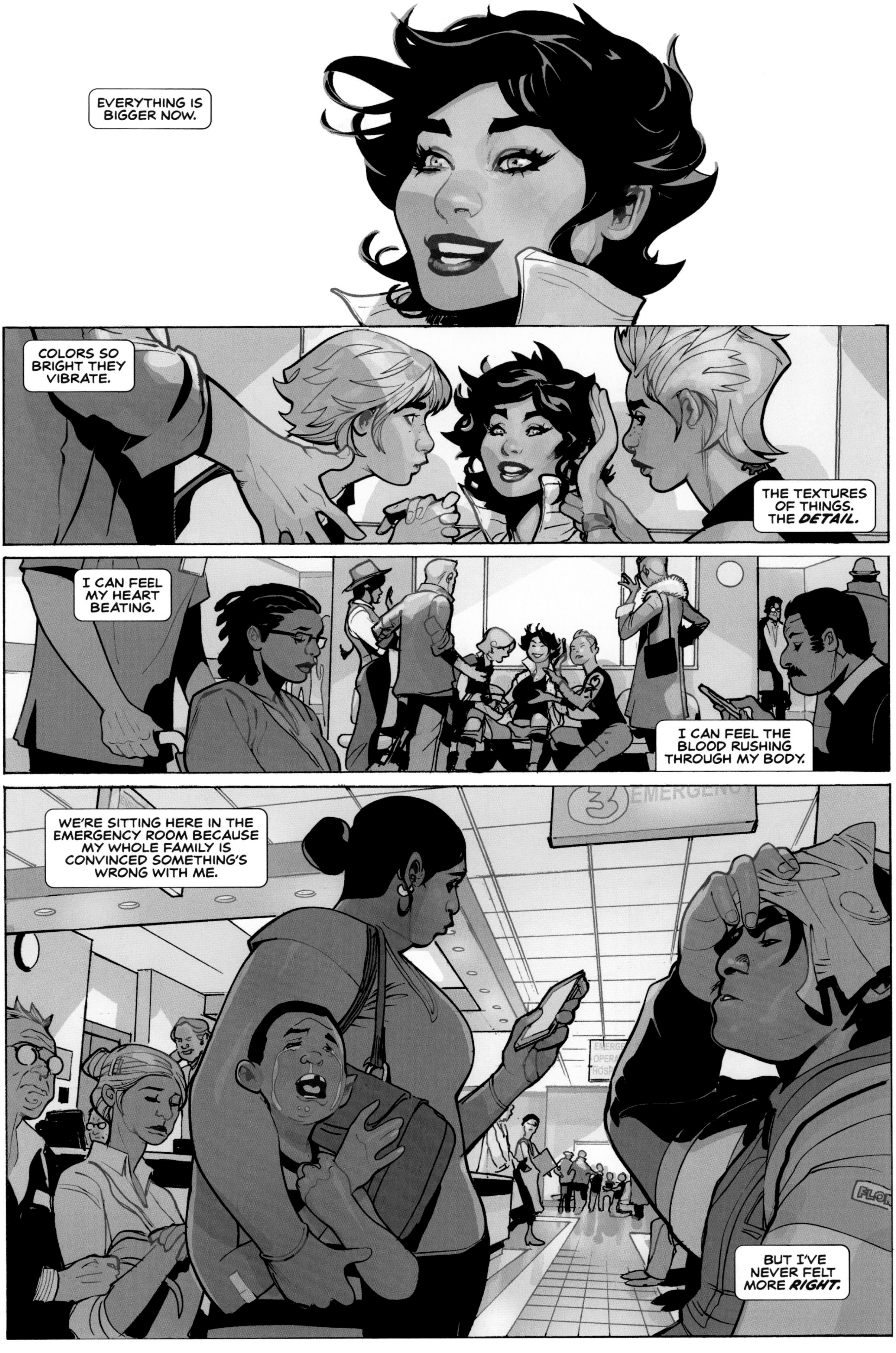
EVERYTHING IS BIGGER NOW.
COLORS SO BRIGHT THEY VIBRATE.
THE TEXTURES OF THINGS. THE DETAIL.
I CAN FEEL MY HEART BEATING.
I CAN FEEL THE BLOOD RUSHING THROUGH MY BODY.
WE'RE SITTING HERE IN THE EMERGENCY ROOM BECAUSE MY WHOLE FAMILY IS CONVINCED SOMETHING'S WRONG WITH ME.
BUT I'VE NEVER FELT MORE RIGHT.

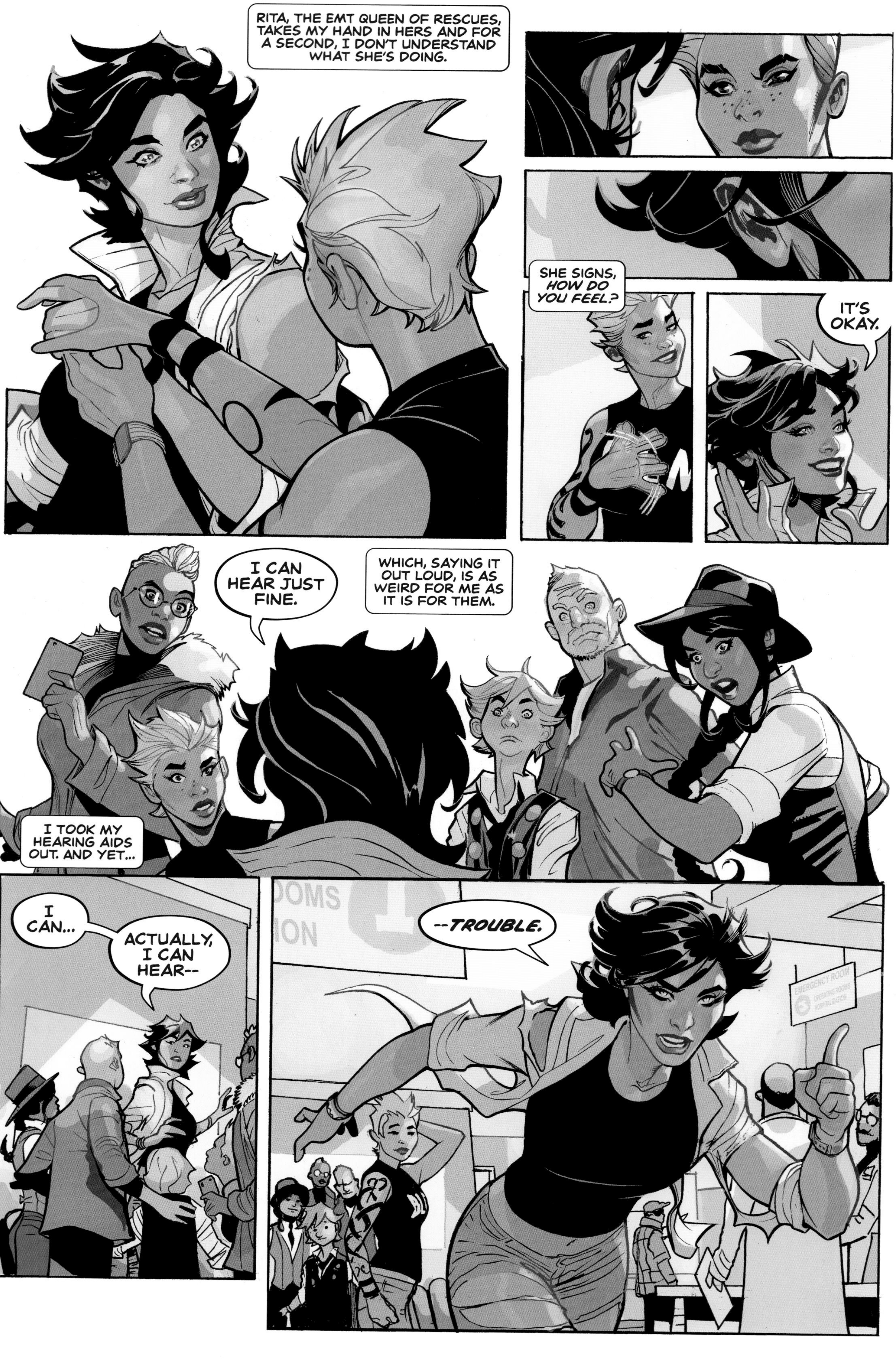
RITA, THE EMT QUEEN OF RESCUES, TAKES MY HAND IN HERS AND FOR A SECOND, I DON'T UNDERSTAND WHAT SHE'S DOING.
SHE SIGNS, *HOW DO YOU FEEL?*
IT'S OKAY.
I CAN HEAR JUST FINE.
WHICH, SAYING IT OUT LOUD, IS AS WEIRD FOR ME AS IT IS FOR THEM.
I TOOK MY HEARING AIDS OUT. AND YET...
I CAN...
ACTUALLY, I CAN HEAR--
--*TROUBLE.*
EMERGENCY ROOM

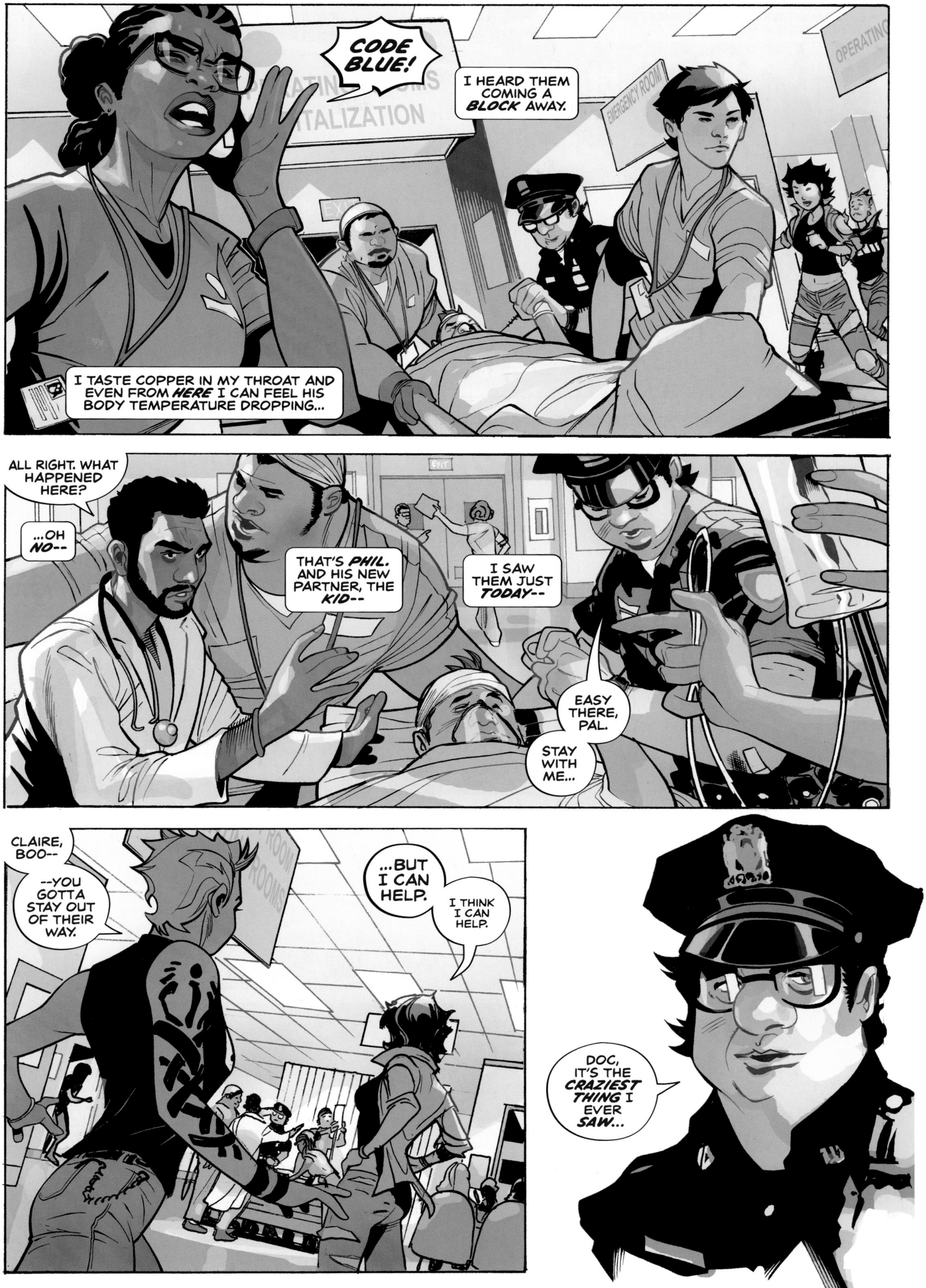

CODE BLUE!
I HEARD THEM COMING A BLOCK AWAY.
I TASTE COPPER IN MY THROAT AND EVEN FROM HERE I CAN FEEL HIS BODY TEMPERATURE DROPPING...
ALL RIGHT. WHAT HAPPENED HERE?
...OH NO--
THAT'S PHIL. AND HIS NEW PARTNER, THE KID--
I SAW THEM JUST TODAY--
EASY THERE, PAL.
STAY WITH ME...
CLAIRE, BOO--
--YOU GOTTA STAY OUT OF THEIR WAY.
...BUT I CAN HELP.
I THINK I CAN HELP.
DOC, IT'S THE CRAZIEST THING I EVER SAW...

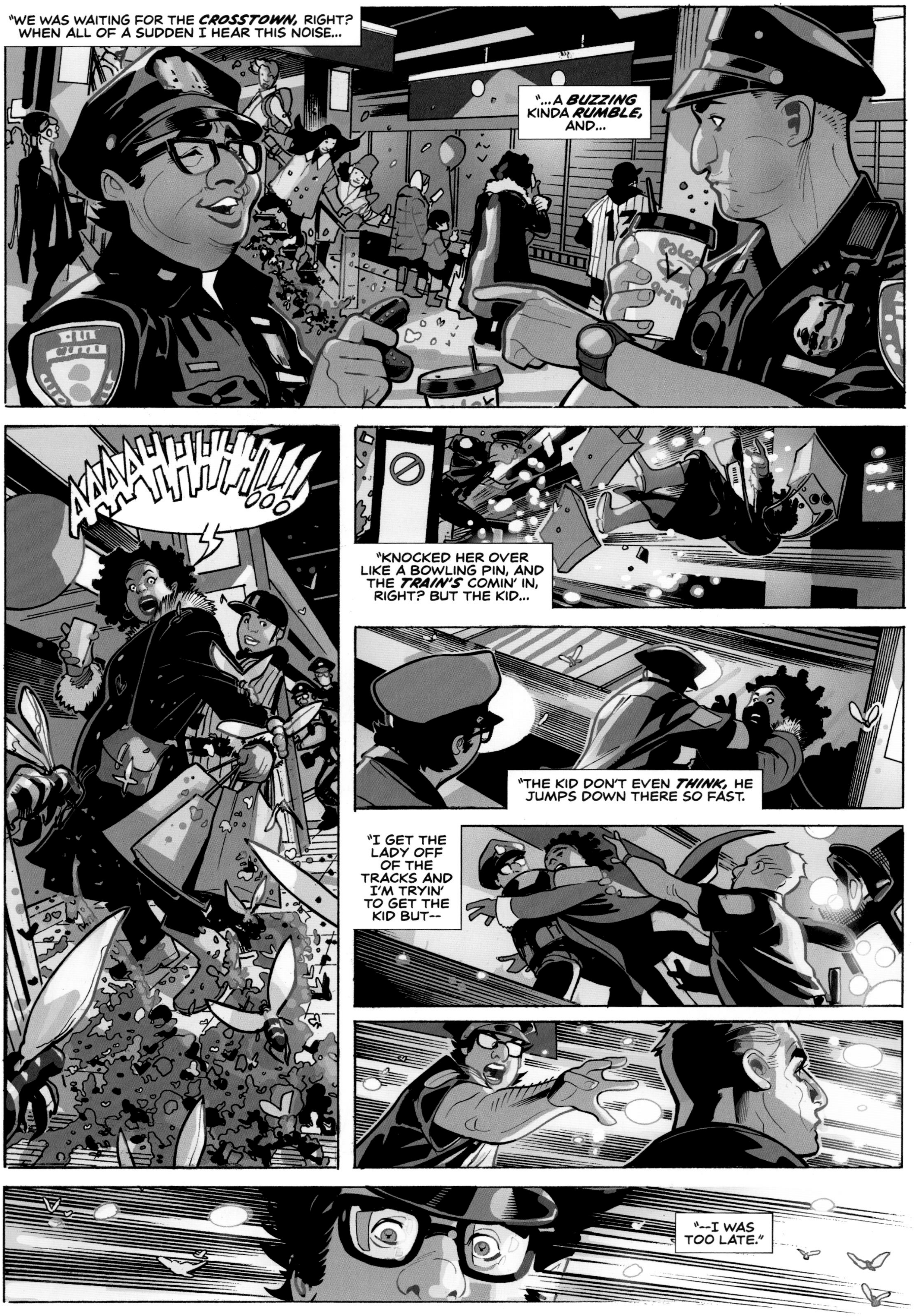

"WE WAS WAITING FOR THE CROSSTOWN, RIGHT? WHEN ALL OF A SUDDEN I HEAR THIS NOISE...
"...A BUZZING KINDA RUMBLE, AND...
AAAAHHHHH!!!!!ooo!
"KNOCKED HER OVER LIKE A BOWLING PIN, AND THE TRAIN'S COMIN' IN, RIGHT? BUT THE KID...
"THE KID DON'T EVEN THINK, HE JUMPS DOWN THERE SO FAST.
"I GET THE LADY OFF OF THE TRACKS AND I'M TRYIN' TO GET THE KID BUT--
"--I WAS TOO LATE."

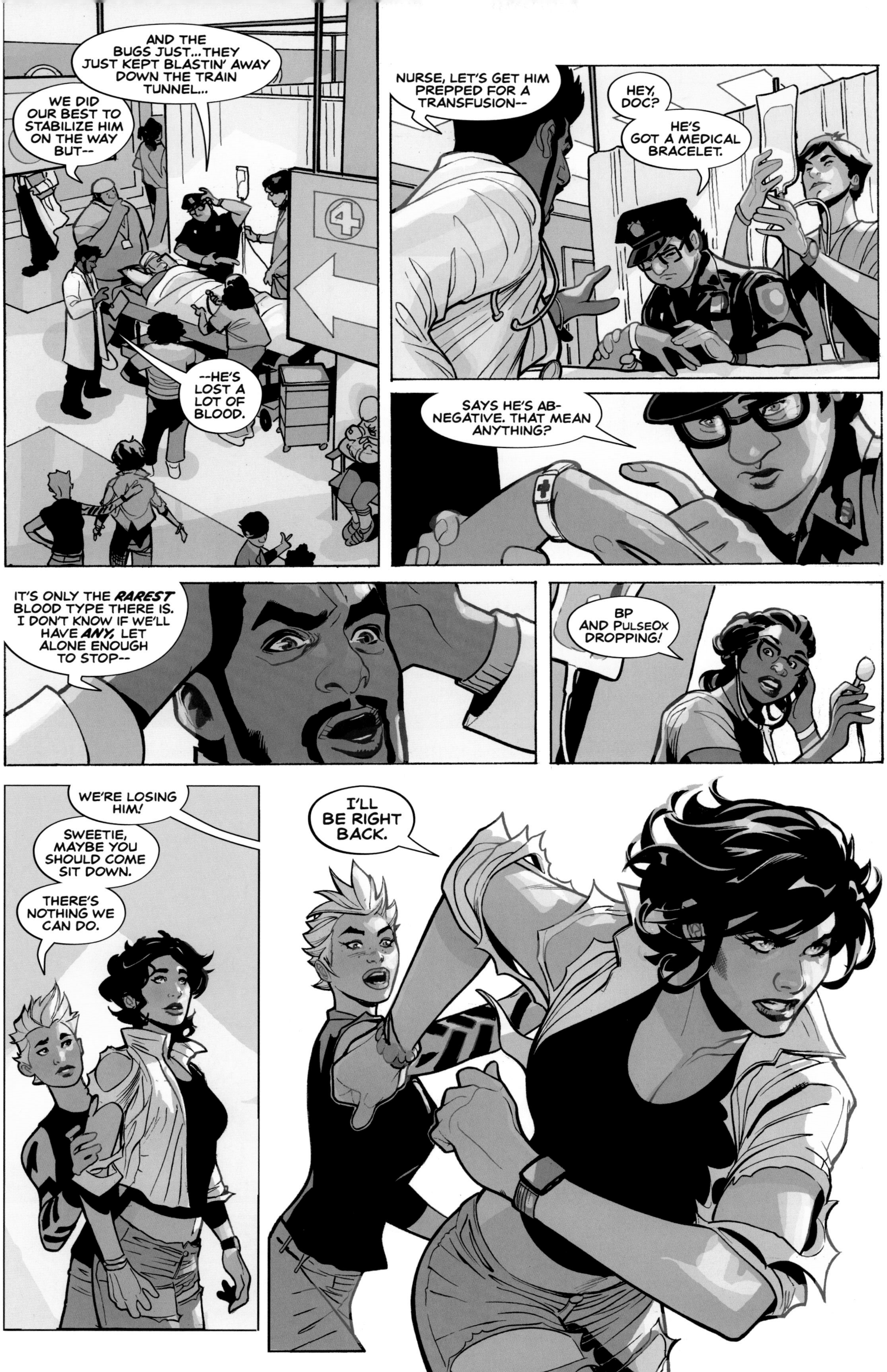
AND THE BUGS JUST...THEY JUST KEPT BLASTIN' AWAY DOWN THE TRAIN TUNNEL...
WE DID OUR BEST TO STABILIZE HIM ON THE WAY BUT--
--HE'S LOST A LOT OF BLOOD.
NURSE, LET'S GET HIM PREPPED FOR A TRANSFUSION--
HEY, DOC?
HE'S GOT A MEDICAL BRACELET.
SAYS HE'S AB-NEGATIVE. THAT MEAN ANYTHING?
IT'S ONLY THE RAREST BLOOD TYPE THERE IS. I DON'T KNOW IF WE'LL HAVE ANY, LET ALONE ENOUGH TO STOP--
BP AND PULSEOX DROPPING!
WE'RE LOSING HIM!
SWEETIE, MAYBE YOU SHOULD COME SIT DOWN.
THERE'S NOTHING WE CAN DO.
I'LL BE RIGHT BACK.

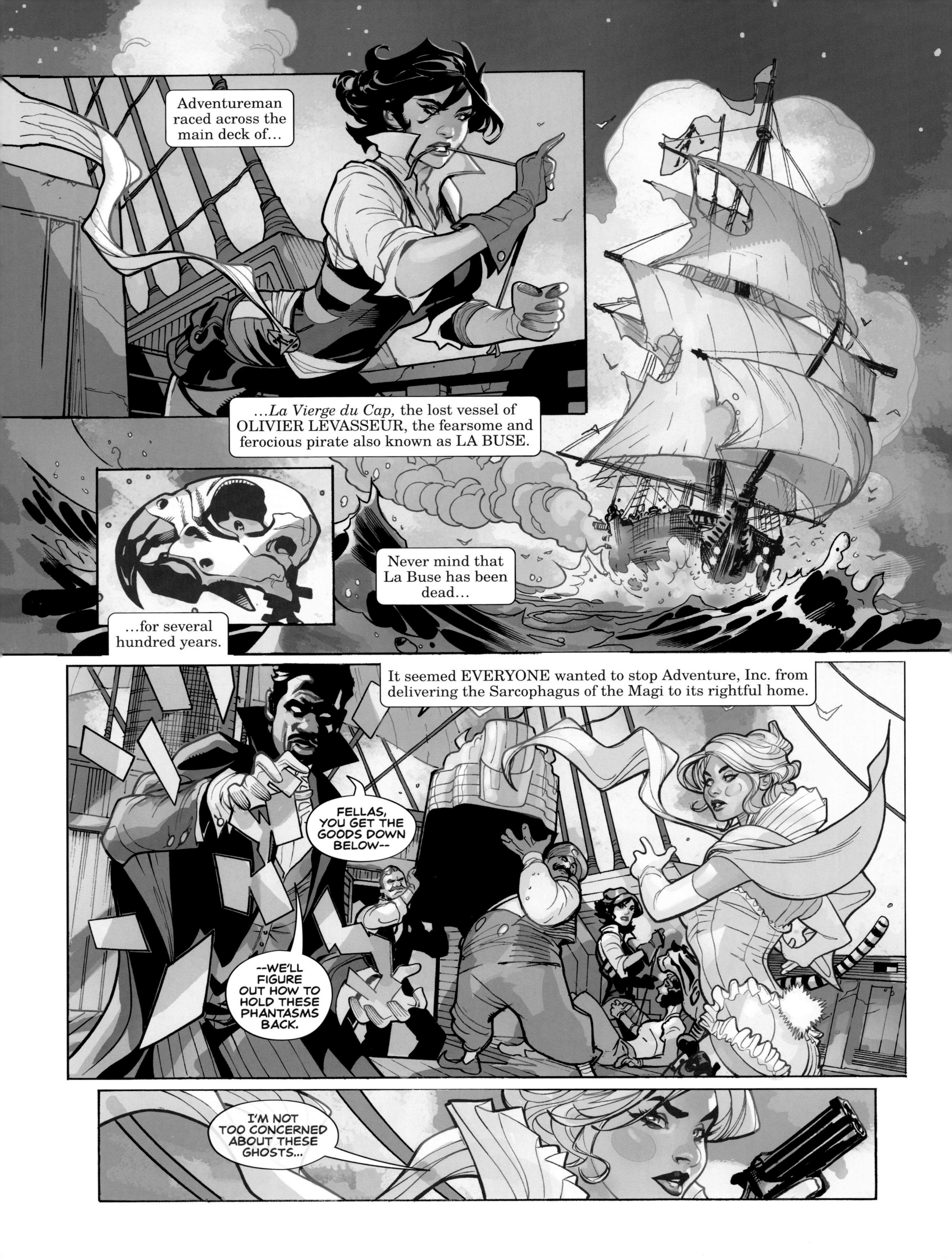

Adventureman raced across the main deck of...
...*La Vierge du Cap,* the lost vessel of OLIVIER LEVASSEUR, the fearsome and ferocious pirate also known as LA BUSE.
Never mind that La Buse has been dead...
...for several hundred years.
It seemed EVERYONE wanted to stop Adventure, Inc. from delivering the Sarcophagus of the Magi to its rightful home.
FELLAS, YOU GET THE GOODS DOWN BELOW--
--WE'LL FIGURE OUT HOW TO HOLD THESE PHANTASMS BACK.
I'M NOT TOO CONCERNED ABOUT THESE GHOSTS...

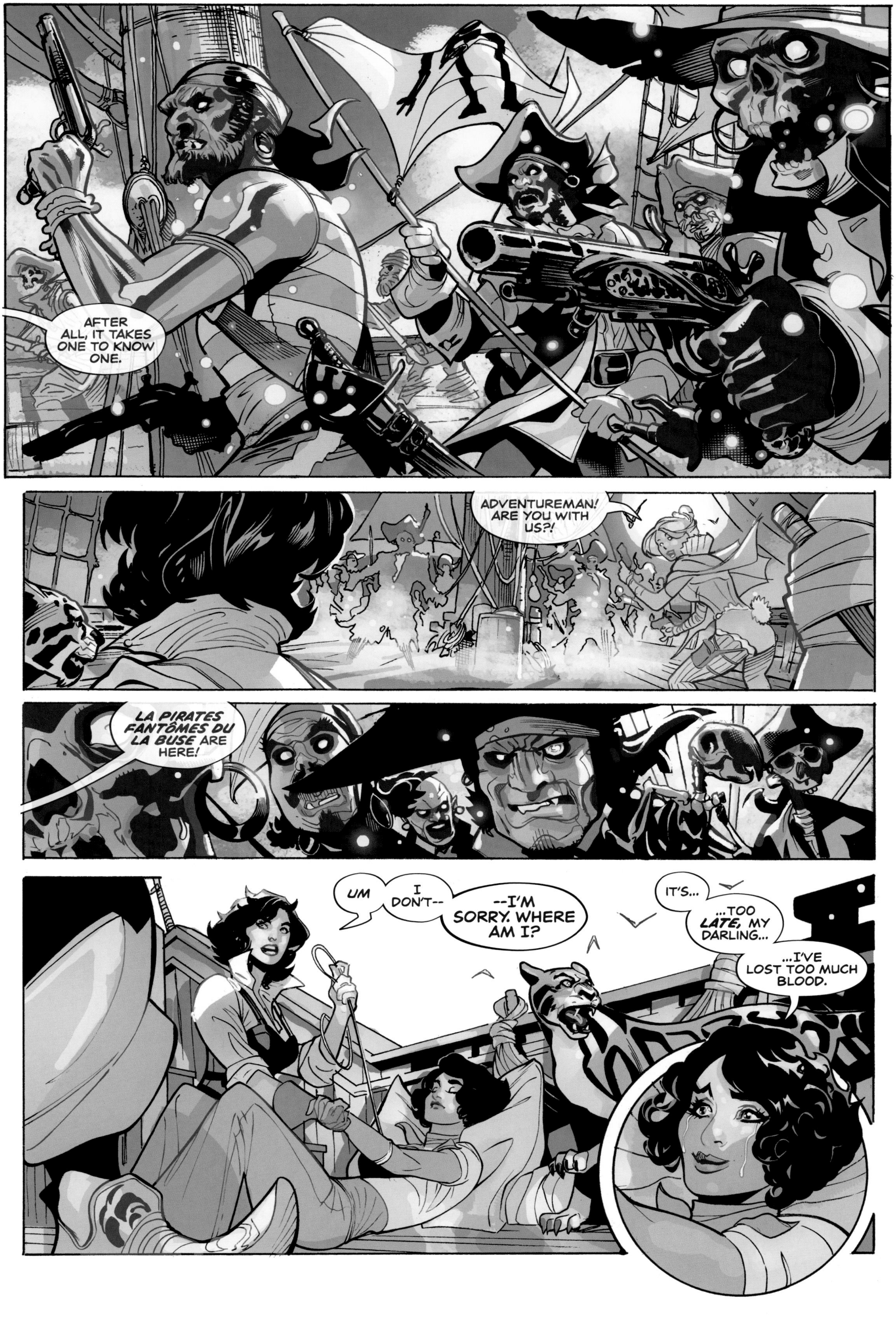
AFTER ALL, IT TAKES ONE TO KNOW ONE.
ADVENTUREMAN! ARE YOU WITH US?!
LA PIRATES FANTÔMES DU LA BUSE ARE HERE!
UM
I DON'T--
--I'M SORRY. WHERE AM I?
IT'S...
...TOO LATE, MY DARLING...
...I'VE LOST TOO MUCH BLOOD.

As Adventureman frantically began to attempt a dangerous field transfusion to save the science-witch of superpharmacology Chagall…

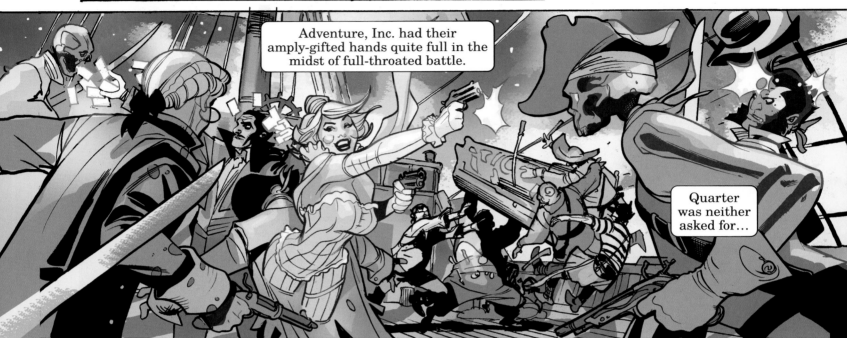

Adventure, Inc. had their amply-gifted hands quite full in the midst of full-throated battle.

Quarter was neither asked for…

…nor given.

HROOOAARRR

AHH! LISTEN, FRIENDS--

ROOOAAAARRRRRR

IT'S THE LOVELIEST SOUND IN THE WORLD…

WWWWWWHOOOO

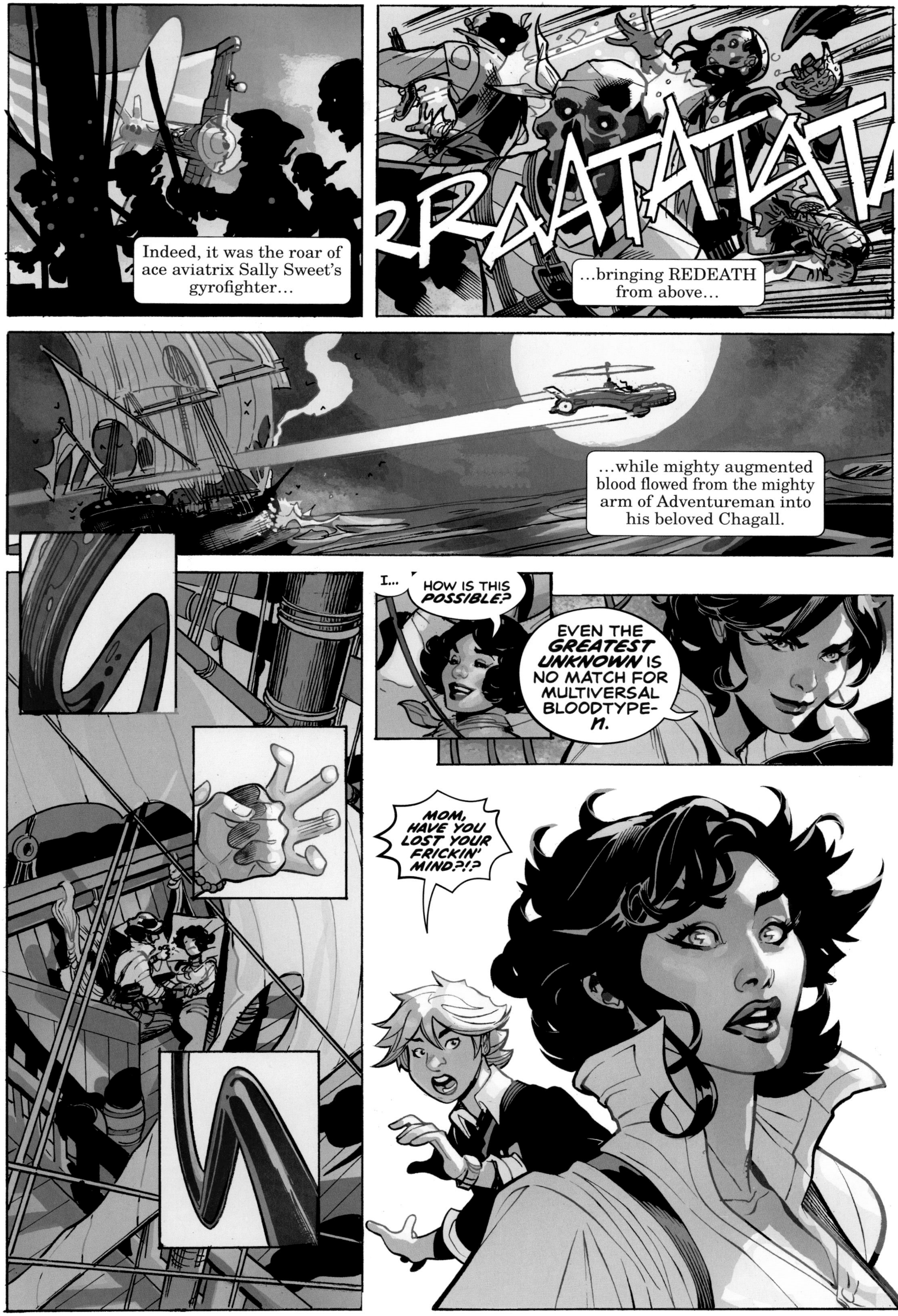
Indeed, it was the roar of ace aviatrix Sally Sweet's gyrofighter…
RRAATATATATA
…bringing REDEATH from above…
…while mighty augmented blood flowed from the mighty arm of Adventureman into his beloved Chagall.
I…
HOW IS THIS POSSIBLE?
EVEN THE GREATEST UNKNOWN IS NO MATCH FOR MULTIVERSAL BLOODTYPE-N.
MOM, HAVE YOU LOST YOUR FRICKIN' MIND?!?

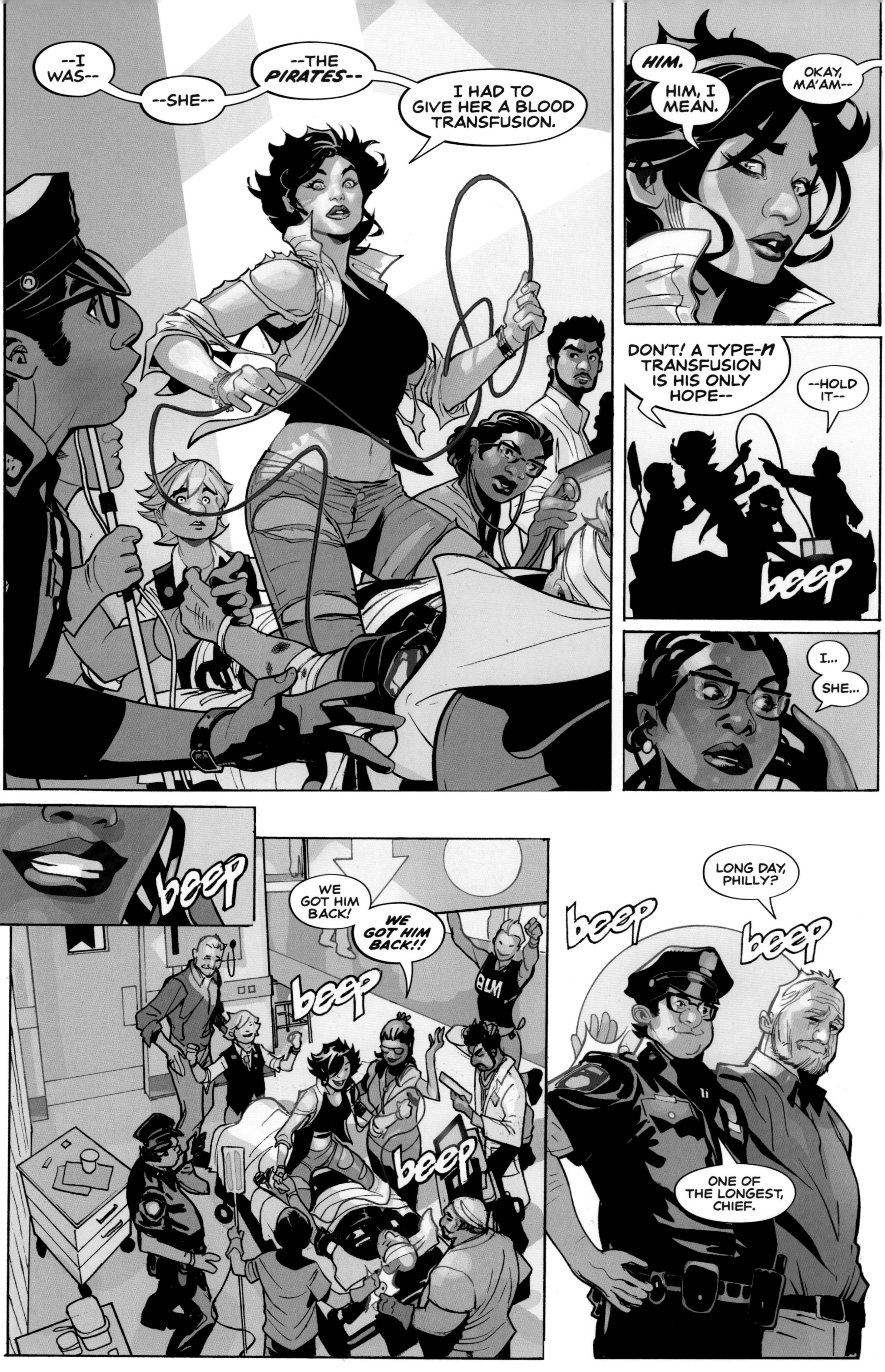
--I WAS--
--SHE--
--THE *PIRATES*--
I HAD TO GIVE HER A BLOOD TRANSFUSION.
HIM.
HIM, I MEAN.
OKAY, MA'AM--
DON'T! A TYPE-M TRANSFUSION IS HIS ONLY HOPE--
--HOLD IT--
beep
I...
SHE...
beep
WE GOT HIM BACK!
WE GOT HIM BACK!!
beep
beep
beep
LONG DAY, PHILLY?
beep
ONE OF THE LONGEST, CHIEF.

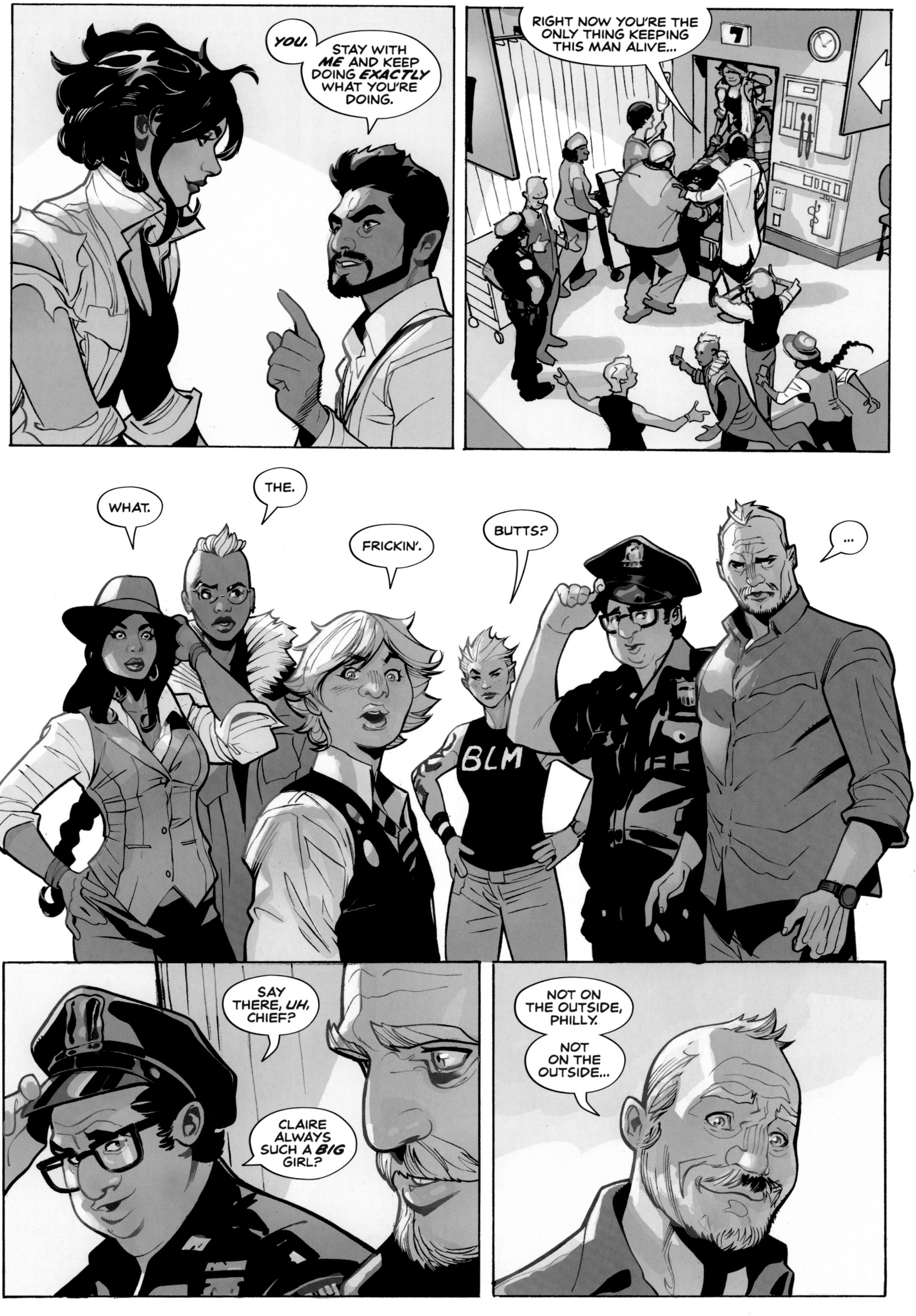
YOU.
STAY WITH ME AND KEEP DOING EXACTLY WHAT YOU'RE DOING.
RIGHT NOW YOU'RE THE ONLY THING KEEPING THIS MAN ALIVE...
WHAT.
THE.
FRICKIN'.
BUTTS?
...
SAY THERE, UH, CHIEF?
CLAIRE ALWAYS SUCH A BIG GIRL?
NOT ON THE OUTSIDE, PHILLY.
NOT ON THE OUTSIDE...

YOU GUYS GETTIN' WHAT YOU NEED OUT THERE?

RRRRRRRRRR RRRRRRRRRR RRRRRRRRRR

UH...PLEASE REMAIN STILL AND TRY NOT TO TALK, MS. CONNELL.

OR...GROW... ANYMORE.

WHAT?

THE MIC, CUT THE MIC--

RRRRRRRRRRRRRRRRRRRRRRRRRRRRRRRRRRRRRRRRRRRRRRRRRRR

YOU EVER SEEN ANYTHING LIKE THIS?

MACHINE'S GOTTA BE BUSTED, RIGHT? I MEAN...

RRRRRRRRRRRRR RRRRRRRRRRRR

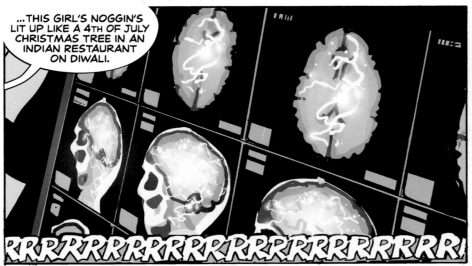
...THIS GIRL'S NOGGIN'S LIT UP LIKE A 4TH OF JULY CHRISTMAS TREE IN AN INDIAN RESTAURANT ON DIWALI.

GUYS? I CAN STILL HEAR YOU.

RRRRRRRRRRRR RRRRRRRRRR

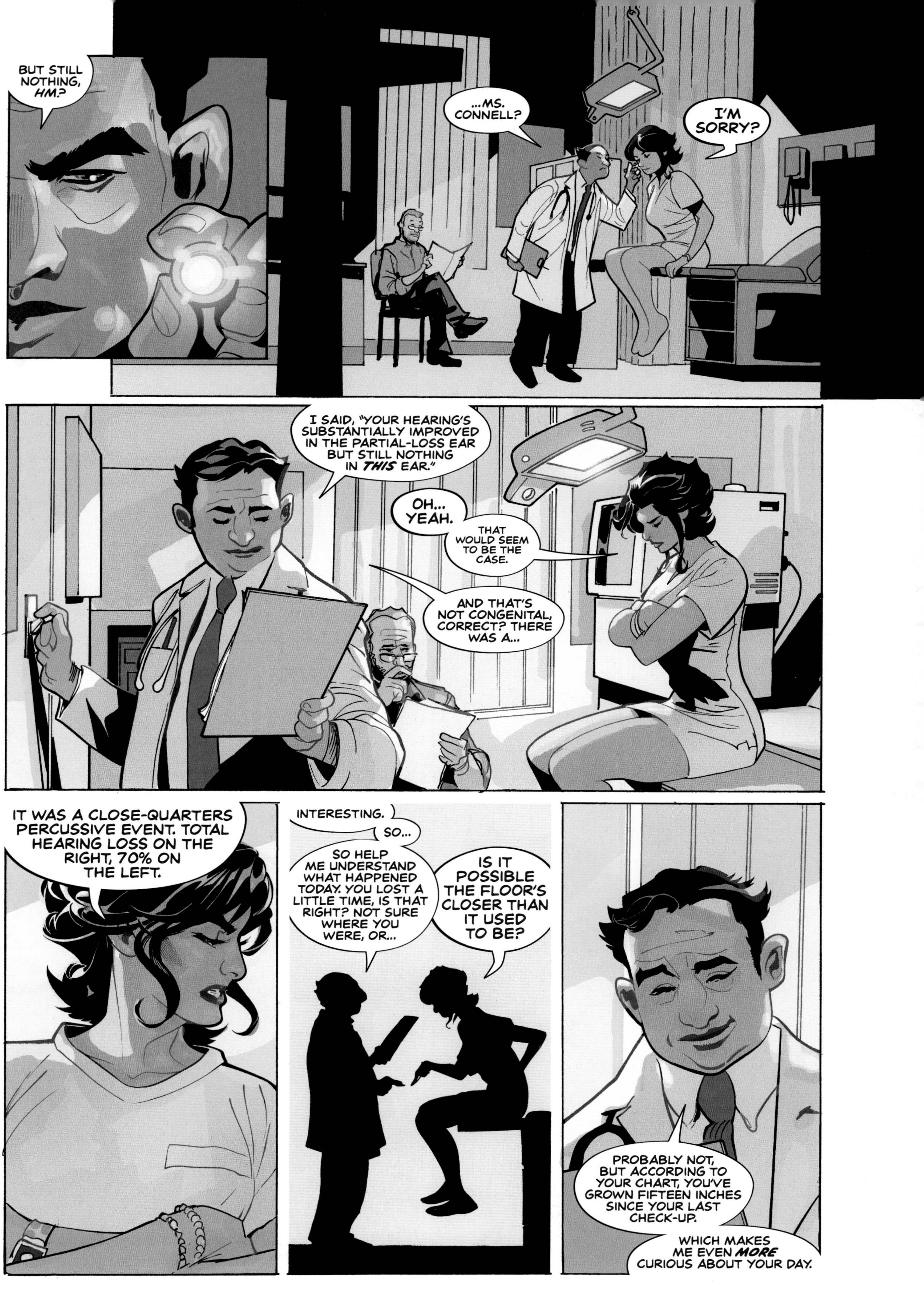
BUT STILL NOTHING, *HM?*
...MS. CONNELL?
I'M SORRY?
I SAID, "YOUR HEARING'S SUBSTANTIALLY IMPROVED IN THE PARTIAL-LOSS EAR BUT STILL NOTHING IN *THIS* EAR."
OH... YEAH.
THAT WOULD SEEM TO BE THE CASE.
AND THAT'S NOT CONGENITAL, CORRECT? THERE WAS A...
IT WAS A CLOSE-QUARTERS PERCUSSIVE EVENT. TOTAL HEARING LOSS ON THE RIGHT, 70% ON THE LEFT.
INTERESTING.
SO...
SO HELP ME UNDERSTAND WHAT HAPPENED TODAY. YOU LOST A LITTLE TIME, IS THAT RIGHT? NOT SURE WHERE YOU WERE, OR...
IS IT POSSIBLE THE FLOOR'S CLOSER THAN IT USED TO BE?
PROBABLY NOT, BUT ACCORDING TO YOUR CHART, YOU'VE GROWN FIFTEEN INCHES SINCE YOUR LAST CHECK-UP.
WHICH MAKES ME EVEN *MORE* CURIOUS ABOUT YOUR DAY.

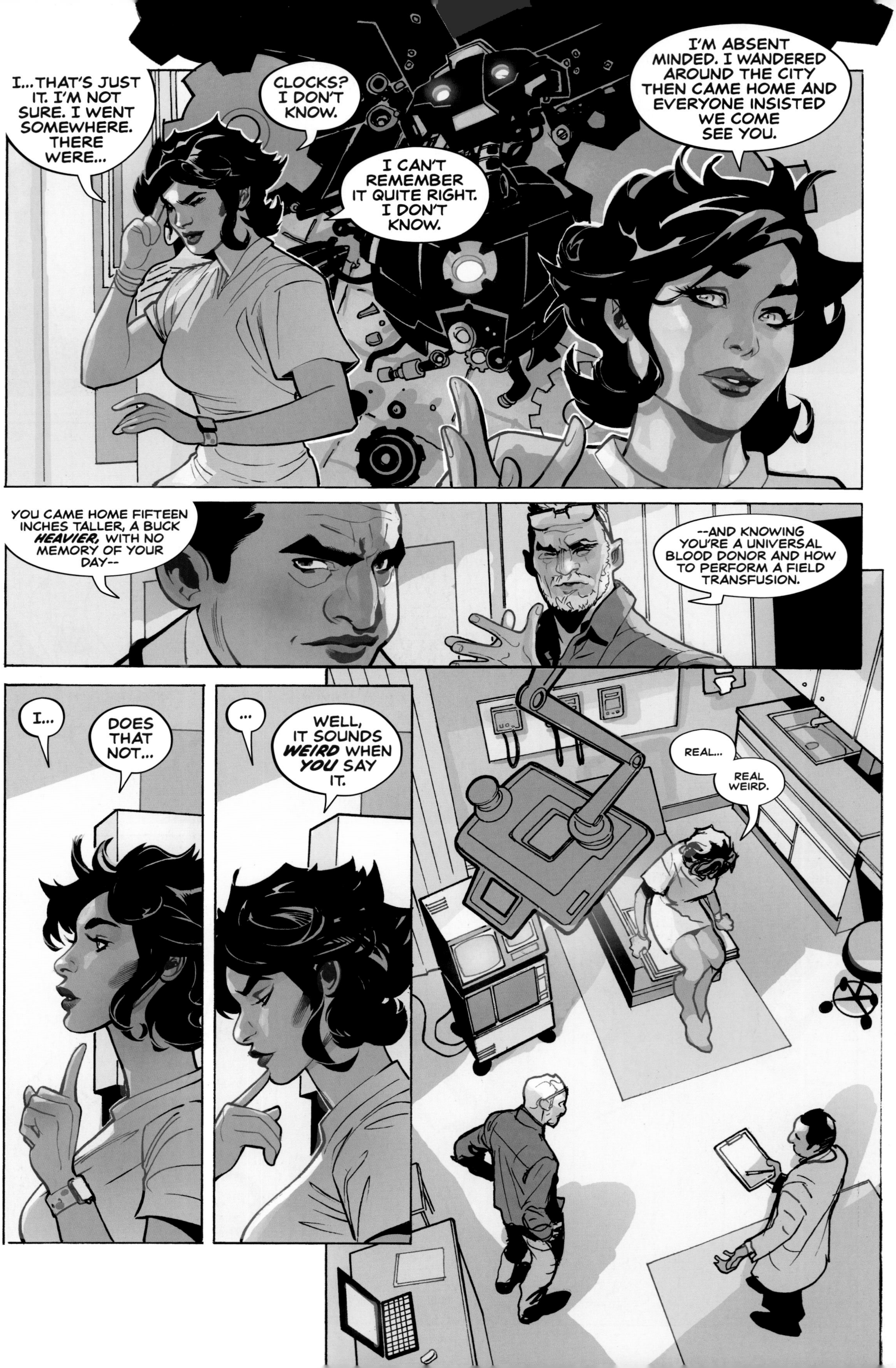

I...THAT'S JUST IT. I'M NOT SURE. I WENT SOMEWHERE. THERE WERE...
CLOCKS? I DON'T KNOW.
I CAN'T REMEMBER IT QUITE RIGHT. I DON'T KNOW.
I'M ABSENT MINDED. I WANDERED AROUND THE CITY THEN CAME HOME AND EVERYONE INSISTED WE COME SEE YOU.
YOU CAME HOME FIFTEEN INCHES TALLER, A BUCK HEAVIER, WITH NO MEMORY OF YOUR DAY--
--AND KNOWING YOU'RE A UNIVERSAL BLOOD DONOR AND HOW TO PERFORM A FIELD TRANSFUSION.
I...
DOES THAT NOT...
...
WELL, IT SOUNDS WEIRD WHEN YOU SAY IT.
REAL...
REAL WEIRD.

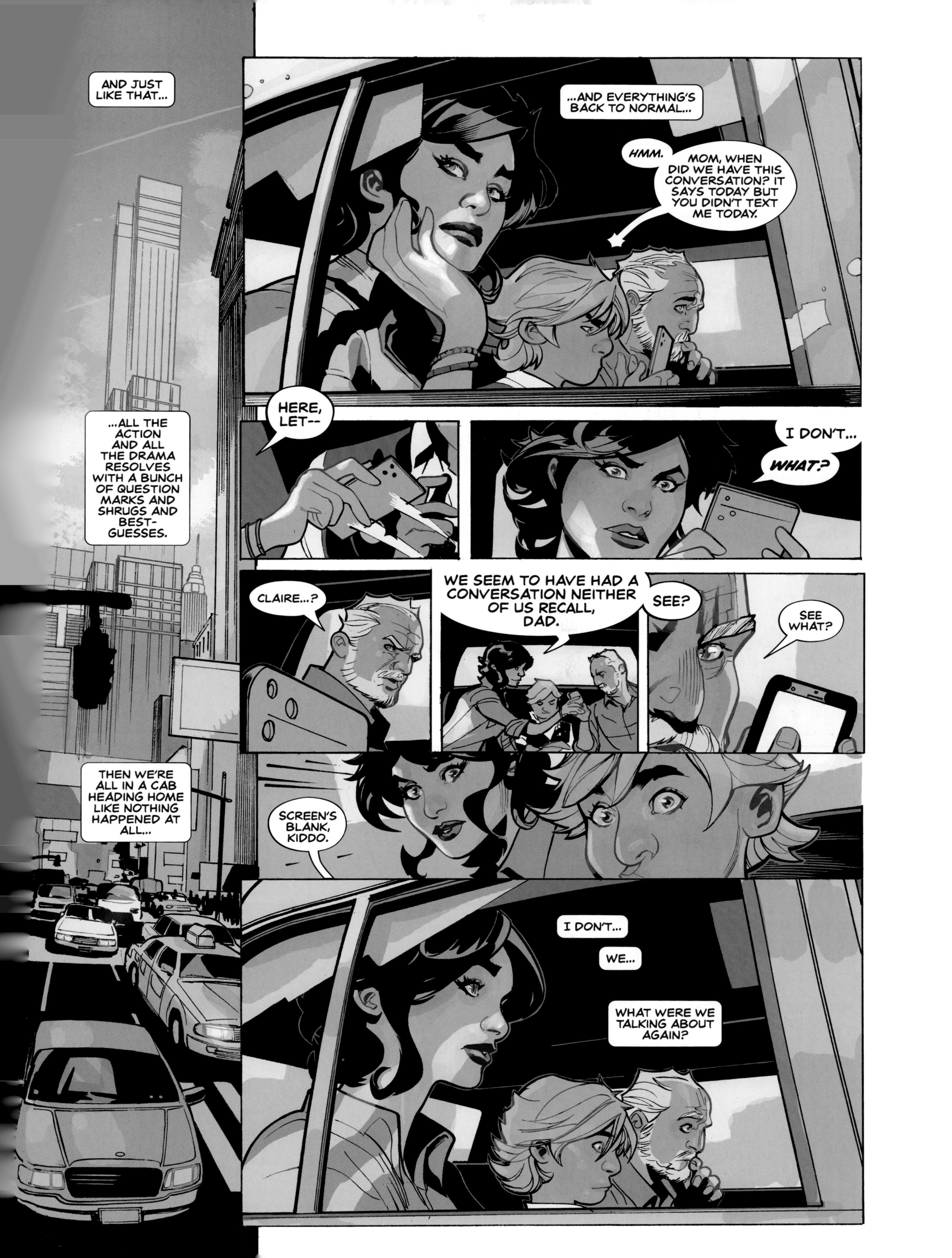
AND JUST LIKE THAT...
...AND EVERYTHING'S BACK TO NORMAL...
HMM.
MOM, WHEN DID WE HAVE THIS CONVERSATION? IT SAYS TODAY BUT YOU DIDN'T TEXT ME TODAY.
...ALL THE ACTION AND ALL THE DRAMA RESOLVES WITH A BUNCH OF QUESTION MARKS AND SHRUGS AND BEST-GUESSES.
HERE, LET--
I DON'T...
WHAT?
CLAIRE...?
WE SEEM TO HAVE HAD A CONVERSATION NEITHER OF US RECALL, DAD.
SEE?
SEE WHAT?
THEN WE'RE ALL IN A CAB HEADING HOME LIKE NOTHING HAPPENED AT ALL...
SCREEN'S BLANK, KIDDO.
I DON'T...
WE...
WHAT WERE WE TALKING ABOUT AGAIN?

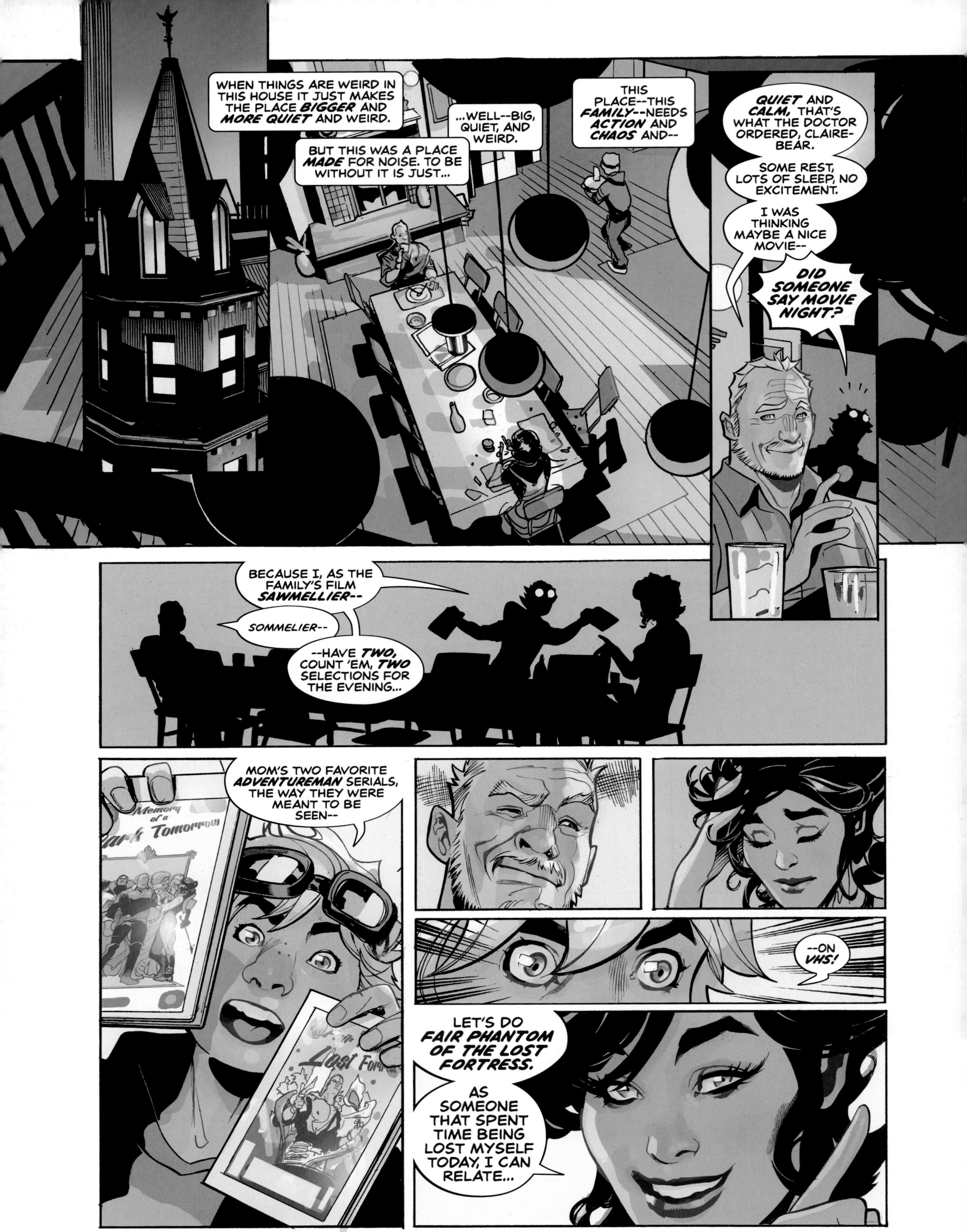

WHEN THINGS ARE WEIRD IN THIS HOUSE IT JUST MAKES THE PLACE BIGGER AND MORE QUIET AND WEIRD.
BUT THIS WAS A PLACE MADE FOR NOISE. TO BE WITHOUT IT IS JUST...
...WELL--BIG, QUIET, AND WEIRD.
THIS PLACE--THIS FAMILY--NEEDS ACTION AND CHAOS AND--
QUIET AND CALM, THAT'S WHAT THE DOCTOR ORDERED, CLAIRE-BEAR.
SOME REST, LOTS OF SLEEP, NO EXCITEMENT.
I WAS THINKING MAYBE A NICE MOVIE--
DID SOMEONE SAY MOVIE NIGHT?
BECAUSE I, AS THE FAMILY'S FILM SAWMELLIER--
SOMMELIER--
--HAVE TWO, COUNT 'EM, TWO SELECTIONS FOR THE EVENING...
MOM'S TWO FAVORITE ADVENTUREMAN SERIALS, THE WAY THEY WERE MEANT TO BE SEEN--
Memory of a Dark Tomorrow
Lost
--ON VHS!
LET'S DO FAIR PHANTOM OF THE LOST FORTRESS.
AS SOMEONE THAT SPENT TIME BEING LOST MYSELF TODAY, I CAN RELATE...

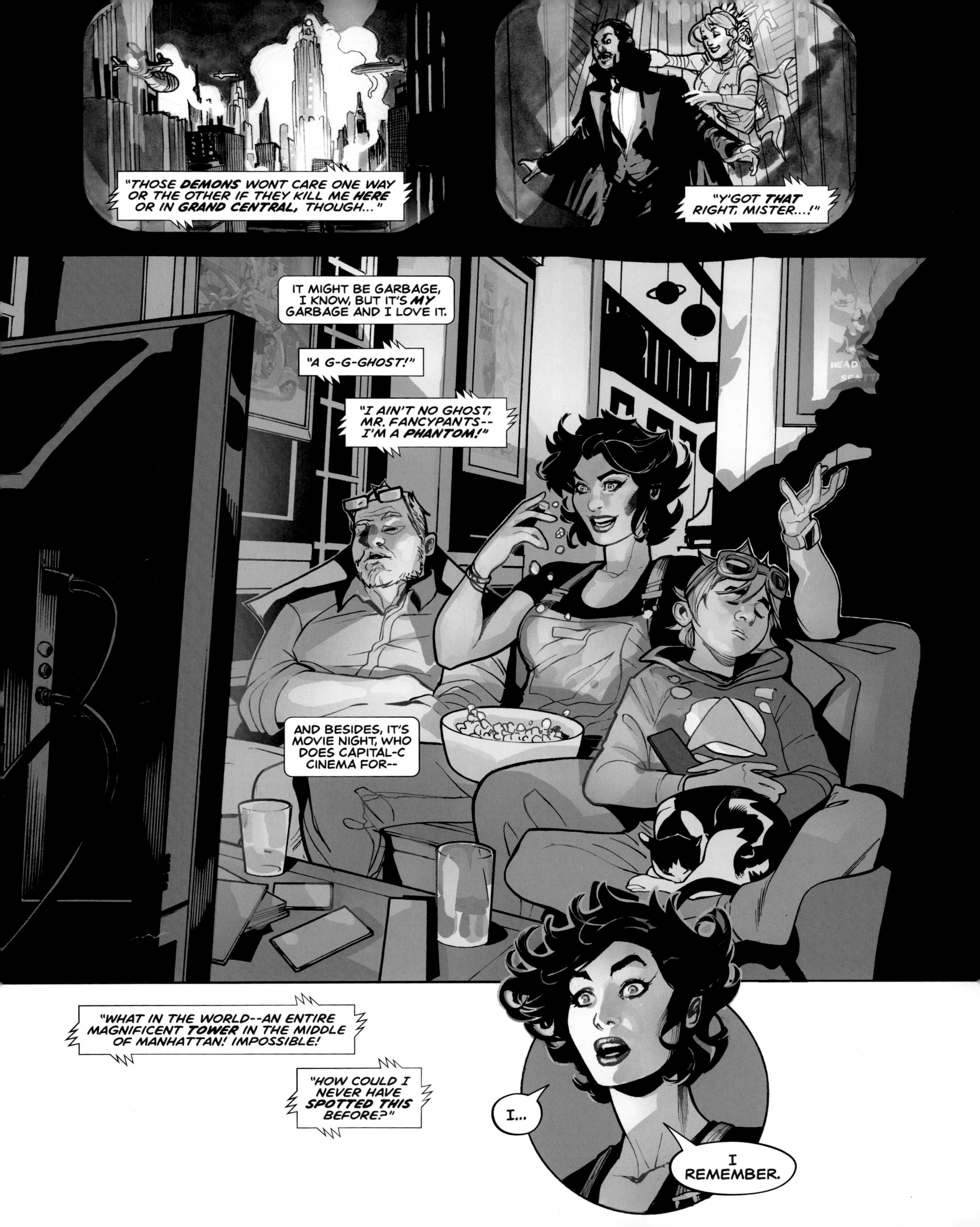
"THOSE DEMONS WONT CARE ONE WAY OR THE OTHER IF THEY KILL ME HERE OR IN GRAND CENTRAL, THOUGH..."
"Y'GOT THAT RIGHT, MISTER...!"
IT MIGHT BE GARBAGE, I KNOW, BUT IT'S MY GARBAGE AND I LOVE IT.
"A G-G-GHOST!"
"I AIN'T NO GHOST, MR. FANCYPANTS-- I'M A PHANTOM!"
AND BESIDES, IT'S MOVIE NIGHT, WHO DOES CAPITAL-C CINEMA FOR--
"WHAT IN THE WORLD--AN ENTIRE MAGNIFICENT TOWER IN THE MIDDLE OF MANHATTAN! IMPOSSIBLE!
"HOW COULD I NEVER HAVE SPOTTED THIS BEFORE?"
I...
I REMEMBER.

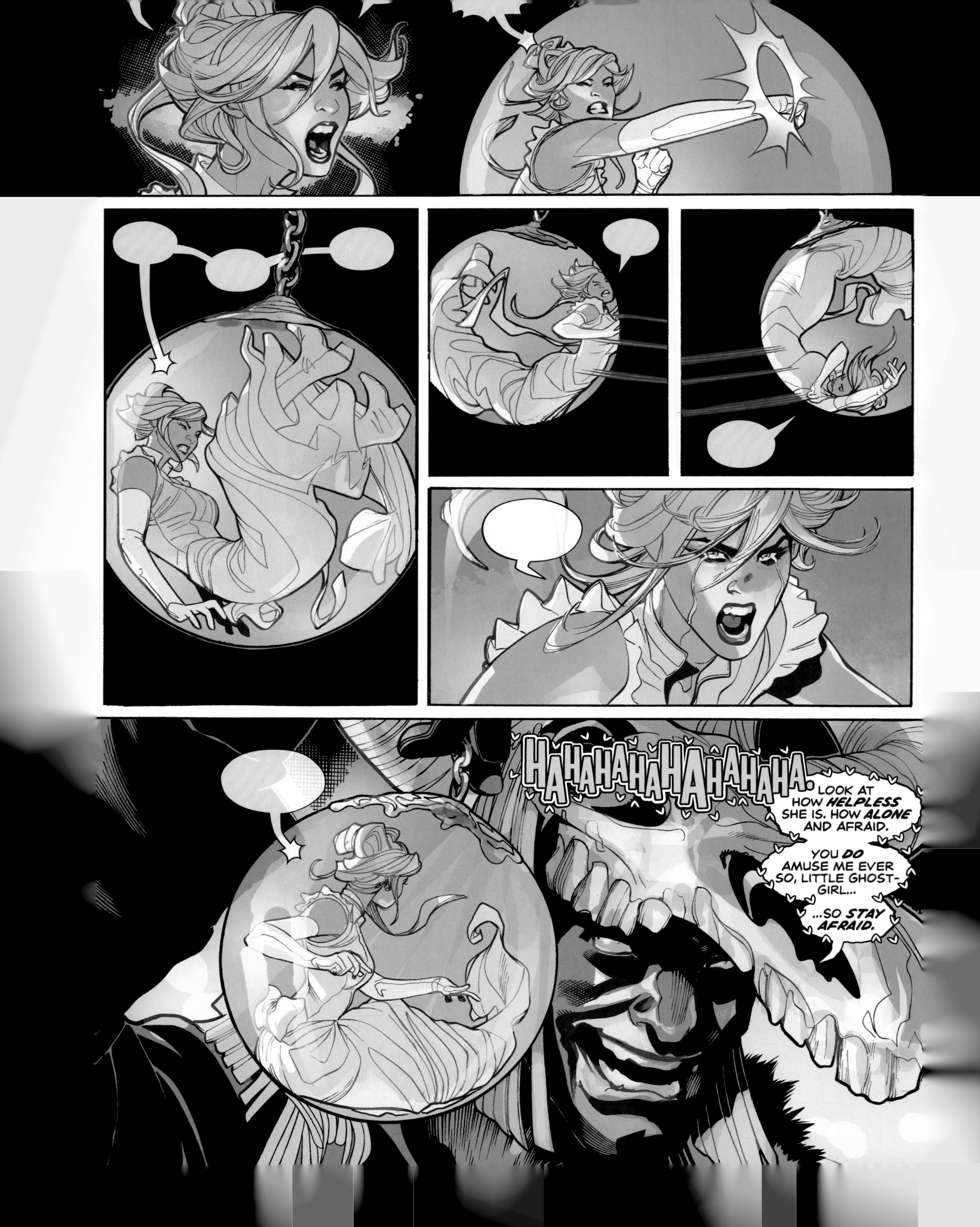
HAHAHAHAHAHAHAHA.
LOOK AT HOW HELPLESS SHE IS. HOW ALONE AND AFRAID.
YOU DO AMUSE ME EVER SO, LITTLE GHOST-GIRL...
...SO STAY AFRAID.

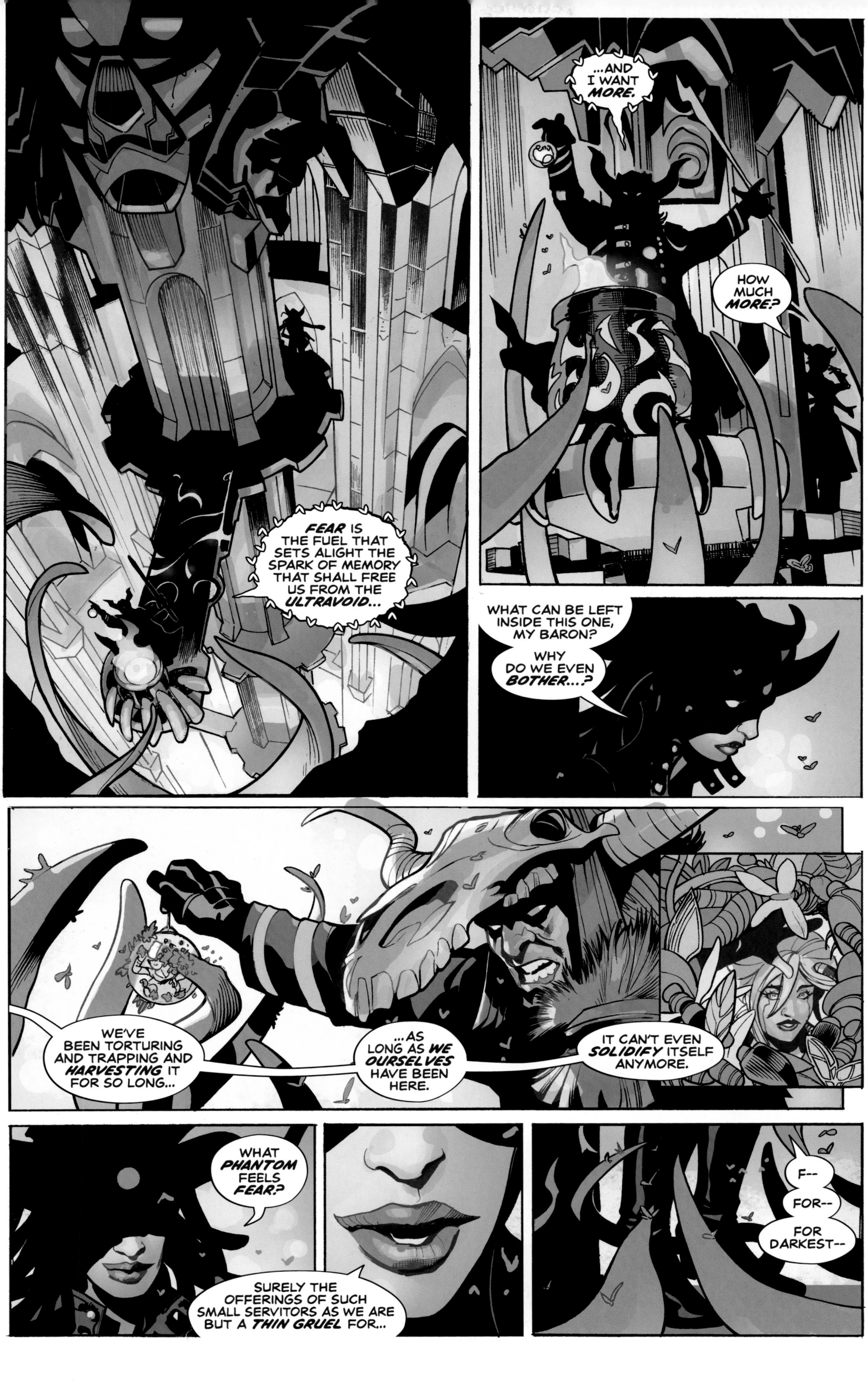
FEAR IS THE FUEL THAT SETS ALIGHT THE SPARK OF MEMORY THAT SHALL FREE US FROM THE ULTRAVOID...
...AND I WANT MORE.
HOW MUCH MORE?
WHAT CAN BE LEFT INSIDE THIS ONE, MY BARON?
WHY DO WE EVEN BOTHER...?
WE'VE BEEN TORTURING AND TRAPPING AND HARVESTING IT FOR SO LONG...
...AS LONG AS WE OURSELVES HAVE BEEN HERE.
IT CAN'T EVEN SOLIDIFY ITSELF ANYMORE.
WHAT PHANTOM FEELS FEAR?
SURELY THE OFFERINGS OF SUCH SMALL SERVITORS AS WE ARE BUT A THIN GRUEL FOR...
F--
FOR--
FOR DARKEST--

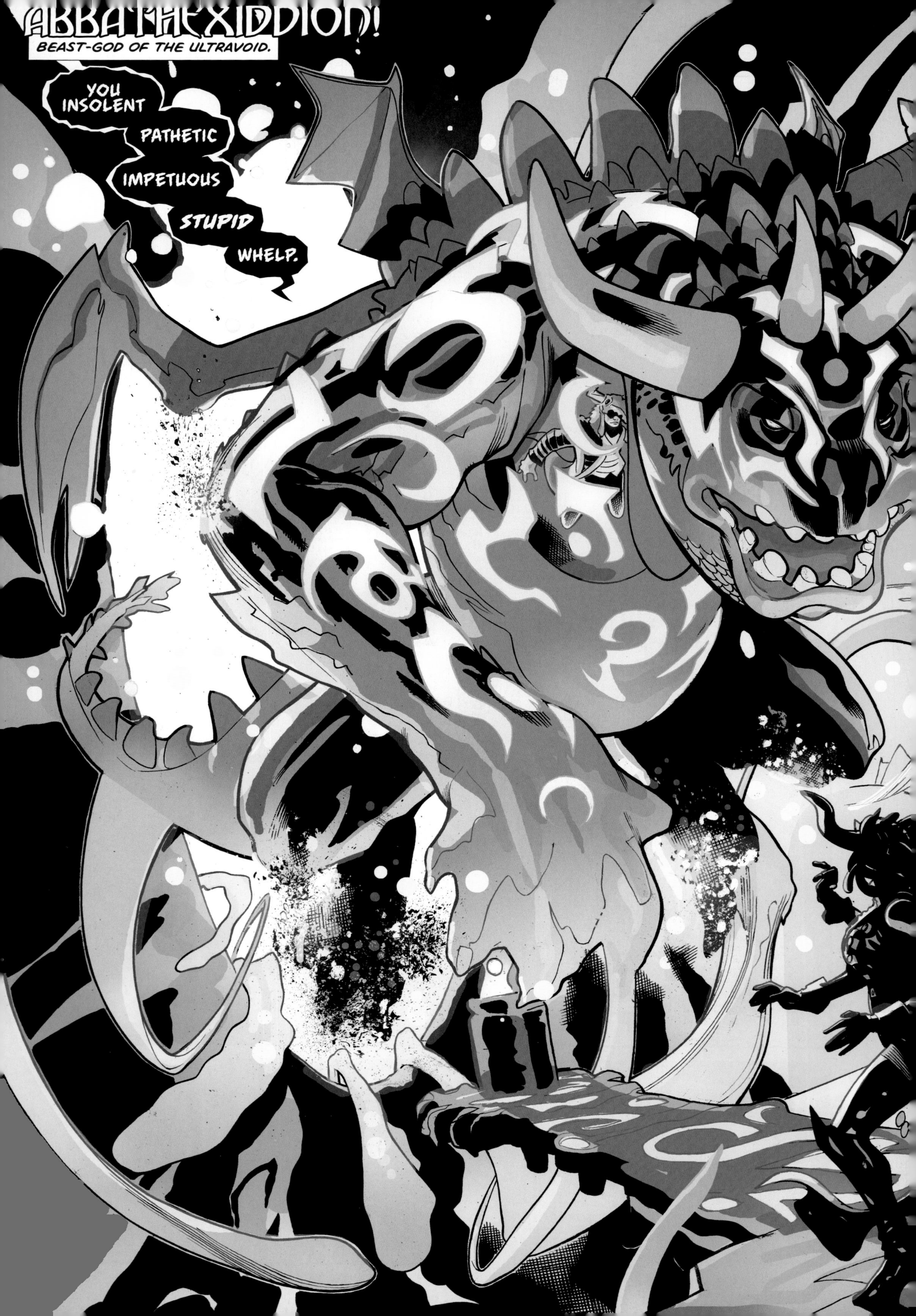
ABBA THE XIDDION!
BEAST-GOD OF THE ULTRAVOID.
YOU INSOLENT PATHETIC IMPETUOUS STUPID WHELP.

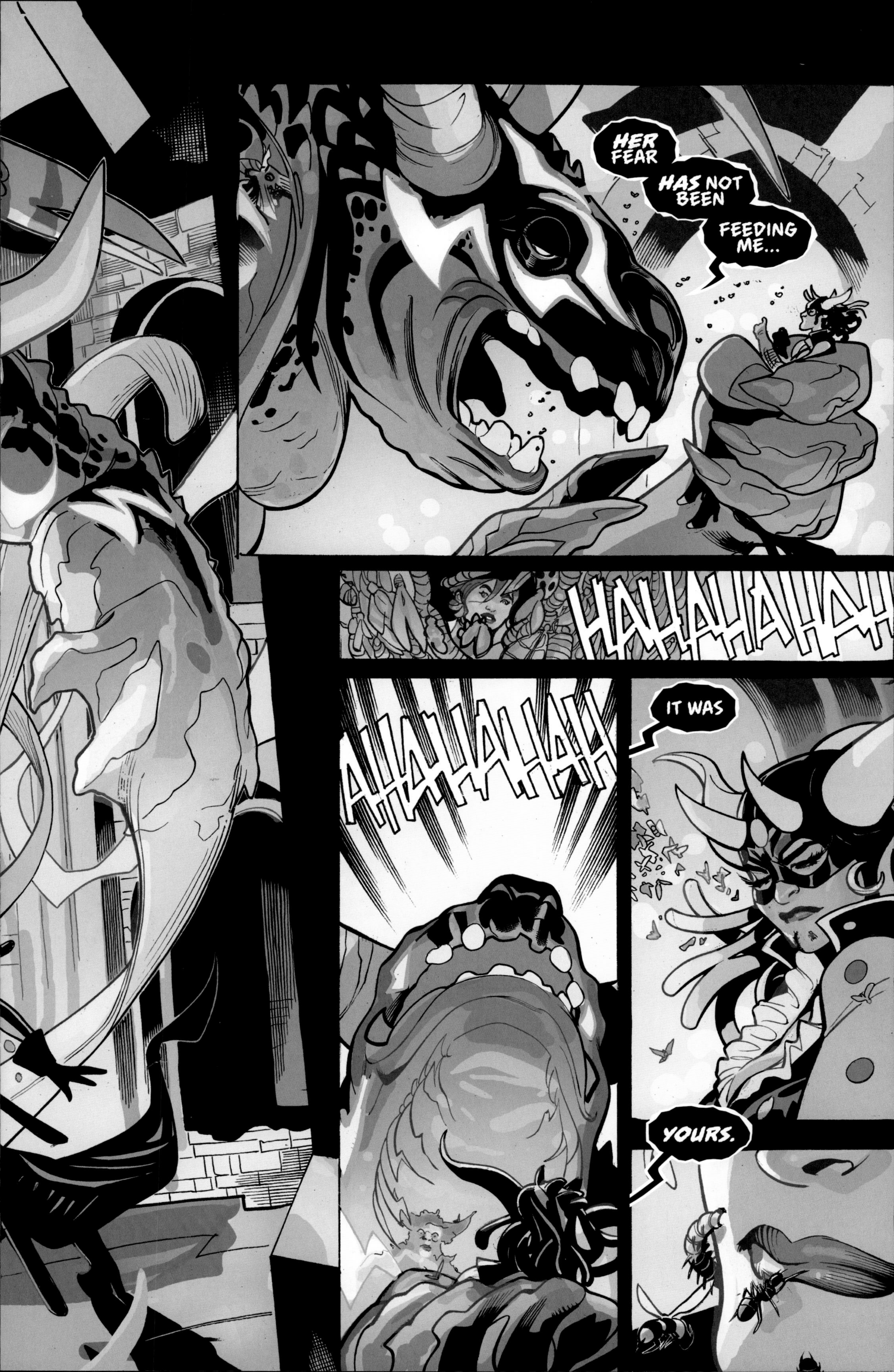
HER FEAR
HAS NOT BEEN
FEEDING ME...
HAHAHAHAH
AHAHAHAH
IT WAS
YOURS.

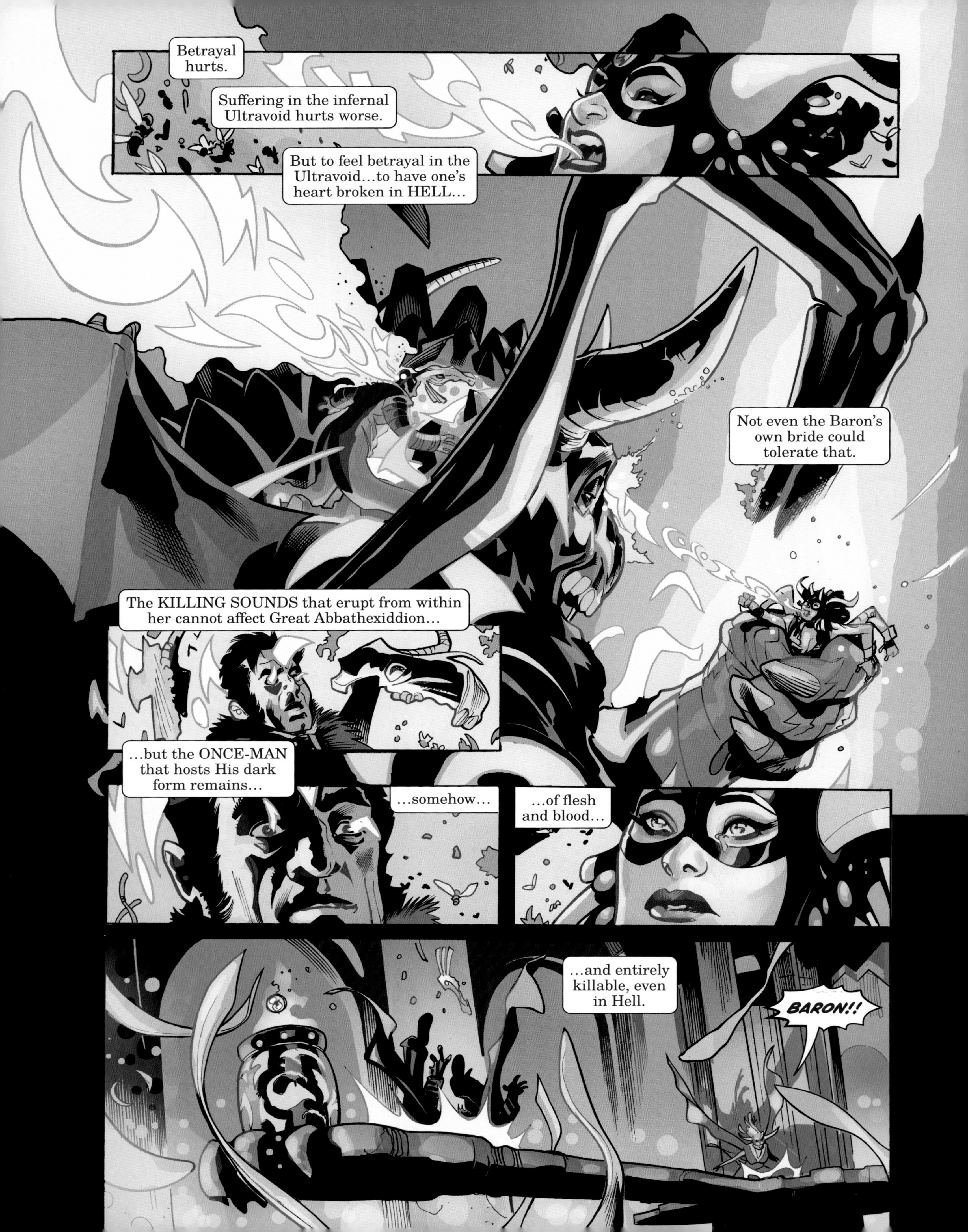
Betrayal hurts.
Suffering in the infernal Ultravoid hurts worse.
But to feel betrayal in the Ultravoid…to have one's heart broken in HELL…
Not even the Baron's own bride could tolerate that.
The KILLING SOUNDS that erupt from within her cannot affect Great Abbathexiddion…
…but the ONCE-MAN that hosts His dark form remains…
…somehow…
…of flesh and blood…
…and entirely killable, even in Hell.
BARON!!

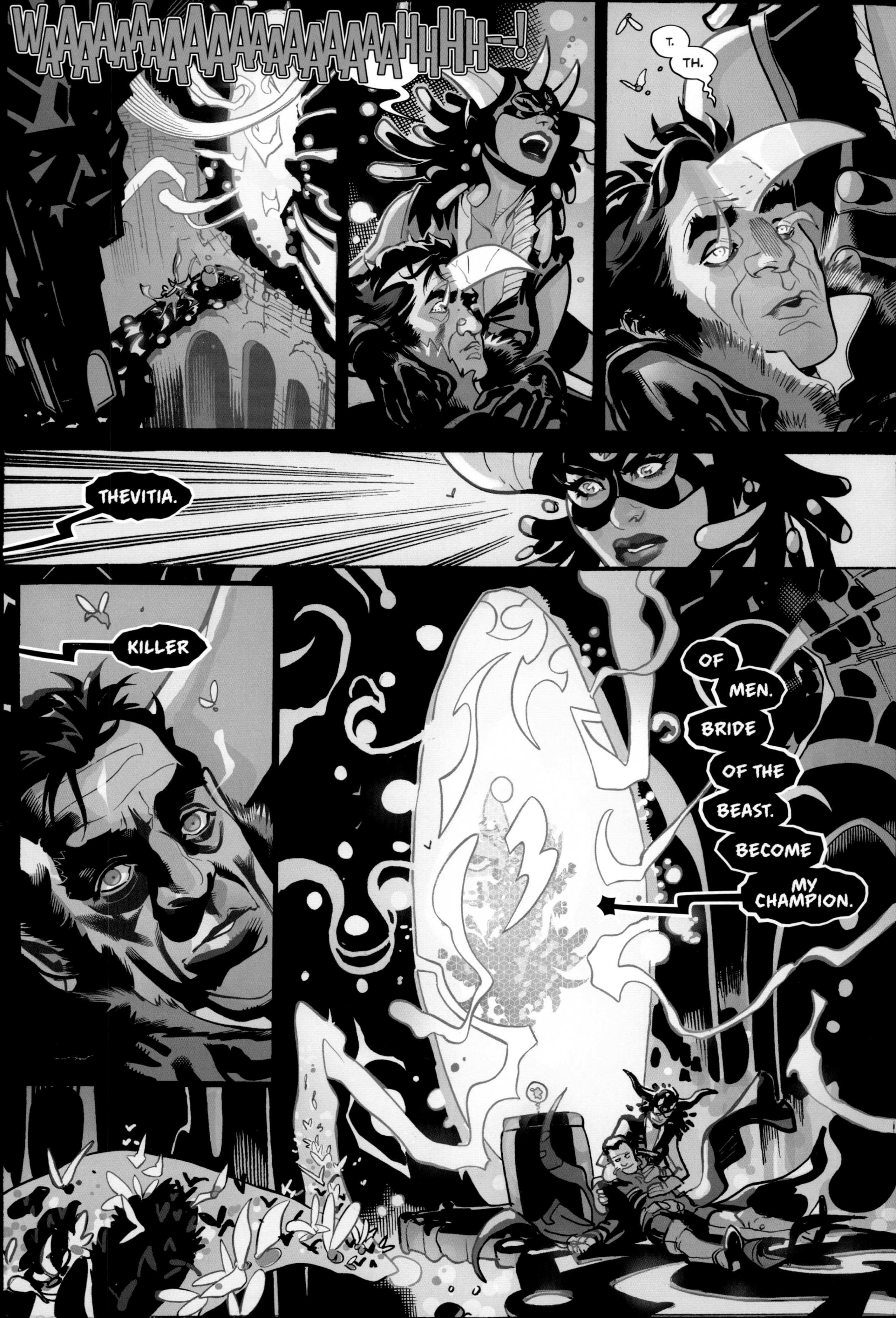
WAAAAAAAAAAAAAAAAAAAAAAAHHHHH--!
T.
TH.
THEVITIA.
KILLER
OF
MEN.
BRIDE
OF THE
BEAST.
BECOME
MY
CHAMPION.

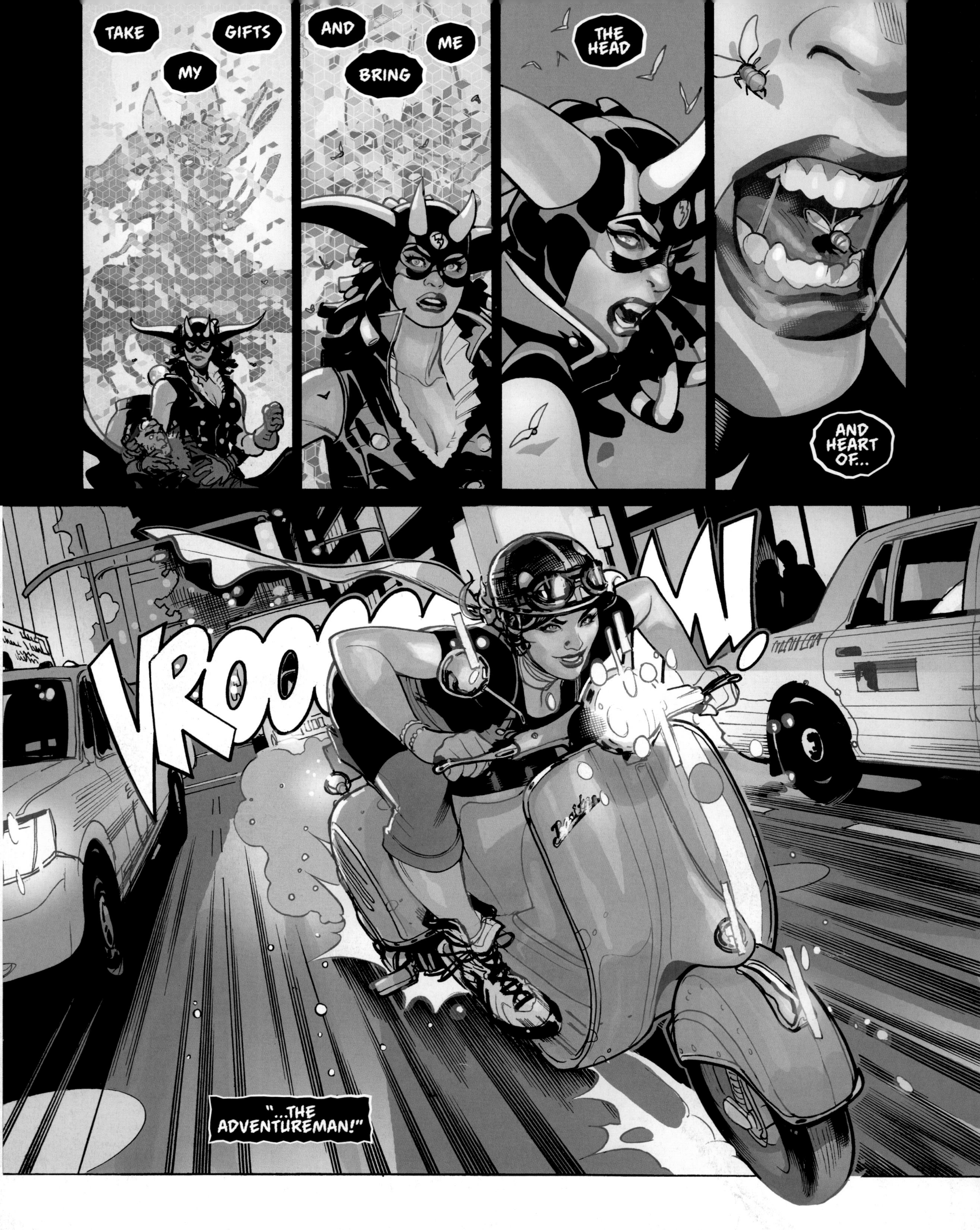
TAKE
MY
GIFTS
AND
BRING
ME
THE HEAD
AND HEART OF...
VROOOM!
"...THE ADVENTUREMAN!"

ADVENTUREMAN

"The END and EVERYTHING AFTER"

VOLUME 1

CHAPTER

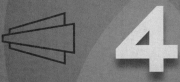 **4**

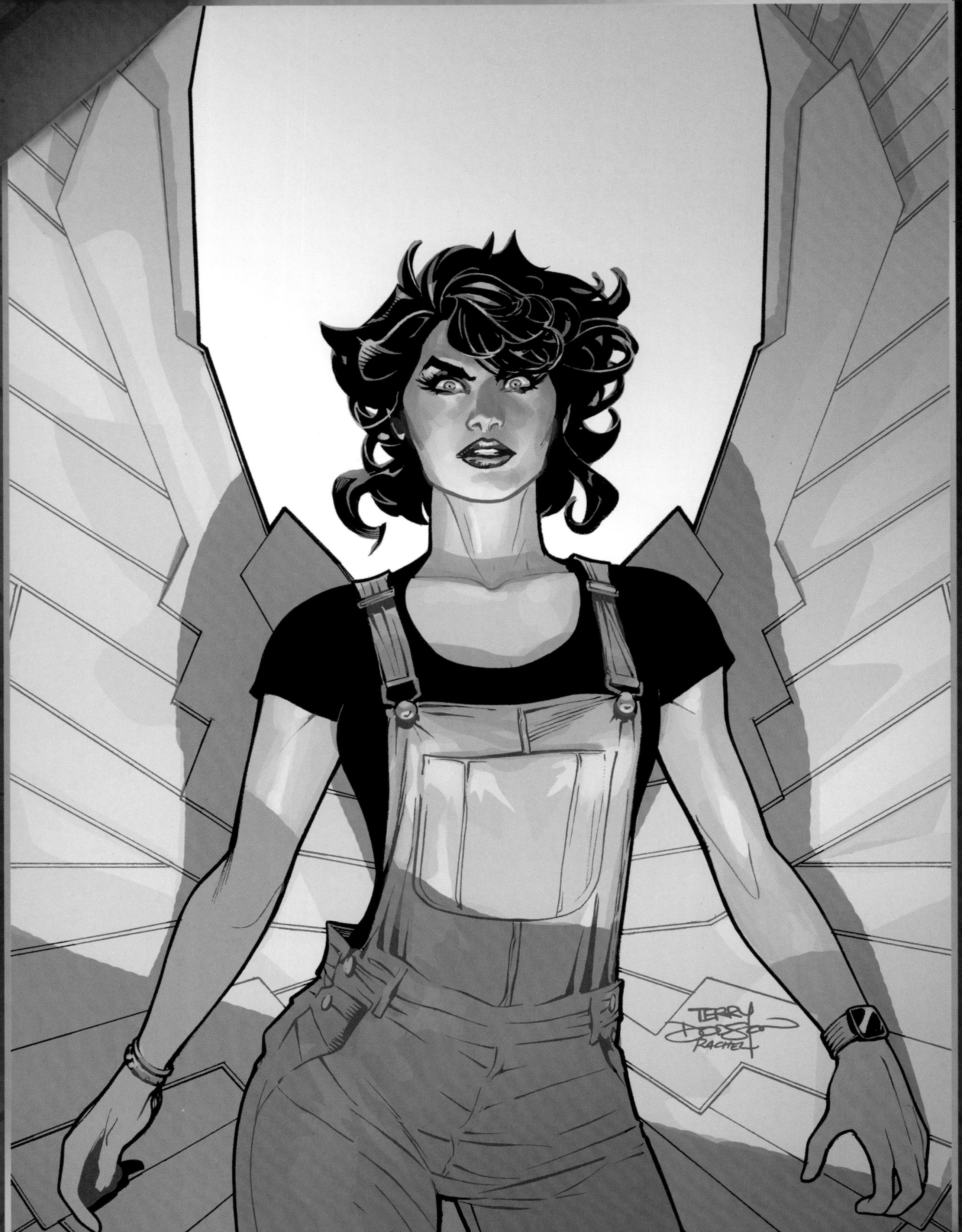

ORIGINAL COVER
FOR ISSUE 4

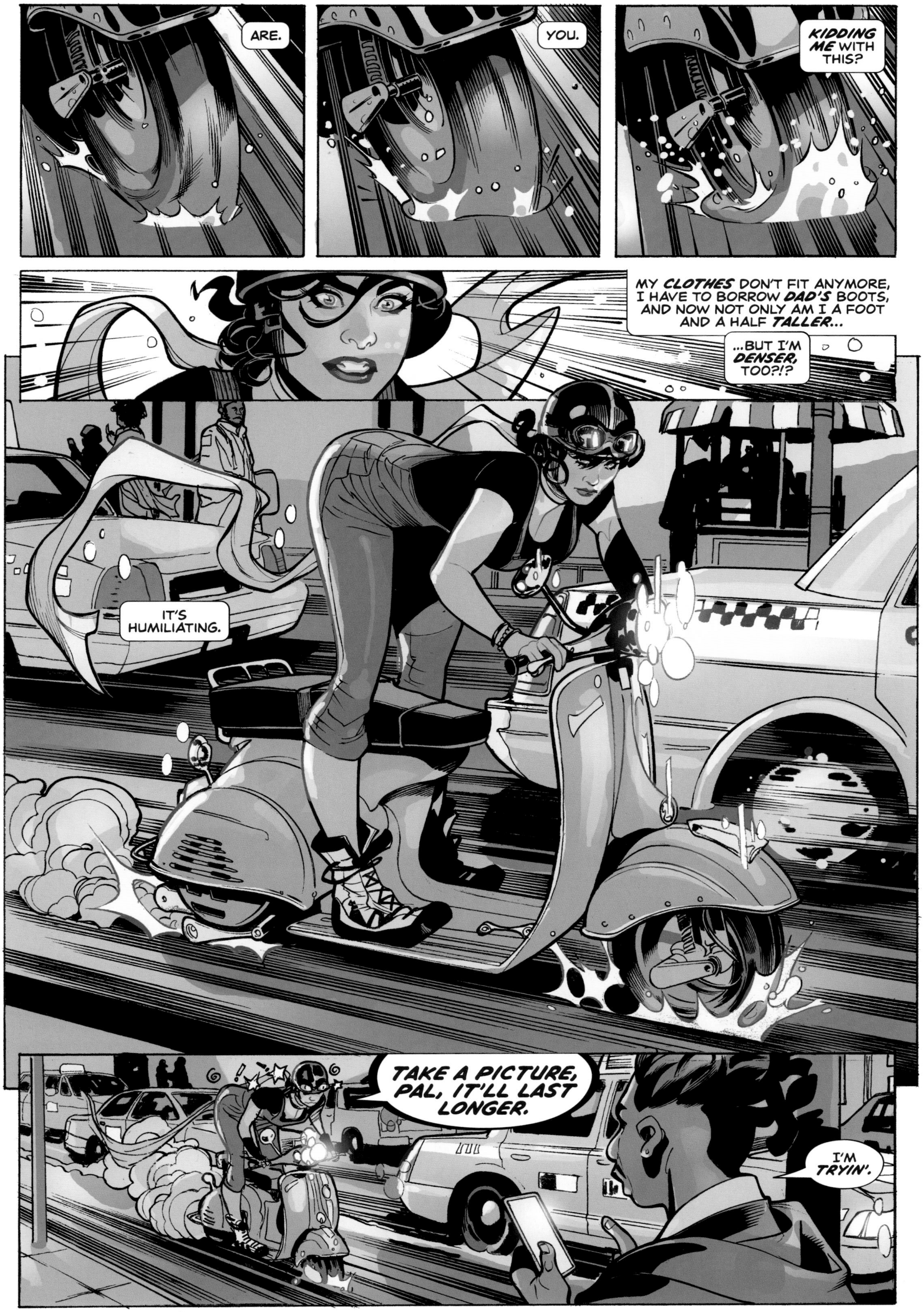
ARE.
YOU.
KIDDING ME WITH THIS?
MY CLOTHES DON'T FIT ANYMORE, I HAVE TO BORROW DAD'S BOOTS, AND NOW NOT ONLY AM I A FOOT AND A HALF TALLER...
...BUT I'M DENSER, TOO?!?
IT'S HUMILIATING.
TAKE A PICTURE, PAL, IT'LL LAST LONGER.
I'M TRYIN'.

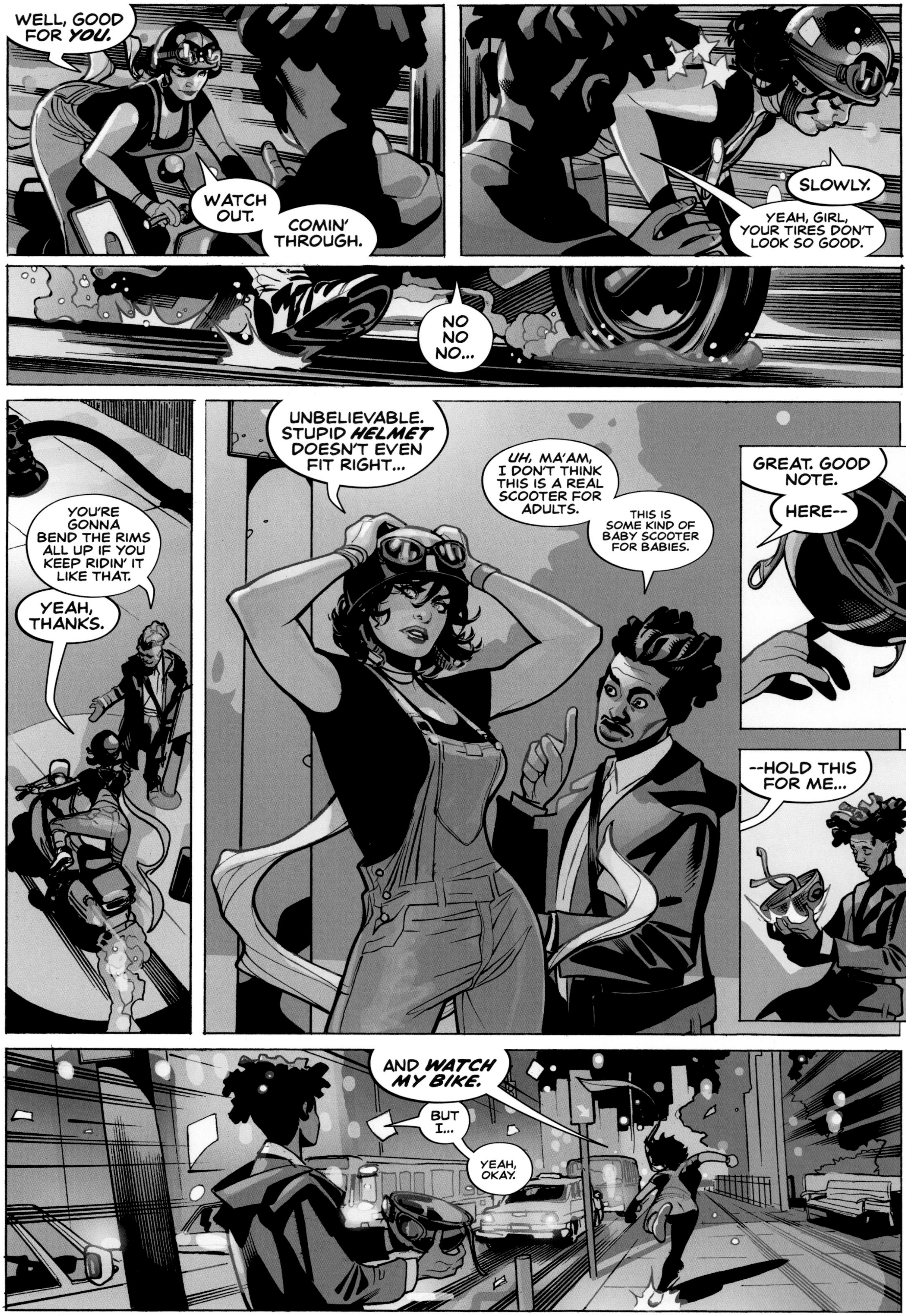
WELL, GOOD FOR YOU.
WATCH OUT.
COMIN' THROUGH.
SLOWLY.
YEAH, GIRL, YOUR TIRES DON'T LOOK SO GOOD.
NO NO NO...
YOU'RE GONNA BEND THE RIMS ALL UP IF YOU KEEP RIDIN' IT LIKE THAT.
YEAH, THANKS.
UNBELIEVABLE. STUPID HELMET DOESN'T EVEN FIT RIGHT...
UH, MA'AM, I DON'T THINK THIS IS A REAL SCOOTER FOR ADULTS.
THIS IS SOME KIND OF BABY SCOOTER FOR BABIES.
GREAT. GOOD NOTE.
HERE--
--HOLD THIS FOR ME...
AND WATCH MY BIKE.
BUT I...
YEAH, OKAY.

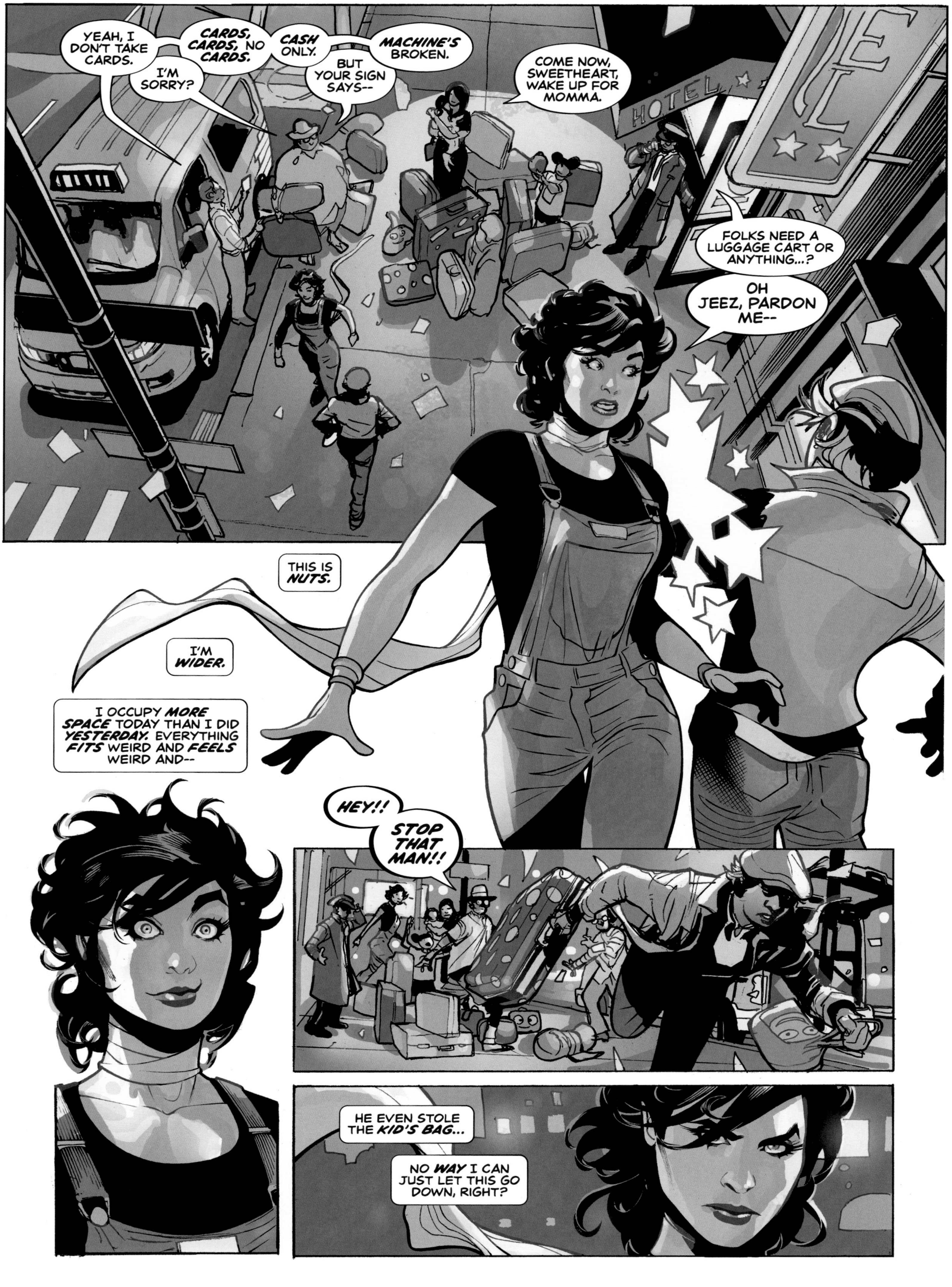

YEAH, I DON'T TAKE CARDS.
I'M SORRY?
CARDS, CARDS, NO CARDS.
CASH ONLY.
BUT YOUR SIGN SAYS--
MACHINE'S BROKEN.
COME NOW, SWEETHEART, WAKE UP FOR MOMMA.
HOTEL
FOLKS NEED A LUGGAGE CART OR ANYTHING...?
OH JEEZ, PARDON ME--
THIS IS NUTS.
I'M WIDER.
I OCCUPY MORE SPACE TODAY THAN I DID YESTERDAY. EVERYTHING FITS WEIRD AND FEELS WEIRD AND--
HEY!!
STOP THAT MAN!!
HE EVEN STOLE THE KID'S BAG...
NO WAY I CAN JUST LET THIS GO DOWN, RIGHT?

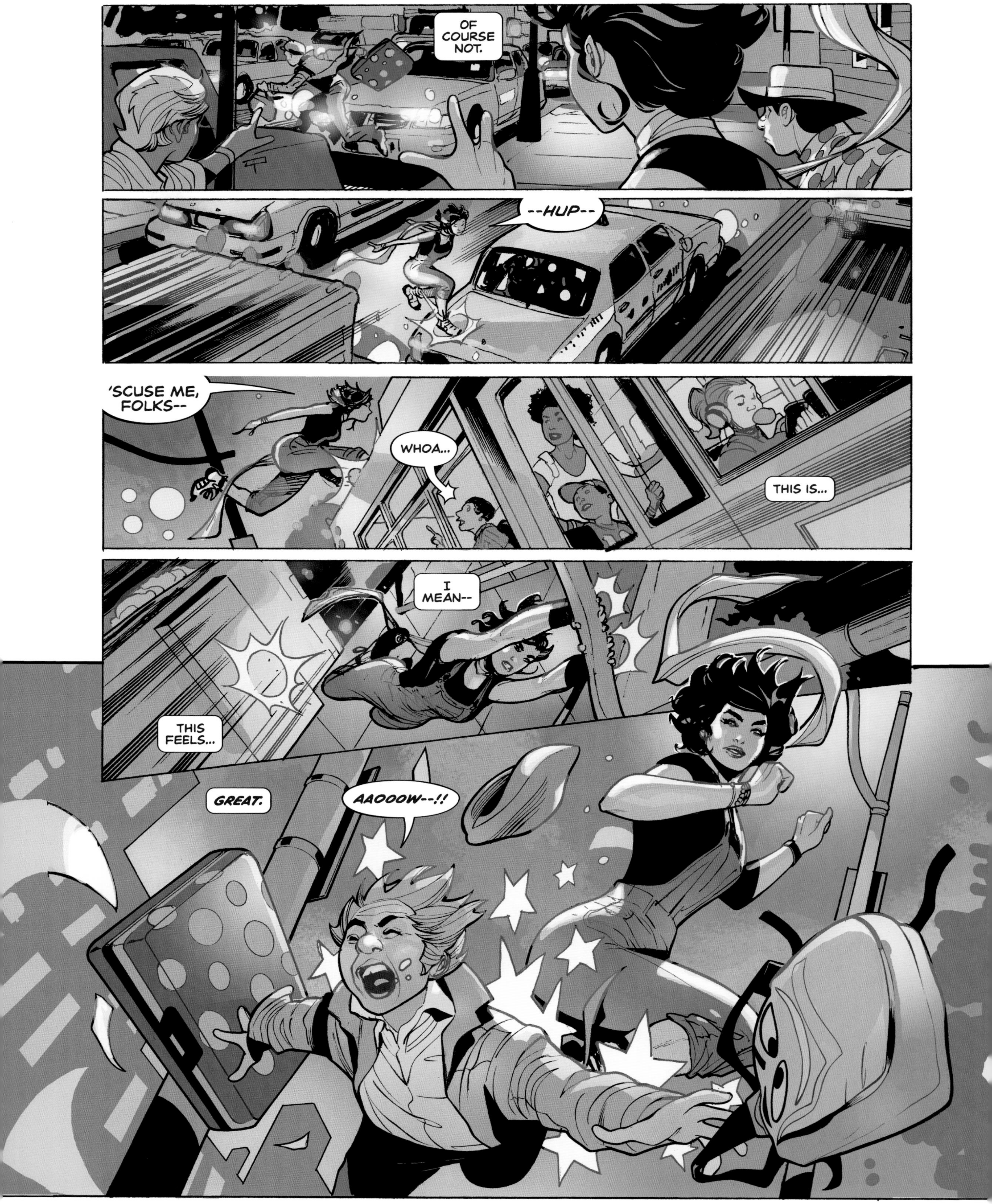
OF COURSE NOT.
--HUP--
'SCUSE ME, FOLKS--
WHOA...
THIS IS...
I MEAN--
THIS FEELS...
GREAT.
AAOOOW--!!

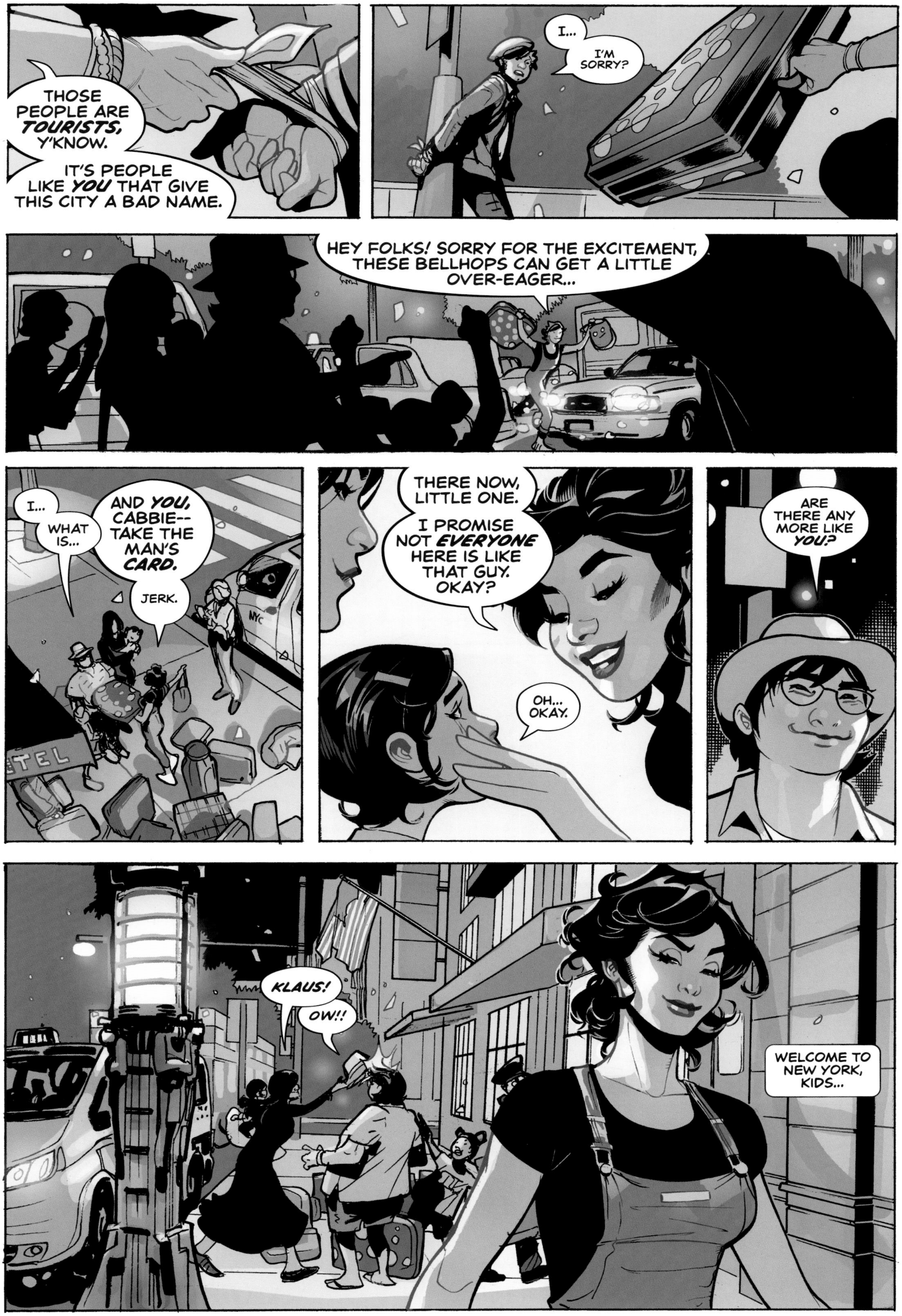
THOSE PEOPLE ARE TOURISTS, Y'KNOW.
IT'S PEOPLE LIKE YOU THAT GIVE THIS CITY A BAD NAME.
I...
I'M SORRY?
HEY FOLKS! SORRY FOR THE EXCITEMENT, THESE BELLHOPS CAN GET A LITTLE OVER-EAGER...
I...
WHAT IS...
AND YOU, CABBIE-- TAKE THE MAN'S CARD.
JERK.
NYC
TEL
THERE NOW, LITTLE ONE.
I PROMISE NOT EVERYONE HERE IS LIKE THAT GUY. OKAY?
OH... OKAY.
ARE THERE ANY MORE LIKE YOU?
KLAUS!
OW!!
WELCOME TO NEW YORK, KIDS...

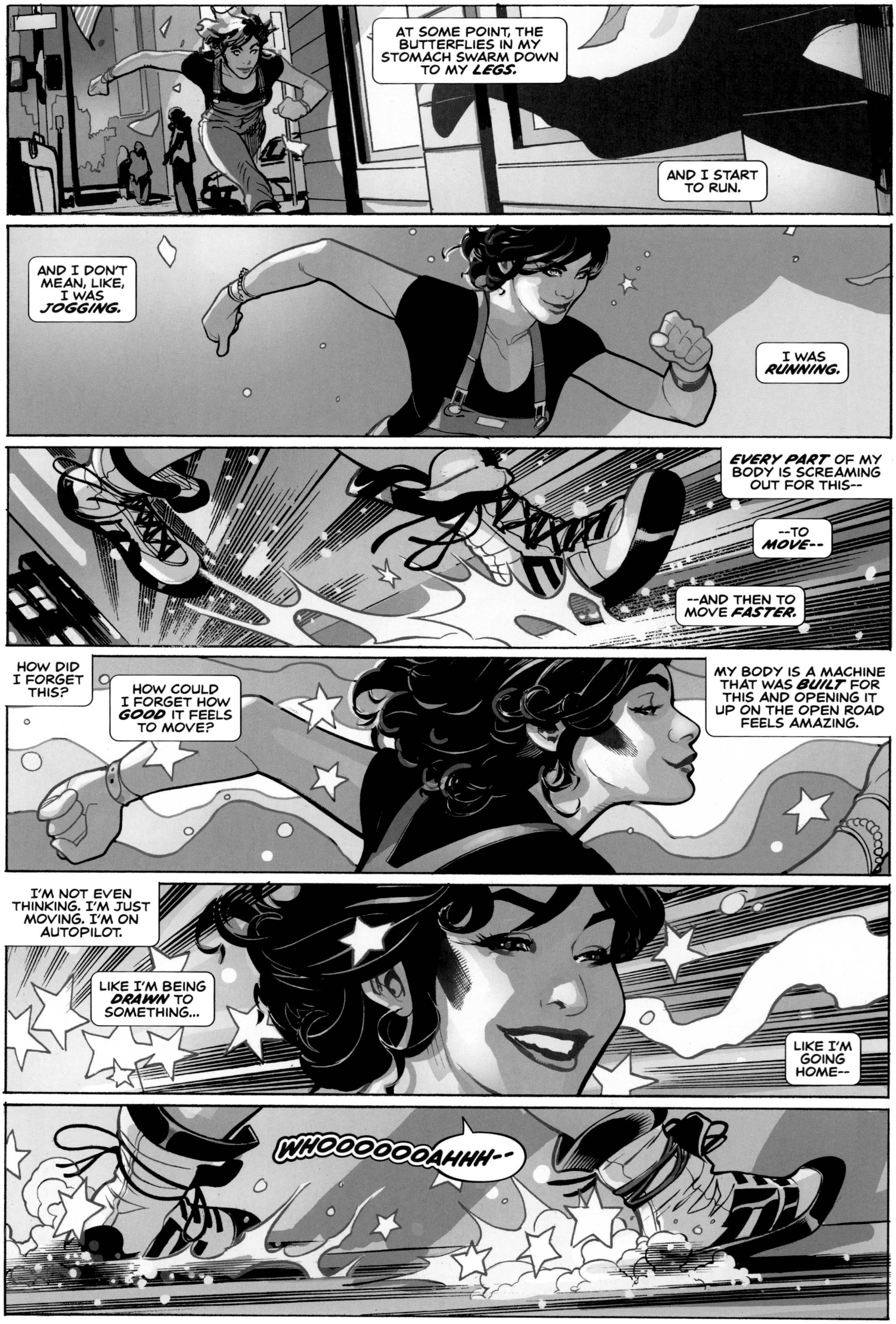
AT SOME POINT, THE BUTTERFLIES IN MY STOMACH SWARM DOWN TO MY LEGS.
AND I START TO RUN.
AND I DON'T MEAN, LIKE, I WAS JOGGING.
I WAS RUNNING.
EVERY PART OF MY BODY IS SCREAMING OUT FOR THIS--
--TO MOVE--
--AND THEN TO MOVE FASTER.
HOW DID I FORGET THIS?
HOW COULD I FORGET HOW GOOD IT FEELS TO MOVE?
MY BODY IS A MACHINE THAT WAS BUILT FOR THIS AND OPENING IT UP ON THE OPEN ROAD FEELS AMAZING.
I'M NOT EVEN THINKING. I'M JUST MOVING. I'M ON AUTOPILOT.
LIKE I'M BEING DRAWN TO SOMETHING...
LIKE I'M GOING HOME--
WHOOOOOOOAHHH--

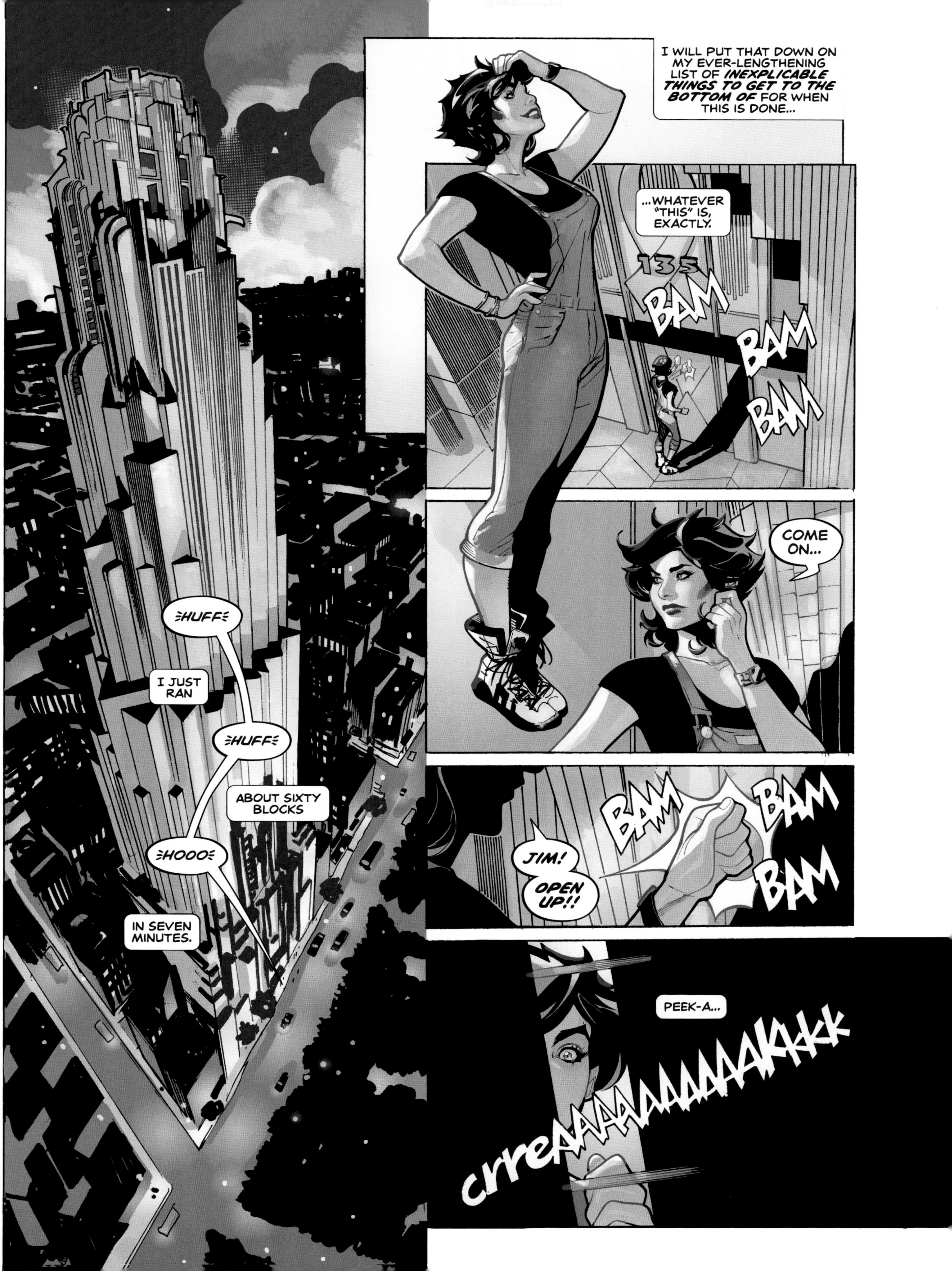

HUFF
I JUST RAN
HUFF
ABOUT SIXTY BLOCKS
HOOO
IN SEVEN MINUTES.
I WILL PUT THAT DOWN ON MY EVER-LENGTHENING LIST OF INEXPLICABLE THINGS TO GET TO THE BOTTOM OF FOR WHEN THIS IS DONE...
...WHATEVER "THIS" IS, EXACTLY.
135
BAM
BAM
BAM
COME ON...
BAM
BAM
BAM
JIM!
OPEN UP!!
PEEK-A...
crreAAAAAAAAAKKKK

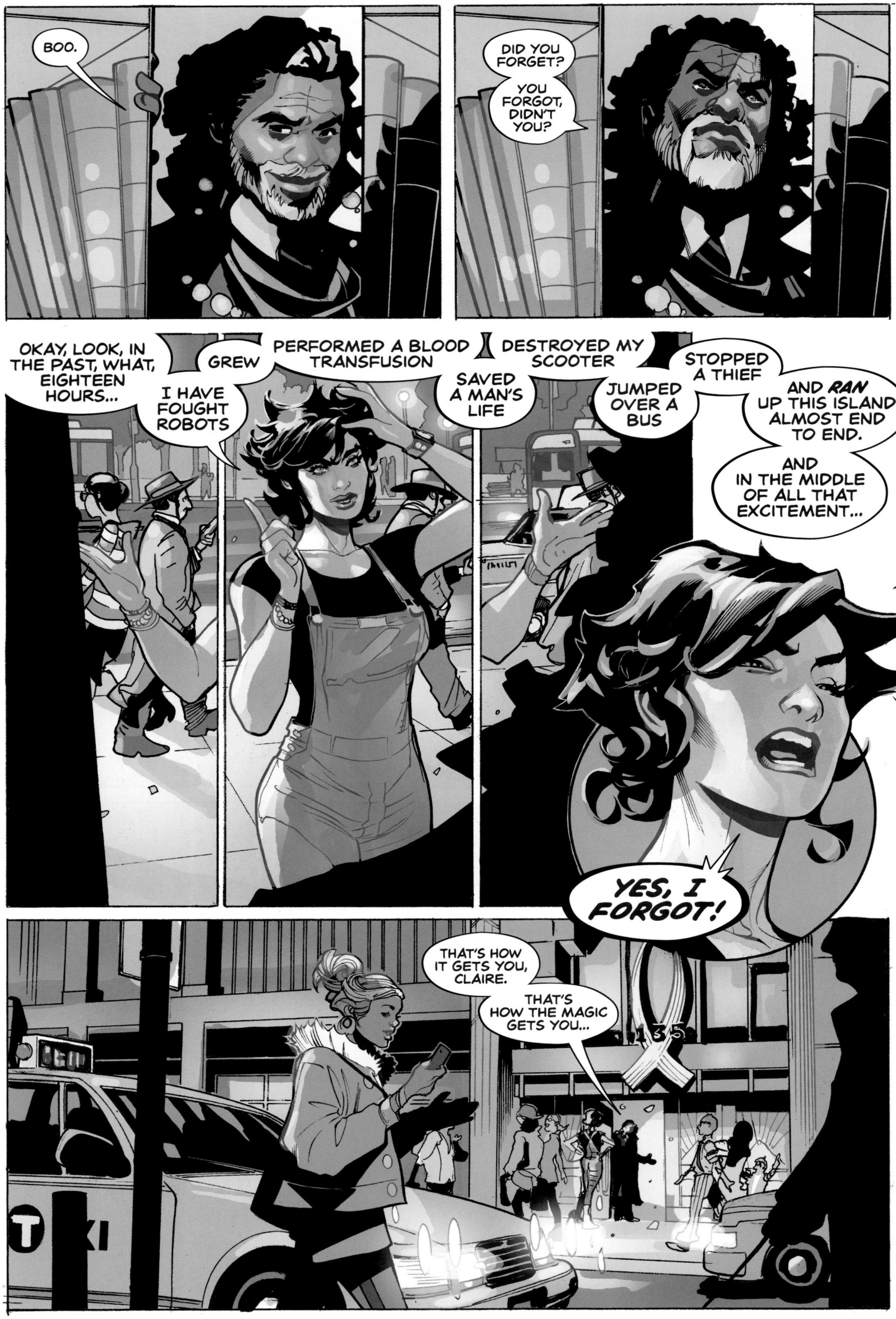
BOO.
DID YOU FORGET?
YOU FORGOT, DIDN'T YOU?
OKAY, LOOK, IN THE PAST, WHAT, EIGHTEEN HOURS...
I HAVE FOUGHT ROBOTS
GREW
PERFORMED A BLOOD TRANSFUSION
SAVED A MAN'S LIFE
DESTROYED MY SCOOTER
JUMPED OVER A BUS
STOPPED A THIEF
AND *RAN* UP THIS ISLAND ALMOST END TO END.
AND IN THE MIDDLE OF ALL THAT EXCITEMENT...
YES, I FORGOT!
THAT'S HOW IT GETS YOU, CLAIRE.
THAT'S HOW THE MAGIC GETS YOU...

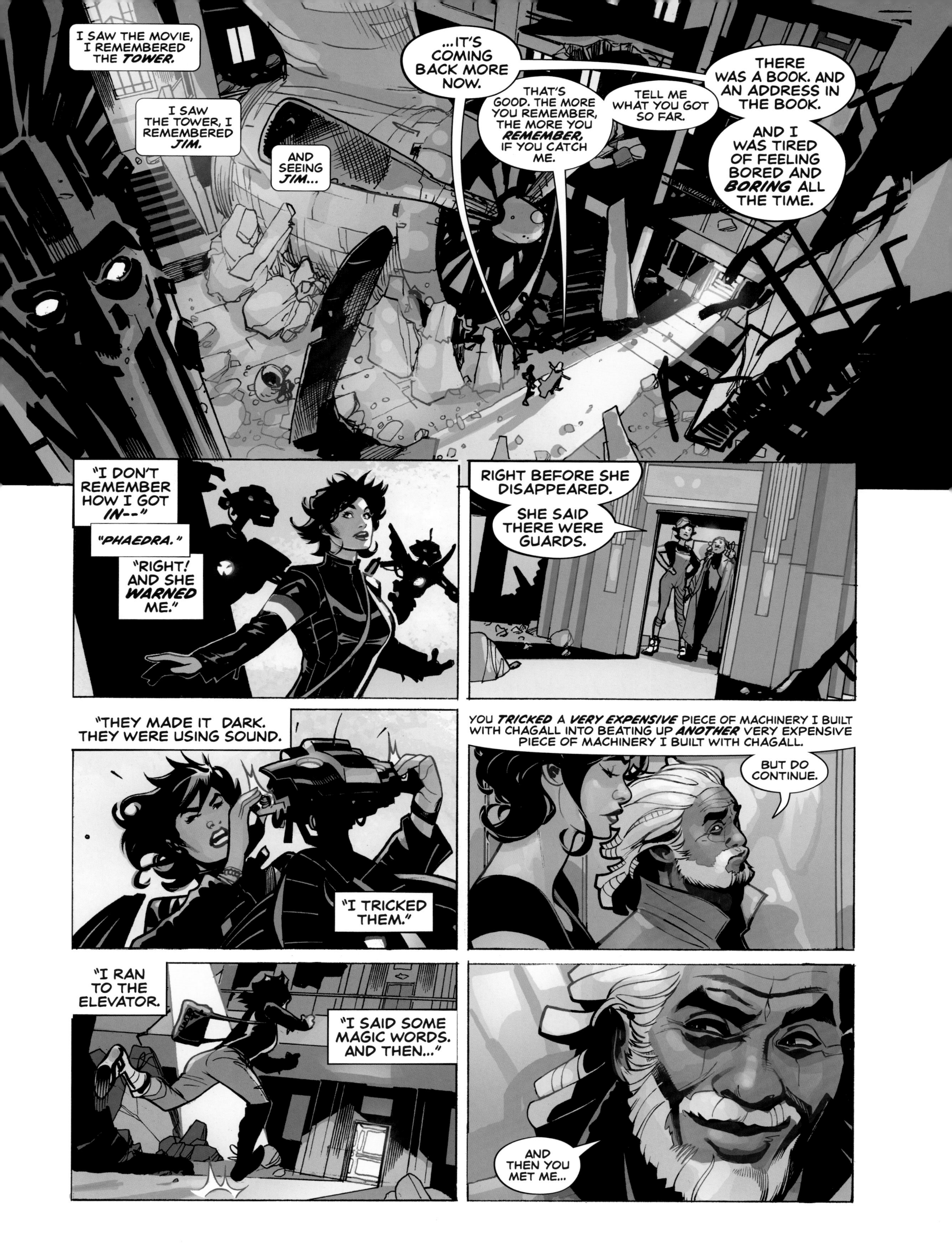

I SAW THE MOVIE, I REMEMBERED THE *TOWER.*
I SAW THE TOWER, I REMEMBERED *JIM.*
AND SEEING *JIM...*
...IT'S COMING BACK MORE NOW.
THAT'S GOOD. THE MORE YOU REMEMBER, THE MORE YOU *REMEMBER,* IF YOU CATCH ME.
TELL ME WHAT YOU GOT SO FAR.
THERE WAS A BOOK. AND AN ADDRESS IN THE BOOK.
AND I WAS TIRED OF FEELING BORED AND *BORING* ALL THE TIME.
"I DON'T REMEMBER HOW I GOT *IN--"*
"PHAEDRA."
"RIGHT! AND SHE *WARNED* ME."
RIGHT BEFORE SHE DISAPPEARED.
SHE SAID THERE WERE GUARDS.
"THEY MADE IT DARK. THEY WERE USING SOUND.
"I TRICKED THEM."
YOU ***TRICKED*** A ***VERY EXPENSIVE*** PIECE OF MACHINERY I BUILT WITH CHAGALL INTO BEATING UP ***ANOTHER*** VERY EXPENSIVE PIECE OF MACHINERY I BUILT WITH CHAGALL.
BUT DO CONTINUE.
"I RAN TO THE ELEVATOR.
"I SAID SOME MAGIC WORDS. AND THEN..."
AND THEN YOU MET ME...

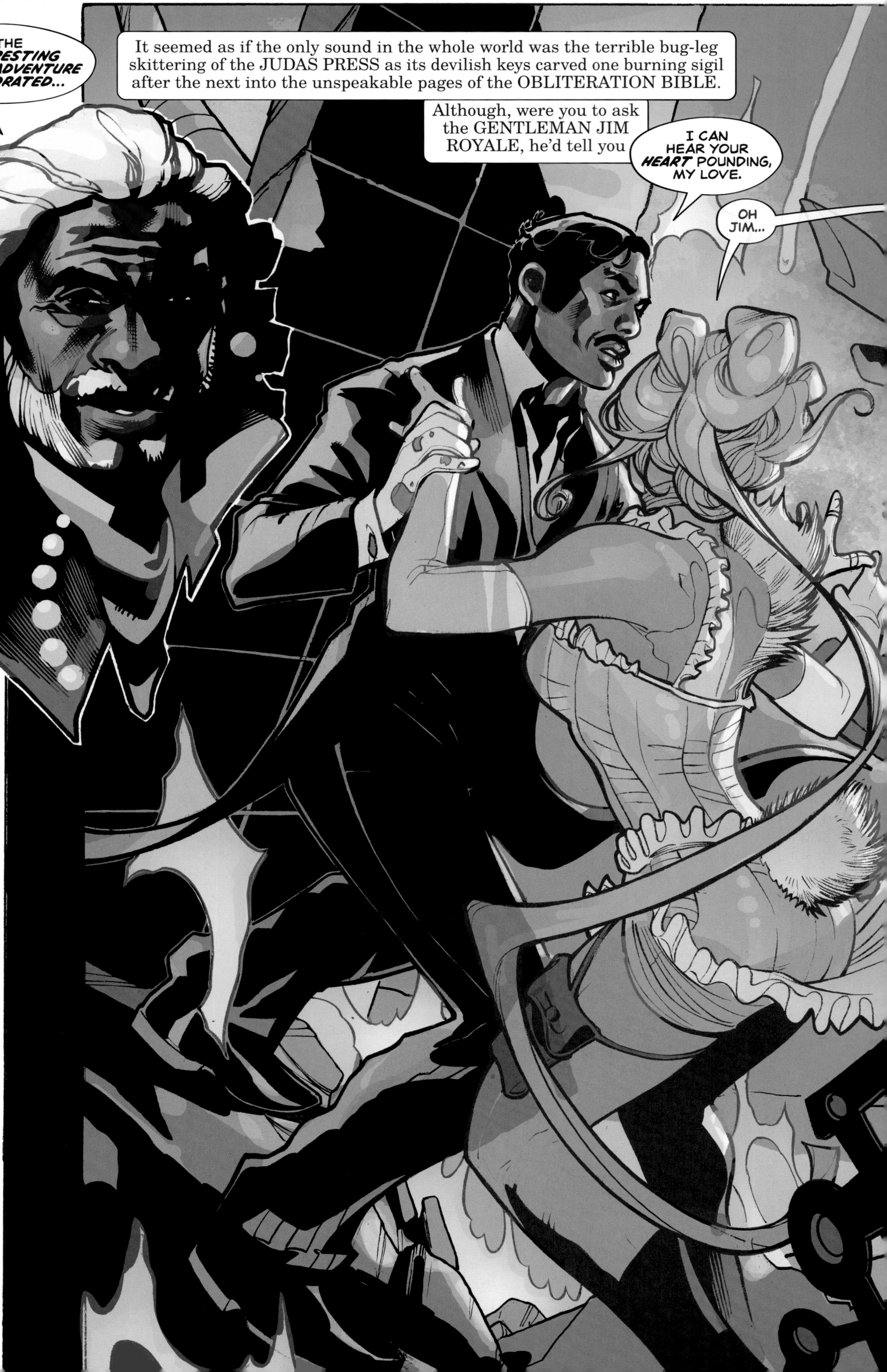

IN THE FINAL RESTING PLACE OF ADVENTURE INCORPORATED...
It seemed as if the only sound in the whole world was the terrible bug-leg skittering of the JUDAS PRESS as its devilish keys carved one burning sigil after the next into the unspeakable pages of the OBLITERATION BIBLE.
Although, were you to ask the GENTLEMAN JIM ROYALE, he'd tell you
I CAN HEAR YOUR HEART POUNDING, MY LOVE.
OH JIM...

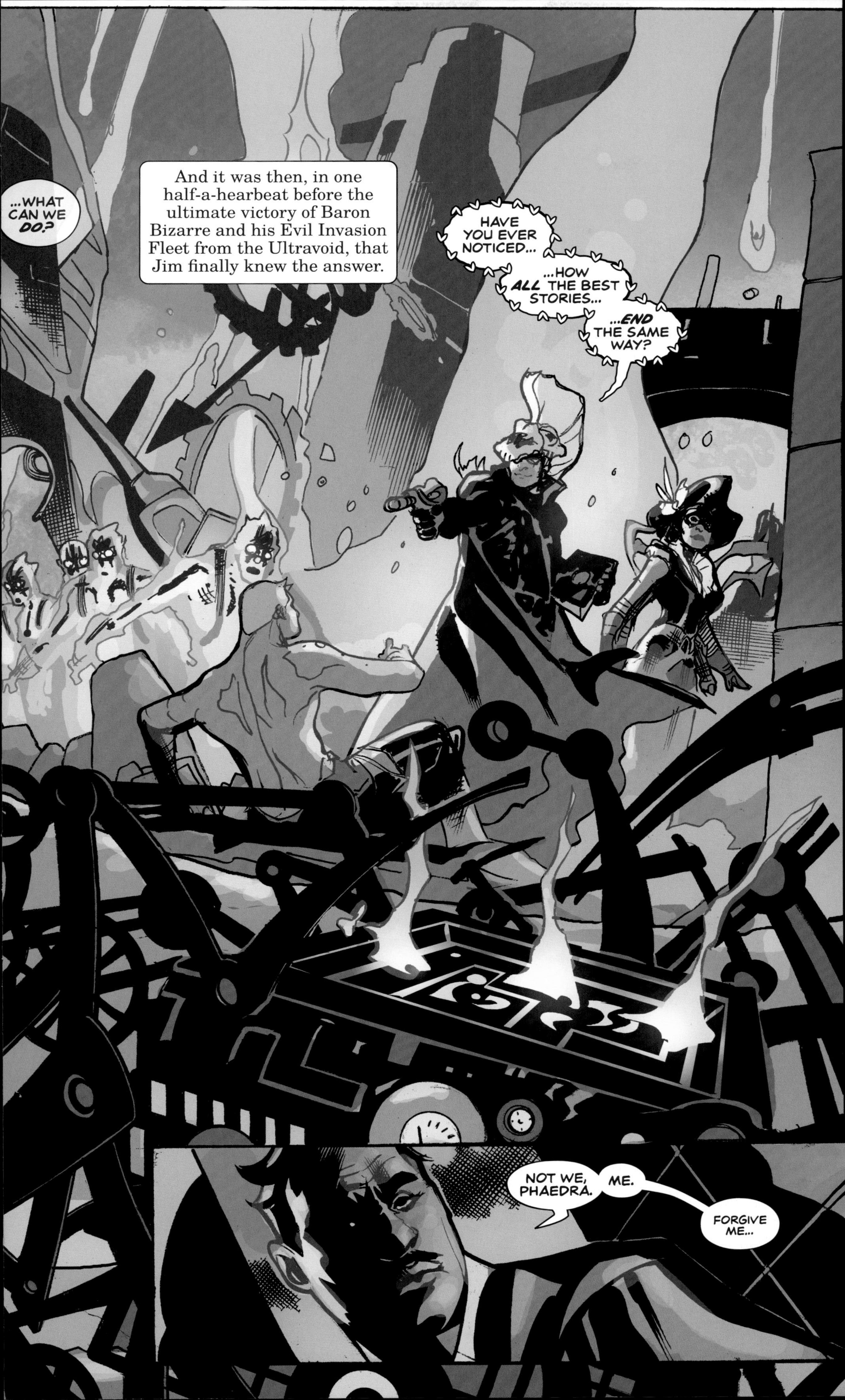

...WHAT CAN WE DO?
And it was then, in one half-a-hearbeat before the ultimate victory of Baron Bizarre and his Evil Invasion Fleet from the Ultravoid, that Jim finally knew the answer.
HAVE YOU EVER NOTICED...
...HOW ALL THE BEST STORIES...
...END THE SAME WAY?
NOT WE, PHAEDRA.
ME.
FORGIVE ME...

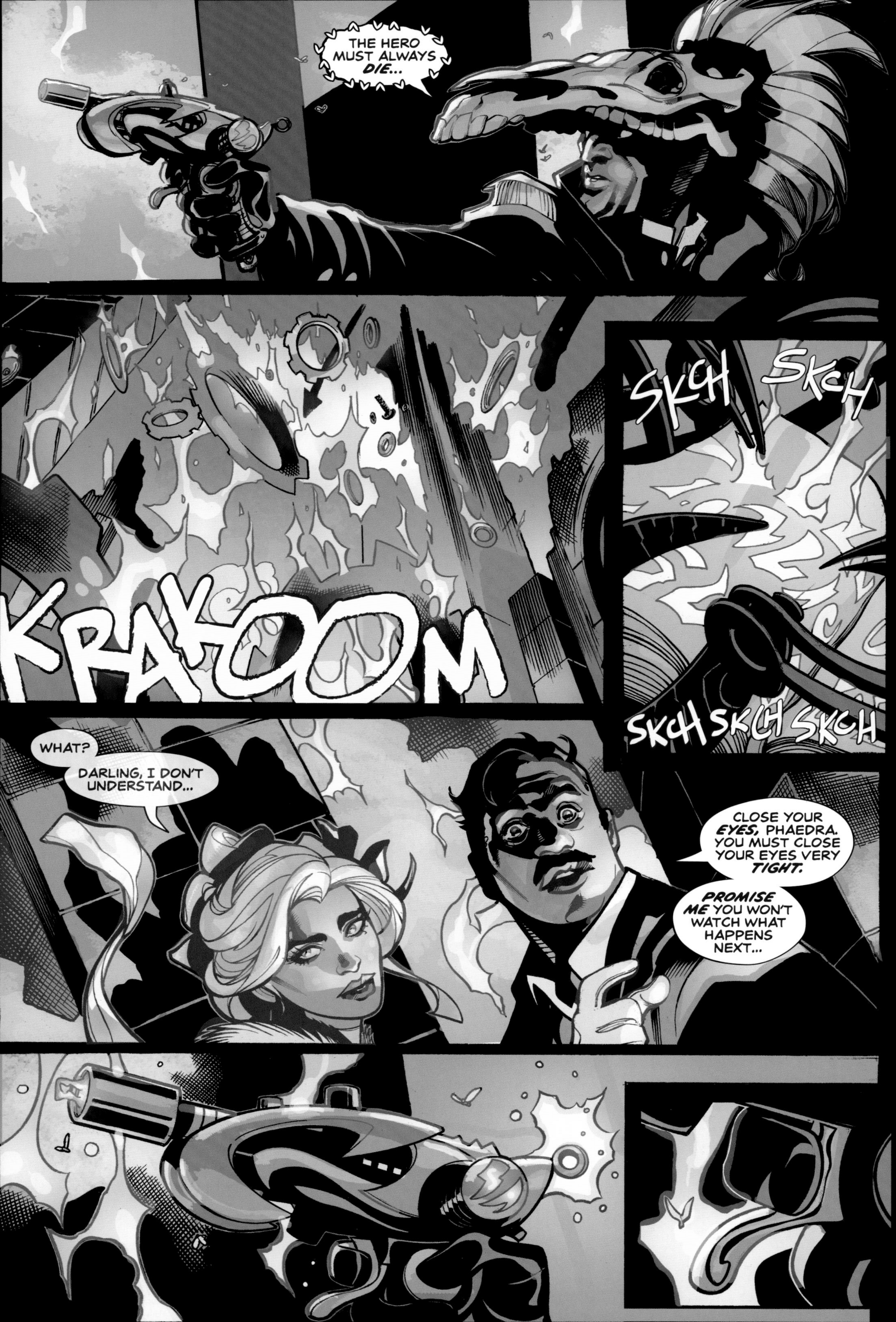
THE HERO MUST ALWAYS DIE...
KRAKOOM
SKCH SKCH
SKCH SKCH SKCH
WHAT?
DARLING, I DON'T UNDERSTAND...
CLOSE YOUR EYES, PHAEDRA. YOU MUST CLOSE YOUR EYES VERY TIGHT.
PROMISE ME YOU WON'T WATCH WHAT HAPPENS NEXT...

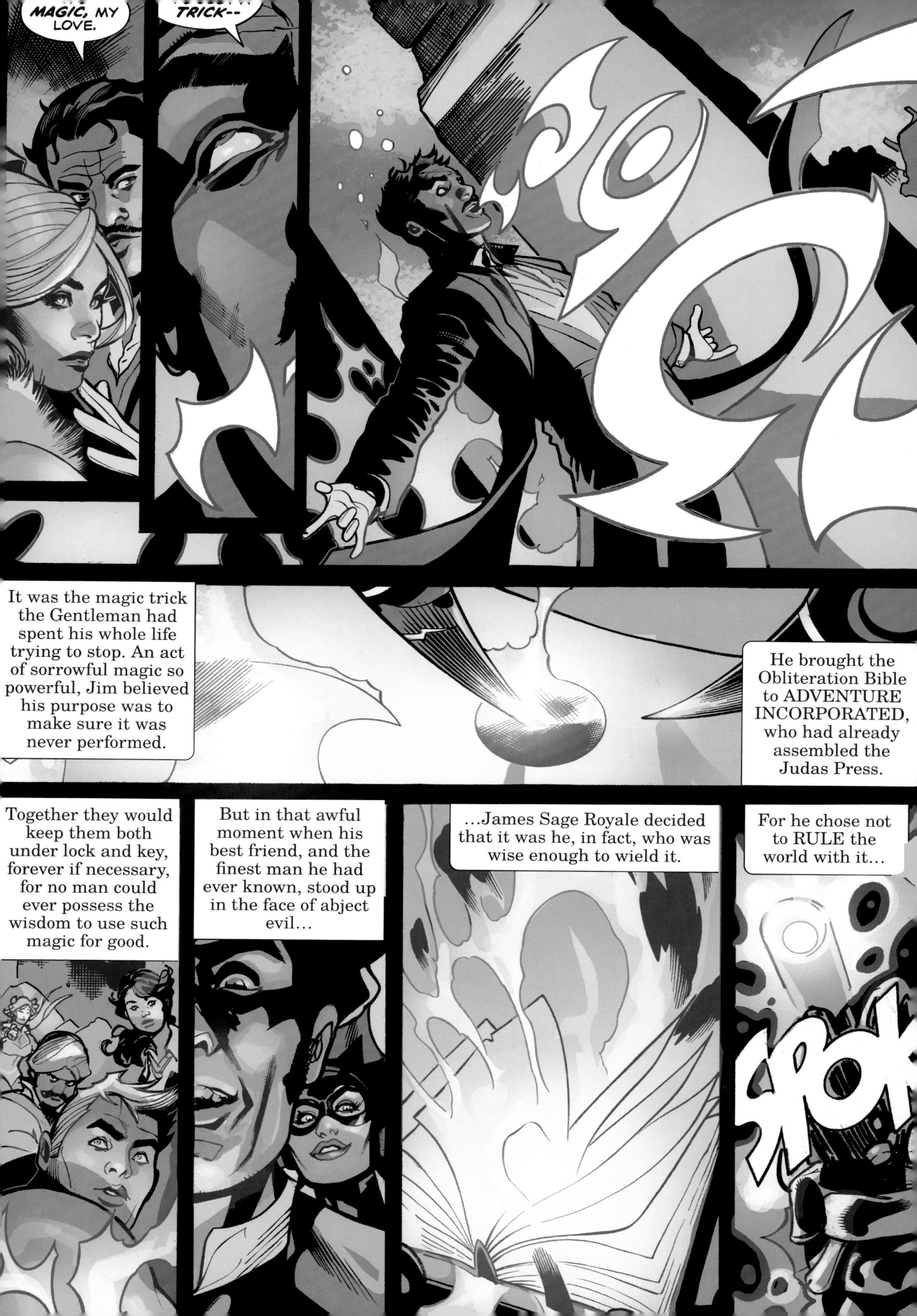
MAGIC, MY LOVE.
TRICK--
It was the magic trick the Gentleman had spent his whole life trying to stop. An act of sorrowful magic so powerful, Jim believed his purpose was to make sure it was never performed.
He brought the Obliteration Bible to ADVENTURE INCORPORATED, who had already assembled the Judas Press.
Together they would keep them both under lock and key, forever if necessary, for no man could ever possess the wisdom to use such magic for good.
But in that awful moment when his best friend, and the finest man he had ever known, stood up in the face of abject evil…
…James Sage Royale decided that it was he, in fact, who was wise enough to wield it.
For he chose not to RULE the world with it…

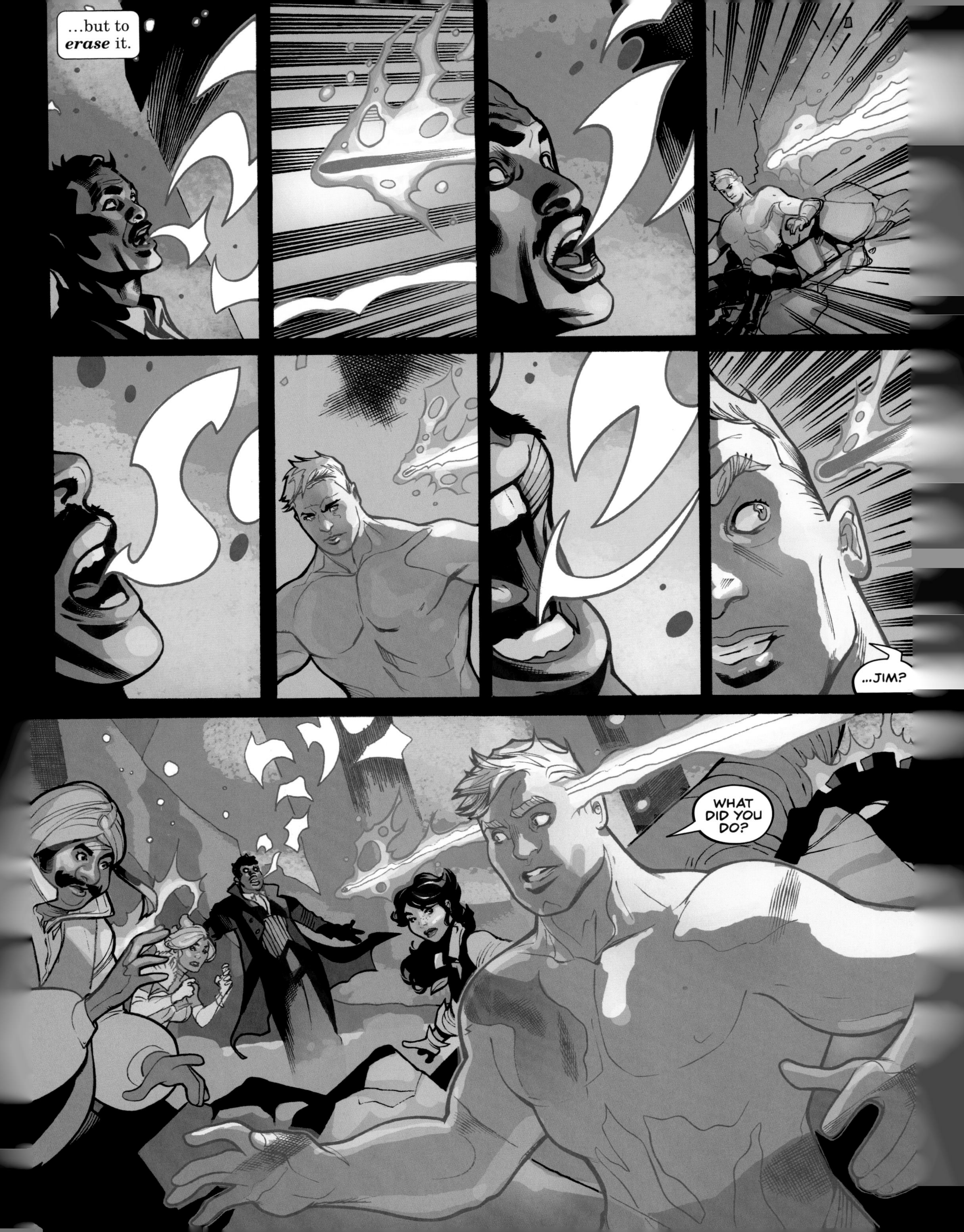
…but to *erase* it.
…JIM?
WHAT DID YOU DO?

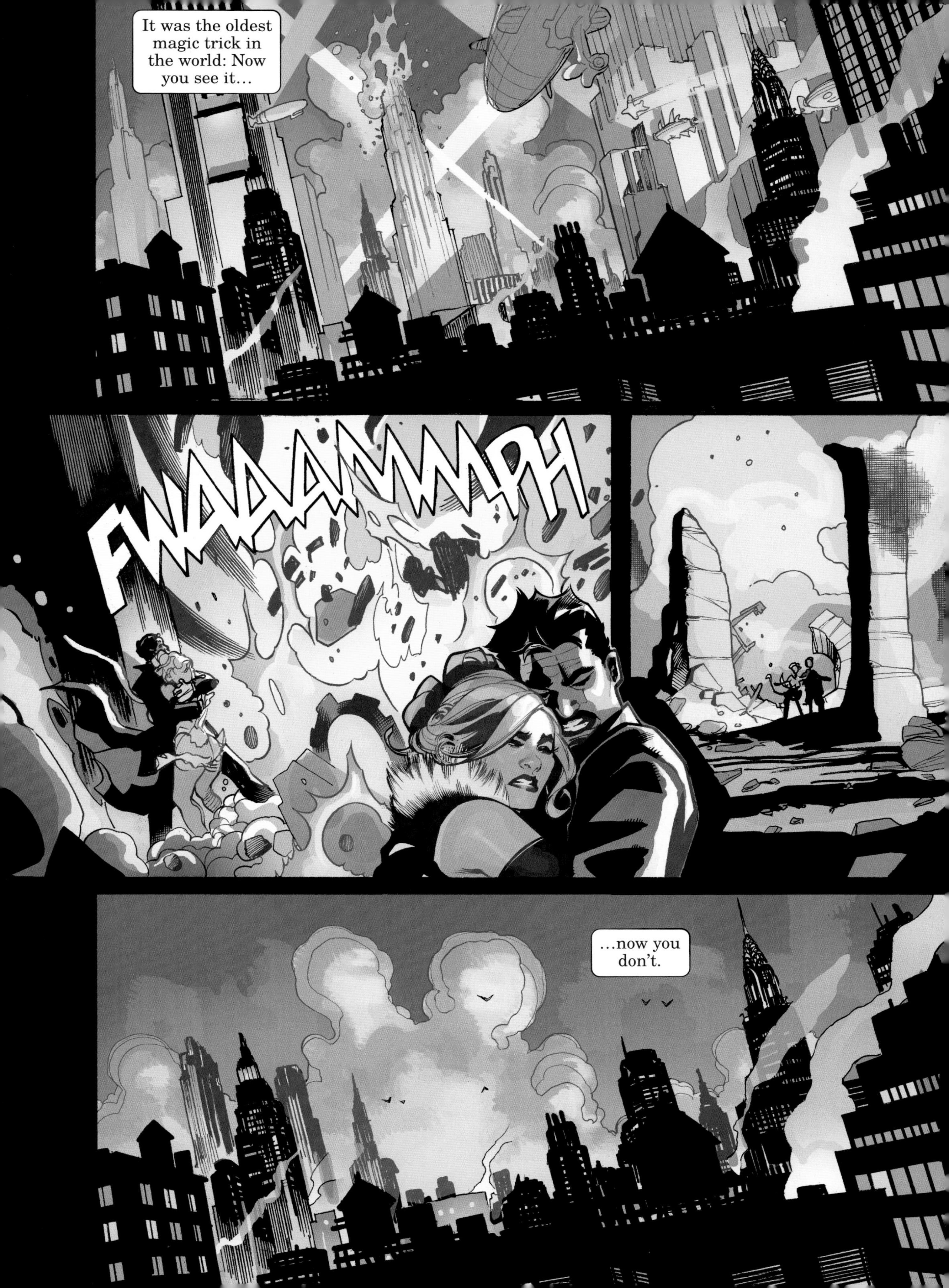
It was the oldest magic trick in the world: Now you see it…
FWADAMMPH
…now you don't.

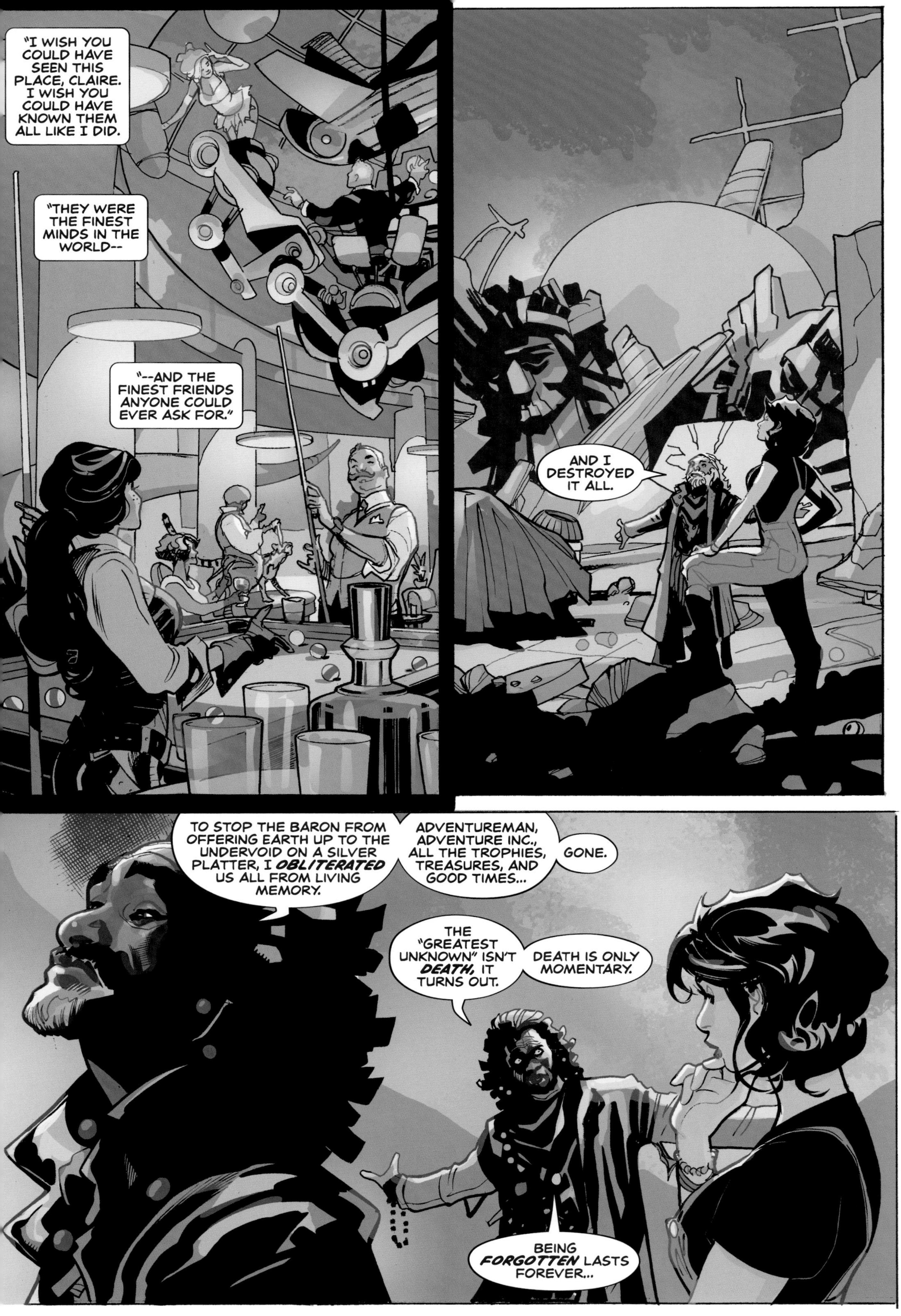
"I WISH YOU COULD HAVE SEEN THIS PLACE, CLAIRE. I WISH YOU COULD HAVE KNOWN THEM ALL LIKE I DID.
"THEY WERE THE FINEST MINDS IN THE WORLD--
"--AND THE FINEST FRIENDS ANYONE COULD EVER ASK FOR."
AND I DESTROYED IT ALL.
TO STOP THE BARON FROM OFFERING EARTH UP TO THE UNDERVOID ON A SILVER PLATTER, I OBLITERATED US ALL FROM LIVING MEMORY.
ADVENTUREMAN, ADVENTURE INC., ALL THE TROPHIES, TREASURES, AND GOOD TIMES...
GONE.
THE "GREATEST UNKNOWN" ISN'T DEATH, IT TURNS OUT.
DEATH IS ONLY MOMENTARY.
BEING FORGOTTEN LASTS FOREVER...

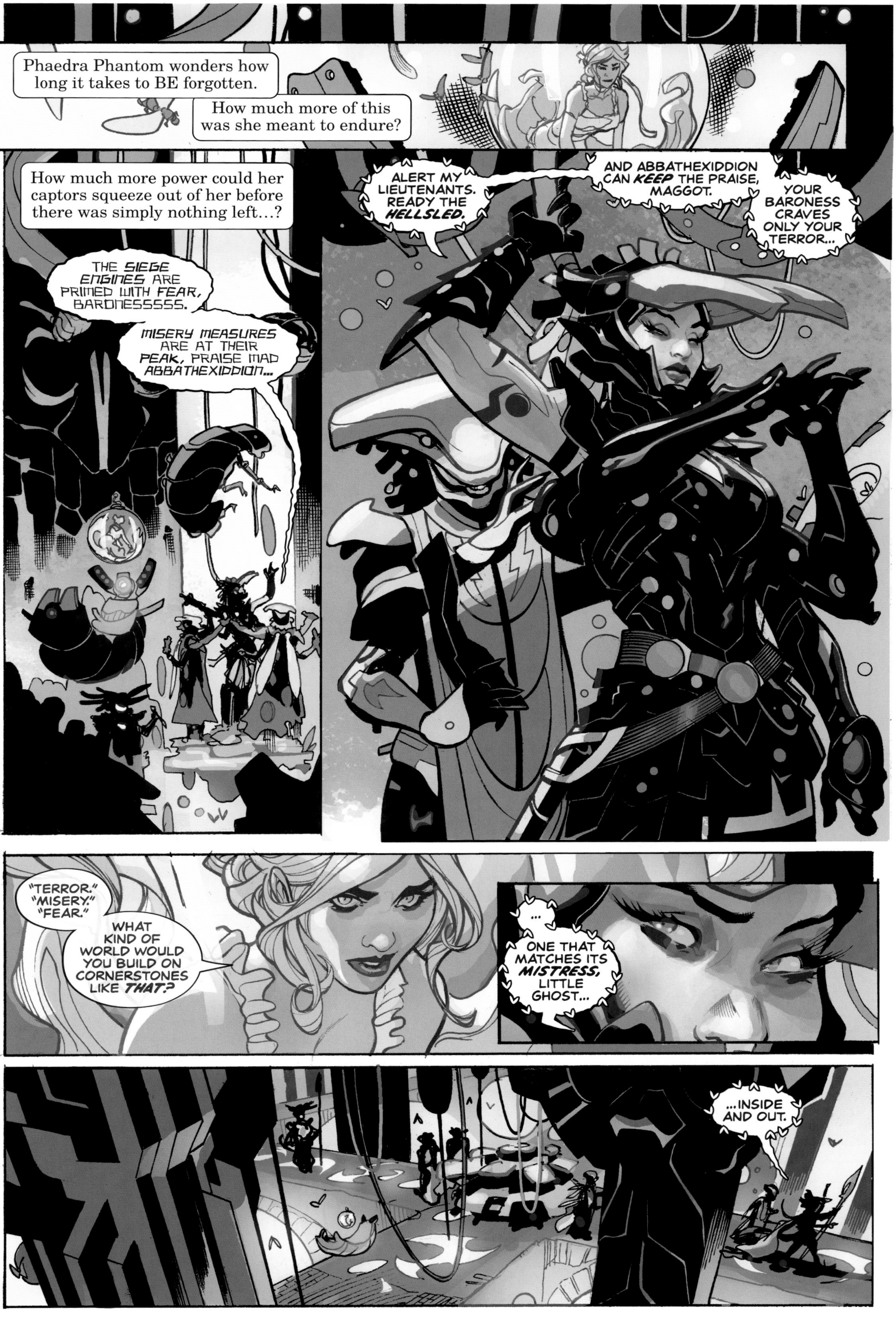

Phaedra Phantom wonders how long it takes to BE forgotten.
How much more of this was she meant to endure?
How much more power could her captors squeeze out of her before there was simply nothing left…?
THE SIEGE ENGINES ARE PRIMED WITH FEAR, BARONESSSSS.
MISERY MEASURES ARE AT THEIR PEAK, PRAISE MAD ABBATHEXIDDION…
ALERT MY LIEUTENANTS. READY THE HELLSLED.
AND ABBATHEXIDDION CAN KEEP THE PRAISE, MAGGOT.
YOUR BARONESS CRAVES ONLY YOUR TERROR…
"TERROR." "MISERY." "FEAR."
WHAT KIND OF WORLD WOULD YOU BUILD ON CORNERSTONES LIKE THAT?
…
ONE THAT MATCHES ITS MISTRESS, LITTLE GHOST…
…INSIDE AND OUT.

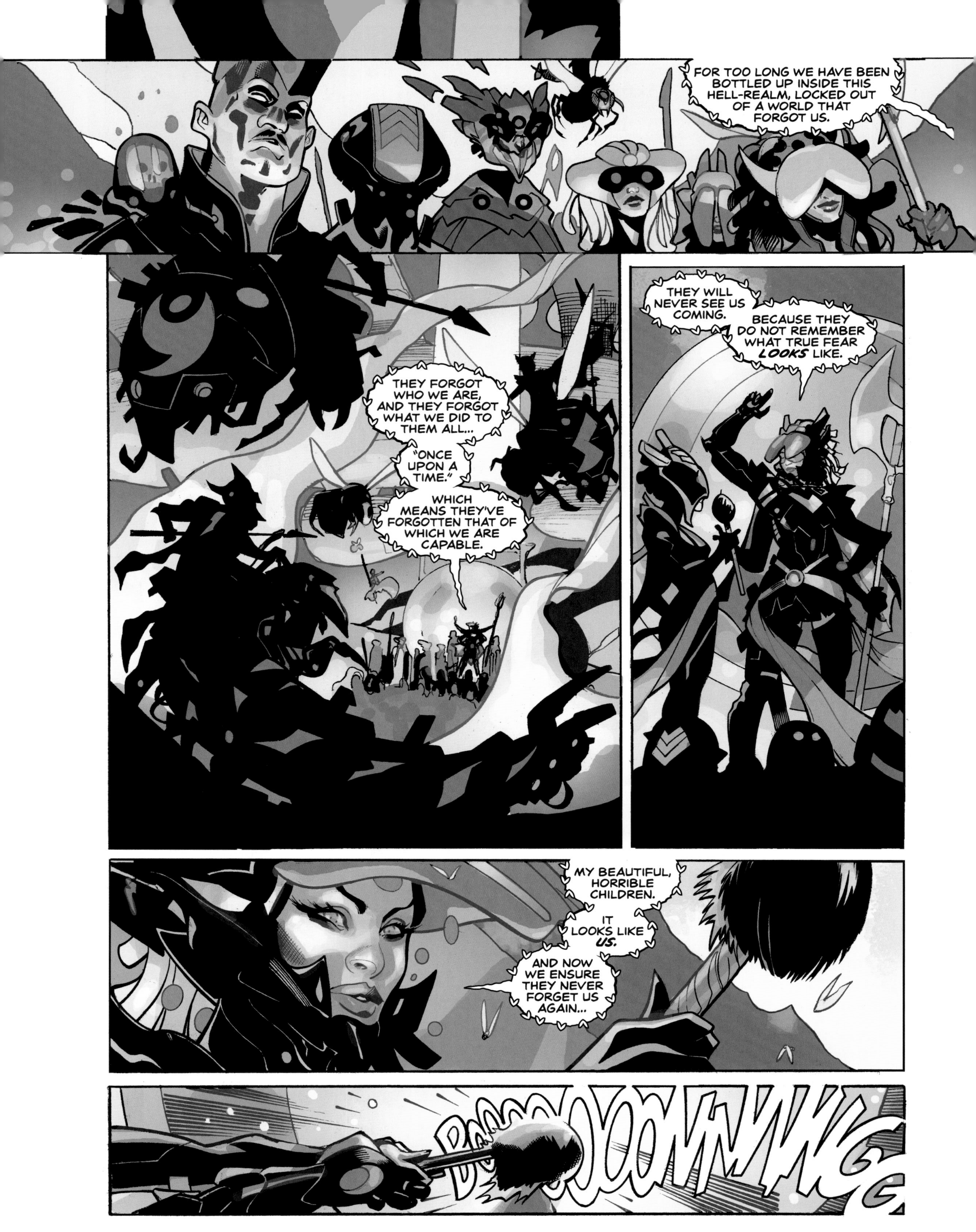
FOR TOO LONG WE HAVE BEEN BOTTLED UP INSIDE THIS HELL-REALM, LOCKED OUT OF A WORLD THAT FORGOT US.
THEY FORGOT WHO WE ARE, AND THEY FORGOT WHAT WE DID TO THEM ALL...
"ONCE UPON A TIME."
WHICH MEANS THEY'VE FORGOTTEN THAT OF WHICH WE ARE CAPABLE.
THEY WILL NEVER SEE US COMING.
BECAUSE THEY DO NOT REMEMBER WHAT TRUE FEAR LOOKS LIKE.
MY BEAUTIFUL, HORRIBLE CHILDREN.
IT LOOKS LIKE US.
AND NOW WE ENSURE THEY NEVER FORGET US AGAIN...
BOOOOOOOMMMNNNG

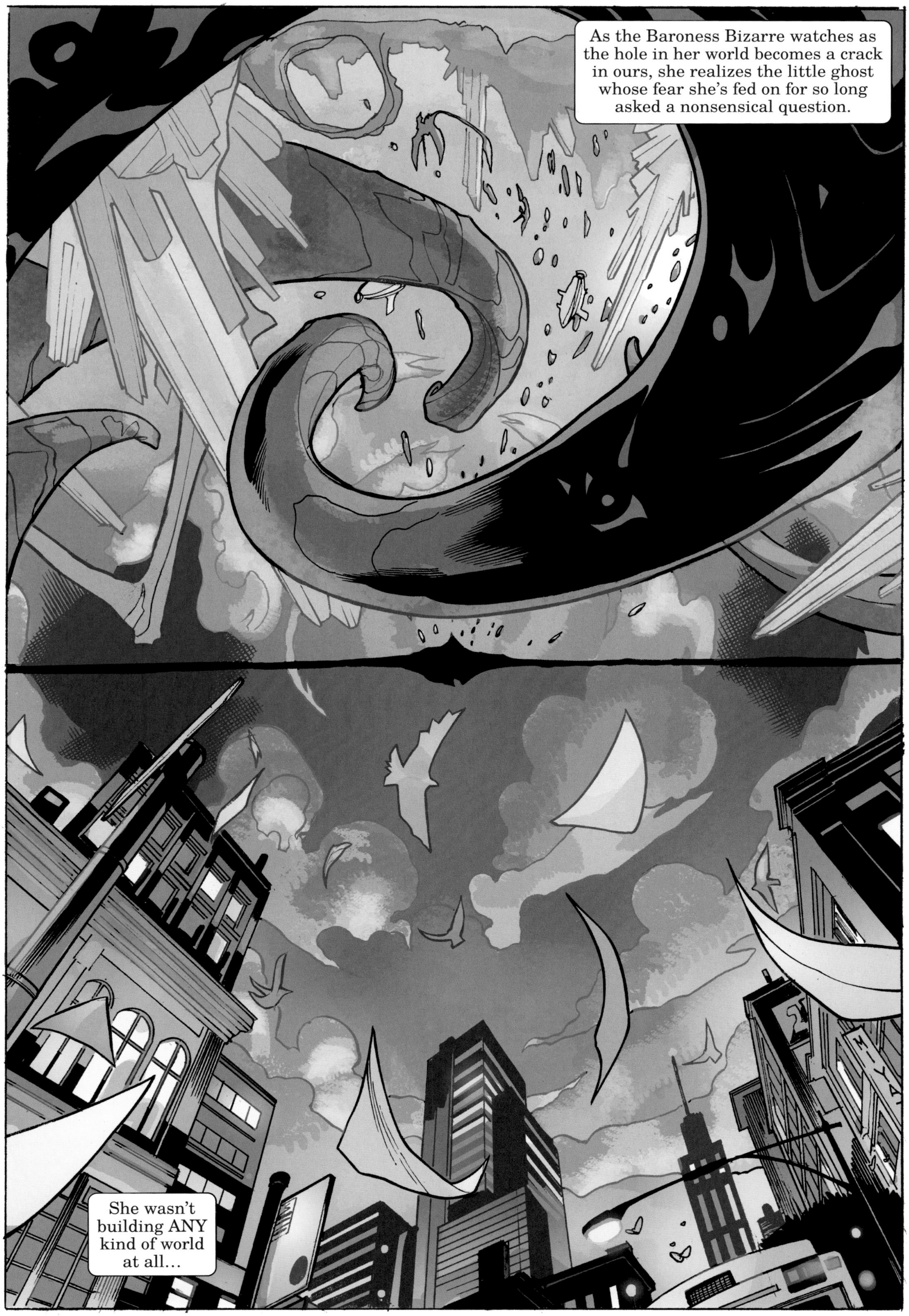
As the Baroness Bizarre watches as the hole in her world becomes a crack in ours, she realizes the little ghost whose fear she's fed on for so long asked a nonsensical question.
She wasn't building ANY kind of world at all...

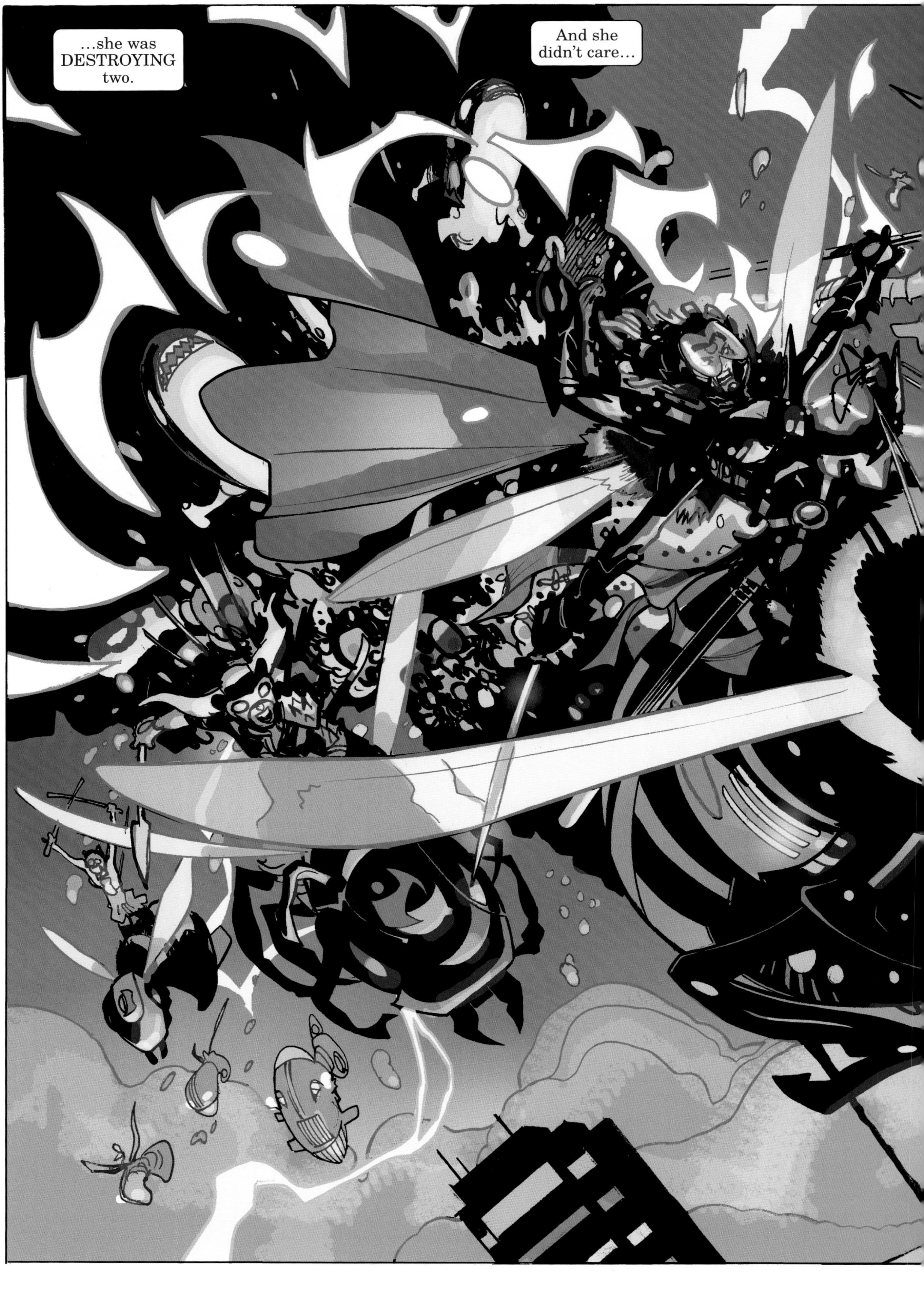
…she was DESTROYING two.
And she didn't care…

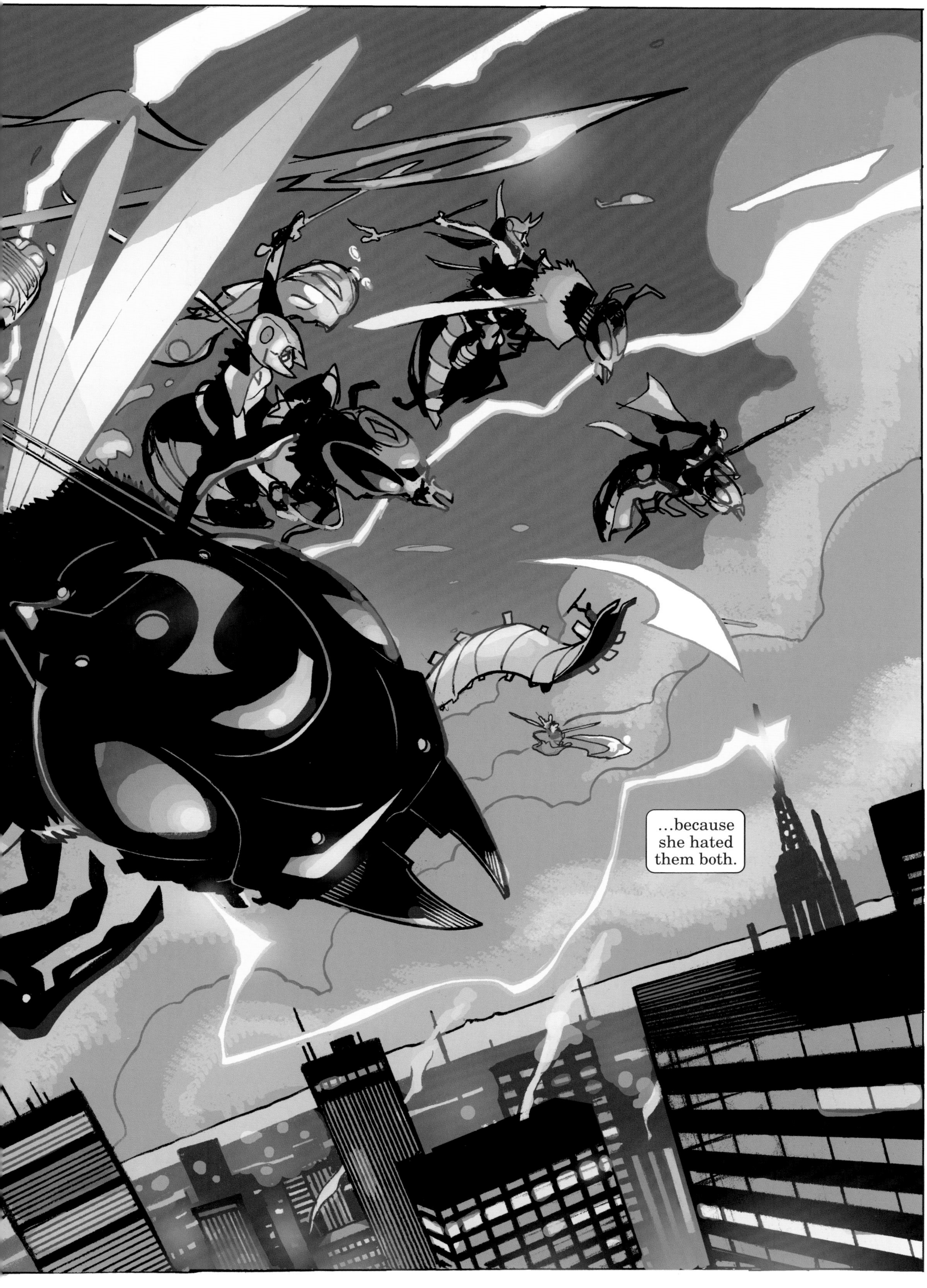
...because she hated them both.

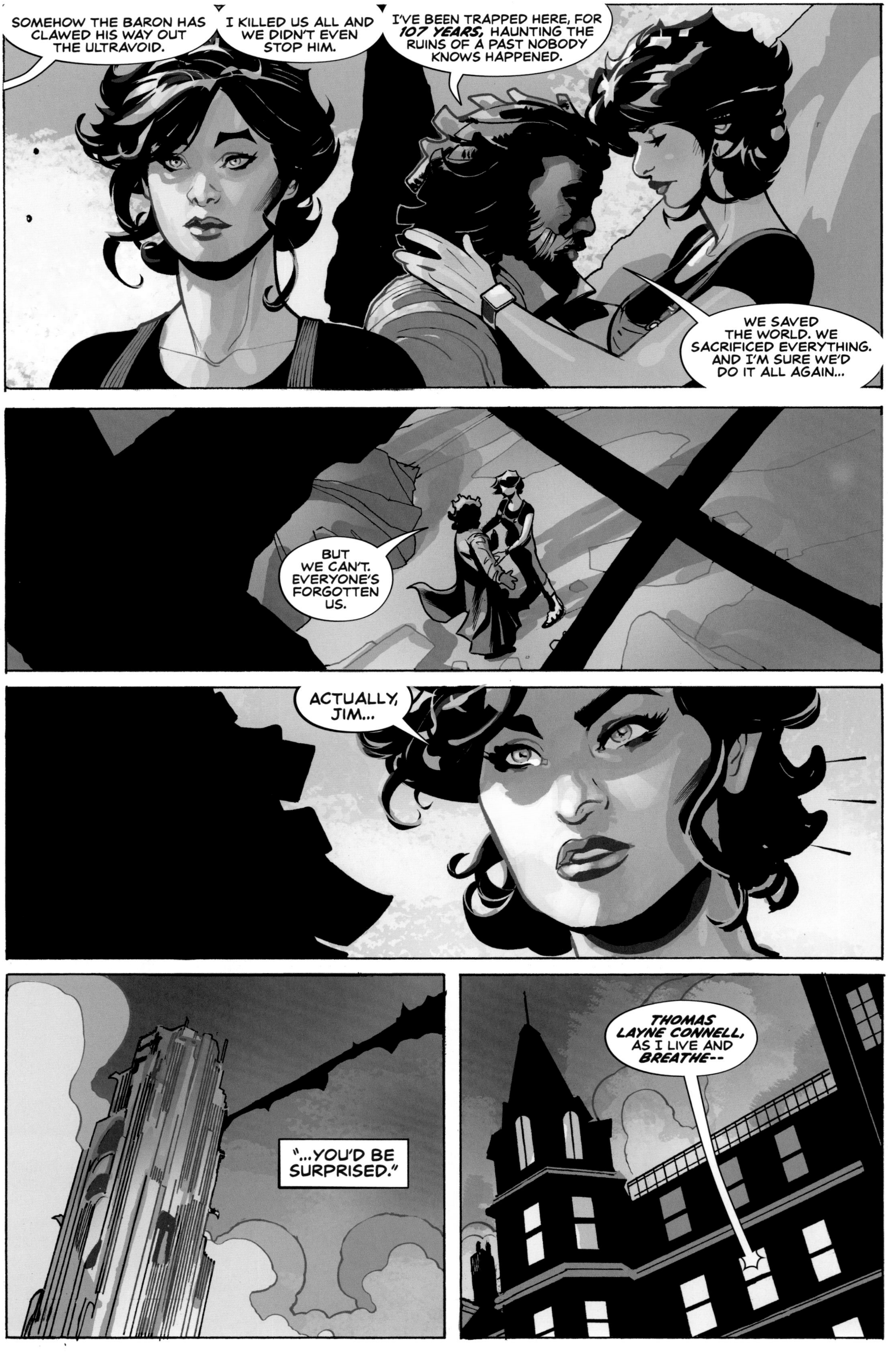
SOMEHOW THE BARON HAS CLAWED HIS WAY OUT THE ULTRAVOID.
I KILLED US ALL AND WE DIDN'T EVEN STOP HIM.
I'VE BEEN TRAPPED HERE, FOR **107 YEARS,** HAUNTING THE RUINS OF A PAST NOBODY KNOWS HAPPENED.
WE SAVED THE WORLD. WE SACRIFICED EVERYTHING. AND I'M SURE WE'D DO IT ALL AGAIN...
BUT WE CAN'T. EVERYONE'S FORGOTTEN US.
ACTUALLY, JIM...
"...YOU'D BE SURPRISED."
THOMAS LAYNE CONNELL, AS I LIVE AND ***BREATHE--***

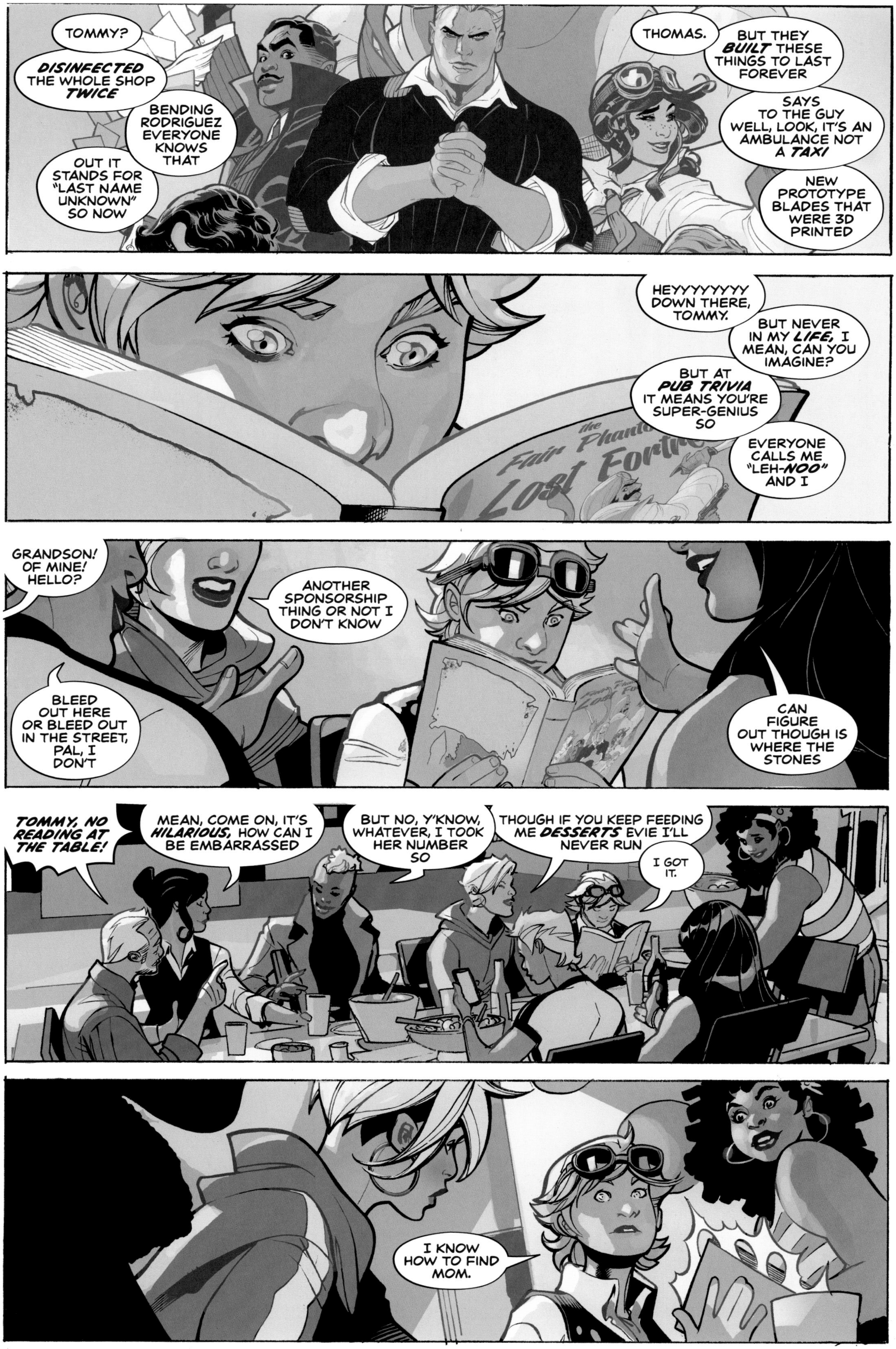
TOMMY?
DISINFECTED THE WHOLE SHOP TWICE
BENDING RODRIGUEZ EVERYONE KNOWS THAT
OUT IT STANDS FOR "LAST NAME UNKNOWN" SO NOW
THOMAS.
BUT THEY BUILT THESE THINGS TO LAST FOREVER
SAYS TO THE GUY WELL, LOOK, IT'S AN AMBULANCE NOT A TAXI
NEW PROTOTYPE BLADES THAT WERE 3D PRINTED
HEYYYYYYYY DOWN THERE, TOMMY.
BUT NEVER IN MY LIFE, I MEAN, CAN YOU IMAGINE?
BUT AT PUB TRIVIA IT MEANS YOU'RE SUPER-GENIUS SO
EVERYONE CALLS ME "LEH-NOO" AND I
GRANDSON! OF MINE! HELLO?
ANOTHER SPONSORSHIP THING OR NOT I DON'T KNOW
BLEED OUT HERE OR BLEED OUT IN THE STREET, PAL, I DON'T
CAN FIGURE OUT THOUGH IS WHERE THE STONES
TOMMY, NO READING AT THE TABLE!
MEAN, COME ON, IT'S HILARIOUS, HOW CAN I BE EMBARRASSED
BUT NO, Y'KNOW, WHATEVER, I TOOK HER NUMBER SO
THOUGH IF YOU KEEP FEEDING ME DESSERTS EVIE I'LL NEVER RUN
I GOT IT.
I KNOW HOW TO FIND MOM.

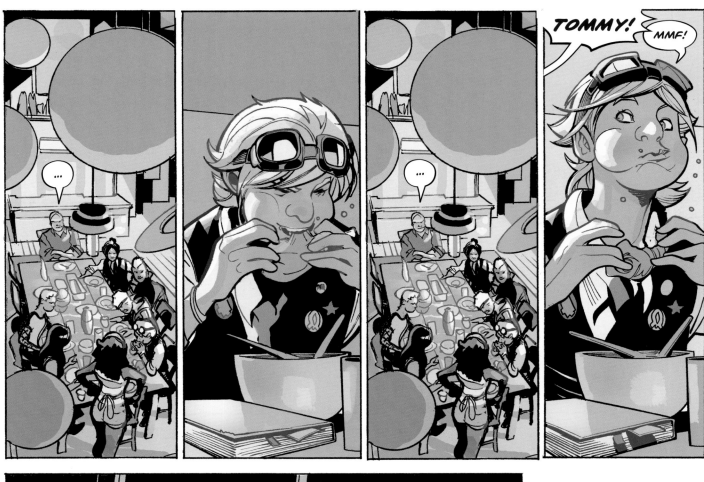

TOMMY!

MMF!

...

...

MOUF FULL. SORRY.

UH. OKAY SO.

SO, UH, IT'S LIKE IN *FAIR PHANTOM OF THE LOST FORTRESS.*

Fair Phantom's Lost Fortress

Y'KNOW. WHERE GENTLEMAN JIM FIRST SHOWS UP?

THE OBLIVIONISTS?

≡SIGH≡ OKAY. AHEM:

The marketplace at high noon was hot and bright and filled with suspicious eyes paying new people too much attention...

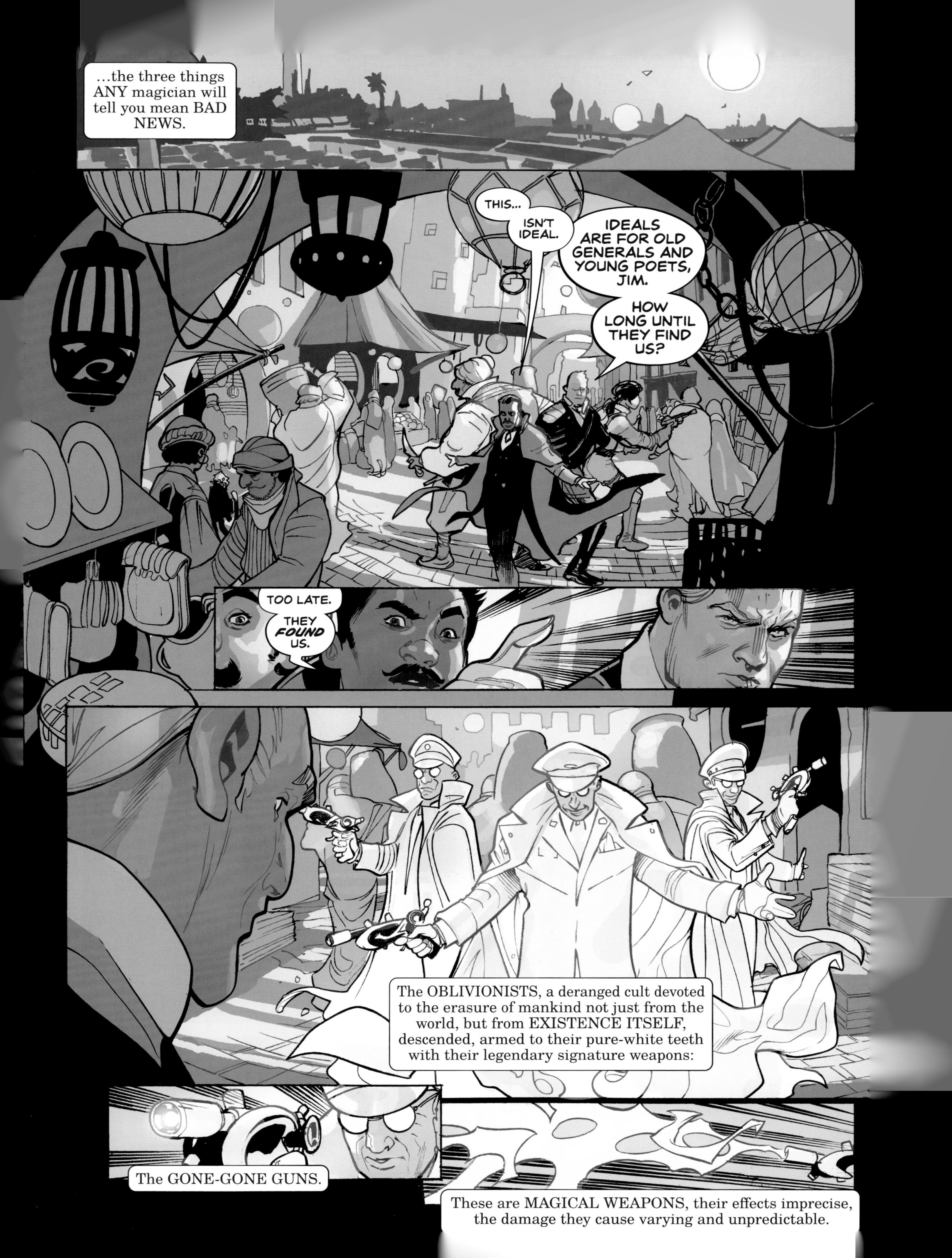
...the three things ANY magician will tell you mean BAD NEWS.
THIS...
ISN'T IDEAL.
IDEALS ARE FOR OLD GENERALS AND YOUNG POETS, JIM.
HOW LONG UNTIL THEY FIND US?
TOO LATE.
THEY *FOUND* US.
The OBLIVIONISTS, a deranged cult devoted to the erasure of mankind not just from the world, but from EXISTENCE ITSELF, descended, armed to their pure-white teeth with their legendary signature weapons:
The GONE-GONE GUNS.
These are MAGICAL WEAPONS, their effects imprecise, the damage they cause varying and unpredictable.

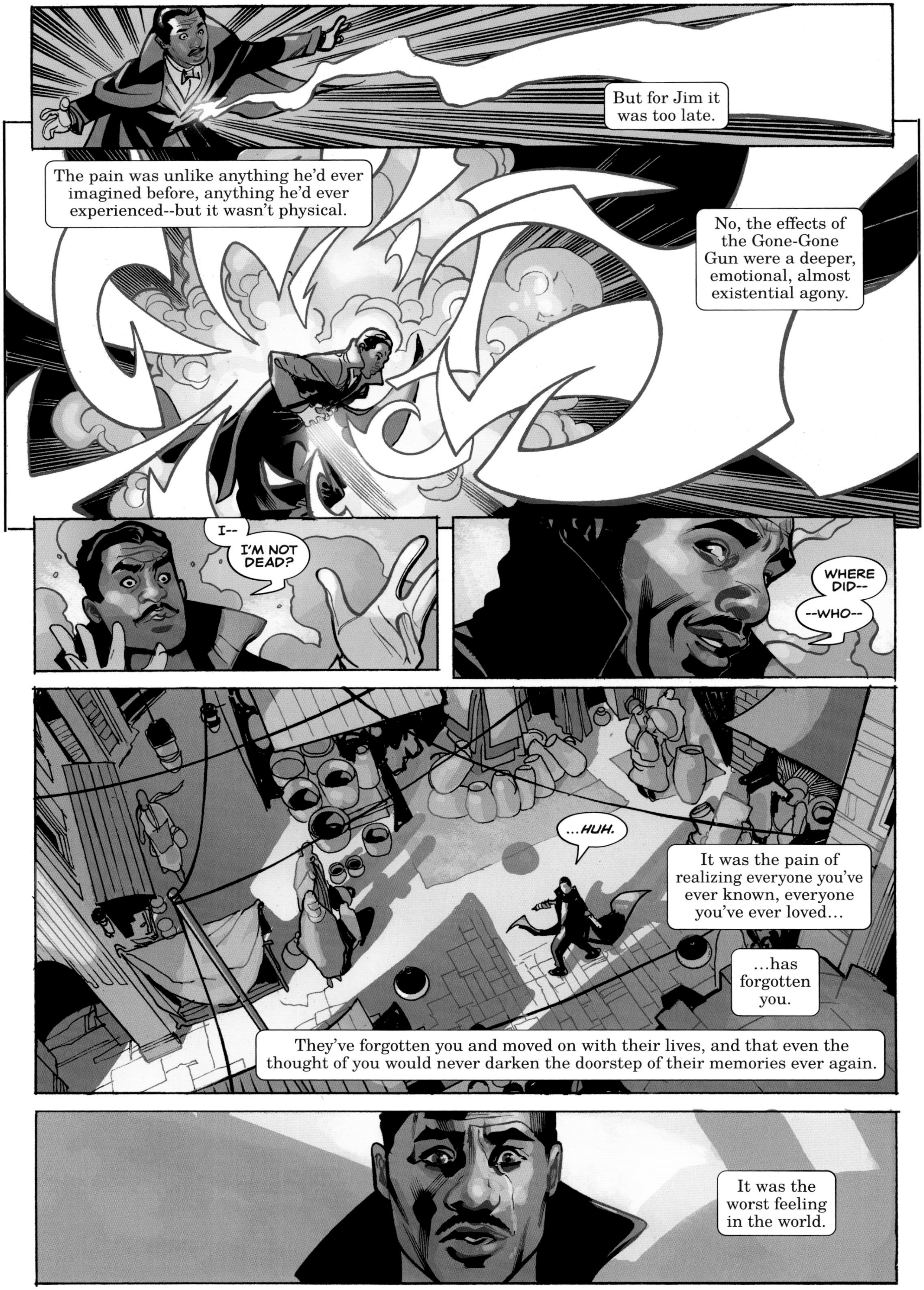
But for Jim it was too late.
The pain was unlike anything he'd ever imagined before, anything he'd ever experienced--but it wasn't physical.
No, the effects of the Gone-Gone Gun were a deeper, emotional, almost existential agony.
I--
I'M NOT DEAD?
WHERE DID--
--WHO--
...HUH.
It was the pain of realizing everyone you've ever known, everyone you've ever loved...
...has forgotten you.
They've forgotten you and moved on with their lives, and that even the thought of you would never darken the doorstep of their memories ever again.
It was the worst feeling in the world.

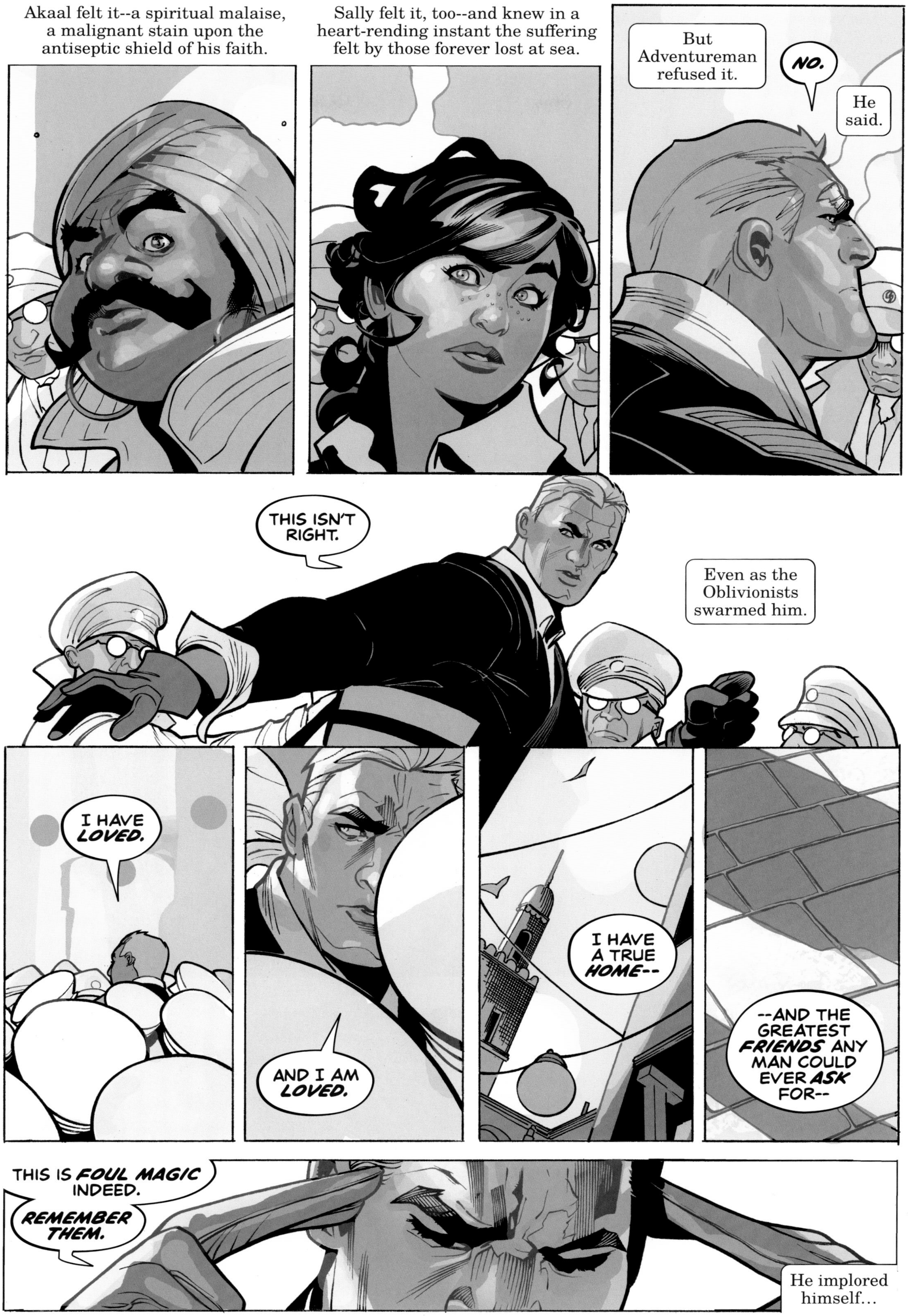

Akaal felt it--a spiritual malaise, a malignant stain upon the antiseptic shield of his faith.
Sally felt it, too--and knew in a heart-rending instant the suffering felt by those forever lost at sea.
But Adventureman refused it.
NO.
He said.
THIS ISN'T RIGHT.
Even as the Oblivionists swarmed him.
I HAVE LOVED.
AND I AM LOVED.
I HAVE A TRUE HOME--
--AND THE GREATEST FRIENDS ANY MAN COULD EVER ASK FOR--
THIS IS FOUL MAGIC INDEED.
REMEMBER THEM.
He implored himself...

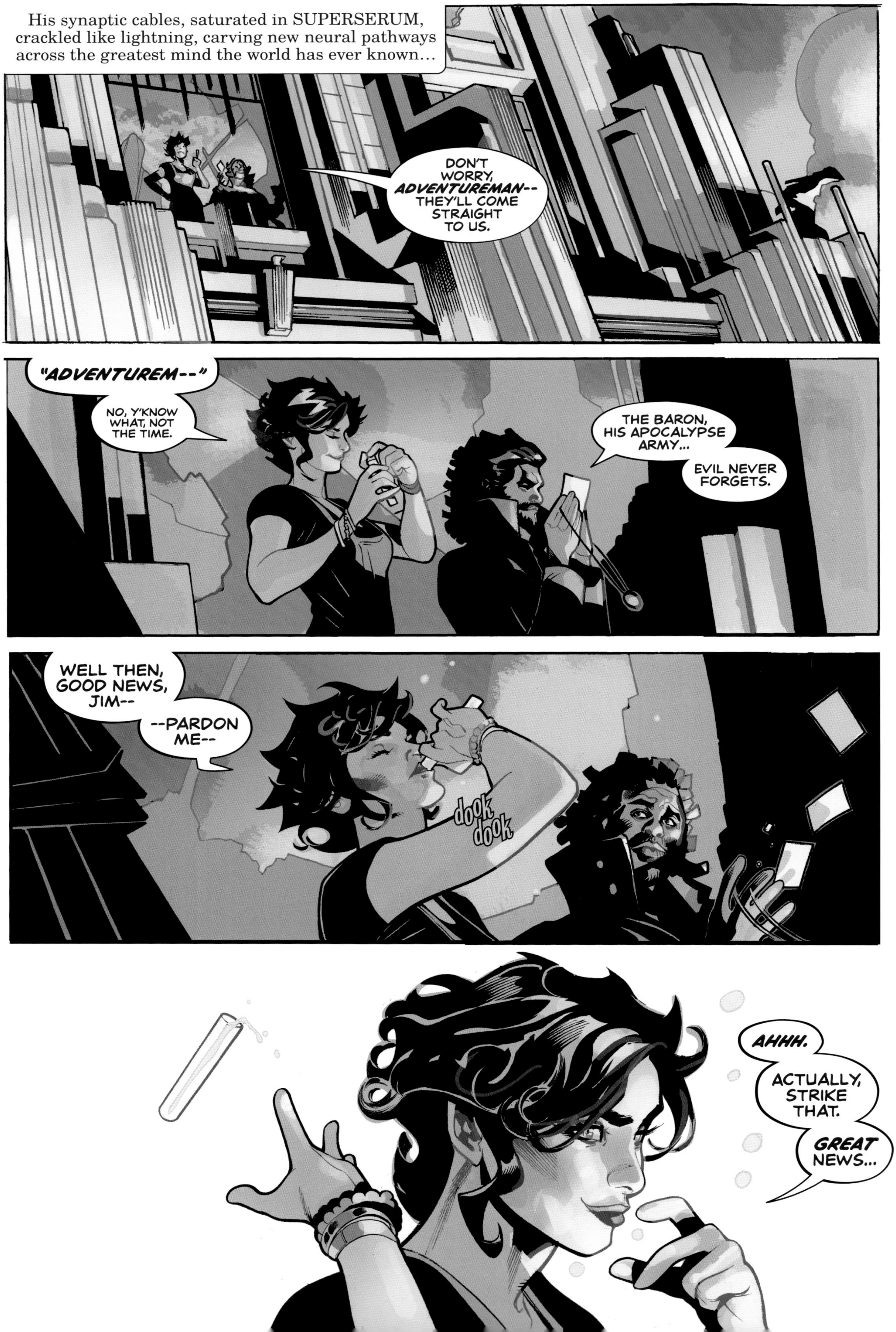

His synaptic cables, saturated in SUPERSERUM, crackled like lightning, carving new neural pathways across the greatest mind the world has ever known…
DON'T WORRY, ADVENTUREMAN-- THEY'LL COME STRAIGHT TO US.
"ADVENTUREM--"
NO, Y'KNOW WHAT, NOT THE TIME.
THE BARON, HIS APOCALYPSE ARMY...
EVIL NEVER FORGETS.
WELL THEN, GOOD NEWS, JIM--
--PARDON ME--
dook dook
AHHH.
ACTUALLY, STRIKE THAT.
GREAT NEWS...

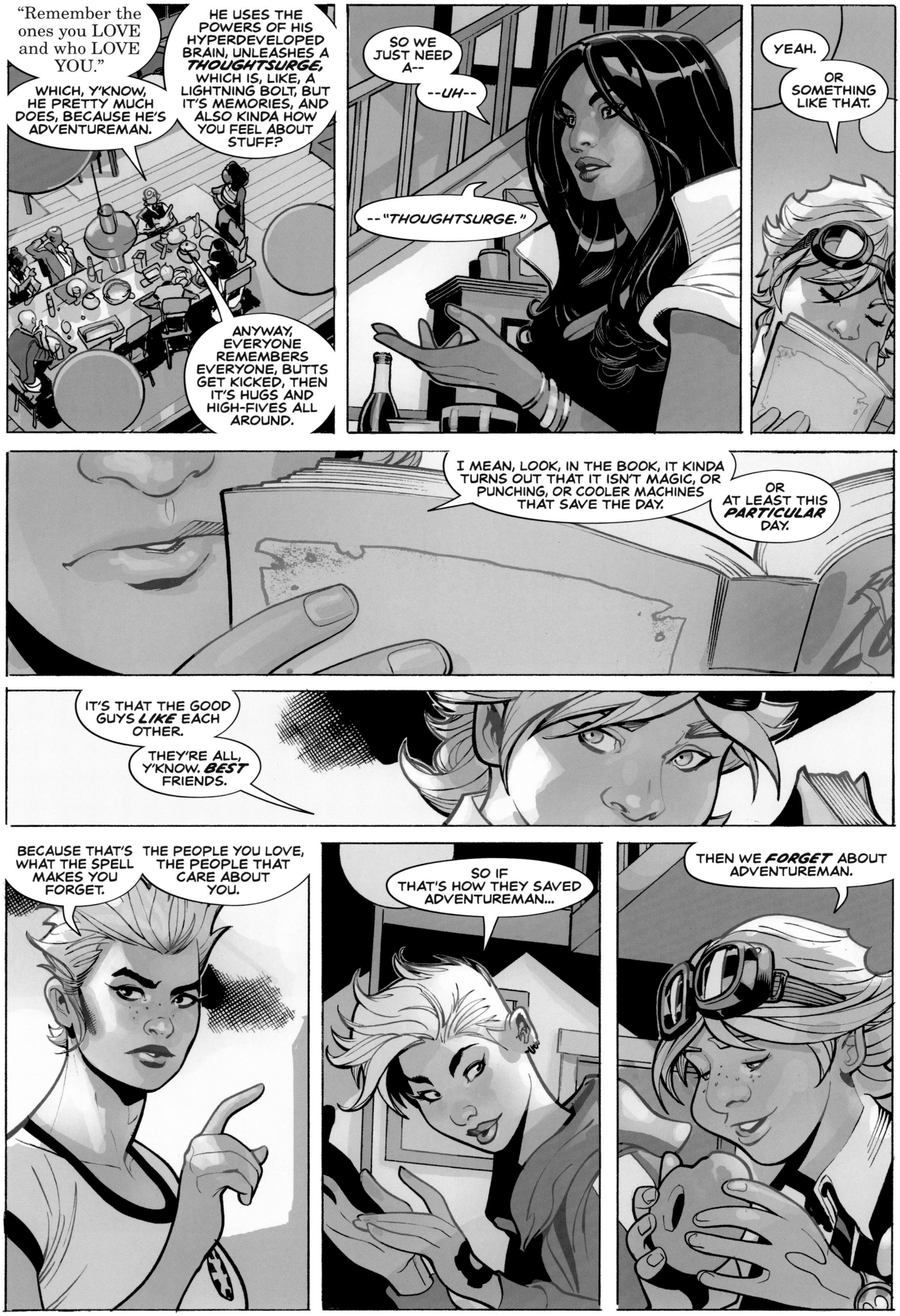
"Remember the ones you LOVE and who LOVE YOU."
WHICH, Y'KNOW, HE PRETTY MUCH DOES, BECAUSE HE'S ADVENTUREMAN.
HE USES THE POWERS OF HIS HYPERDEVELOPED BRAIN, UNLEASHES A *THOUGHTSURGE,* WHICH IS, LIKE, A LIGHTNING BOLT, BUT IT'S MEMORIES, AND ALSO KINDA HOW YOU FEEL ABOUT STUFF?
ANYWAY, EVERYONE REMEMBERS EVERYONE, BUTTS GET KICKED, THEN IT'S HUGS AND HIGH-FIVES ALL AROUND.
SO WE JUST NEED A--
--UH--
--*"THOUGHTSURGE."*
YEAH.
OR SOMETHING LIKE THAT.
I MEAN, LOOK, IN THE BOOK, IT KINDA TURNS OUT THAT IT ISN'T MAGIC, OR PUNCHING, OR COOLER MACHINES THAT SAVE THE DAY.
OR AT LEAST THIS *PARTICULAR* DAY.
IT'S THAT THE GOOD GUYS *LIKE* EACH OTHER.
THEY'RE ALL, Y'KNOW. *BEST* FRIENDS.
BECAUSE THAT'S WHAT THE SPELL MAKES YOU FORGET.
THE PEOPLE YOU LOVE, THE PEOPLE THAT CARE ABOUT YOU.
SO IF THAT'S HOW THEY SAVED ADVENTUREMAN...
THEN WE *FORGET* ABOUT ADVENTUREMAN.

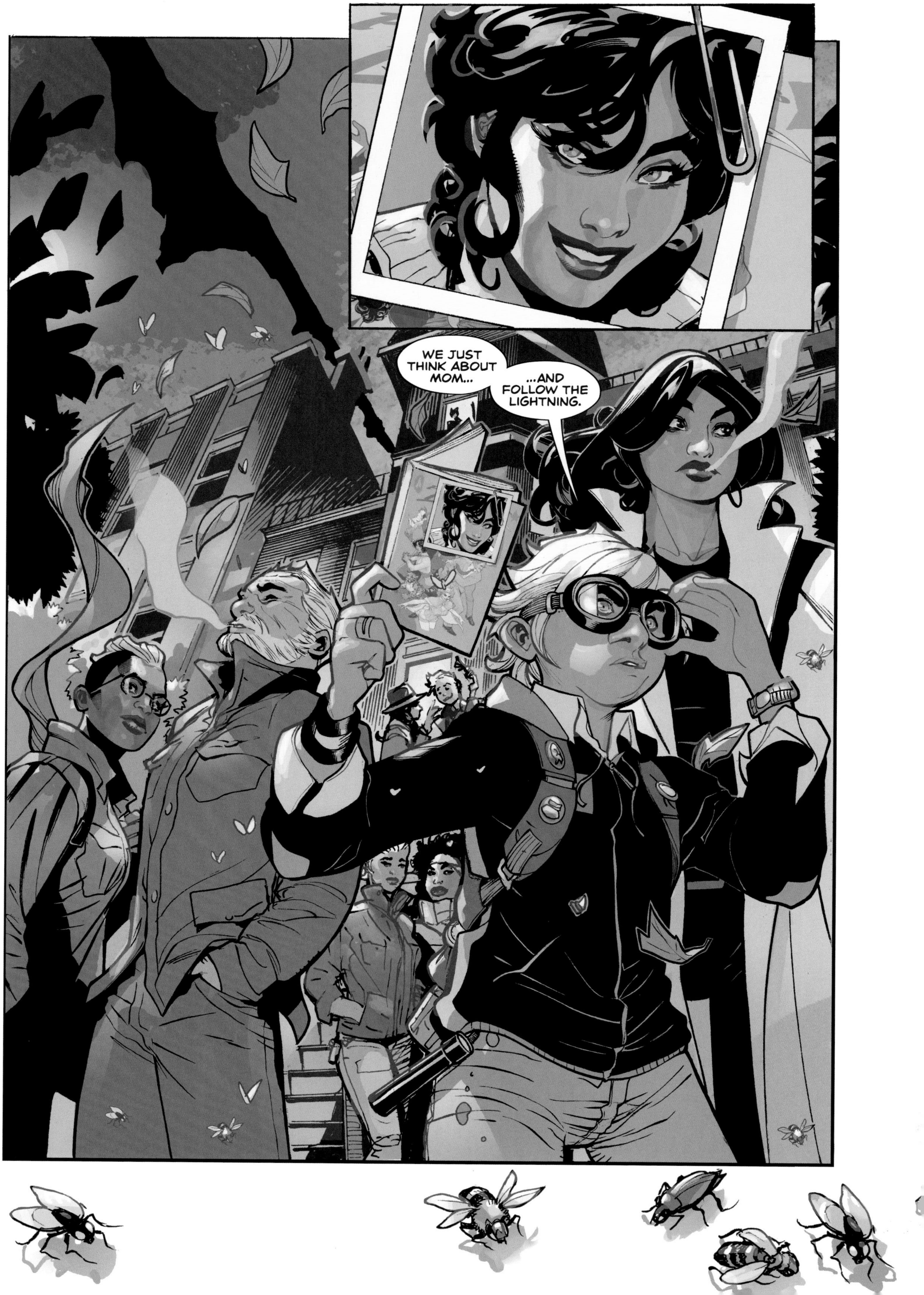
WE JUST THINK ABOUT MOM...
...AND FOLLOW THE LIGHTNING.

THE LONG ROAD FROM PAST TO PRESENT

ADVENTUREMAN™

ORIGIN STORY

WORDS BY MATT FRACTION
ART BY TERRY DODSON

The origins of ***ADVENTUREMAN!***, for me, started with the gift of working with Terry and Rachel on ***UNCANNY X-MEN*** around 2008. I learned a lot from that book -- most important, how much I enjoyed working with **Team Dodson** (second-most important: don't write X-Men). It feels like we maybe promised each other around then that, one day, we'd figure something out together to do as an original project, when we could take our time and get it right. Whatever we were gonna do, whatever world we wanted to build together, we wanted to build well and right (as evidenced by our eagerness to start talking about ADVENTUREMAN! far before we were ready for print, and evidenced yet again by how good the pages you've just read look). Take ALL the words and all my nonsense out: the caliber of work **Terry** and **Rachel** [and **Clayton Cowles**, letterer supreme, and **Leonardo Olea** who designs the books so gorgeously] have done here simply can't exist on the meatgrinder schedule work for hire conglomerate comics demand.

FIRST CLAIRE SKETCH FROM 2011.

Writer and pal **Greg Thompson** gave me a copy of **Philip José Farmer's *DOC SAVAGE: HIS APOCALYPTIC LIFE***. A concordance-biography of **Lester Dent's *MAN OF BRONZE***, it's kind of like a pocket encyclopedia that tracks all of Doc's adventures, powers, friends, foes, etc. (Farmer did one for Tarzan, too.) Along with **Kingsley Amis' *THE BOOK OF BOND*** (another favorite of mine, leave me alone, I'm weird) which does the same thing for 007 (under the auspices of being a How-To).

In 2009, I left Kansas City, MO and moved to Portland, OR. The last movie I saw in KC, alongside writer/party uncle **Chris Sebela**, was **Pete Docter's *UP***. I mention this because all the stuff with **Christopher Plummer's** character, the old colonial adventurer living lost to history, stuck with me. That guy is still out there. What if he came back now?

5.19.15

FIRST DEFINITIVE LOOK FOR ADVENTUREMAN.

At some point, those strands of thinking all tied together. In my head, it was when I got into Sebela's car after the movie. And the idea of naming the hero in such a definitively masculine way but having the new incarnation of that hero be a woman, was there too; that the modern incarnation of the character would be everything the Pulp heroes, at their imperial/colonial/and sexist worst, couldn't be, or weren't.

So I had **Claire**, right away. The last name changed a couple times, but Claire was always Claire. And what's interesting (to me, sitting here looking at the dates and times on these files, anyway) is that she was hard of hearing right away. Until now, when I made myself go through it all and think it through, I would've sworn my work with another hard-of-hearing character, **Clint Barton** in ***HAWKEYE***, predated Claire. But this book was cooking a couple years before Hawkeye -- the thinking about how to portray deafness in comics started for me with ADVENTUREMAN! and that I'd happen to get to write Hawkeye as hard of hearing meant those ideas were cooking in these pages first. Huh.

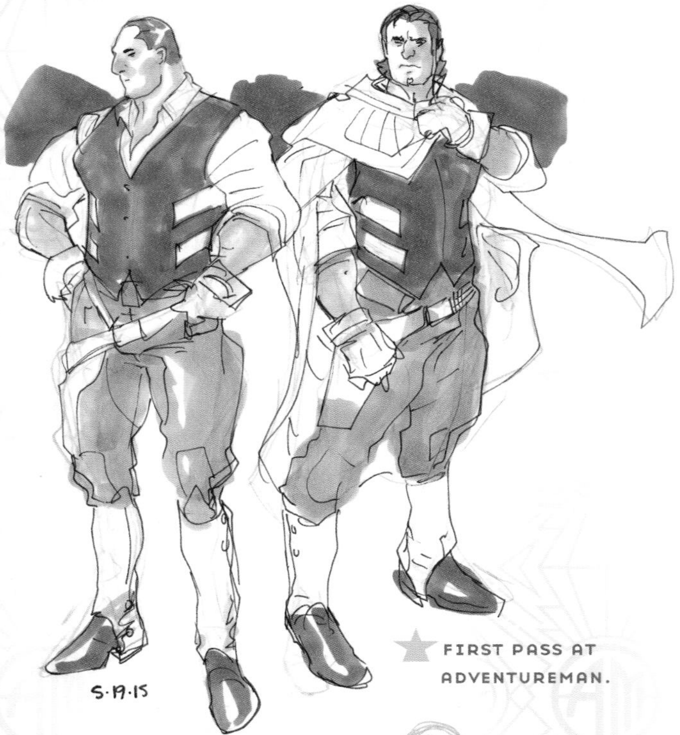
5.19.15

FIRST PASS AT ADVENTUREMAN.

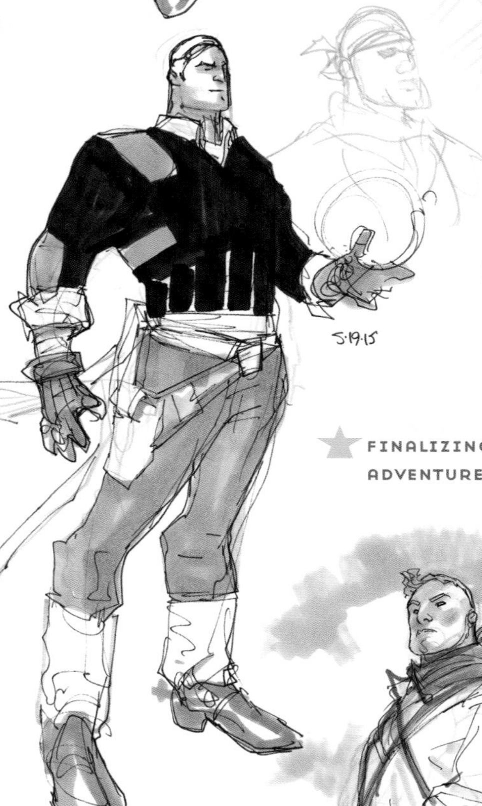
5.19.15

FINALIZING ADVENTUREMAN.

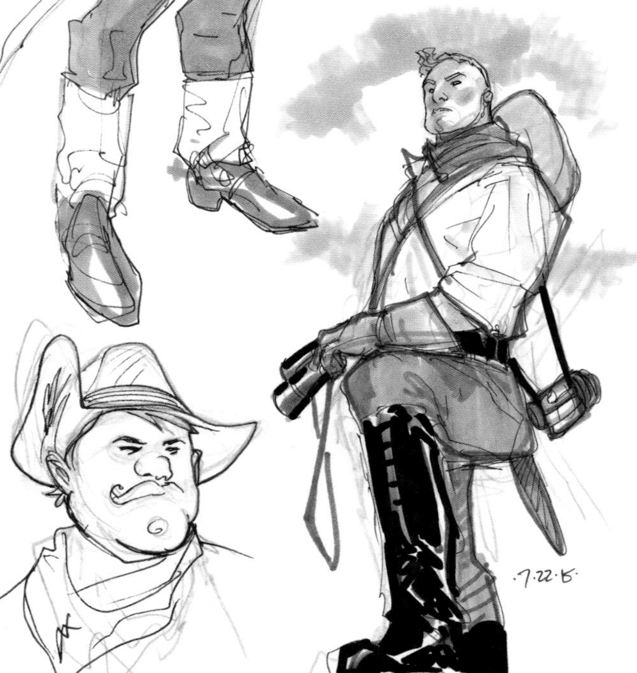
7.22.15

SAFARI ADVENTUREMAN.

Beyond that, I knew she was a single mother. I knew she had a big family. I knew she was one of seven adopted sisters. And I think I had the scooter -- although if you told me Terry gave her the scooter and I wrote into it, that wouldn't surprise me.

The earliest document I can find in the ADVENTUREMAN! file is dated 2009, so that all fits. I left Missouri for Oregon with the Farmer in my back pocket and ADVENTUREMAN! taking root in my head.

Most times when I have an idea, I'm not sure right away if it's a story-sized idea or a series-sized idea. With ADVENTUREMAN! though, I knew right away -- this was a world the Dodsons and I could live in, and make a meal out of, and tell as many stories about this adventurer reborn as we wanted, for a long as we liked.

Ideas like that, cats and kittens, are worth their weight in gold.

To start in the middle of end of the past -- to give it half our first issue! -- meant we had to develop, define, and design not just the world of the original ADVENTUREMAN!, but we needed to develop, define, and design his entire supporting cast of characters. And the bad guys. And all their stuff.

AND THEN WE WERE LEAVING IT ALL BEHIND.

Sort of.

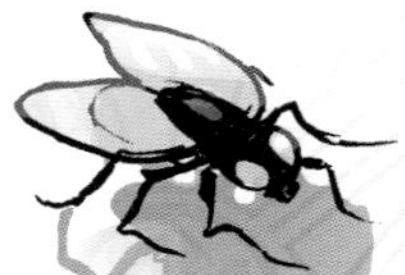

THE FORGOTTEN GENERATION

I'm a pulp fiction dilletante and can't claim anything more than a casual familiarity with the pulp world (for my money, for prosody, pacing, and just-plain bonkers plotting, you can't beat ***THE SPIDER***, especially the ones written by **Norvell Page**. ***THE SPIDER VS THE EMPIRE STATE and CITY OF DOOM*** are a blast and have a samurai movie-level body count). And while I may have been born yesterday, I stayed up all night -- I used Farmer as my guide.

Doc had a crew, so **Adventureman** would have a crew. As the pulp magazines laid out so many of our adventure archetypes, I steered into that. There'd be a brawler, a pilot, a scientist, a mystic and the like. Doc's crew was made up of **Monk**, a chemist; **Ham**, a lawyer-swordsman (as one does); **Renny**, a two-fisted engineer; **Long Tom Roberts** the pilot; and **Johnny**, the archeologist with a large vocabulary. The Spider ran with **Nita van Sloan**, his fianceé and one-time replacement; **Ram Singh**, the knife-weilding manservant (sigh); Sgt. Ronald Jackson, his chauffer; **Harold Jeykins**, a proto-Pennyworth; and **Kirk**, his proto-Jim Gordon. There were others, of course; you get the idea.

Something else that appealed to me about "doing" Pulp was having the chance to reclaim some of the ignorance too much entertainment of that era carries: the racist, sexist, colonial, imperial nonsense that makes so much of pop culture's past hard to stomach at best. It would start in how we created the supporting cast in the past, and Claire's family in the present. Who they were, what they looked like, spoke, behaved and were treated by one another became as paramount as what they did within the story itself. We created our casts -- in each era -- with rich backstories and worlds and adventures of their own and, as time goes on and more ADVENTUREMAN! sees print, the more of those stories we'll learn. It doesn't seem like beginning with the ambition of presenting a group of men and women racially and ethnically diverse, with a diverse array of body-types and histories as the best in the world at what they do, who would sacrifice themselves to save the world in anonymous heroism should be any kind of great victory. At the same time, compared to some pulp material, it's downright revolutionary.

It's a start, anyway.

I want to share this, from the original ADVENTUREMAN! #1 plot document, with a few edits for spoilers and coherence:

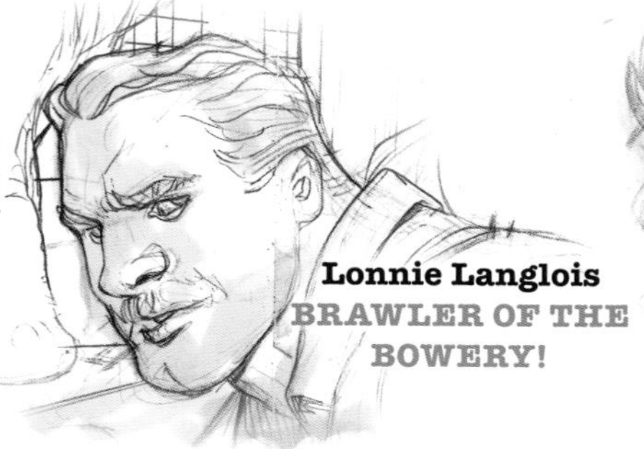

Lonnie Langlois
BRAWLER OF THE BOWERY!

A great big slab of fighting Irish guy that came from a prominent and wealthy family on the upper West Side. He split with them once he fell in love with the Sweet Science though. The kind of boxer that does 12 rounds then goes and fights at underground clubs after and reads French philosophy and poetry. T[redacted]

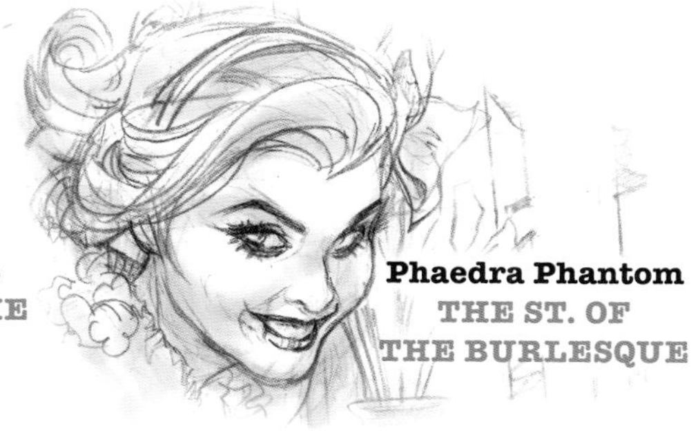

Phaedra Phantom
THE ST. OF THE BURLESQUE

A burlesque girl turned protector of society's unfortunates, Lily St. Cyr as con woman and vigilante,[redacted] She rattles off battle-bander a mile-a-minute. She can seemingly vanish, to turn into smoke and phase through walls, all while firing off her ferocious GHOST GUNS. Pale white, Phaedra may actually be a ghost of a murdered showgirl...

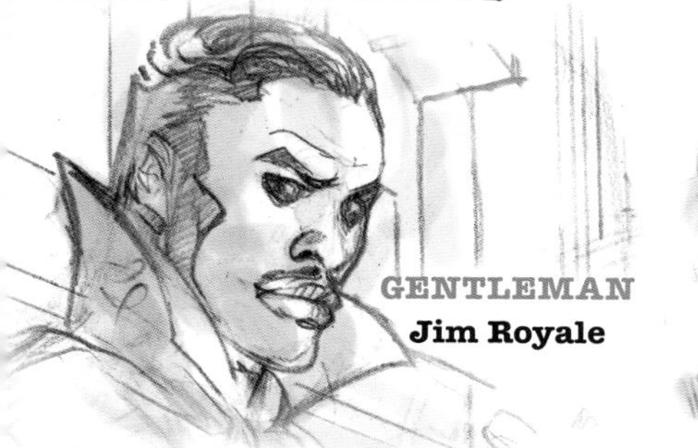

GENTLEMAN
Jim Royale

Master of arcane mysteries and close magic. One eyebrow would seem permanently arched[redacted] He could easily have slept in his tux. He hasn't shaved in a week. Always wears a waistcoat and can seemingly procure anything from within it. (As an aside, I named this character after my friend, the late Jim Royal, an artist, inker, father and friend gone too soon. Giving him immortality in the pages of the artform he loved seemed as good a way as any to tell him goodbye.)

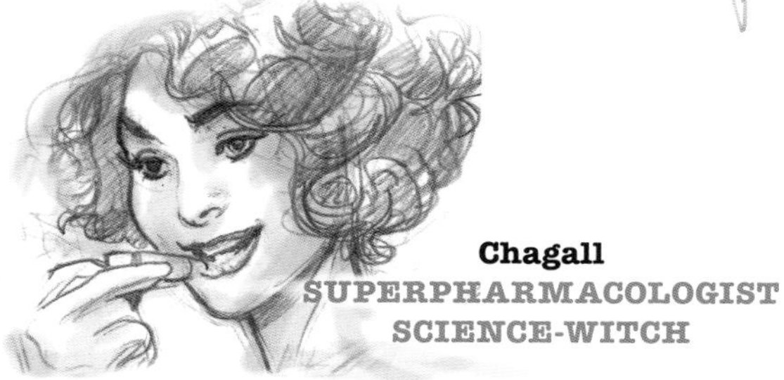

Chagall
SUPERPHARMACOLOGIST SCIENCE-WITCH

Our science-adventurer,[redacted]white labcoat (fur lined!), red shirt, and white slacks, might be a perfect outfit. She's a chemist and superpharmacologist -- preparer of Adventureman's Superelixr. There's an unspoken understanding that she and Adventureman are a couple; psychologically this maybe affects the closeness to which they stand or their physical comfort around one another but there's no outward indications -- no kisses or hand-holding or anything.

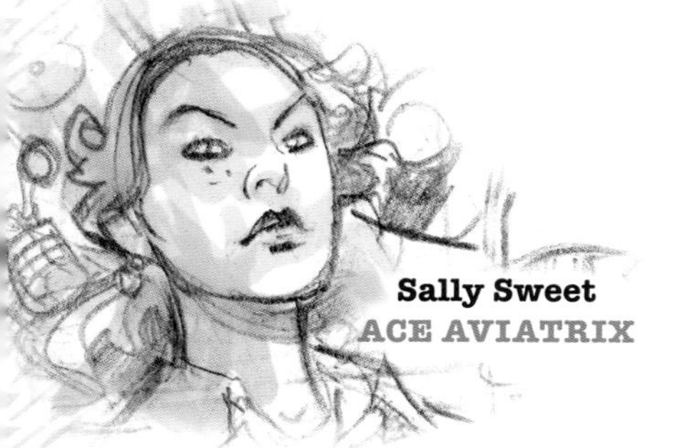

Sally Sweet
ACE AVIATRIX

The Magnificent Matron of the Morning, the Sweet Sister of the Skies, Sally's never seen a machine she couldn't drive or pilot. A barnstormer turned Canadian fighter pilot in the first World War (women weren't allowed to fly for the states) she was our Red Baron before the Armistice. She's[redacted]

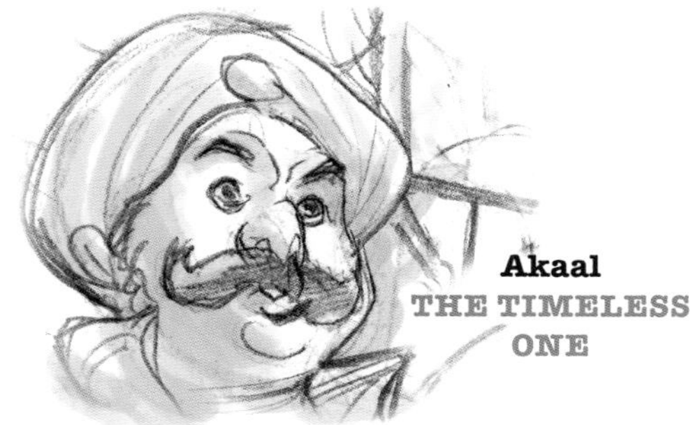

Akaal
THE TIMELESS ONE

A Sikh superkiller from the Punjab regions. He believes that positive actions in this life is the key to salvation and peace; he believes he must help to make this life more worthwhile. A human balancer of the scales.[redacted]He is pragmatic and realistic in all things and usually clashes, good-naturedly, with The Gentleman.

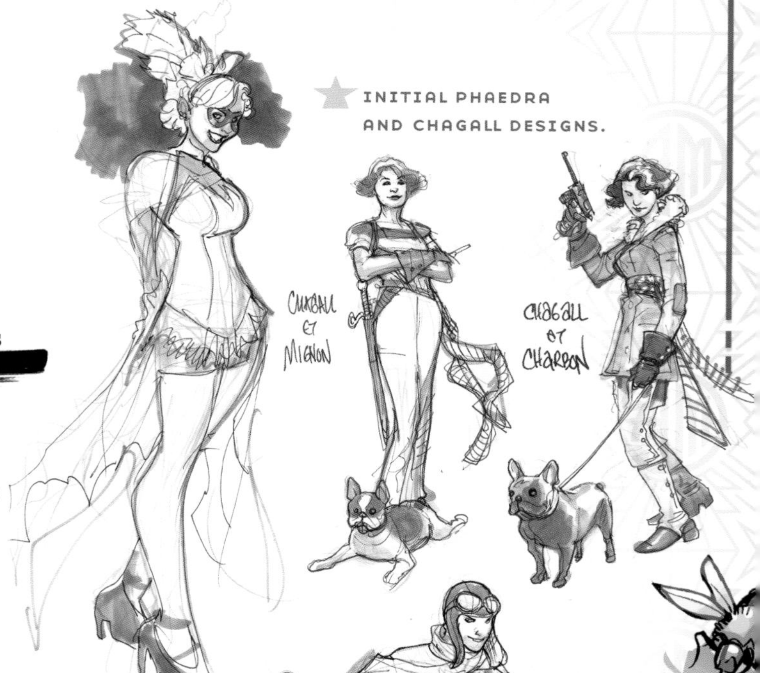

CHAGALL ET MIGNON
CHAGALL ET CHARRON

INITIAL PHAEDRA AND CHAGALL DESIGNS.

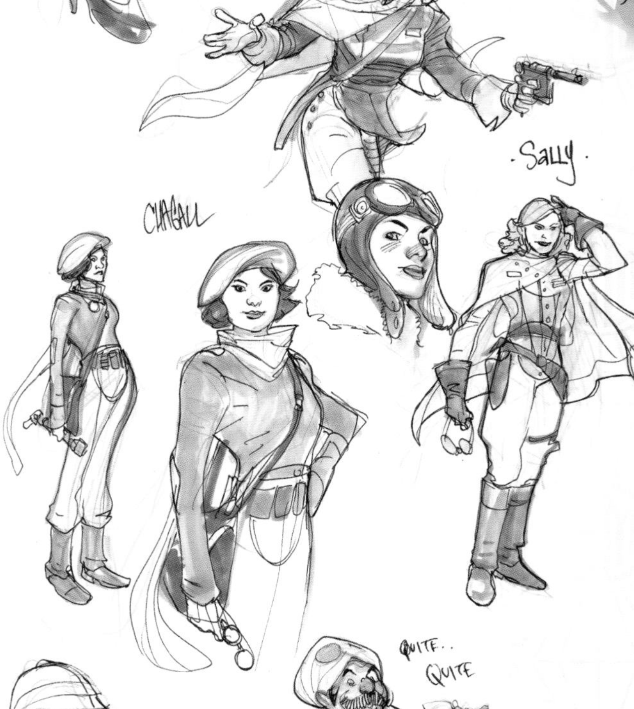

CHAGALL
SALLY

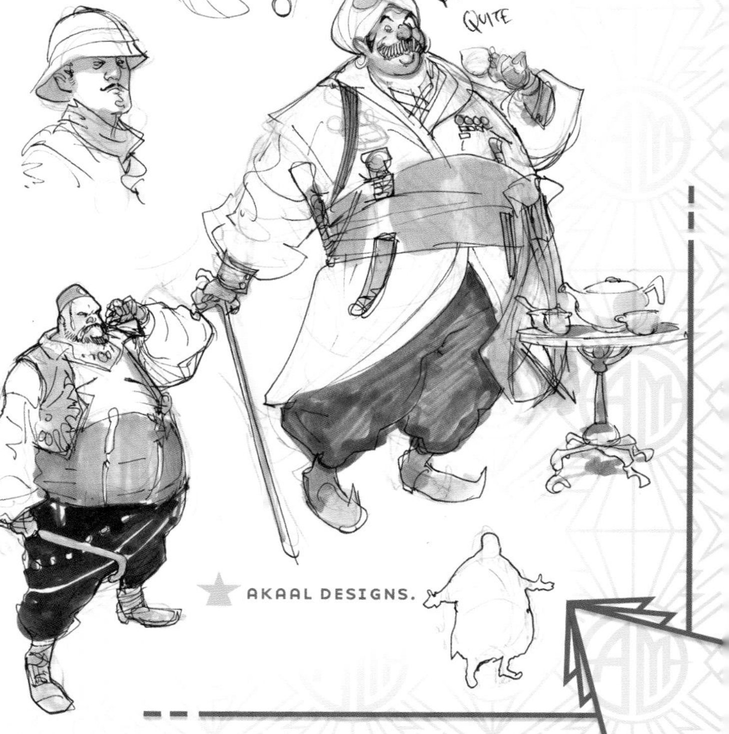

QUITE.. QUITE

AKAAL DESIGNS.

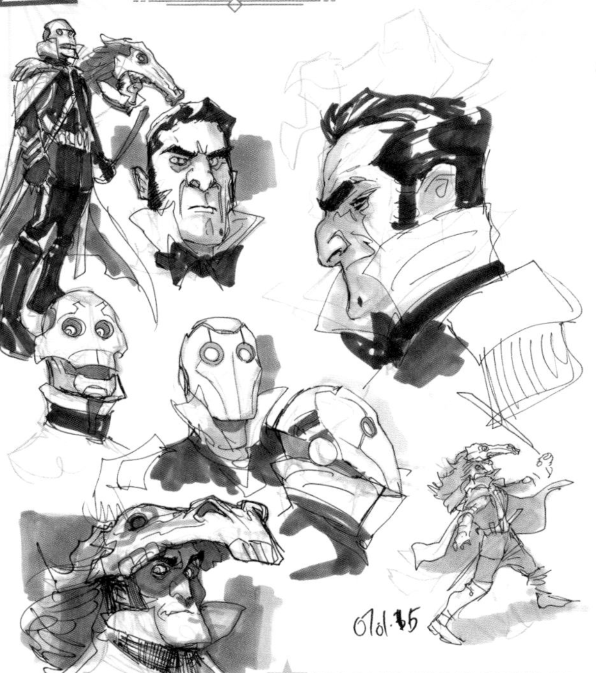

VARIOUS INCARNATIONS OF BARON BIZARRE.

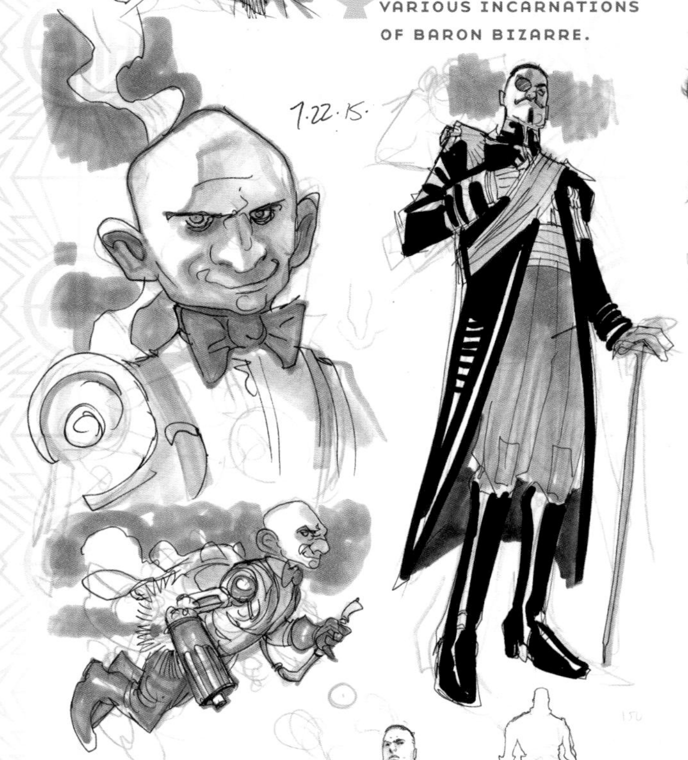
7.22.15.

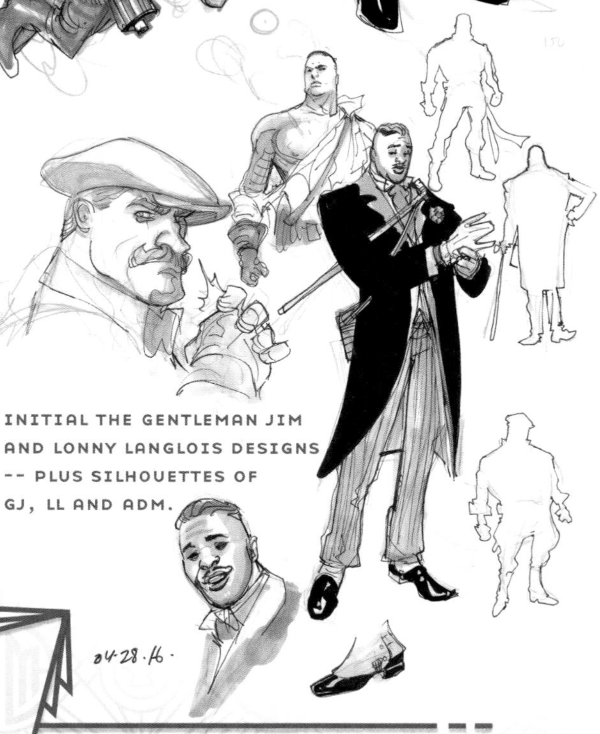

INITIAL THE GENTLEMAN JIM AND LONNY LANGLOIS DESIGNS -- PLUS SILHOUETTES OF GJ, LL AND ADM.

The bad guys would be opposite numbers -- but also, like, Nazis pirates from hell? That were also bugs? Here's their initial descriptions...

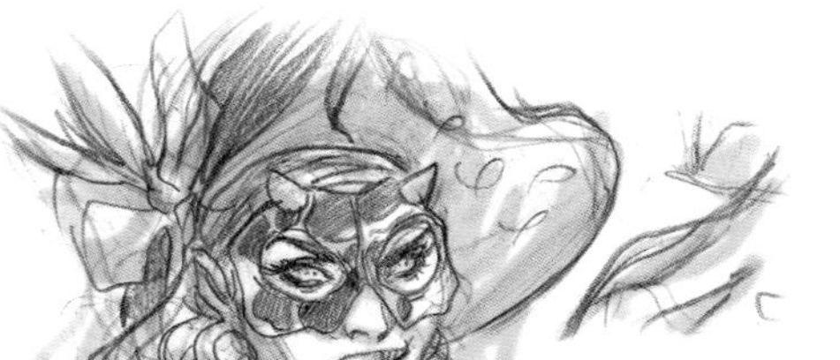

BARONESS BIZARRE

Would she be his bride? I suppose so. The bride of the Bad Guy. [redacted], she should definitely have military touches to her outfit. Or maybe not. Maybe like Fletcher Hanks' FANTOMAH, she's got a bombshell body and GILDA head of hair and a skull for a face. Maybe she wears insane gowns like in the film MADAME SATAN (http://bit.ly/1VbRTey which... Which I'm kinda loving...).

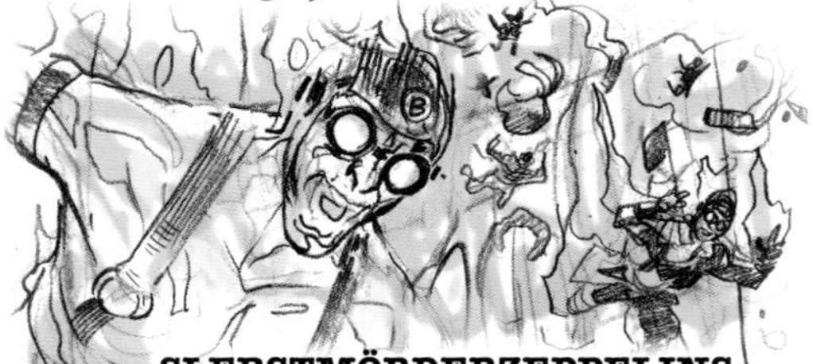

SLEBSTMÖRDERZEPPELINS /THE OFENDÄMON

SO these are the great big Suicide Zepplins that are piloted by insane kamikaze-like dudes. The zeppelins are like deliberate Hindenbergs but after they ignite, their pilots are REBORN as OFENDÄMON—sorta literally furnace demons—like burning zombies in Baron Bizarre-approved pilot garb. So we should get a hint of a suicide-zep in the distance, and these guys sorta leaping out of them, ready to fight.

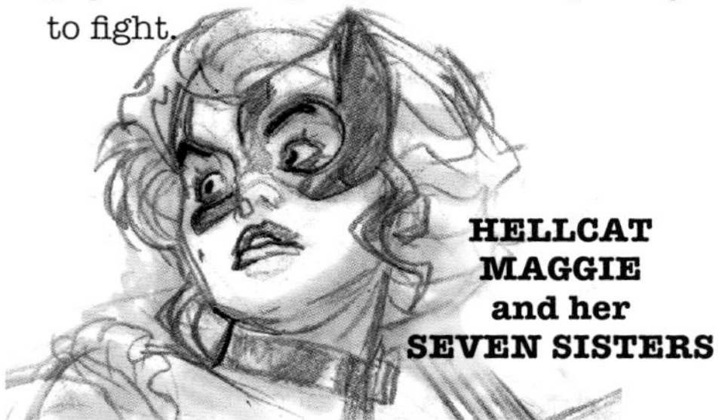

HELLCAT MAGGIE and her SEVEN SISTERS

"Hellcat Maggie" was real; or at least, people claim she was real, and was a member of the Dead Rabbits gang of Five Points (she had a blink-and-you'll-miss-her cameo in GANGS OF NEW YORK). She (it's been said) wore on each hand a pair of leather gloves she outfitted with steel claws or razors on the fingertips. I like the idea of Maggie and the Sisters being [redacted] And similar outfits and styles of dress—I guess maybe like a bloodthirsty version of your Coraline.

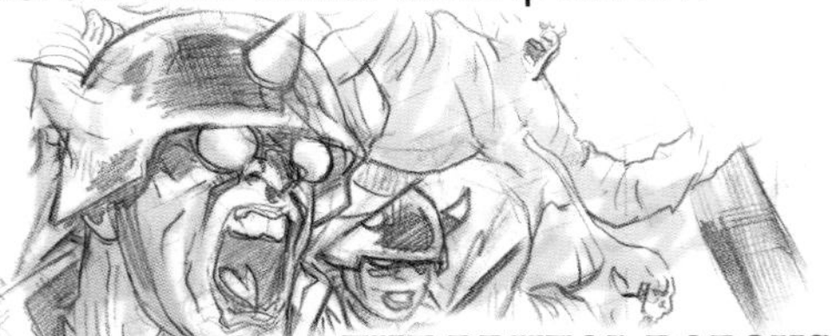

THE BRUTAL BARONS /BARONETTES

BB/Ms. BB's flunkies and thugs. The footsoldiers of the Bizarrmy. I just thought about Catwoman's thugs on the old BATMAN TV show, with the tiger-stripe blazers and the weird ear hats? These should be her, like, personal security phalanx. Maybe the Baronettes are like a roller derby team of Lady Linebackers, half-cheerleader, half-thug squad.

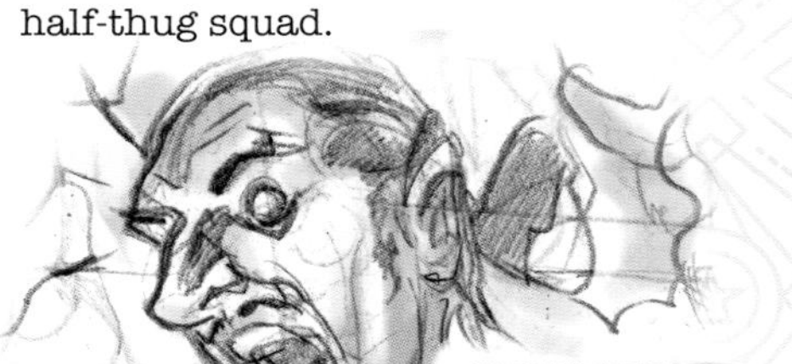

SLUGGER DUMPHEE

Sorta the nightmare bizarro (err... Bizarre) version of Lonnie—a living Mr. Hyde wall of a violent nightmare. Or maybe we go the opposite way—maybe he's like one of those early boxers, whip thin with a mustache, and gnarly, magically-enhanced, brass knuckles... either way: this dude's a fighter, a brawler. Crazy strong, whether he looks it or not.

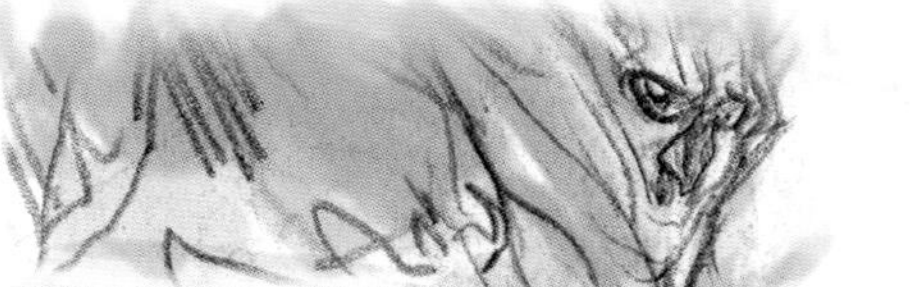

THE METAMAGE

Can, uh—this was supposed to be, y'know, their Arcane Occult Warrior guy—what if it's just, like, a giant eyeball with tentacles? What if it used to be a man but now is more like a monster? What if it has ten-thousand mouths and hovers and radiates weird ultraviolet light...? Something more like an HP Lovecraft-ian entity than a Voldemoort...

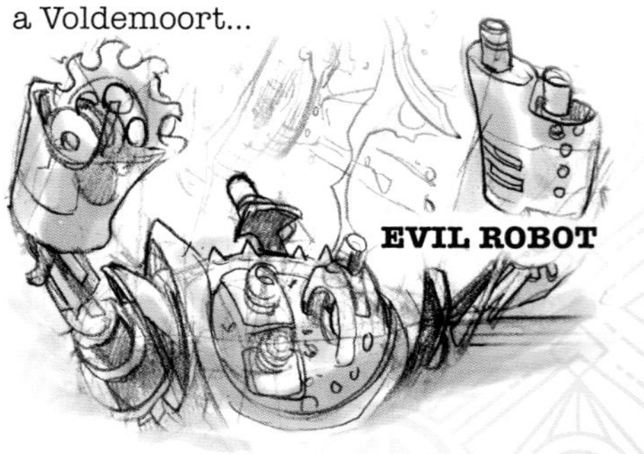

EVIL ROBOT

...is an evil robot.

So -- so we're playing in the realm of lawyer-swordsman, right? Right. Something occurred to me early on in the writing process, and I realized it would be the primary joy of playing in the world of ADVENTUREMAN!, and I'm going to share it with you now: Everything fits.

I didn't know what ANY of that stuff meant when I typed it; it just came out. I didn't know what the Berserker Bible was, or the big clock (the name of it changed until our literal last pass of lettering, when I finally landed on APOCALYPSYDRA). I didn't know where the bugs were coming from or what they meant. I stood out of the way and dreamed it all out of my fingertips in real time and trusted Terry and I would figure out why it mattered and what it did later (also I trusted Terrya would make it look amazing). It sounds funny but somewhere along the way, ADVENTUREMAN! became an exercise in pure imagination and let's-pretend and makin'-stuff-up.

And after all this time I am SO glad we're finally able to share all that let's-pretend with you.

LETTERHEAD
ADVENTUREMAN

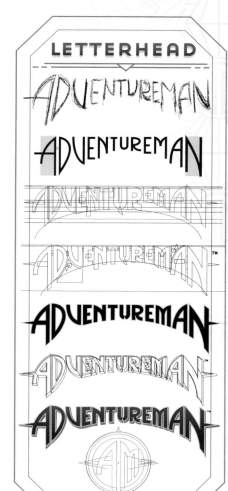

SOME OF THE PROCESS OF ADVENTUREMAN'S LOGO FROM HAND TO VECTORS BY OLEA.

FUTURE ALERT!

Gentle implications towards future stories lie ahead. Not quite spoilers but at the same time... not NOT spoilers. So if you're spoiler-adverse (to the point of, say, not even wanting to see a movie trailer), maybe come back to this section after, oh, the next couple volumes..

FAMILY

As a friend's daughter approached the age of her bat-mitzvah, she started to interrogate what it meant to her to be Jewish and what the rituals and ceremony of her faith meant to her. One part of this for her meant she wanted to honor the tradition of dinner on Shabbat Eve -- Friday nights -- and so a tradition among a cluster of us, friends and family, found or otherwise, began.

I was raised irreligious, you could say; I'm also an only child. The idea of a meal steeped in an observance of faith at a table with a dozen people, with maybe a dozen more with plates on their laps in the living room was all new to me when it became a semi-recurring event in my life.

So much of ADVENTUREMAN is about this great big Connell family; the idea of a mandatory Shabbat dinner, though, came from those Fridays spent with a great big bunch of people over all kinds of food, all of us shouting over one another and catching up and simply being together.

A great big dinner scene gave us a great chance to throw all the Connell girls around a dinner table and have 'em start doing exactly that by way of introduction. It also meant throwing ourselves into the middle of a scene with... nine characters all at once.

Adventure Family
SHOT / PAGE KEY
PAGE 36
PAGE 37
PAGE 38
PAGE 39
PAGE 40
REGGIE
DAD
EMPTY
EVIE
RITA
URSULA

Here's the floor plan I thumbnailed for myself during the writing. It represents where you'd put your actors (the circles in the center of ovals = heads on top of shoulders) and where you'd put the cameras (the little angle signs that look like Vs). Terry took it one step further and added thumbnails of the characters to help us both keep track. I am horrible with names in real life; in stuff I write I am, somehow, even worse. So this was AWESOME.

I even think that, to make things more complicated, a couple of the sisters' names changed a few times. Uh, so did the "Connell" surname. I am a joy to work with tell everyone you know.

ADVENTURE FAMILY GUIDE.

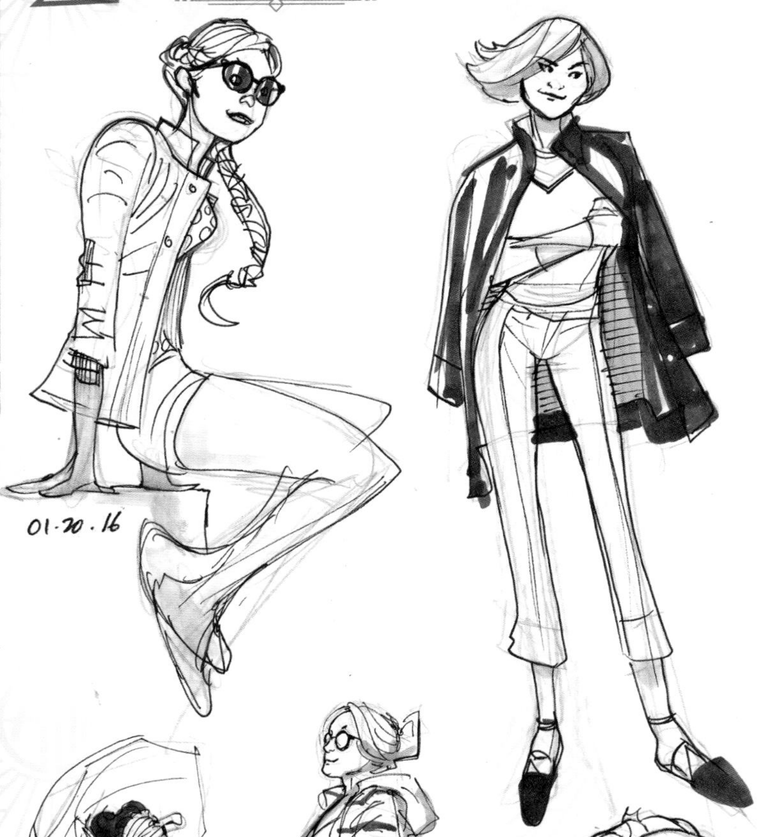
01.20.16

The work started with Terry exploring character, and that meant sketching to find who these women were. We knew we wanted a group at that Shabbat night table as diverse as the heroes that stood and fell with Adventureman in the past -- since the **Connell sisters** were brought together by adoption there was literally no reason to do otherwise.

(At one point in the Shabbat scene in issue 1 there were... four different languages spoken around the table? Our initial editor Lauren Sankovitch did the hard work of finding speakers willing to help us out, Clayton even lettered it as specified. Getting it all right though ended up spooking me and I changed it back.)

I'm as inspired by Terry's drawings as I think he gets from whatever half-understandable blather I write. Having the chance to watch him daydream through a pencil-tip helps grow and inform who these people would become.

Part of the agony of this book -- and part, honestly, of the reason these early issues have been so big -- is that we have so much of this world in our heads and we want all of it out now. All of these remarkable women have stories we can't wait to tell. Even here we only have space for five of 'em...

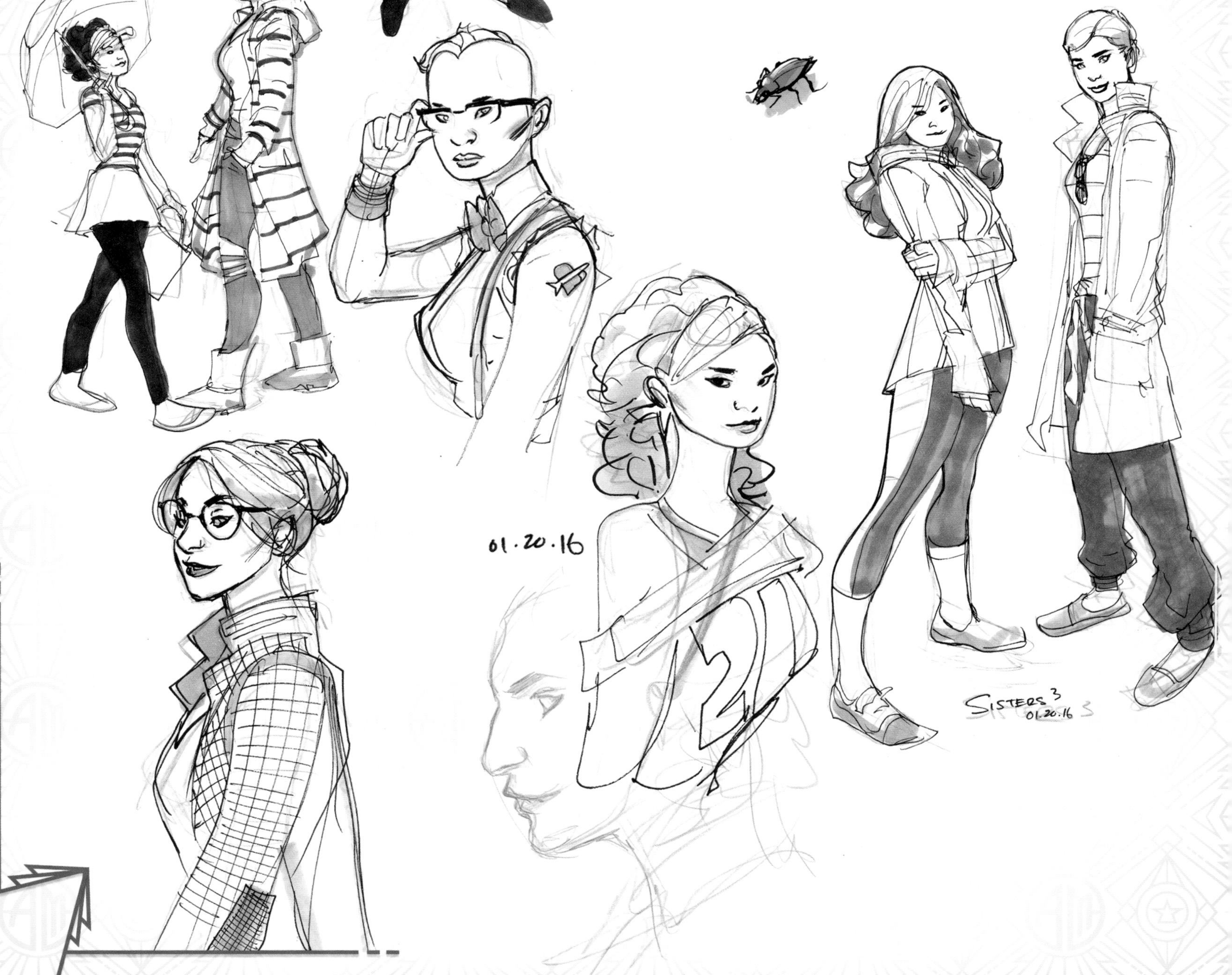
01.20.16
SISTERS 3
01.20.16

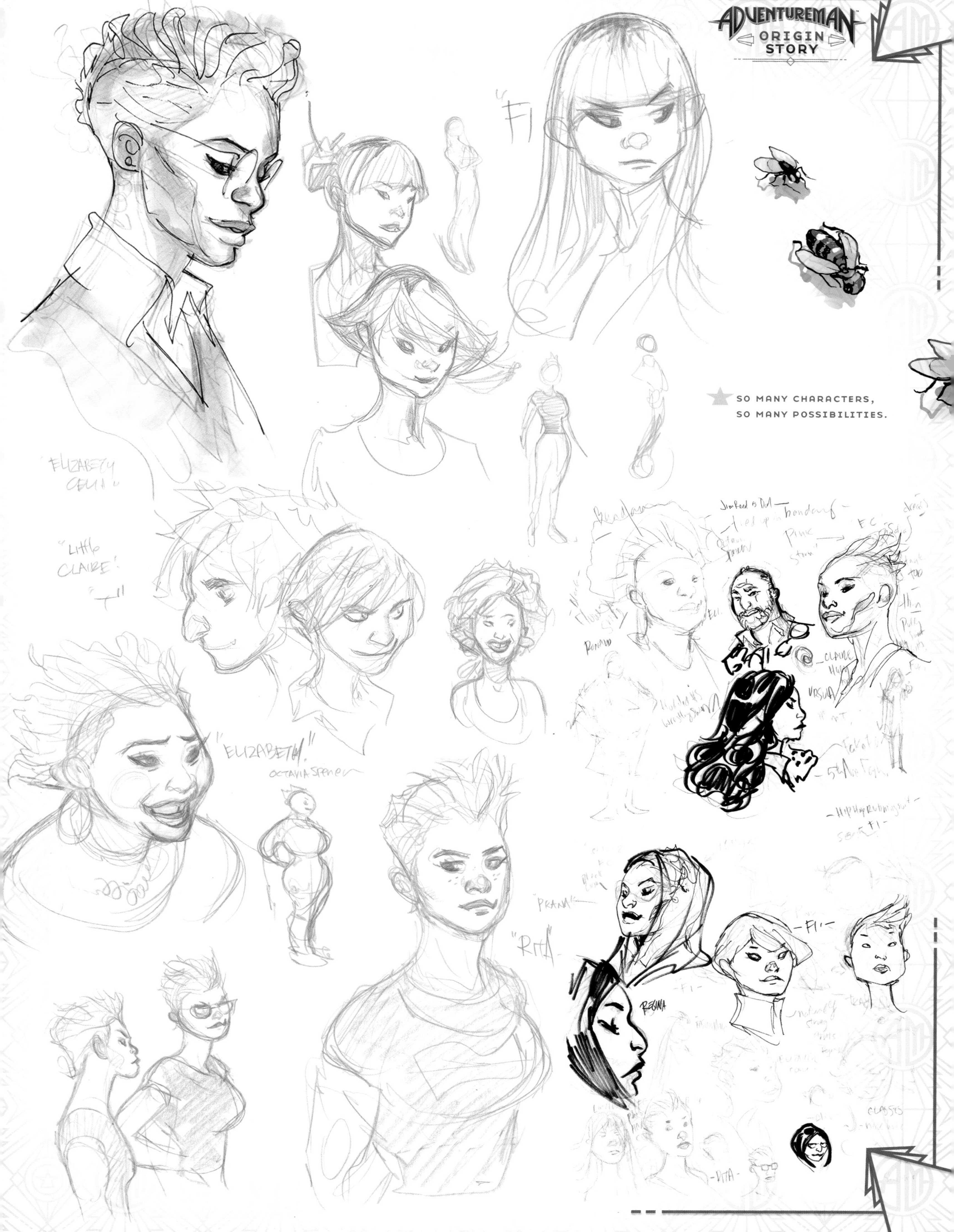
"ELIZABETH CELIA"
"FI"
"Little CLAIRE"
"ELIZABETH!"
"RITA"
"PRANA"
REGINA
-FI-
RONALD
URSULA
-RITA-
CLASSES

★ SO MANY CHARACTERS, SO MANY POSSIBILITIES.

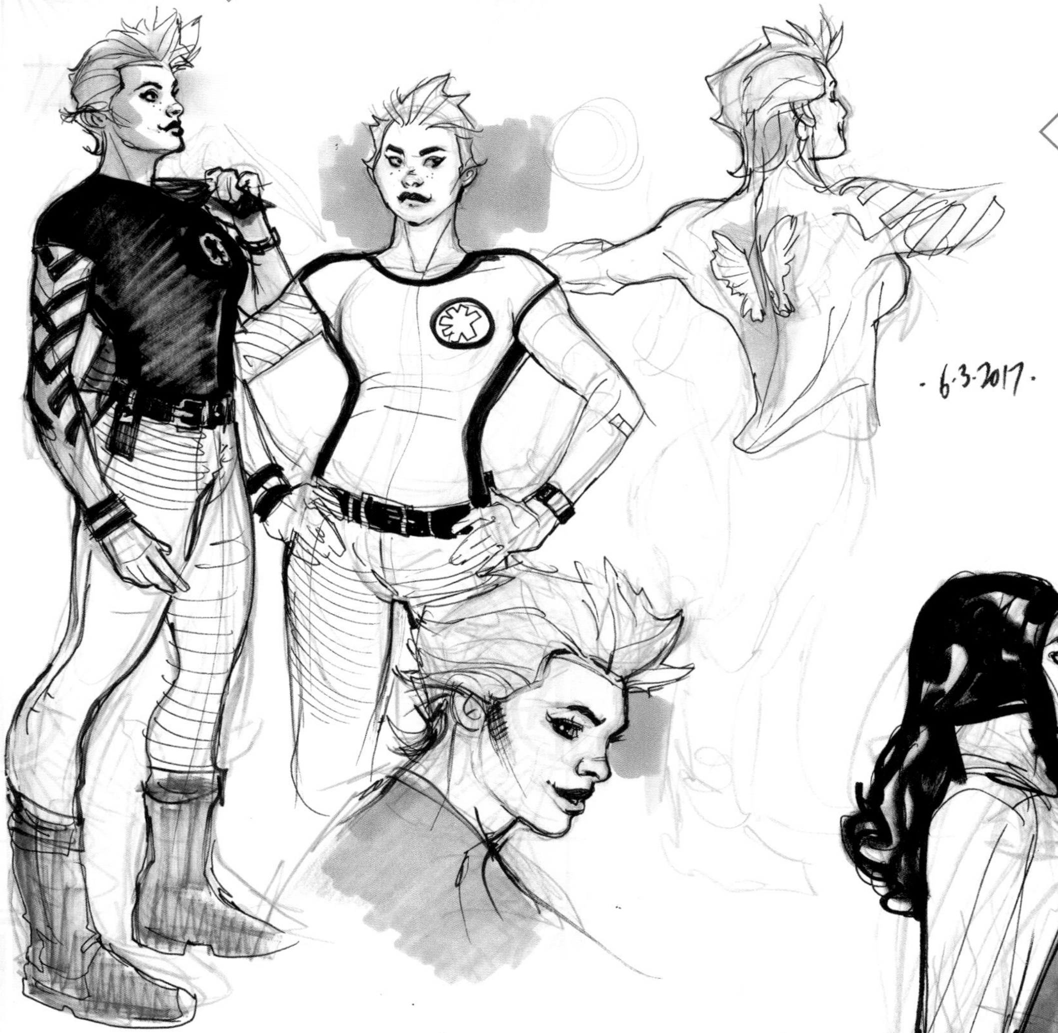
6.3.2017.

RITA

Is a Brazilian woman and combat medic turned EMT. Maybe she was a firefighter at some point. Maybe she still is, in the reserves. In love with an EMT driver, but trying to keep it a secret...

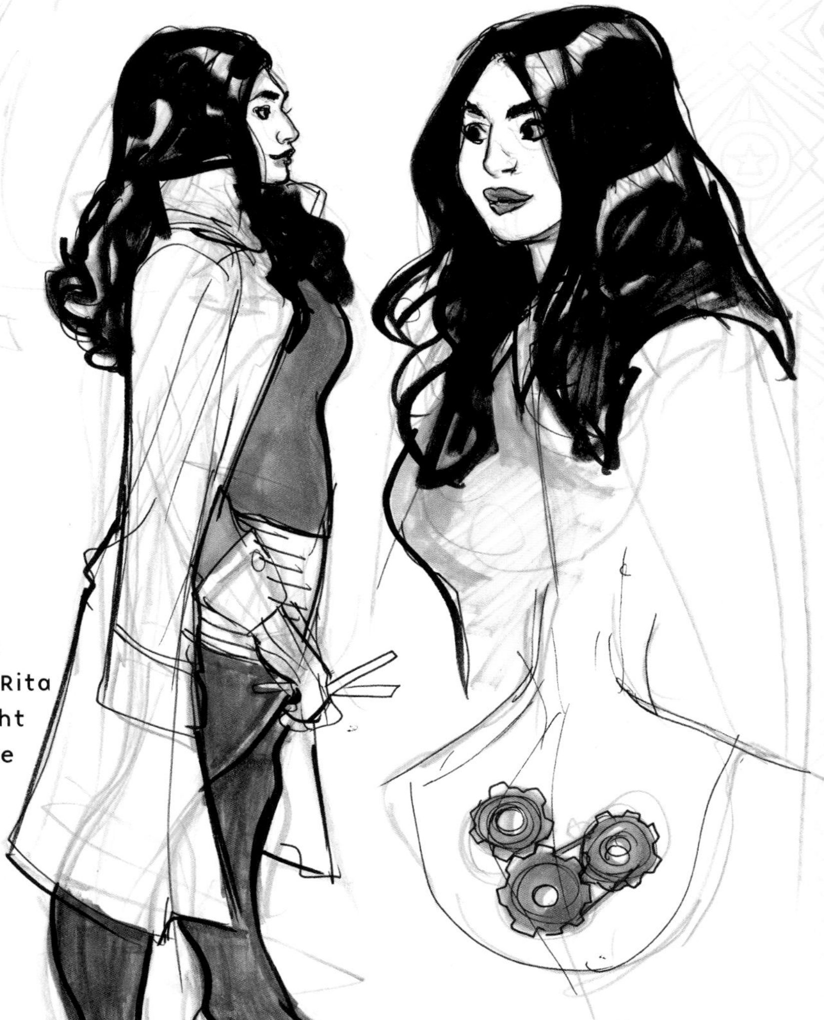

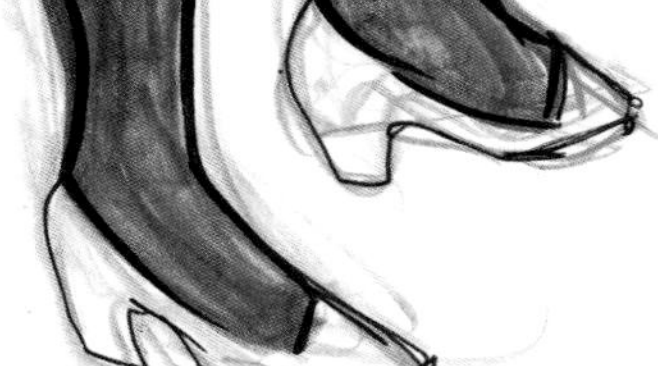

REGINA

An Indian woman and worshiping Hindu that works in poverty law. Rita and Regina are thought of as "the twins" since they came into the Connell family at the same time, but they could not be more different...

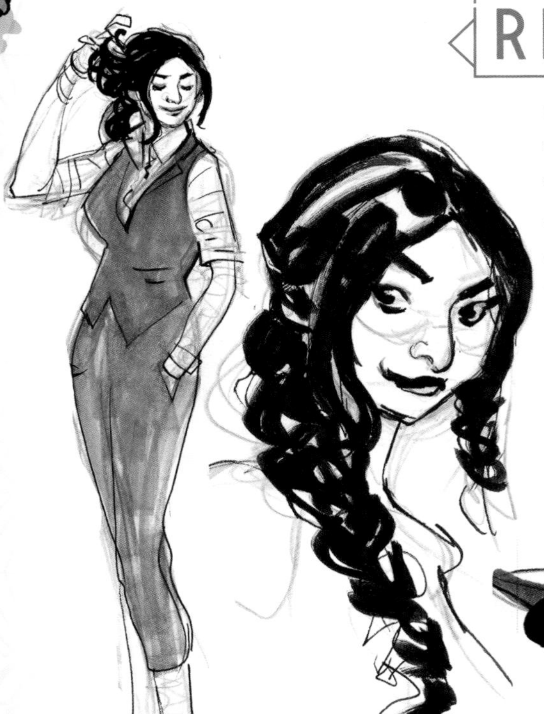

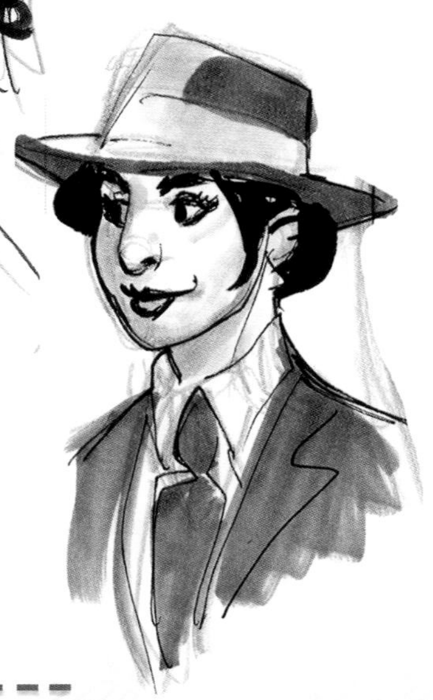

URSULA

A Persian woman and teacher/scientist. Engineer. Wants to rebuild the world with a 3D printer. I like the idea of her having a team of interns/grad students to turn to, like the **Baker Street Irregulars**...

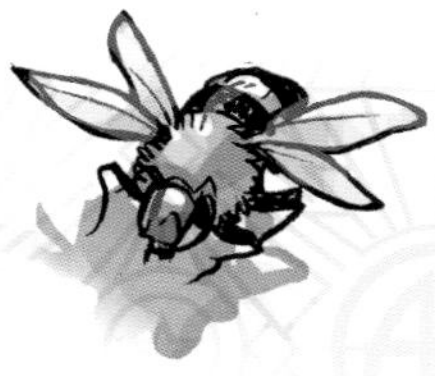

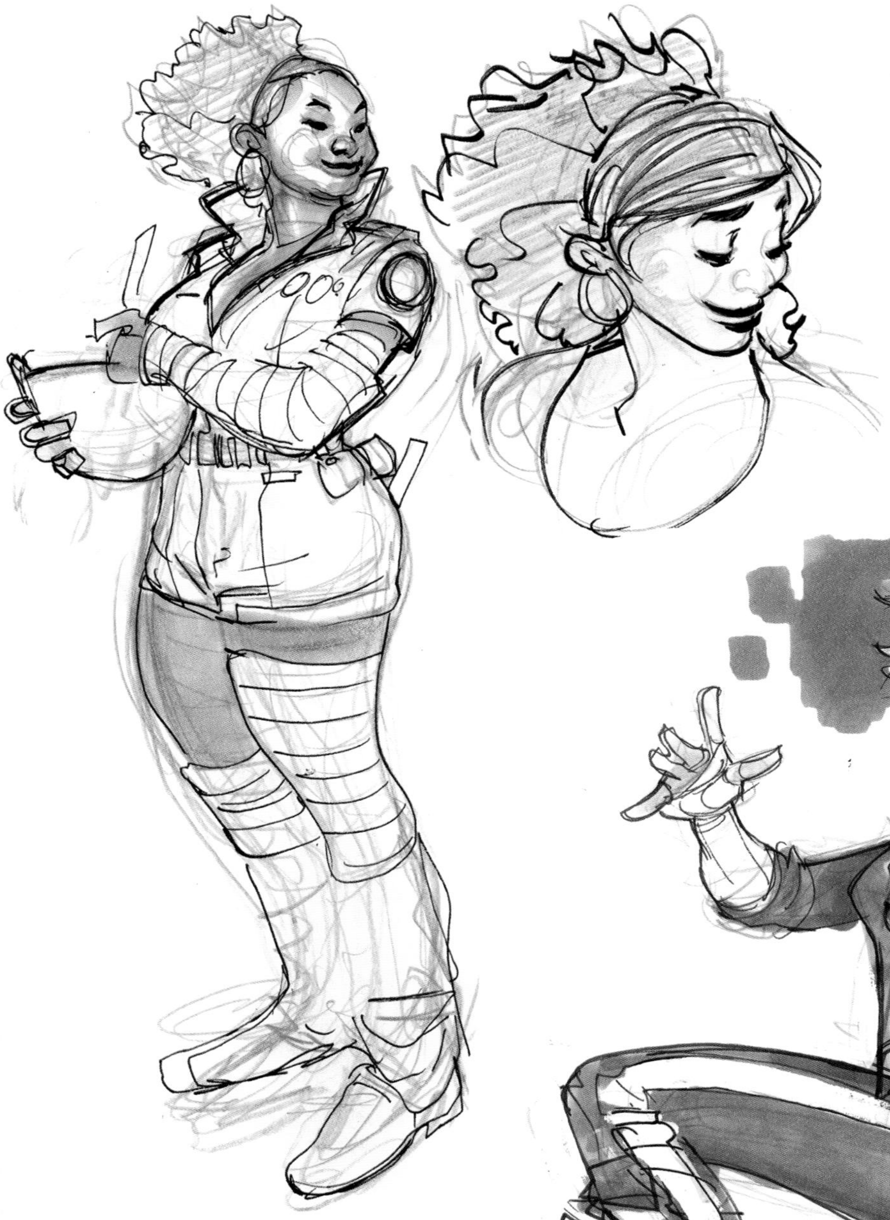

EVIE

A Caribbean woman that bakes the best French pastries in Manhattan. Maternal, caregiving, warm, soft. Boundless love. And pastries (The **pain aux framboises** from issue one is Rachel Dodson's favorite, so we had to pop that in)...

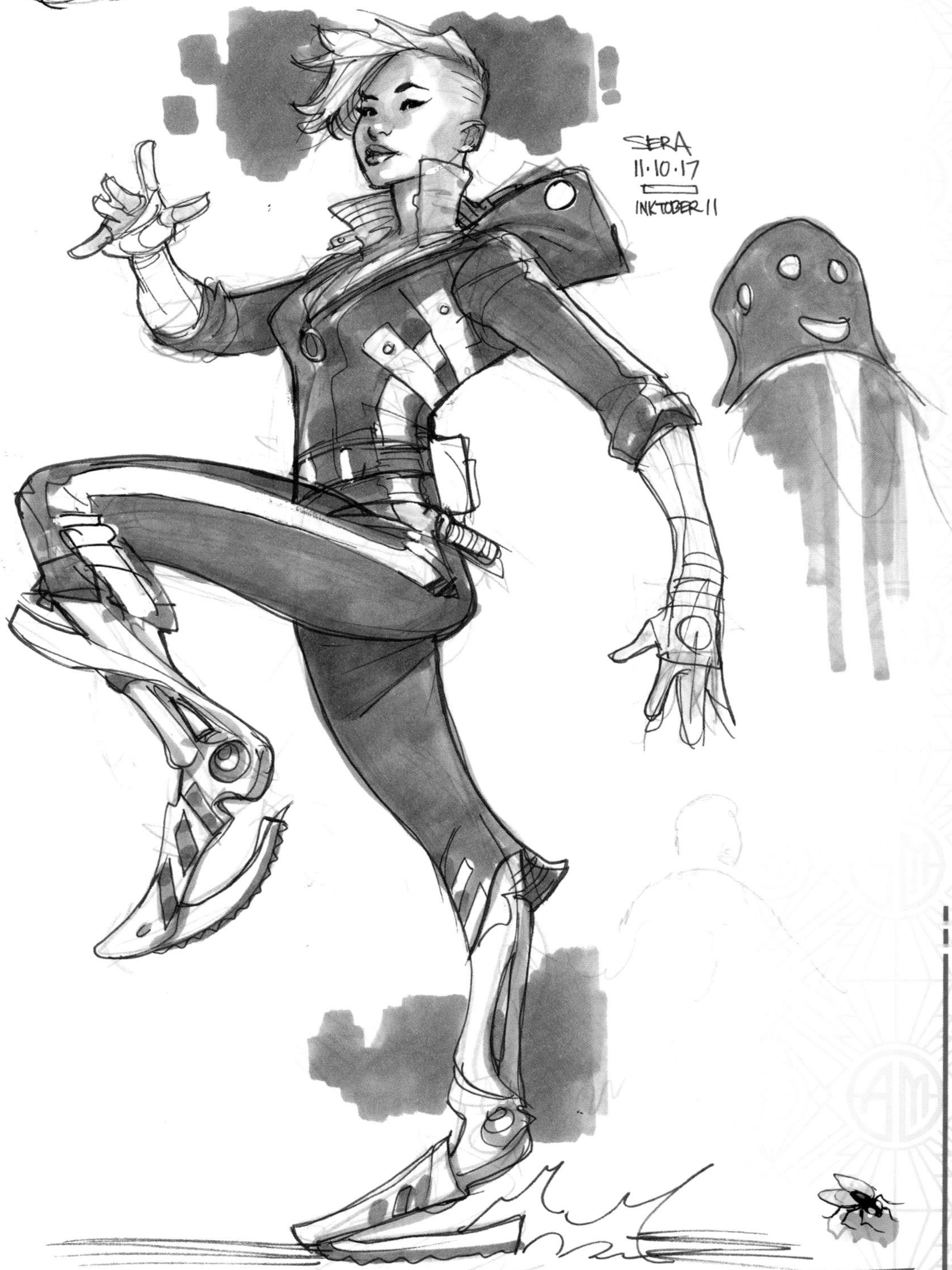
SERA
11.10.17
INKTOBER 11

SERAFINA

("Fi" said as 'Fee') Korean by birth. A congenital birth defect saw her legs being amputated at the knee shortly after birth. Gets by on fiberglass blade prosthetics (a la **Aimee Mullins**). When she ingests superserum she'll crush the legs under her own weight and will rely on superscience to build stronger ones. **Han Solo** on ceramic cheetah calves...

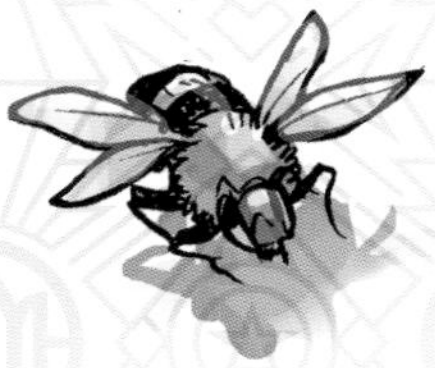

CLAIRE

~~Shasta Fay Chuzzlewit~~

The **Connell Family** were, for a while there, the... ***O'Donnells***, and maybe even the ***O'Conners*** at one point. **Tommy** was ***Timmy*** and ***Denny*** and maybe even ***Casey*** at one point; everybody's names wiggled around some before settling, except **Claire**. I wish I could say it was because none of the names had quite fit yet, and that as Terry discovered who everyone was on the outside, my grasp of who they were on the inside changed too. And while that's true, the ugly truth is it's because I am terrible with names -- especially with the names of characters I myself have created. Left to my devices, I'd go full **Dickens/Pynchon** and populate everything I do with ***Cherrycokes***, ***Sweedlepipes***, ***Benny Profanes*** and ***Horatio Fizkin*** -- they'd at least be easier for me to track. Shoulda called Claire "***Shasta Fay Chuzzlewit***" and been done with it.

I landed on **Connell** (kahn-ELL) after the ⋆ checks Wikipedia ⋆ "*guitar-oriented, melodic, jangle pop style of rock*" band ***The Connells***, out of North Carolina. I used to cut through the Connell family's backyard, once upon a time, being out and about and up to no good in the world back in the days when one would do things like trespass lightly through someone else's property. Surely that means something but for the life of me I can't tell you what that might actually be. Ah, fun and games.

Come to think of it, this would not be the first subconscious and oblique reference to a regional band of my youth that's bubbled up in my work. I wonder what that's about.

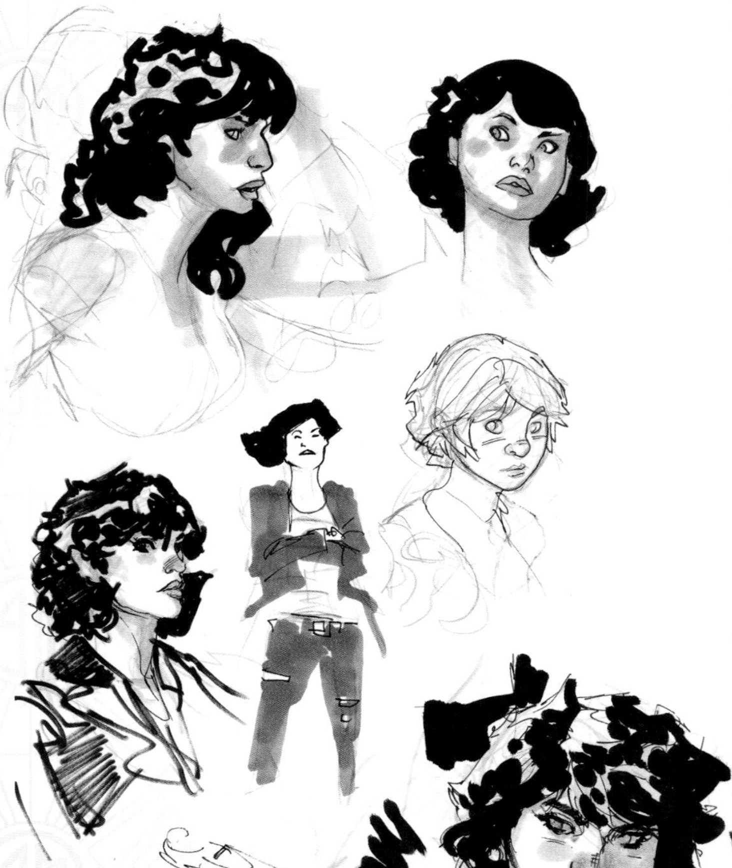

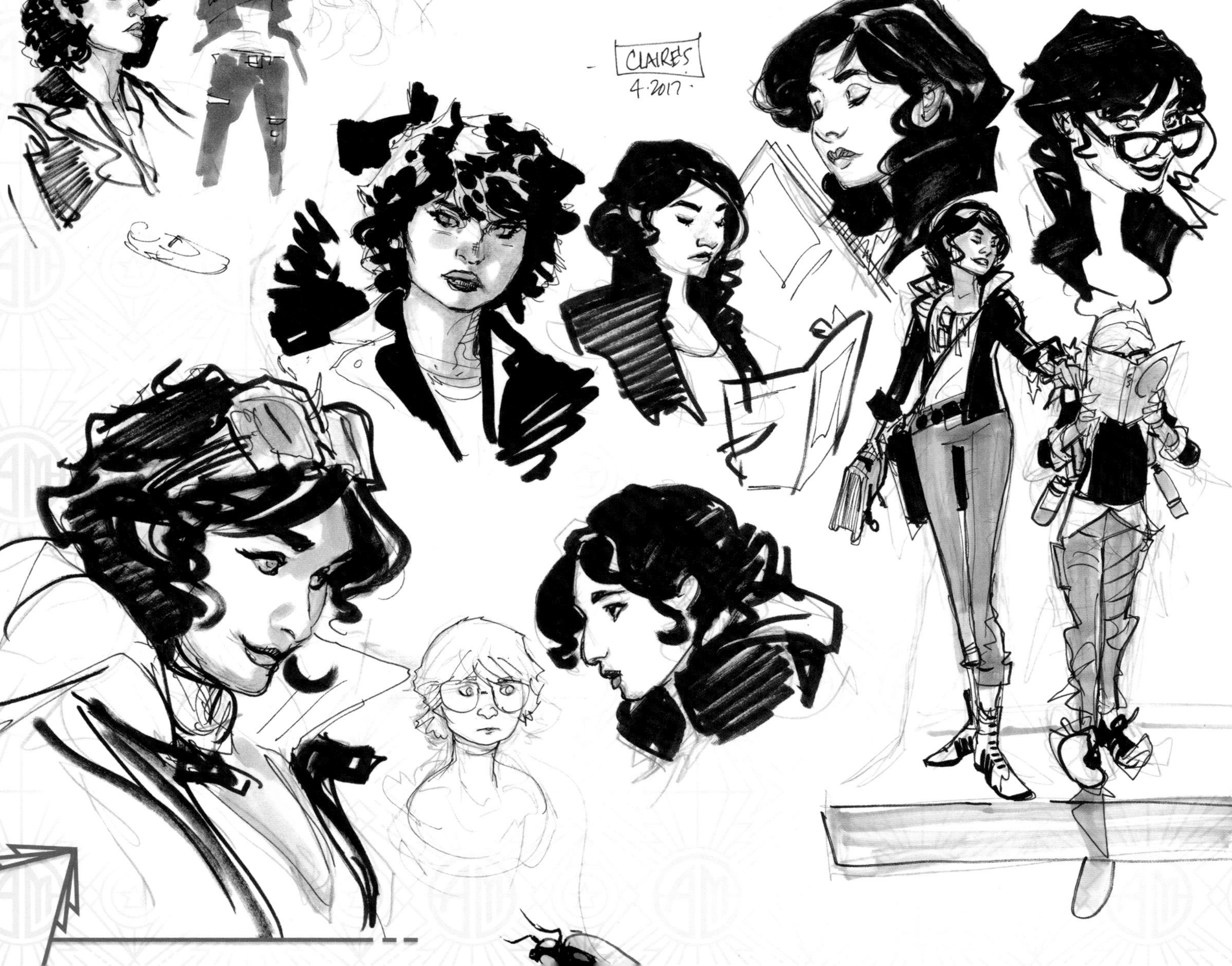
CLAIRE'S
4.2017.

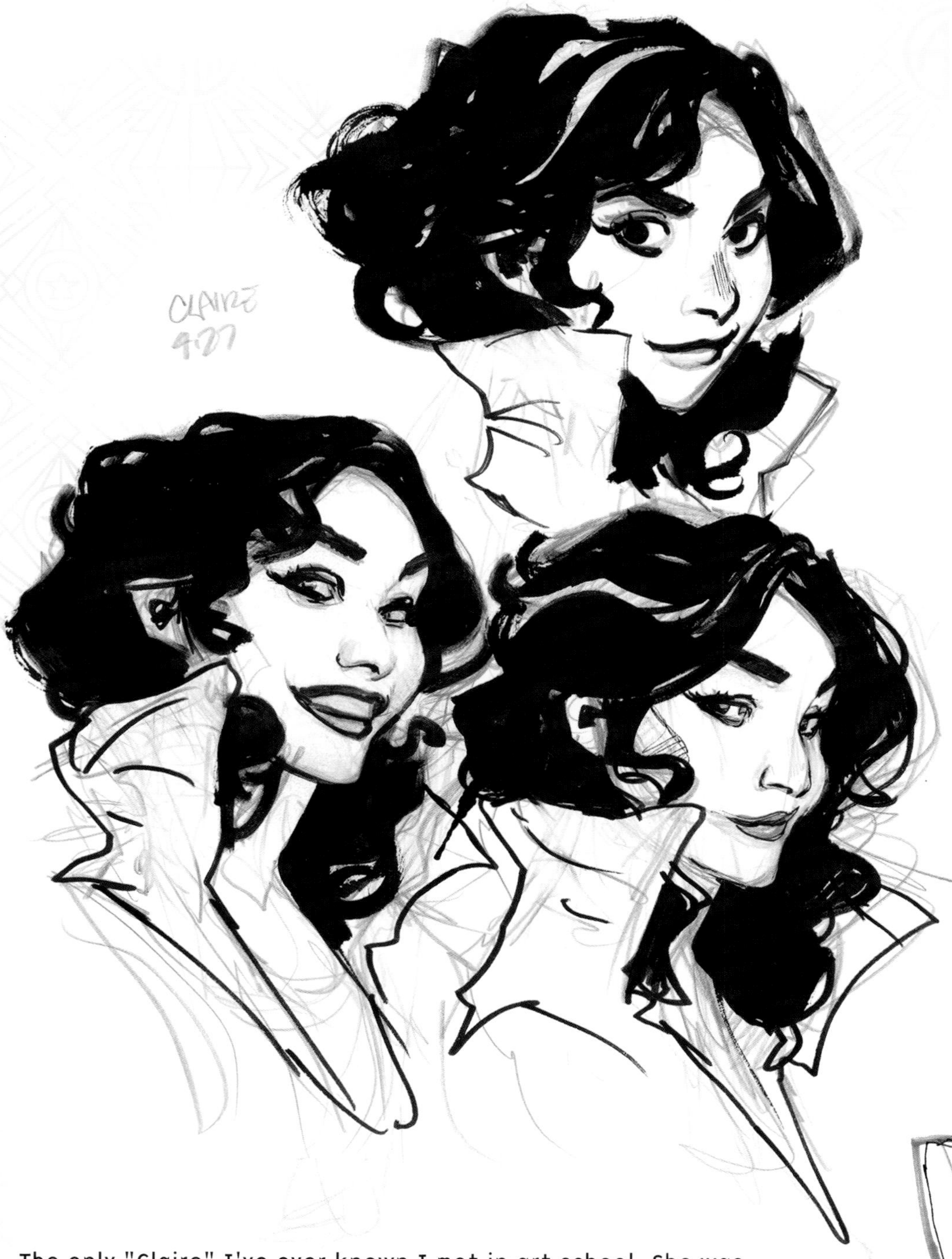
CLAIRE
4/27

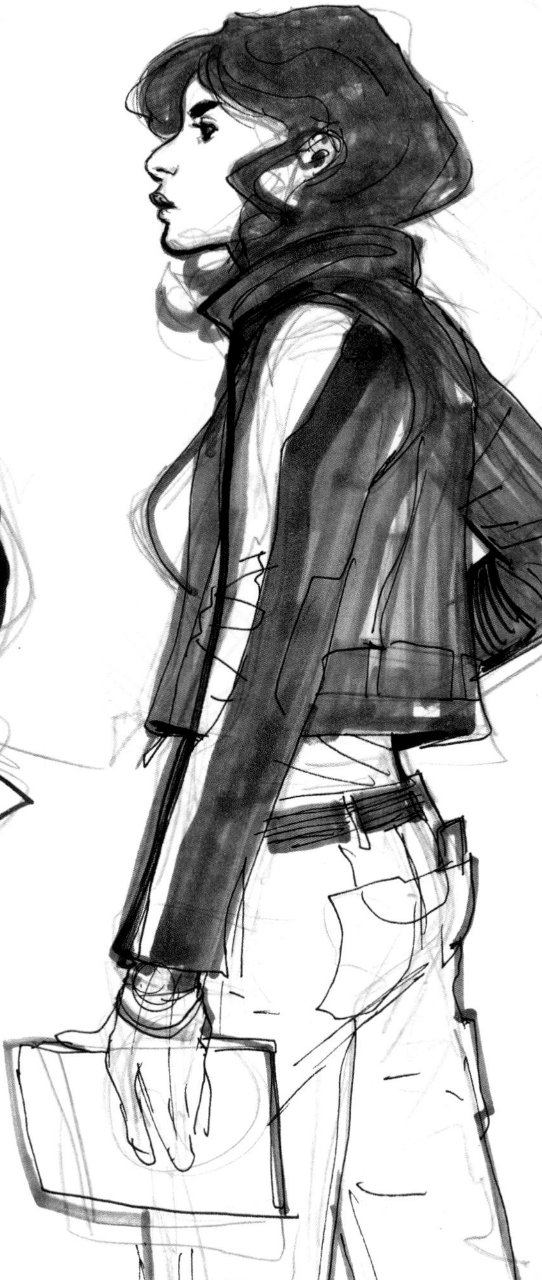

The only "Claire" I've ever known I met in art school. She was the first artist I'd ever met. I don't mean the first art student. I was an art student. She was an artist. I remember watching her make a pinch pot the day I met her, the little dumb throwaway bowl you squish out to make slip when working with clay. Not art! A thing crafted in service of making art -- and when I looked at my weird lumpy hollowed out tumor of a pot compared to the elven and delicate shell Claire held in palm almost absent-mindedly, I realized, oh... THAT'S an artist.

They're a different species, artists; they leave different footprints than the rest of us. Everything Claire touched -- and touches still -- she infuses with... I don't know. Art dust. Some kind of singular signature, whether it was in a drawing or a sculpture or the way she signed her name.

I don't know if any of this means anything to the creation of ADVENTUREMAN! or anything else. But if everything here does indeed fit then, well, surely disparate connections like this are why.

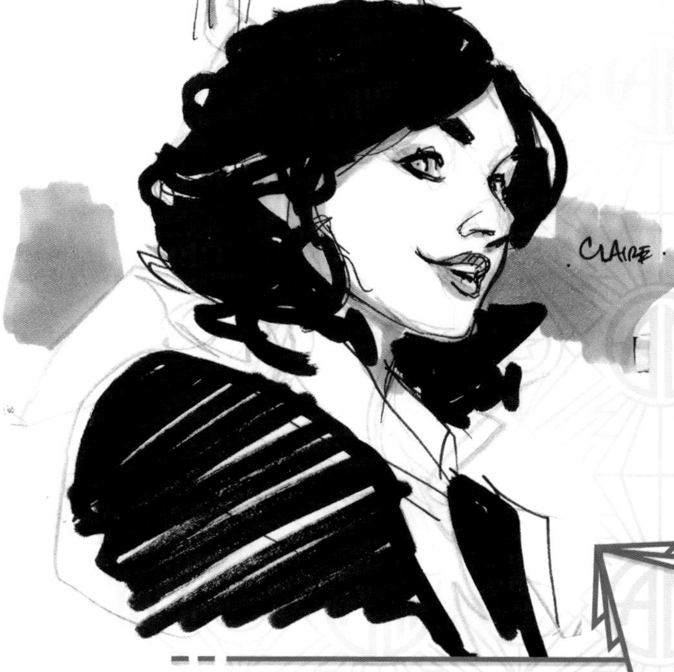
CLAIRE

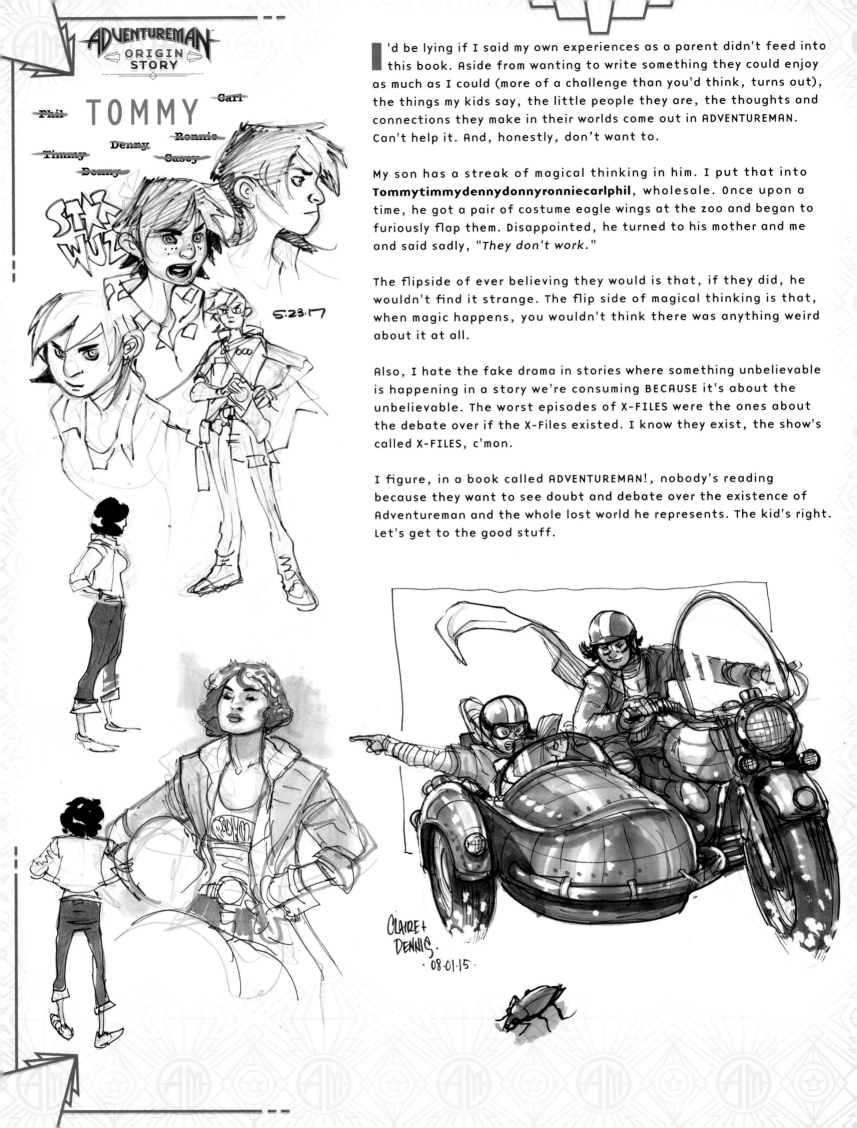

ADVENTUREMAN ORIGIN STORY

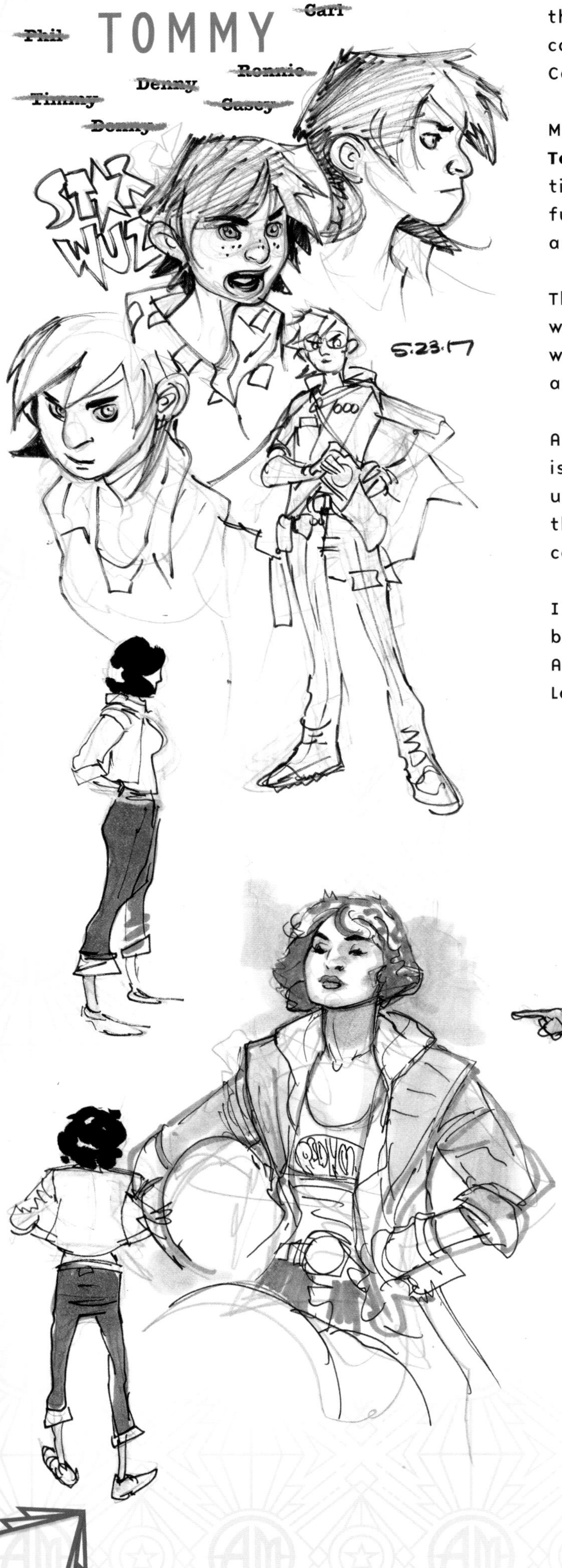

Carl
Phil
TOMMY
Ronnie
Denny
Timmy
Casey
Donny
5.23.17

I'd be lying if I said my own experiences as a parent didn't feed into this book. Aside from wanting to write something they could enjoy as much as I could (more of a challenge than you'd think, turns out), the things my kids say, the little people they are, the thoughts and connections they make in their worlds come out in ADVENTUREMAN. Can't help it. And, honestly, don't want to.

My son has a streak of magical thinking in him. I put that into **Tommytimmydennydonnyronniecarlphil**, wholesale. Once upon a time, he got a pair of costume eagle wings at the zoo and began to furiously flap them. Disappointed, he turned to his mother and me and said sadly, "*They don't work.*"

The flipside of ever believing they would is that, if they did, he wouldn't find it strange. The flip side of magical thinking is that, when magic happens, you wouldn't think there was anything weird about it at all.

Also, I hate the fake drama in stories where something unbelievable is happening in a story we're consuming BECAUSE it's about the unbelievable. The worst episodes of X-FILES were the ones about the debate over if the X-Files existed. I know they exist, the show's called X-FILES, c'mon.

I figure, in a book called ADVENTUREMAN!, nobody's reading because they want to see doubt and debate over the existence of Adventureman and the whole lost world he represents. The kid's right. Let's get to the good stuff.

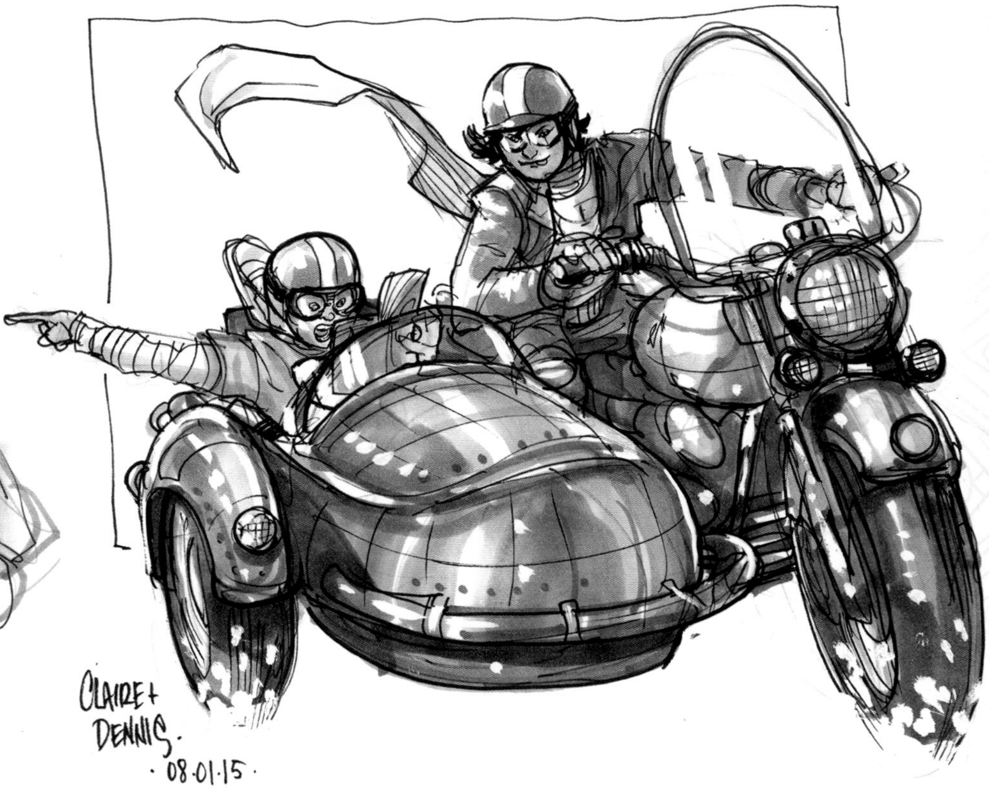

CLAIRE + DENNIS.
· 08.01.15 ·

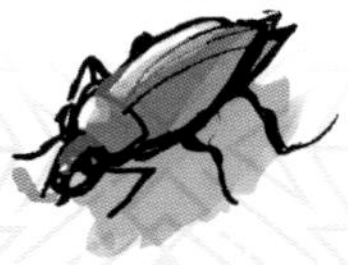

The last sister -- the one we've spent the least amount of time with (so far) is **BITSY** -- **Elizabeth Cecille**.

(Look, there I go again -- I just changed her name. Because "Elizabeth Cecille" has a better meter than 'Elizabeth Cecillia' which is what she had been in my notes. Sometimes it just takes reading a thing out loud to hear it right...)

She was the first girl the Connells adopted, named after **St. Elizabeth**, "the patron saint of difficult marriages." Coming into her parents' life saved theirs, and formed the cornerstone of her glorious and raucous sprawl of a family. She's a folklorist and storyteller and, in a couple issues' time, she's gonna have to sit down with her nephew and get up to speed real real fast...

RONALD CONNELL. Dad. Grandpa. A great big barrel of a man. A retired cop, a widower, a father and focal point around which the family orbits. I don't think I gave Terry too much more of a description of the guy other than that -- then, boom, there he was on the page and I could even hear his voice in my head. He started as a plot function, as a story note, and -- like the sisters, like Tommy, like Claire -- Terry's drawings woke them up. Everything he puts down hums with an inner life that could've only come from him. He finds these characters and shares them with me and suddenly I know all these things about them: who they are, how they move, what they daydream about, why they're in the story and what they're gonna do.

Y'know my favorite thing about working with Terry?

He's an artist.

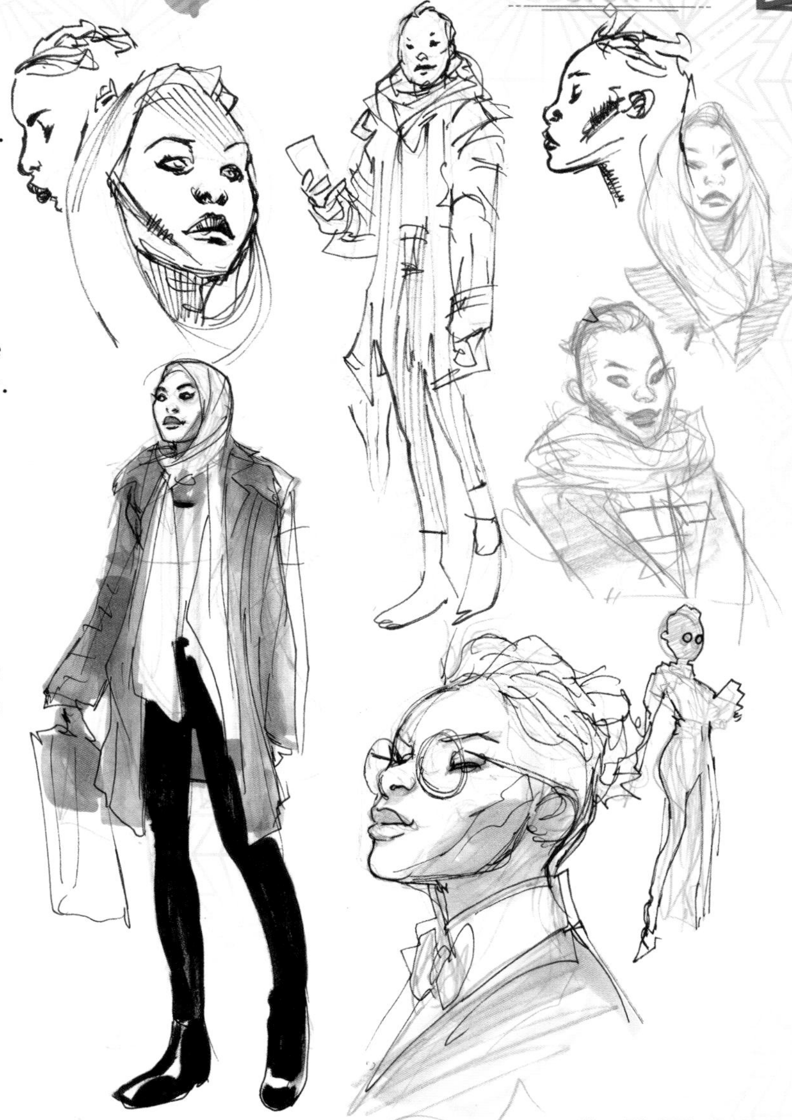

BITSY

Elizabeth ~~Cecillia~~ Cecille

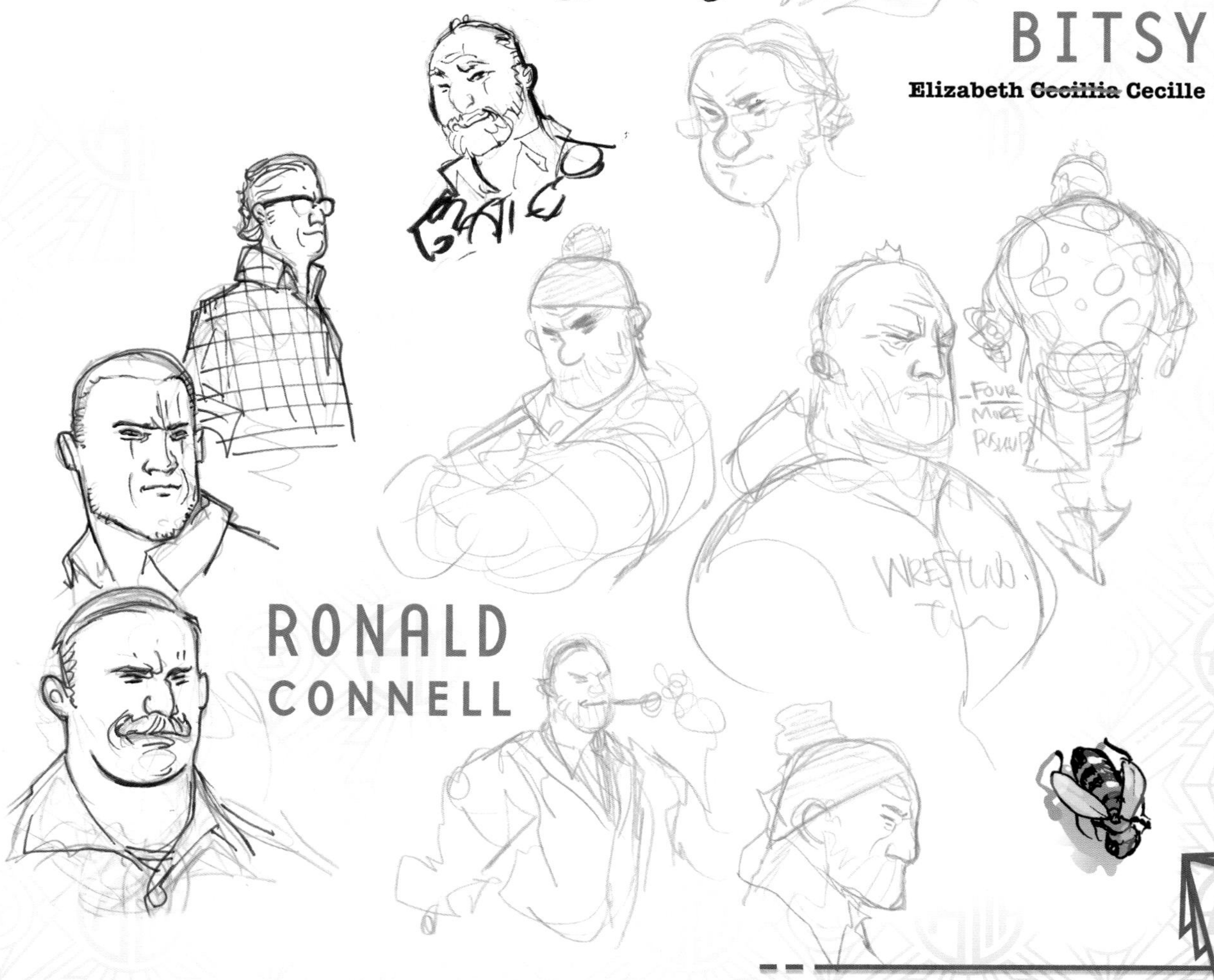

RONALD CONNELL

MATT FRACTION

Writes comic books somewhere out in the woods where he lives with his wife, writer **Kelly Sue DeConnick**, his two children, two dogs, a bearded dragon, and a yard full of coyotes, deer, and crows.

TERRY DODSON

Has worked on about every character in mainstream comics and continues as a cover artist. Terry is the co-creator of *Red One* with **Xavier Dorison** and *Adventureman* with **Matt Fraction**. He's worked in toy and statue design, animation and video games and has had gallery exhibitions featuring his paintings. The *Native Oregonian* shares his life with **Rachel Dodson** and their three cats by a lake on the Oregon coast.

RACHEL DODSON

Received her *Interior Design* degree from *Bassist College*, which lead her on a path to inking comics 9 to 5, and allowed her a life of leisure - riding horses, open water swimming, guitar plucking and landscape gardening.

CLAYTON COWLES

Is a 2009 graduate of the *Joe Kubert School*. He has lettered numerous books for *Marvel*, *DC*, *Valiant*, and *Image Comics*, including *Defenders*, *Red One*, and *Superman's Pal Jimmy Olsen* with his *Adventureman* collaborators. He has twice been nominated for the *Eisner* and *Ringo Awards* for "Best Lettering." He lives in upstate **New York** in a house with two cats.

LEONARDO OLEA

As a man of many hats, he has worked with major entertainment brands, publishers and artists around the globe. He was one of the head organizers of a comic book festival, went as a title designer for an **Oscar** nominated short film and even owned a bar. Olea has worked on comics like *Superman*, *Run Love Kill*, *Fairy Quest* and *Revelations* among others. At the moment, he is working with the intriguing brand *MAFUFO*. He lives in a secret facility and loves chocolate.